FIRST BURMA CAMPAIGN

FIRST BURMA CAMPAIGN

THE JAPANESE CONQUEST OF 1942

BY COLONEL E.C.V. FOUCAR MC
COMPILED AND INTRODUCED BY JOHN GREHAN

FRONTLINE
BOOKS

FIRST BURMA CAMPAIGN
The Japanese Conquest of 1942

This edition published in 2020
and reissued in this format in 2024 by

Frontline Books,
An imprint of
Pen & Sword Books Ltd,
47 Church Street, Barnsley, S. Yorkshire, S70 2AS,

This book is based on file reference CAB 44/324 , which is held at The National Archives, Kew, and is licensed under the Open Government Licence v3.0.

Introduction Copyright © John Grehan
Text alterations and additions © Frontline Books

The right of John Grehan to be identified as
the author of the introduction has been asserted by him in accordance
with the Copyright, Designs and Patents Act 1988.

ISBN: 9 781 52679 764 3

All rights reserved. No part of this publication may be reproduced, stored in or introduced into a retrieval system, or transmitted, in any form, or by any means (electronic, mechanical, photocopying, recording or otherwise) without the prior written permission of the publisher. Any person who does any unauthorized act in relation to this publication may be liable to criminal prosecution and civil claims for damages. CIP data records for this title are available from the British Library

Typeset in 10.5/13 pt Palatino
by SJmagic DESIGN SERVICES, India

Printed and bound by CPI UK

Pen & Sword Books Ltd incorporates the imprints of Air World Books, Pen & Sword Archaeology, Atlas, Aviation, Battleground, Discovery, Family History, History, Maritime, Military, Naval, Politics, Social History, Transport, True Crime, Claymore Press, Frontline Books, Praetorian Press, Seaforth Publishing and White Owl

For a complete list of Pen & Sword titles please contact:

PEN & SWORD BOOKS LTD
47 Church Street, Barnsley, South Yorkshire, S70 2AS, UK.
E-mail: enquiries@pen-and-sword.co.uk
Website: www.pen-and-sword.co.uk

Or

PEN AND SWORD BOOKS,
1950 Lawrence Road, Havertown, PA 19083, USA
E-mail: Uspen-and-sword@casematepublishers.com
Website: www.penandswordbooks.com

Contents

Introduction by John Grehan   x

Chapter 1   1
Burma – Its physical features – Resources and Industries – Main towns – Communications – Lack of Communications with neighbouring countries.

Chapter 2   10
Early history of Burma – British associations with the country – The wars with Burma – British Rule – Self Government and its results – Japanese influences.

Chapter 3   20
Events in the Far East – Japanese aims and aggression – Military forces in Burma – Military effect of the Separation from India – Creation of the Army in Burma – Expansion from 1939 onwards – State of preparedness of Burma on outbreak of war with Japan in December 1941 – Other Allied Forces in Burma – Forces employed by Japan in Burma.

Chapter 4   40
Appreciations of a possible Japanese attack on Burma – View of Singapore Defence Conference – View of Burma Army – Dispositions made in accordance with these views – Reconsideration of situation after outbreak of war with Japan – Changes of Command affecting Burma – The Reinforcement problem.

Chapter 5   50
Opening of the Campaign in December 1941 – Early Operations – F.F.2 raid on Prachuab Girikhan – Japanese occupation of Victoria Point and Bokpyin – F.F.2 attack on Bokpyin – Other Operations in Tenasserim, Karenni, and in the Shan States – Internal conditions in Burma – Air raids on Rangoon and their serious results – Civil Defence in Burma.

Chapter 6   57
Detailed appreciation of the military situation by Lieut.-General Hutton – Events in Tenasserim in January 1942 – Signs of an early Japanese advance – Evacuation of Mergui – Japanese attack and capture Tavoy – Advance of Japanese 55th Division on Kawkareik – Operations in that area – Withdrawal of 16 Brigade.

Chapter 7   70
The Japanese advance on Moulmein – Operations leading up to the attack on that town on January 30th 1942 – The defence of Moulmein – British withdrawal on January 31st, 1942.

Chapter 8   79
Operations on the west bank of the Salween river – Defence of and withdrawal from Martaban – Attack on the 7th Battalion 10th Baluch Regiment at Kuzeik – Decision to withdraw to the Bilin river – Evacuation of Thaton on February 15th, 1942.

Chapter 9   93
British dispositions on the Bilin river line – Operations on that line – Heavy enemy attacks held – Japanese infiltrate round both flanks and carry out coastal landings – Withdrawal of 17 Division to Kyaikto.

Chapter 10   104
Operations carried out by 17 Division on February 21st, 22nd and 23rd, 1942 – The withdrawal from Kyaikto – Japanese attacks on the Sittang bridgehead and on our force east of the river – Battle of the Sittang – Withdrawal of 17 Division across the Sittang.

Chapter 11   123
Operations in the Pegu area between February 26th and March 8th, 1942 – The Japanese attack on Pegu – Establishment of a road block south of Pegu – British withdrawal from Pegu and successful attack on the road block.

Chapter 12   136
Situation in Rangoon during January and February 1942 – Labour shortage – Evacuation of non-essential population – Outbreak of lawlessness and looting – Decision of General Alexander to abandon the port – Demolitions – Final withdrawal from Rangoon – The enemy establish a road block on the road to Prome – Operations in the Taukkyan area on March 7th and 8th, 1942.

CONTENTS

Chapter 13   149

Effects of the loss of Rangoon – Regrouping of British forces in the Irrawaddy valley – Formation of Burcorps – Minor operations at Henzada and Letpadan – Japanese attacks on A.V.G. and R.A.F. at Magwe and the serious results thereof – Formation of a striking force by Burcorps – Operations of striking force at Padigon and Paungde – Enemy establish a road block at Shwedaung – Action at Shwedaung – Attack on our force at Padaung.

Chapter 14   165

Operations in the Shan States and Karenni in January and February 1942 – Relief of 1 Burma Division by Chinese VI Army – Concentration of 1 Burma Division south of Toungoo – Decision by Army Commander to release unreliable elements in Battalions of Burma Rifles – Our attacks on Pyuntaza and Shwegyin – Decision to withdraw 1 Burma Division to the Irrawaddy front – Actions at Kyauktaga and Gonde.

Chapter 15   175

Entry into Burma of the Chinese Expeditionary Force – Organisation and equipment – Problems of Transport and Supply – Formation of Chinese Liaison Mission – Chinese system of Command – Operations until the end of March 1942 – The loss of Toungoo.

Chapter 16   185

The situation at Prome – Decision to evacuate the town – Dispositions of 17 Division in the area – Japanese attack on Prome on April 1st, 1942 – Our Withdrawal – Actions at Ainggyaunngon and Hmawza – March to Dayindabo – Plan for the defence of the oilfields – Withdrawal of Burcorps to line Minhla-Taungdwingyi.

Chapter 17   195

Defence of the Minhla-Taungdwingyi line – Failure of Chinese to assist – Operations about Kokkogwa and Alebo – Enemy take Migaungye – Result of this and withdrawal of 1 Burma Division to Yin Chaung line – Action near Mingyun – Japanese attack Yin Chaung line – Withdrawal to Pin Chaung begun – Operations on west bank of Irrawaddy – Decision to retain Taungdwingyi.

Chapter 18   211

Denial Scheme for Yenangyaung and Chauk oilfields – Orders issued for the destruction of the oilfields – Japanese establish themselves on the Pin Chaung – Operations at Yenangyaung between April 16th, and 21st, 1942 – Withdrawal of 1 Burma Division – Operations by columns of 17 Division from Natmauk and Taungdwingyi – Plans for an offensive against the Japanese in the Yenangyaung area.

Chapter 19   227

Effect of the Japanese advance through the Shan States – General Alexander's plans in the event of the loss of Mandalay – Decision to fall back to Kalewa to protect India – Supply problems – Withdrawal to west bank of Irrawaddy begun – 2 Burma Brigade ordered to cover Myittha valley – Successful delaying actions at Meiktila and Kyaukse – Decision to withdraw Chinese V Army to Katha – Destruction of the Ava bridge.

Chapter 20   244

Japanese appear unexpectedly at Monywa – Attack on Headquarters of 1 Burma Division – Attack on and capture of Monywa – Serious results – Our attempts to recapture the town – Decision to break off the action and withdrawal of 1 Burma Division on Ye-U – Minor operations north of Monywa – Japanese move up the Chindwin – 16 Brigade hurried to Kalewa – March of 2 Burma Brigade by Pauk and Tilin to Kalemyo.

Chapter 21   255

General Alexander ordered to withdraw his force north of Tamu – The withdrawal to Shwegyin – Action at Shwegyin – Final stages of the withdrawal north of Tamu – 4 Corps assumes operational control of all Burma Army troops.

Chapter 22   266

Operations carried out by Chinese Expeditionary Force in April and May 1942 – The Japanese thrust through Karenni and the Shan States – Collapse of the VI Army – Occupation by the enemy of Bhamo and Myitkyina – Chinese operations south of Mandalay – Withdrawal of V Army and 38th Division to China – Conduct of Chinese forces during withdrawal – Failure of British and Chinese to co-operate fully.

Chapter 23   277

Events in Arakan and more particularly in Akyab – Civil unrest – Air attacks on Akyab – Japanese advance – Encounters with Japanese – Evacuation of Akyab – Organisation of Karen Levies – Resistance by Karen Levies and Karens of Burma Rifles – Commando units – Evacuation of Myitkyina – Indiscipline of members of armed forces on the northern evacuation routes to India.

Chapter 24 286

The Air Garrison of Burma – Its inadequacy – Strength of Japanese air force opposed to it – Air attacks on Rangoon – Our successes – Air support for early operations of 17 Division – Withdrawal from Rangoon – Formation of Burwing and Akwing – Heavy reverses at Magwe and Akyab – Termination of R.A.F. activities based on Burma – Operations from Loiwing and India – Our air losses and those of the Japanese.

Chapter 25 303

Civil administration in so far as it affected the military situation – General failure to place civil and military administration on a war time basis before opening of hostilities – Evacuation problems – Work on the Burma-Assam road – Military administration and other matters – The Base – Transport and Supply – Ordnance – Transportation and Movement Control – Denial of Railways and River services – No general Denial Scheme – Signals – Medical stores – Matters affecting discipline and morale – Morale of Burma units – Casualties.

Chapter 26 326

Careful Japanese preparations for invasion – Unscrupulous methods – Wearing of native dress – Burmese assistance to the enemy – General attitude of the Burmese – Japanese treatment of prisoners – Japanese tactical methods – Causes of our failure to hold Burma – Conclusion.

APPENDICES

Appendix A	Army in Burma Location Statement for December 1st, 1941.	338
Appendix B	Army in Burma outline Order of Battle for December 8th, 1941.	349
Appendix C	State of 17 Division Infantry Battalions on evening of February 24th, 1942.	352
Appendix D	Chinese Expeditionary Force Order of Battle.	354
Appendix E	Army in Burma – Order of Battle for April 1st, 1942.	357

Introduction

On 17 May 1944, the men of the Burma Army staggered and limped towards Tamu near the border with the eastern Indian state of Manipur. Watching them reach the end of their 900-mile march from Rangoon was Lieutenant General Bill Slim, commander of the Burma Corps: 'All of them, British, Indian and Ghurkha were gaunt and ragged as scarecrows. Yet, as they trudged behind their surviving officers in groups pitifully small, they still carried their arms and kept their ranks. They might look like scarecrows but they looked like soldiers too. They did not expect to be treated like heroes, but they did expect to be met as soldiers, who, even if defeated, were by no means disgraced.' Slim expected his men to be applauded for accomplishing what was, and remains, the longest fighting withdrawal in the 300-year history of the British Army. But there was no fanfare for the malaria- and dysentery-riddled troops as there had been for those that had been rescued from Dunkirk, and the battle for Burma would become regarded as a forgotten war and the men that fought in the steep jungle-clad mountains and the arid plains (as, indeed my father did) would become part of what became known as the Forgotten Army.

Memoirs and histories of the First Burma Campaign are not to be found in abundance. There are two reasons for this. The first is that there were, in truth, relatively few British regiments in Burma at the time of the Japanese invasion. The second, is that narratives of the war in Burma tend to concentrate upon the subsequent success of the Fourteenth Army and the great battles of Kohima, Imphal, the Irrawaddy and Mandalay. Yet there were battles a plenty in 1942.

The conquest of Burma began in December 1941 with air attacks, the Japanese 5th Air Division striking at Rangoon, the Burmese capital, and British airfields. This Japanese force numbered around 150 aircraft to oppose which Air Vice-Marshal Stevenson had just thirty-seven combat aircraft (from the RAF, the Indian Air Force and the American Volunteer Group). There was only one battery of anti-aircraft guns for airfield defence other than Browning machine guns.

Stevenson called for reinforcements and by 1 January 1942, Stevenson's force numbered fifty-three aircraft – of Curtiss P-40s and Hawker Hurricanes – but the Japanese had also been reinforced and now could count up to 200 machines. Stevenson wrote that: 'Fighter for fighter we were superior and it was only when heavily outnumbered, and without warning and proper airfield facilities, that the enemy were able to get a decision. Their bombers were "easy meat" for our fighters if interception took place.' Though the Japanese had been unable to gain air superiority, on 15 January, General Shojiro Iida's Fifteenth Army invaded the southern Burmese province of Tenasserim.

The main Japanese thrust, however, came from the east, with General Shōzō Sakurai's 33rd Division moving across the border from Thailand. The Japanese were clearly aiming for Rangoon, but in their way ran the 600-yard-wide River Sittang and British hopes of stopping the Japanese rested on holding the line of this important waterway. The first clash of arms took place on the banks of another river, the Bilin between 14 and 18 February. The 17th Infantry Division of the British Indian Army, which was holding the river, was overwhelmed by two Japanese divisions and forced to retreat. It pulled back towards the Sittang with the Japanese close on its heels. What happened next still divides opinion. The 16th and 46th Indian infantry brigades had still not reached the bridge over the Sittang by 22 January while enemy efforts to take the bridge had mounted. Brigadier Sir John George Smyth, V.C. was faced with an agonising decision. If he tried to hold onto the bridge to give his two missing brigades chance to fight their way through to the river, he risked the bridge being taken by the Japanese who would then be able to race directly to Rangoon. If he destroyed the bridge, the Japanese advance towards the Burmese capital would be seriously delayed. Smyth decided that he could not risk the Japanese storming the bridge and at 05.30 that morning, the bridge was destroyed.

Bill Norman was one of those troops stranded on the wrong side of the Sittang: 'On reaching the river bank I was surprised to see it deserted, not a soul in sight. While making up our minds as to how we could cross, a man appeared from nowhere who was from our platoon. He told me that the platoon had made rafts but they fell apart and he was able to scramble back to the shore. He feared that many had drowned.' One of Norman's comrades found a very thick bamboo pole which he threw into the water: 'Clad in only our shorts we had a good drink out of the river and set off on our pole. It was nice to discover that we could wade about two hundred yards before we got out of our depth, pointing a pole at a landmark we swam ... Once again, we lost all sense of time, we just swam and swam, resting every now and then.' They eventually reached the other bank, so exhausted they were barely able to stand. 'We had done it,' wrote Norman, 'and the feeling of relief was something I could never describe.'[1] In fact quite a number of men were able to cross the Sittang and re-join their regiments.

Historian Jon Latimer called the disaster at the Sittang Bridge 'a defining moment in the decline and fall of the British Empire,' and Wavell immediately dismissed Smyth who was never given another command.[2]

It was later revealed that Smyth had sought permission from General Officer Commanding Burma Command, General Thomas Hutton, to retire behind the Sittang ten days earlier. Hutton denied Smyth's request and as a result two-thirds of the 17th Division was stranded on the wrong side of the river. Hutton was superseded by General Harold Alexander. In all fairness to Hutton, he was merely following the orders of Wavell, who after passing on the appeal from Smyth had told him: 'I have every confidence in judgement and fighting spirit of you and Smyth, but bear in mind that continual withdrawal, as experience in Malaya showed, is most damaging to morale of troops, especially Indian troops. Time can often be gained as effectively and less expensively, by bold counter-offensive. This especially so against Japanese.'

The Japanese eventually found an alternative crossing point and they reached Rangoon on 9 March. The British had evacuated the capital two days earlier – Wavell was determined to make sure there was no repeat of the embarrassing surrender of tens of thousands of British troops in Singapore just a few weeks earlier.

Though reinforcements, in the form of the British 7th Armoured Brigade and the 63rd Indian Infantry Brigade, had reached Rangoon after the Sittang Bridge debacle, this was not enough to hold back the Japanese who, by 6 March, had virtually surrounded the city. It was

---

1. W. Norman, *The Battle of Sittang 16-23 February 1942*, www.euxton.com/Army-Battle-for-Sittang-16-23-February-1942.htm
2. Join Latimer, *Burma: The Forgotten War* (John Murray, London, 2004), p.58.

INTRODUCTION

Wavell's and Alexander's intention to withdraw to Prome, on the River Irrawaddy, some 200 miles north of Rangoon.

Rangoon was the main port for supply of goods to the British army in Burma and its loss meant that the retreating troops were cut off from their supply base. As there was no road from Burma to India, Alexander's force was virtually isolated with no possibility of outside assistance other than from the Chinese in the north, who Alexander hoped to join forces with.

The British drove away from Rangoon with the last lorries carrying the more robust of the wounded. Those that were unlikely to survive the journey were left behind. A medical officer gave those hopeless cases a final injection of morphine before the army pulled out. Four very courageous orderlies volunteered to stay behind to care for the wounded, placing their lives in the hands of the Japanese. The M3 Stuart tanks of the 7th Armoured Brigade lined the road as protection for the departing convoy as the enemy was rapidly approaching Rangoon.

In fact, the Japanese could easily have trapped the retreating British. Colonel Takanobu Sakuma with the Japanese 214th Regiment had already blocked the main highway to Prome. Alexander's men attacked the roadblock and were thrown back. Yet, seemingly inexplicably, a second attempt met with no opposition at all. It was later learnt that Sakuma's commanding officer, Sakurai, did not expect the British to retreat northwards. He thought that Alexander would mount a strong defence of Rangoon and then withdraw to the west. Sakurai, therefore, ordered the 214th Regiment to join the main body of the 33rd Division – and the British were allowed to escape. This was possibly the first bit of good luck the British had had since the start of the war. Had the roadblock remained in place, the British column, strung out for forty miles on a single road, would have been annihilated. As it was, the route north to Prome was nothing more than a narrow tarmac road which severely restricted the speed of the British withdrawal. Worse terrain, much worse, would later follow.

Alexander's luck, however, held a little longer. The Japanese had advanced so rapidly that they had outstripped their supplies and their operations ground to a temporary halt. This allowed Alexander the chance to establish positions along the Irrawaddy while the Chinese 6th and 66th armies (the equivalent of two British divisions) held a front to the south of Mandalay.

Every movement, though, by the British was hampered by the flood of refugees in their hundreds of thousands. To add to the chaos this caused, numbers of Burmese soldiers deserted to join the ranks of the Burma Independence Army which had joined the Japanese invasion, hoping to drive the colonialists from their country. The Burmese independence movement – the Freedom Bloc – had been increasingly active since the start of the war and the British troops could not rely on cooperation from the natives. It was not only the civilians who turned their backs on the British; the men of the Burma Frontier Force deserted in large numbers.

As well as losing Burmese support, the Chinese leader, Chiang Kai-shek, withdrew three of his armies after being attacked by the Japanese on 29 March. The Japanese also bombed Mandalay into virtual oblivion, with thousands of civilians killed: 'Every house was burned down or still flaming and smouldering,' wrote American reporter Clare Boothe Luce. 'A terrible stink arose from 2,000 bodies in the ruins of brick, plaster and twisted tin roofing. Only the smoke-grimed stone temple elephants on the scarred path were watching guard over the Road to Mandalay, while buzzards and carrion crows wheeled overhead. Bodies were lying on the streets and bobbing like rotten apples in the quiet green moat around the untouched fort.'[3]

The Japanese started a major attack against the British on 1 April near Prome, and on 2 April, the Japanese commander, General Iida, established his headquarters at Toungoo deep in the heart of Burma.

Fierce fighting held up the Japanese, but it could not alter the final outcome. The other major Chinese contingent, the Chinese Expeditionary Force, which achieved a notable success against the Japanese at Hopong-Taunggyion south of Mandalay, also abandoned Burma and headed back into western China.

General Alexander then made the decision on 26 April to withdraw all his men to India. One of the great territories of the British Empire was about to be given up. Along with Hong Kong and Singapore, it seemed that British influence in the Far East, which had been nurtured for generations, was about to be swept away in a matter of just a few weeks.

The retreating troops faced three great threats. The first was that the Japanese might cut them off and push a strong force between them and India. The second was that their food supplies might run out. The third fear was the monsoon: 'This was the worse danger of all,' wrote Lieutenant General Bill Slim who had been placed in command of

---

3 Quoted in Rupert Clarke, *With Alex at War* [Kindle Edition], (Pen & Sword, Barnsley, 2014).

INTRODUCTION

Burma Corps consisting of the 17th Indian Infantry Division and 1st Burma Division. 'If it came while we were still struggling hundreds of miles from safety, the track would turn to the most glutinous mud, vehicles would be bogged [down], and all movement practically impossible. Immobilized, we should be in imminent danger of starving. Even a heavy shower or two might have disastrous consequences. The odds were we might escape either the Japanese, the failure of our supplies, or the monsoon, but our chances of avoiding all three were slender.'[4] As Wavell put it: 'operations were now a race with the weather as with the Japanese and as much a fight against nature as against the enemy.' The men faced a 130-mile trek through the most difficult of conditions along dusty paths that were destined to become quagmires when the rains came.

The conditions were such that the cohesion of many units fell apart: 'There were parties of troops that marched out in formed bodies under officers,' wrote Colonel E.C.V. Foucar, the author of this book, 'Chins [one of the major ethnic nationalities in Burma] of the Frontier Force were particularly good in this respect. They retained their discipline to the last. On the other hand, many, and particularly Indians of the Burma Frontier Force, were only too ready to shoulder aside civilians in their anxiety to reach safety. Stores and villages were looted, and refugees robbed, and the threat of arms was freely employed.'

This, of course, led to reprisals and sometimes men would simply disappear overnight, no doubt murdered. It was easy for men to go missing in such circumstances as no one would spend time or effort searching for them. The Burmese also took advantage of the helplessness of the Indian and Anglo-India refugees, murdering and robbing them.

Equally, the Japanese showed no mercy to Indian soldiers who fell into their hands. They were rounded up, their hands tied and placed in bamboo huts, which were doused in gasoline and then set on fire. Even British officers who were captured, were stripped, tied to trees and used for bayonet practice.[5]

In his official report Wavell described the road between Ye-U and Kalewa: 'This road was nothing more than a sandy track ... which caused the abandonment of the major portion of the Motor Transport and all tanks. The track from Ye-U passed through innumerable chaungs or nullahs [a riverbed or ravine] some of which were dry

---

4 Field Marshal Viscount Slim, *Defeat into Victory* (Pan, London, 1999), pp.98-9.
5 See Pike, p.286.

and sandy and some of which were wet ... there was a difficult hill section with many rickety bridges constructed only of brushwood or bamboo. Anyone seeing this track for the first time would find it difficult to imagine how a fully mechanised force could possibly move over it.'[6]

The last stage of the march proved the most punishing, with the men ill and exhausted. Apart from wading through rivers and clambering up steep gorges, the men had to deal with poisonous insects and snakes – including King Cobras that could grow up to eighteen feet long.

Though for much of the withdrawal the British, Indian and Burmese troops had had to fight the Japanese, often hand-to-hand, the last stage of the retreat was without incident, the only fear being that the enemy might move up the River Chindwin and cut the army off from the India border. So difficult was the track the troops had to negotiate, even a small body of Japanese could have fatally delayed the weary troops, but that last, arduous march was conducted without interference from the enemy.

The fear of being cut off from India, however, meant that there was no rest for the men, and as they trudged on, sleep, and efforts to overcome it, became a principal factor: 'all anyone wanted to do was just to sink down wherever one could and go to sleep,' wrote Lieutenant John Randle of the 7th Battalion, 10th Baluch Regiment. He recalled that one portly staff officer simply sat down and said to Randle: 'I'd rather die, than march any more,' and die he did.[7]

The majority persevered and finally reached the Indian border: 'They were filthy, bearded, ragged and in the uttermost extremes of exhaustion,' wrote one of those survivors. 'Their shirts – those that still had shirts – were black with sweat, and tomorrow they would be white from the dried sweat of perspiration ... Some were lucky enough to still have their boots and in most cases the soles were flapping with a melancholy rhythm ... Some were barefoot ... There were men with bright and burning eyes which told of malaria and men with the yellow faces and eyes which are the forerunners of jaundice ... There were others ... that staggered blindly on, leaving a melancholy trail of blood in their wake.'[8]

---

6 John Grehan & Martin Mace, *The Fall of Burma 1941-1943* (Pen & Sword, Barnsley, 2015), p.81.
7 John Randle, *Battle Tales From Burma* (Pen & Sword, Barnsley, 2004), p.20.
8 Tim Carew, *The Longest Retreat, The Burma Campaign 1942* (Hamish Hamilton, London, 1969), p.5.

INTRODUCTION

Colonel E.C.V. Foucar wrote the first, and exceptionally detailed narrative of this campaign in 1942, not to highlight the horrors of the retreat or the courage of the men, but as an objective, impartial assessment of the circumstances which led to the desperate situation the British Army found itself in when the Japanese invaded in 1942. He had an intimate knowledge of Burma and he wrote other books about this intriguing country, its climate, terrain and people – all of which played important parts in the First Burma Campaign.

John Grehan
Storrington
October 2019

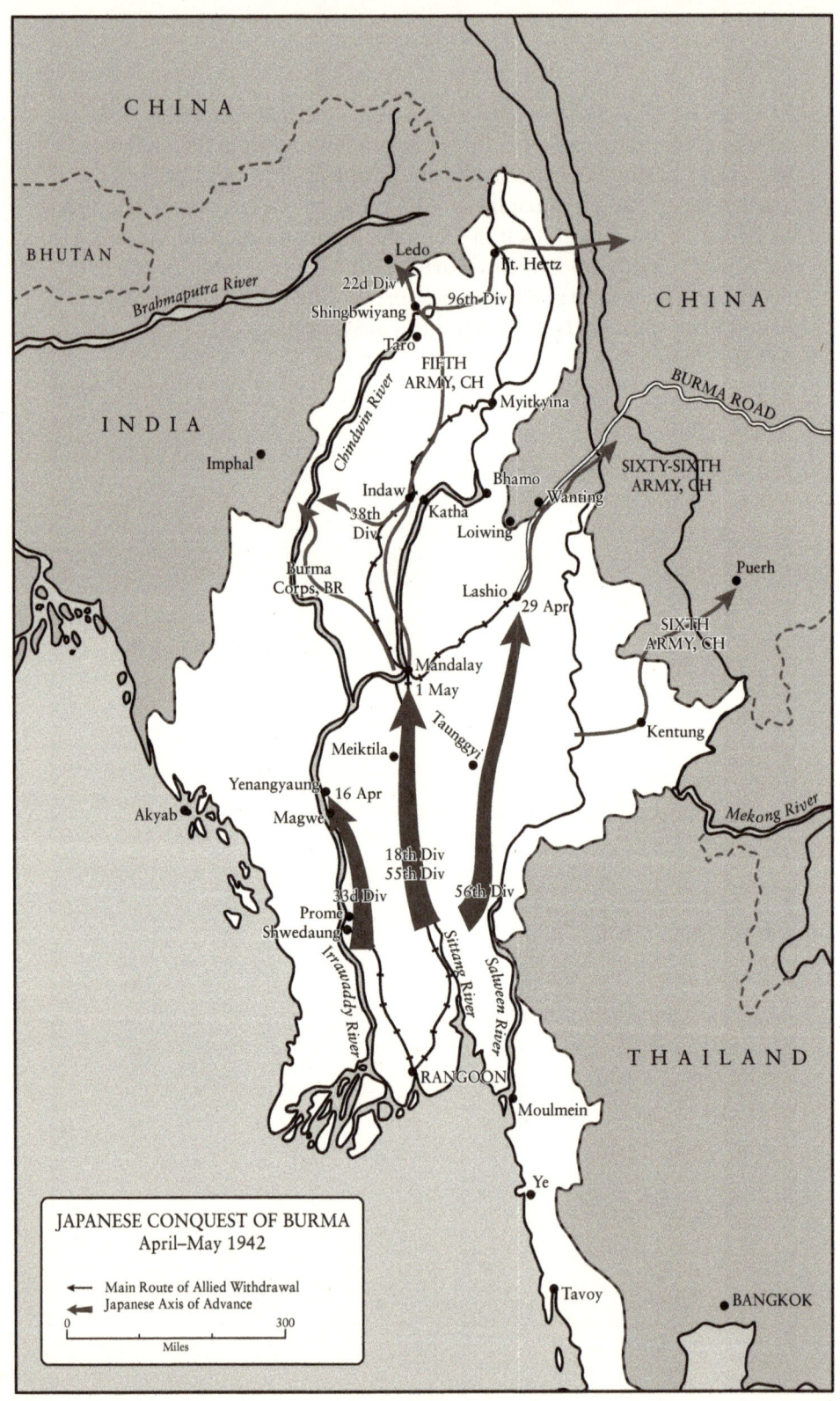

The Japanese conquest of Burma, April-May 1942.

Chapter 1

Burma – Its physical features – Resources and Industries – Main towns – Railways, roads and waterways – Lack of Communications with neighbouring countries.

Burma lies to the east of the Bay of Bengal. On the north-west and north it adjoins Tibet, the Indian State of Manipur, and the provinces of Assam and Bengal. On the north-east it is bordered by Chinese territory, and on the east by French Indo-China and Thailand. Its coastline from the mouth of the Naf river in the Akyab district in the west to Maliwun in the extreme south is about twelve hundred miles in length. The total area of the country is about two hundred and forty thousand square miles. It is approximately the same size as Spain and Portugal. Roughly speaking, its shape may be likened to that of the conventional diamond with a long thin tail projecting south. This tail forms the greater part of the Tenasserim division and is the north-western portion of the Malay peninsula.

Burma falls into three natural divisions, the Arakan and the Chin Hills, the Irrawaddy and the Sittang basins, and the province of Tenasserim together with those Shan and Karenni States lying in the basin of the Salween. These three natural divisions run north and south.

The Arakan Yomas, steep and jungle clad, thrusting south from the Chin Hills cut off the coastal belt of Arakan from the most fertile and populous part of Burma, the Irrawaddy valley.

The Irrawaddy is one of the great rivers of Asia and it is navigable as high as Myitkyina about one thousand miles from the sea. The river rises beyond the confines of Burma in the Himalayas, and in its long course through Burma traverses very varying tracts of country. First there is the hilly country at the sources of the Chindwin, its main tributary, and in the stretches north of Mandalay. It drains much of the northern Shan States, a mass of rugged hills and deep gorges. Next it traverses the dry zone of Burma. This extends from the north of Mandalay to Thayetmyo and consists mostly of open undulating lowland, broken in the south-east by the Pegu Yomas, a considerable range of comparatively low hills running north and south and separating the Irrawaddy and Sittang rivers.

In the dry zone, as the name implies, rainfall is lower than in the rest of Burma. In general, this tract is arid, and vegetation is scanty as compared with other portions of the country. Below the dry zone from just south of Prome is the Irrawaddy delta, a vast and fertile plain, unbroken by hills, and extending to the sea. This delta consists almost entirely of a rich alluvial deposit and is the main rice-growing area of the country. It supports many prosperous towns and villages.

Although cut off from it by the Pegu Yomas the valley of the Sittang geographically forms part of the Irrawaddy basin. The mouth of the Sittang lies within the deltaic area of the Irrawaddy, and like the Irrawaddy it flows through the central plain of the country.

The third natural division of Burma comprises in its southern portion the administrative division of Tenasserim, that narrow strip on the Malay peninsula lying between the river Salween and the Bay of Bengal on the west and the hills forming the Thai Frontier. From these hills run many streams and rivers, several of them flowing into the Salween or its tributaries, others into the Bay of Bengal. The low-lying land in the Tenasserim area is mainly under rice or other cultivation, but there are vast areas of dense jungle. Further north the Salween traverses the Shan States and Karenni. It is also one of the great rivers of the world rising in Tibet north of Lhasa. It is too swift to be navigable, except to a limited extent near its mouth, and much of its course runs through deep gorges, save where it is crossed by the Burma road, in Chinese territory, it is unbridged. In its lower reaches it is on or near the frontier with Thailand and is a formidable natural obstacle.

Burma is encircled on three sides by mountain ranges, all forming part of the eastern Himalayan chain. In the north are the Naga Hills and the Kumon range. The Naga Hills are continued on the south-west by the Chin Hills which are then prolonged southwards by the Arakan Yomas. These follow the Arakan coast to its south-west extremity at Cape Negrais. East of the Kumon range are the Kachin, Shan, and Karen Hills extending from the Irrawaddy valley into China far beyond the Salween and thence south towards Thailand. From these hills a long narrow range known as the Dawnas thrusts further south to form the eastern watershed of the Salween and to separate Tenasserim from Thailand. Also running north and south through central Burma and dividing the valleys of the lower Irrawaddy and the Sittang are the

CHAPTER 1

Pegu Yomas. Although somewhat detached from the other ranges they are geographically a part of them. All these hills, save for certain areas of open plain and down-land in the Shan States, are forest clad and steep. On the east of the Shan States the frontier with Indo-China is demarcated by the broad Mekong river.

Burma has two very clearly defined seasons. During the period of the south-west monsoon from mid-May to the end of September the greater part of the country is subject to a very heavy rainfall. This is heaviest in the coastal regions of Arakan and Tenasserim where it exceeds two hundred inches. It is also very heavy along the Assam border region. In the dry zone the average is between twenty and thirty inches. During the dry season between October and May little or no rain is experienced, and from the end of March until the break of the monsoon the heat in the plains is very great. This is particularly so in the dry zone.

In 1941 the population of the country probably exceeded fifteen million. The last available figures were those of the 1931 census. The indigenous races accounted for about thirteen and a half millions, these being nearly ten million Burmans, a million and a half Karens, and a million Shans. Of the non-indigenous population, the most important communities in 1941 were the Indians (one million) and the Chinese, probably two hundred and fifty thousand. Much of the coolie labour in the country was provided by the Indian population which was also engaged to a large extent in trade. Many Indians, too, had settled in the country as cultivators, more particularly in the fertile rice growing districts of Lower Burma. The Chinese were an industrious and important community long settled in the country, and upon the opening of the Burma road and the development of overland communications with China their numbers had rapidly grown.

Cultivation is the most important industry in Burma and the greater part of the population is engaged directly or indirectly in it or in connected occupations. The staple crop is rice.

A characteristic feature of Burma is its extensive paddy lands. They cover the Delta and a great part of Lower Burma, but almost every available piece of suitable flat land throughout the country is under rice cultivation. In the rainy season these lands are under water. In the dry weather after the harvest they are sun-baked and dusty. Each filed is surrounded by a low bund of earth which serves to retain water on it during the planting and cultivating periods.

The export trade in rice has been very great for many years. Other crops grown, particularly in Upper Burma, are sugar cane, tobacco, cotton, ground nuts, maize and some wheat.

Following the example of Malaya and the Dutch East Indies, rubber cultivation was successfully introduced into Burma. In 1941 large areas in Tenasserim and around Rangoon and Toungoo were planted with rubber, and the rubber production of Burma was by no means inconsiderable.

The forests of the country are large and very fine, and Burma produces the worlds main supply of teak. The timber industry is, after cultivation, the most important.

The mineral wealth of Burma is great. It has oil, tin and wolfram, lead and silver, amber, jade and precious stones. Much of this still remains to be exploited, but the oil industry has been carried on for over a hundred years. At first oil was extracted by the Burmese by primitive methods, but in 1889 the Burmah Oil Company Ltd., began operations on modern lines. The principal oil-bearing areas are situated along the Irrawaddy at Thayetmyo, Yenangyaung, Chauk, Lanywa and Yenangyat. In 1941 several large companies were interested in oil production. There were some small refineries on the oilfields but the important refining plants were at Syriam, Thilawa, and Seikgyi near Rangoon. The largest of these was the Burmah Oil Company's plant at Syriam. To this refinery oil was brought direct by a pipe line from the fields at Yenangyaung and Chauk.

The production of tin and wolfram was developed during the first World War, and thereafter the industry was considerable in Tenasserim. In this area numerous large mines and dredging areas were being worked in 1941. There was also an important tin and wolfram mine at Mawchi in the Karenni state of Bawlake.

At Namtu in the northern Shan States was the silver lead mine of the Burma Corporation. Here lead was produced on a very large scale and Namtu was connected by the private railway of the Burma Corporation with the northern Shan States branch of the Burma Railways at Namyao twenty-five miles distant from Namtu.

Rangoon, the capital city and main port, is situated on the Rangoon river in the Irrawaddy delta. It is about twenty-five miles from the sea. It may well be termed the gateway of Burma since from it radiate all the lines of communication through the country. In 1941 it had a population of about half a million, of which the largest part was Indian. It was the commercial and industrial centre and through the port passed by far the greater part of the country's imports and exports. In it or in its environs were housed large rice and timber mills and a great part of such minor industrial activities as had been established in Burma.

CHAPTER 1

Moulmein, Bassein and Akyab, the only other seaports of any size, were in 1941 badly served by land communications and therefore of very minor importance. From them was exported rice, and Moulmein in addition exported timber and some of the rubber and mineral ore of Tenasserim. Kyaukpyu, Sandoway, Tavoy, and Mergui were still smaller ports utilised mainly by country craft and coastal shipping.

In 1941 the inland communications of Burma were, generally speaking, bad. Away from the main centres of population they were practically non-existent. No railway or road connected the country with India or Malaya.

The Burma Railways, recently taken over by the Government, operated on the metre gauge. With a small exception it was of single track throughout its length. The main line ran from Rangoon to Mandalay, a distance of three hundred and eighty-six miles. Of this the first hundred and seventy-six miles consisted of a double track, the remainder and all branch lines being single.

From Pegu, forty-seven miles north of Rangoon on the main line, ran two branch lines. One ran south to Thongwa through a rich paddy growing district. The other ran east to Martaban on the west bank of the Salween above Moulmein. A ferry connected it with Moulmein and the line then ran south from that place to Ye.

From Pyinmana, two hundred and twenty-six miles north of Rangoon, a branch line ran north-west to Taungdwingyi and Kyaukpadyaung, the nearest rail point to the oilfields at Yenangyaung and Chauk.

At Thazi junction, three hundred and six miles north of Rangoon, began two branch lines. The southern Shan States branch ran east to Kalaw and terminated at Shwenyaung just west of Taunggyi, the capital of the Shan States. The other branch was a loop to Meiktila and Myingyan, an important centre on the Irrawaddy. It rejoined the main line at Paleik, twelve miles south of Mandalay.

From Rangoon a second line ran north-west via Tharrawaddy to Prome, a hundred and sixty-one miles distant, on the Irrawaddy. From this line a branch at Letpadan connected by ferry with Henzada, on the right bank of the Irrawaddy, and from Henzada a branch ran north to Xyangin whist another ran south to Bassein to serve the western portion of the Irrawaddy delta.

Mandalay, after Rangoon, was in 1941 the most important railway and communications centre in Burma. It had a population of over one hundred thousand and was the second city in size in the country. Its population was predominantly Burmese. From this city ran the railway through the Northern Shan States to Lashio. Another short line ran north, seventeen miles to Madaya. A third line ran to the Irrawaddy a few miles south of the city opposite Sagaing. Crossing the river by the recently completed road and rail Ava Bridge, it turned north to Shwebo and Myitkyina. From Sagaing there was a branch line to Monywa and Alon on the Chindwin river. It terminated at Ye-U.

There was under construction a new line which was to link Lashio with a Chinese railway also then being constructed from Kunming to the Burma frontier. This new line, known as the Burma-China Railway, did not form part of the Burma Railways but was directly controlled by the British Government. A few miles of the permanent way had been laid at the end of 1941.

The railway system also had two or three other branch lines of minor importance. To these it is unnecessary to refer.

There were several important railway bridges. On the main line there were the bridges over the Pazundaung creek just outside Rangoon, and across the Myitnge river a few miles south of Mandalay. The Ava Bridge over the Irrawaddy has already been mentioned. This bridge had only recently been completed and was approximately thirteen hundred yards in length.

On the Martaban branch was the important bridge across the Sittang river at Mokpalin, and a smaller bridge across the Bilin river at Hninpale.

The Gokteik viaduct on the northern Shan States line must also be mentioned. This viaduct, a steel trestle structure, carried the railway across the deep Gokteik gorge, the bottom of the gorge being several hundred feet below the track. The tallest steel pier of the viaduct was three hundred and twenty feet in height.

The road system in Burma in 1941 was very poor. There was no real overland communication between the Arakan division and the rest of the country. A single unfrequented track unfit for motor transport from the right bank of the Irrawaddy near Prome ran west across the Arakan Yomas to Taungup, a village on the coast. Otherwise, the only available routes were by sea or air from Rangoon.

Elsewhere there were few main roads, and those that existed had few feeder roads. Of the main roads the most important was the all-weather road from Rangoon to Mandalay. From Pegu onwards it followed the railway fairly closely. Twenty miles north of Rangoon at Taukkyan this road forked, the other fork running north-west to Tharrawaddy, Prome, Allanmyo and Taungdwingyi. Beyond Taungdwingyi the road deteriorated. Traversing the oilfields, it turned east near Kyaukpadaung and rejoined the main Mandalay road to Meiktila. This road was only metalled and bridged in parts, and many

CHAPTER 1

difficult and dangerous chaungs (water-courses) were unbridged. One of these was the treacherous sandy Pin Chaung just north of Yenangyaung.

There was no road link between Rangoon and Moulmein, and the bridge over the Sittang river was not a road bridge. The road gap extended from Waw, norther-west of Pegu, to Kyaikto, sixteen miles beyond the Sittang. From Kyaikto there was a motor road through Thaton to Martaban, the ferry station for Moulmein.

The Tenasserim Division was well-nigh roadless. From Moulmein a road ran south to Amherst through Thanbyyuzayat from which latter place a short branch went to Pangna. South of this there was no road to Ye, but beyond the Ye river a road led to Tavoy and Mergui. This was cut by numerous wide streams and rivers traversed by primitive ferries. Beyond Mergui the normal means of communication with Victoria Point was by sea. There were no roads.

The Military Defence programme contemplated an all-weather road connecting Rangoon with Mergui. This work was begun by the Public Works Department in 1941. It involved the completing of gaps in the existing road system and much bridging and resurfacing. Little progress had been made before the Japanese invasion of the country.

There were no road links between Moulmein, Tavoy or Mergui with Thailand, but there were three recognised routes. The easiest approach was from Moulmein by the Gyaing river to Kyondo, and onwards from that point by road to Kawkareik. In 1941, the inferior road between Kawkareik and the frontier village of Myawaddy had been improved. At Myawaddy the Thaungyin river, a tributary of the Salween, formed the frontier line. Beyond lay the Thai town of Mesohd where there was a landing ground. A good cart track connected Mesohd with the important Thai centre of Raheng. Another cart track from Thailand entered Burma by the Three Pagodas Pass, south-east of Moulmein. This track continued until it joined the Kawkareik-Kyondo road. The third route was from Tavoy, from which place a road ran east to Myitta, not many miles from the frontier. Beyond Myitta a track went on into Thailand.

From the large town of Toungoo on the main Rangoon-Mandalay road there had recently been constructed a road running east to Mawchi and Kemapyu on the Salween. On the outskirts of Toungoo this road crossed the Sittang by an important bridge. At Kemapyu near which it traversed a high suspension bridge the road turned north to Bawlake and Taunggyi.

Meiktila, north of Toungoo on the main Mandalay road, was an important road junction. Eastward went the road through the Southern

Shan States to Taunggyi, Loilem, Kengtung and the frontier village of Tachilek, where it joined the Thai road system linking up with Chiang Rai. This road crossed the Salween by a difficult ferry at Takaw. It had several feeder roads running north and south. Some of these connected with the important Mandalay-Lashio-Wanting road through the Northern Shan States. This last-named road had recently been considerably improved on the stretch between Maymyo and Lashio and had also been extended from Lashio to the Chinese frontier at Wanting, where it linked up with the new Burma road to Kunming and the Chinese capital at Chungking. It had come into prominence since 1938, forming the main line of communication between China and the outside world after the cutting of the Hankow Canton Railway by the Japanese. From the end of 1938 onwards, it carried an immense amount of traffic.

The Shan States were better served with roads than the rest of Burma, and the Mandalay-Lashio-Wanting road also had several feeder roads running to the north. The most important of these went to Bhamo and thence by a poor track to Myitkyina.

From Mandalay a road led to Sagaing beyond the Irrawaddy, crossing the river by means of the Ava Bridge. It continued north to Sawebo and Kinu, thence west to Ye-U on the Mu river, a tributary of the Irrawaddy. At Ye-U it went south to Alon and Monywa on the Chindwin river, then ran east to Myinmu on the Irrawaddy. West of Monywa and Ye-U there were no roads. This Sagaing-Shwebo-Monywa road was the most important on the west side of the Irrawaddy which was almost roadless. There were a few minor roads in the neighbourhood of the towns of Minbu and Pakokku, but in the main communications were here maintained by tracks. In the dry weather many of the tracks in these districts and also throughout the country were motorable, the flat paddy lands affording a tolerably level surface. These tracks carried an appreciable amount of traffic and to some extent remedied the paucity of roads throughout the country. In the rainy season, however, with the paddy lands under water, wheeled traffic in Burma became confined to the all-weather roads where it was also often interrupted. Un-bridged chaungs were frequently impassable. Washouts on the railways were no uncommon occurrence.

The Irrawaddy has always been an important line of communication in Burma. From earliest times its valley has been the most populous area in the country, and before roads were built the river was the one convenient highway. It carried men and merchandise, it determined plans of campaign, and formed the main line of advance or retreat for

CHAPTER 1

armies; and down its waters from Central Asia came the early invaders of the country. Its delta area is intersected by innumerable streams and here water transport necessarily remained the only form of conveyance.

The Burman relies largely on his streams and rivers for communications. Particularly in the season of the monsoon, small boats of shallow draught penetrate innumerable small streams, and at all times country craft of every size are to be found on all inland waters. On these, too, ply many river steamers, cargo boats, flats, and launches. In 1941 the Irrawaddy Flotilla Company operated a very large fleet. The Company's vessels maintained regular services on the Irrawaddy and throughout the Delta, on the lower reaches of the Salween and its tributaries around Moulmein, and on the Chindwin.

The Chindwin is the main tributary of the Irrawaddy. Rising in the far north of Burma on the borders of Assam it flows south-west on the eastern side of the Naga and Chin Hills. Turning south-east it joins the Irrawaddy just above Pakokku, south of Mandalay. Through the greater part of its length until reaching Monywa its course is through rugged and dense jungle country very sparsely populated. Much of its valley is malarial. In 1941 this area had no road connection with the rest of Burma and the river was the only link. It is navigable by very shallow draught steamers for a very considerable part of its length.

From Kalewa, Mawlaik, and Sittaung on the west bank of the river, rough tracks led into the Kabaw valley where flows the Yu river, a tributary of the Chindwin. From the Kabaw valley difficult tracks led over the hills to Imphal in Assam. The most important of these tracks ran from Tamu to Imphal, via Lokchao and Palel. At Imphal terminated a motor road from Dimapur (Manipur road) on the Bengal and Assam Railway. Another track from Kalemyo in the Kale valley keeping west of the Chindwin connected with Pakokku on the Irrawaddy.

Upon the development of commercial aviation in the period following the first Great War, Burma became an important link in the Imperial route from Great Britain to Australia. The airport of Mingaldon near Rangoon was built, and a landing ground at Akyab was constructed. Flying boats used Rangoon and Akyab as ports of call. Indian, Dutch and French commercial aircraft also called at these two places, and in 1941 an air service was operating between Chungking and Rangoon. There was an intermediate stop at Lashio where an airfield had been built. There were emergency landing grounds at Moulmein, Tavoy and Mergui, and in connection with the defence scheme for Burma other airfields had either been completed or were being built.

Chapter 2

Early history of Burma – British associations with the country – The wars with Burma – British Rule – Self Government and its results – Japanese influences.

The Burmese are an Indo-Chinese people with the physical characteristics of the Mongoloid races who originally came from the eastern Himalayas and western China. They are supposed to have formed part of the vast migratory swarm that spread outwards to Tibet, Assam, Burma, Malaya and Thailand. In Burma they followed the course of the Irrawaddy to the plains.

Their early history is obscure, but by the eleventh century they were firmly established with a splendid capita at Pagan on the Irrawaddy. The magnificent architecture of this capital city is still evidenced by its ruins. They lie some twenty miles north of Chauk on the east bank of the river. The city and the dynasty were destroyed in a Mongol invasion during the reign of Kublai Khan in 1284 A.D.

Thereafter for a long period the country was divided into petty, warring kingdoms, until in the 16th century the kingdom of Pegu rose to power. Its supremacy was later challenged by a new dynasty in Ava in Upper Burma. Eventually Ava under the leadership of Alompra, a native of the Shwebo district, subdued Pegu. Alompra united Burma and embarked on a scheme of foreign conquest. He took Mergui and Tenasserim from Thailand, then laid siege to Ayuthia, the capital of Siam. He fell ill and retreated to Burma where he died. In the years that followed his death his son, Sin-Byu-Shin, also sought to enlarge the kingdom. The war with Siam was continued and Manipur was invaded.

Prior to the time of Alompra there were European settlements in Burma. The Portuguese had been the earliest to enter the country and had established themselves at Syriam. They had been followed by the Dutch, the French, and the English who set up trading stations.

CHAPTER 2

In 1759 Alompra massacred the English in their settlement of Negrais, suspecting them of aiding his enemies.

The growth of Burmese power and expanding British interests in India inevitably led to frontier disputes. The first of these was in 1795 when a large body of Burmese troops entered the district of Chittagong. The matter was amicably settled and for a time peace prevailed. But the arrogance of the Burmese and their belief that the rich city of Calcutta would be an easy prize led them into further frontier encroachments. They carried off British subjects and attacked a military post. Eventually in 1824 the British Government declared war, and an invading force sailed up the Rangoon river. Rangoon was speedily taken and the Burmese Tenasserim provinces of Tavoy and Mergui were then reduced. Other operations were carried out in Assam and Arakan. The main difficulty facing the British troops was climate, and the ranks of the expedition were sadly thinned by disease.

Late in 1824 the Burmese general, Maha Bandula, assembled a large army and marched on Rangoon. He was defeated, and later when retreating on Prome was killed by a bomb. The British occupied Prome, remaining there for the rainy season of 1825. By the end of the year the Burmese were suing for peace but they employed the respite they thus obtained to prepare for a renewal of the war. Consequently, Sir Archibald Campbell who was in command of the British forces advanced up the Irrawaddy. When he was within four days march of Ava, the capital, the Burmese accepted his peace terms and a treaty was concluded. By this treaty Burma inter alia surrendered to the British the province of Arakan, and Ye, Tavoy, and Mergui. Burma gave up all claims to Assam and its contiguous petty states, agreed to pay an indemnity, and to receive a British Resident at the capital. British ships were no longer to be required to unship their rudders and land their guns when calling at Burmese ports.

This treaty had been made by King Ba-gyi-daw and whilst he reigned it was observed in the main. He was deposed by his brother Tharawadi who made no attempt to conceal his hatred and contempt for the British. His example was followed by the Court, and the British Resident was eventually withdrawn from Burma. Tharawadi's successor, Pagan, maintained the same attitude. Acts of violence were committed at Rangoon on British ships and seamen. Protests were of no avail. The result in 1852 was the Second Burmese War.

From Moulmein, in British Tenasserim, Martaban on the west bank of the Salween river was bombarded, then attacked and captured. A force sailed for Rangoon under General H.T. Godwin. The town was taken on March 14th after a sharp fight round the Shwe Dragon Pagoda. Bassein was seized, and after some resistance Pegu was taken. The British advanced to Prome and in 1853 King Pagan was informed that thenceforth the Province of Pegu was British territory. There was no treaty.

King Pagan was deposed by his brother Mindon who was wise enough to realise the power of the British and avoided a fresh conflict. At the same time, he bitterly resented the annexation of Pegu and long refused to acknowledge it by a formal treaty. But his relations with the British were not otherwise wholly unfriendly although they deteriorated in later years. He built himself a new capital at Mandalay and died there in 1878. He was succeeded by one of his younger sons, Thibaw, who began his reign by the arrest and massacre in the Palace of all possible rivals to the throne. Relations with the British became strained. Once more the Resident was withdrawn. The government of the country fell into disorder and the peace of the British frontier was disturbed. British subjects in Burmese territory were subjected to violence. Embassies were sent by Thibaw to Europe to contract alliances with France and Italy, and British interests were threatened. Matters came to a head when the Burmese Government quite unjustifiably imposed a huge fine of £230,000 on the Bombay Burma Trading Corporation which held certain forest concessions in its territory. The Indian Government suggested that the matter should be referred to arbitration. Thibaw, urgently in need of money and determined to obtain it, rejected the suggestion. In October 1885 the British Government delivered an ultimatum. Thibaw was obdurate, and war followed.

A British force had been assembled at the frontier station of Thayetmyo on the Irrawaddy. Under command of Major General H.N.D. Prendergast V.C., it moved up the river on steamers and flats provided by the Irrawaddy Flotilla Company. The Burmese fort at Minhla was carried after a brisk engagement, and after this there was little resistance. On November 28th, in less than a fortnight from the declaration of war, Mandalay had fallen and Thibaw was a prisoner. Upper Burma was formally annexed on January 1st 1886.

Thibaws soldiery, accustomed to conditions of anarchy and rapine, dispersed. Many took their arms with them and began to prey upon the countryside. The suppression of these bands and the pacification of the country was a far more difficult task than had been the defeat of Thibaw. Reinforcements had to be sent to Burma and for some years the British were engaged in Jungle Warfare against large gangs of dacoits and malcontents.

They had been faced with a somewhat similar task, on a smaller scale, after the Second Burmese War. Then it had been the area about Tharrawaddy where order had to be re-established.

These two periods of pacification clearly illustrated the readiness of the Burmese to take advantage of any relaxation of authority. This trait in their character was to find expression again on more than one occasion in later years.

From the time when Arakan and Tenasserim had been annexed after the First Burmese War, British Burma was included in the administrative charge of the Governor General of India. In 1862 British Burma became a province of India, and was administered first by a Chief Commissioner, and later, from 1897, by a Lieutenant Governor with a Legislative Council of nine nominated members, of whom five were officials. This form of government continued substantially unchanged until 1923.

Meanwhile Burma developed steadily. After the Second Burmese War and the annexation of Pegu large numbers of people attracted by settled conditions had entered British territory from the Kingdom of Ava. Additional great areas of land were brought under cultivation, and with the opening of the Suez Canal there had been a rapid increase in the rice export trade. The port off Rangoon expanded and a railway was built to Toungoo. This was extended to Mandalay after the Third Burmese War; later it continued north to Myitkyina along the west bank of the Irrawaddy. Branch lines were constructed. The establishment of a stable government throughout the country attracted British and Indian capital. Rice milling and export, timber extraction, and the oil industry were developed and made important contributions to the revenues of Burma.

The Government of India Act in 1919 conferred a certain measure of self-government on the people of India. It provided each of the major provinces, which did not include Burma, with a Legislative Council consisting of a large majority of elected members. There was also created a Central Legislature composed of elected and nominated representatives of each province. The field of Government was divided by the Act into Central and Provincial subjects. The latter again, were sub-divided into 'transferred' and 'reserved' subjects. Reserved subjects were the responsibility of the Governor of a Province, whilst transferred subjects were under the control of the Legislative Council. Broadly speaking, matters relating to the administration of law and order and to finance were not transferred. Of course, the Defence of India and matters connected with the armed Forces, foreign affairs, and other subjects of intimate interest to India as a whole were entirely removed from Provincial control.

In 1923 Burma became a Governor's province and obtained a Legislative Council in accordance with the provisions of the Act of 1919. For the first time in the history of the country representatives elected by popular vote had a definite part in the government of Burma. The result was a great political awakening, and younger Burmans in particular became active in political matters. But personalities rather than parties dominated the scene. Leaders collected about them small groups of followers, but the loyalties of these frequently changed. They were rarely able to agree on matters of internal policy but united, on occasions, against the British Government. The spoils of office were eagerly sought and very liberally interpreted. Politicians encouraged youth movements of various kinds, and politics were introduced into school life. Pupils and University students were regularly employed to further political aims. Hpongyis (members of the Buddhist priesthood) entered into politics. The priesthood or wearers of the yellow robe, had always formed a very large and influential class wielding considerable authority. Many of its members with anti-British sentiments were active trouble makers.

Burma had only been linked to India as a matter of administrative convenience. Historically and geographically she was not a part of India. Her people, predominately Buddhist, were entirely distinct from the people of India. There was a general feeling in the country that a disproportionate share of Burma's revenues went to India and that little was received in return. Furthermore, the Burmese considered that as Self Government developed, they would find themselves under the rule of Indians unless detached from their neighbours. They had, rightly or wrongly, always considered themselves superior to the Indians. These factors led to a wide demand for separation from India, and this demand became insistent after the introduction of the reforms in 1923. The Indian Statutory Commission, popularly known as the Simon Commission, appointed to inquire into the development of representative institutions in British India was satisfied that the claim of Burma for separation from India was justified. This finding was embodied in the Report of the Commission published in 1930.

The Burmese as a race are inclined to improvidence and indolence. Content to exist as cultivators they played little part in the development of their country after its occupation by the British. When the cultivated areas increased, much of the work of harvesting was carried out by Indian immigrant labour. The economic pressure of a surplus population on the other side of the Bay of Bengal found a ready outlet in Burma. Indian coolies worked in the ports and in the rice and timber mills. Many of them returned to India after each harvest or at regular periods, but some remained to settle on the land. More industrious and frugal-minded than their Burmese neighbours, they prospered. Much of the trade in towns and villages was in Indian hands, and the Indian moneylender established himself throughout the country. Loans were made on the security of land, and when Burma was faced with a period of depression much land passed into possession of Indians.

In 1930 Burma suffered from economic troubles. Many Burmans could no longer extract an easy living from their paddy fields. Seeking means of livelihood, the poorer classes found that Indian labour had firmly established itself. The result in Rangoon was an outbreak of fierce racial riots, in which Indian coolies were attacked with great ferocity. At the end of the year there followed the Burma rebellion. This although directed against the Government was also largely anti-Indian. Numbers of peaceful Indian cultivators were slaughtered.

The rebellion was at its worst in the Tharrawaddy district, always a centre of unrest. Here a Burmese astrologer and so-called magician named Saya San proclaimed himself king. He purported to confer on his adherents the powers of invulnerability and invincibility. Magic talismans were distributed and many rebels were tattooed with allegedly protective designs. Saya San had a large following and for some time defied authority. There were also outbreaks in neighbouring districts and additional troops had to be drafted into Burma before the rising could be quelled.

Violent crime had always been exceedingly prevalent in the country. The passions of the Burman are easily roused and he is over ready to make use of his dah, a heavy broad bladed knife which serves equally well as a household implement or a dangerous offensive weapon. The rebellion of Saya San demonstrated that the British occupation had done little to alter the uneducated, rural Burman. He remained as easy prey for any plausible rogue who promised him loot and immunity from punishment. Saya San, like leaders in Burma before and after him, followed well-established precedents in distributing charms and causing his men to be tattooed. These credulous, superstitious men were not readily disillusioned. In this rebellion, as in all movements against the British Government, the Hpongyis played their part.

The year 1938 witnessed another outbreak of anti-Indian feeling. There were serious riots in Rangoon, and again numbers of Indians were attacked and killed.

In 1935 the British Parliament passed the Government of Burma Act. This came into force in April 1937 and effected the separation of Burma from India. It also conferred on the people of Burma a much-increased measure of self-government. The defence of Burma, the control of the armed forces, and some other matters were under the direct control of the Governor, but the important subjects of law and order and finance were now placed in charge of Ministers who were taken from the members of the Legislature. This comprised two Chambers, the House of Representatives and the Senate. The House of Representatives or lower house was composed entirely of elected members. Of the Senate half the members were elected by the House of Representatives whilst the remainder were non-officials nominated by the Governor. The Act provided for a maximum of ten Ministers and the members of the Ministry were drawn from the majority parties or groups in the Legislature.

Between the years 1937 and 1941 the Government was never stable. The Burmese members who held the greatest number of seats in the House were always divided into small groups. Coalitions of these never held together for long, and there were frequent changes of Government. They were only united in demands for the independence of Burma. Corruption and personal jealousies were rife with the result that no settled line of policy was pursued. No doubt these are features common to most infant democratic institutions. They were accentuated in a country that had been unaccustomed to anything even approximating to a popular form of government and where people were uneducated and without an understanding of the fundamentals of democracy. In the event it was unfortunate that the change took place so shortly before the outbreak of the Second World War.

Burmese politicians proved themselves remarkably insular in their outlook and had little regard to what was happening beyond their frontiers. When China was attacked by Japan and it was proposed to extend the Mandalay-Lashio road to the frontier to further the import of war material and supplies generally into China, they opposed the project. And whilst, as a political cry, they advocated the Burmanisation of the Armed Forces they criticised defence expenditure on the ground that Burma had no enemies. The Imperial aspect of the matter left them unmoved.

On the outbreak of war with Germany in 1939, the Burmese regarded the conflict as of little concern to themselves. Their politicians still continued to be occupied with purely local matters and the continual intrigue for office. The Burmese Press was either indifferent or anti-

British in tone. It had no sense of responsibility. It indulged largely in scurrility and harped continuously on the theme of injustice to Burma. Inspiration was drawn from communist and anti-British sources and there can be little doubt that here, as elsewhere, Japanese influences were active. These Burmese newspapers, with little counter-opinion circulating amongst their ignorant readers, were the source of much mischief.

It was not in the Burmese Press alone that Japanese propaganda was at work. Several leading Burmese politicians were in close touch with Japan, and it was freely stated that some of these were in receipt of funds from the Japanese. Such a fact, if true, would certainly explain many of their public utterances and actions and the general lack of enthusiasm for active co-operation in the war effort. There were notable exceptions, but this was the general attitude. It caused considerable attention in the case of U-Saw the Premier, who in 1936 had visited Tokyo and for a time was reported to be in receipt of Japanese money. When in December 1941 he was absent from Burma on a visit to Great Britain and America, the British Government, satisfied that he had made contact with the Japanese in the course of his travels, refused to allow him to return and detained him. Again, there was the ex-Premier Dr. Ba Maw who was reported in 1940 to have been among political leaders approached by the Japanese Consul. It was alleged that the Japanese offered to pay him for a lecture tour in Japan. In 1941 he resigned his seat in the House of Representatives and then made a speech advocating no help for Britain in the war, unless independence was promised to Burma. For this he was imprisoned and was in custody when the Japanese invasion of Burma began. He escaped on April 14th 1942. Later, when the enemy occupation was complete, he was appointed Chief Administrator of Burma by the Japanese.

At the first General Election held in 1936 for the newly constituted House of Representatives, the Thakin Party secured a few seats. This party had been formed during the troubled year of 1930. Its policy was frankly communist and violently anti-British and the merits of the participants in the recent rebellion were extolled by it. All its members were young men and many were of the student class. Oddly enough, and in spite of their alleged communist views, the members of the party throughout Burma feted a Japanese millionaire, Mr. Jirozaemon Ito, when he toured the country in 1934.

In the election of 1936, the Thakins secured well over seventy thousand votes, a significant result for a new party ill-equipped with funds. Subsequently the party made considerable headway, always obtaining active recruits and organisers from the students of Rangoon University and the High Schools. It won a number of seats at municipal elections, became increasingly involved in labour and agrarian disputes and agitation, and began to form volunteer corps throughout the country. These corps were declared to exist for the promotion of the moral, intellectual, and physical welfare of members, but party leaders constantly spoke of ejecting the British from Burma by force. Methods of violence and sabotage were freely advocated and detailed.

After the outbreak of war in 1939 the party repeatedly asserted its opposition to British interests and a determination to secure the freedom of Burma by force whilst the British were engaged in fighting elsewhere. More volunteer and student corps were formed by the Thakins and other political bodies, and paraded regularly. Thakins now began freely to express pro-Japanese sentiments because Japan agreed to help them in their fight for Independence. In 1940 at least one Thakin leader went to Tokyo where he was stated to be assisting the Japanese Government in the preparation of Burmese broadcasts. These were of a dangerous anti-British nature. A secret instruction was sent from Japan that Thakins should listen for 'significant messages' in these broadcasts.

Finally, during the course of 1941 several well-known Thakins and a number of young men, totalling some thirty odd in all, disappeared from Burma. They were receiving from the Japanese, military training and instruction in Fifth Column and sabotage activities. It is believed that Colonel Minari who trained these men and was later to lead the Burma Independence Army spent some months in Burma where he passed as the Secretary of the Japan-Burma Association.

Doubtless, numerically, the disaffected element was comparatively small until Japanese successes swelled its numbers. But it had powerful support from persons of influence like U-Saw, Dr. Ba Maw, and other political leaders. It had no particular love for Japan, but was ready to accept Japanese aid and did not pause to consider what that implied. The Japanese posed as the champions of Asiatic Independence and did not reveal their own plans. Yet it is difficult to understand how men like U-Saw and Dr. Ba Maw, were misled if, in fact, they were misled. The rank and file could be easily fooled.

The Japanese in Burma were themselves a small but prosperous community. In Rangoon they carried on several large business undertakings, and a considerable trade existed between Burma and Japan. Manufactured goods from that country found a ready market in Burma, whilst rice, cotton, and other products were largely exported in return. In Rangoon as well as in every town of any importance were to be found Japanese doctors, dentist, and photographers. These professions provided ideal opportunities for contact not only with Thakins but with people of all classes. They enabled much vital information to be collected. The Japanese in Burma made full use of their opportunities and every one of them reported to his Consul what he saw and heard. Undoubtedly road reconnaissances were made, and the traffic along the Burma Road to China was checked. Men who had lived in Burma and knew it well are reported to have returned with the invading army. It is interesting to note, too, that many experienced Police Officers held the view that the Japanese had a far greater share in Burma's internal troubles, than was generally known. They were suspected of fomenting the anti-Indian riots in 1938 and a subsequent serious strike in the oilfields in which the Thakin element was active.

Chapter 3

Events in the Far East – Japanese aims and aggression – Military forces in Burma – Military effect of the Separation from India – Creation of the Army in Burma – Expansion from 1939 onwards – State of preparedness of Burma on outbreak of war with Japan in December 1941 – Other Allied Forces in Burma on outbreak of hostilities – Forces employed by Japan in Burma.

Before passing to a consideration of the Army in Burma in 1941 and of the expansion that had taken place before that date it is necessary to review briefly the general situation in Eastern Asia. In the years following the termination of the First World War in 1918 the power of Japan had risen. With it had developed her expansionist aims and her hostility to European and American interests in China and throughout the Far East.

In 1921 the long-standing Anglo-Japanese alliance was terminated, and in the same year the British Parliament took the decision to enlarge and modernise the naval base of Singapore for the protection of the Eastern trade routes of the Empire. The work on the naval base was continued with some interruption for sixteen years and was completed in 1938.

The Burmese, if they considered the matter at all, regarded their country as safe from external aggression. This was not an entirely unjustified error. In its report made in 1930 the Simon Commission stated – 'The land frontier of Burma on the east is so difficult that it seems scarcely possible for any large body of men to cross it. In contrast, therefore, with the North Western Frontier, the defence of which is the constant anxiety of the Government of India and a vast drain upon its resources, the land frontiers of Burma are so

CHAPTER 3

comparatively secure that their defence has been entrusted principally to the Provincial Government.'

The British and other people within the Empire were slow to realise that there was any likelihood of attack from Japan. When they did so they visualised the struggle as one to be fought at sea with Singapore forming an impregnable bastion against the enemy.

Yet Japan was busily extending her interests in China. In 1931 she invaded Manchuria which in the following year, as the state of Manchukuo, declared its independence from China. This move was sponsored by Japan.

After an uneasy period of tension Japan again invaded Chinese territory. Shanghai, the business centre of China, was occupied and the Yangtse river was closed to navigation. British, American and other commercial interests were severely affected, but the protests of Great Britain, America and France brought no satisfaction.

The Canton-Hangkow Railway, China's main supply route, was cut in October 1938. To counter this move, the Chinese had constructed a great highway linking Chungking, their war-time capital in Western China, via Kunming and Paoshan with Wanting on the Burma frontier. Thence the road went on to Lashio where it made contact with the road and railway system of Burma. The Burma Road, as it came to be known, gave China direct access to the Port of Rangoon. This enabled China to continue her fight for existence.

The Burma Road did not permit of the passage of heavy artillery or the bulkier material of war; but large convoys of motor transport carried along its lighter arms, other munitions, petrol, and essential supplies. In addition, England and America helped China with credits. Thus encouraged, Generalissimo Chiang Kai Shek, China's leader, rejected a peace offer made by Japan at the end of 1938 and continued to oppose the invader. England and America had advanced a step nearer to war with Japan.

Many of the world's markets had been closed to Japan by the raising against her of high tariff walls. As a reply to this she evolved a long-cherished plan for the Mutual Prosperity Sphere which was to embrace all Eastern Asia and Oceania including Thailand and Burma. It was to be a new Order of the East and was held out as a scheme that would make this particular quarter of the world an economic entity. In reality Japan's intention was to secure freedom from competition and economic pressure and complete ascendancy over the countries surrounding her.

After the declaration of war by the British Empire and France against Germany in September 1939 events in the Far East also moved steadily towards a crisis. Japanese sympathies and self-interest favoured Germany and her Axis ally Italy. The latter country entered the war in June 1940 at a moment when a complete German victory seemed certain. There followed the Armistice between France and her enemies, and Great Britain was left to carry on the war alone.

Japan, like Italy, was not slow to take advantage of the situation. In June 1940 she established a blockade of Hongkong, preventing the transit of goods to China. In July Great Britain, hard pressed by the defeat of France, closed the Burma Road for three months. In September Japan entered into a ten-year pact with Germany and Italy for mutual support against any country not yet at war becoming involved in the European or Sino-Japanese conflicts. Almost simultaneously she compelled French Indo-China to permit the entry of her troops and the occupation of air bases in the northern part of the country. She made immediate use of her newly acquired rights, and now was within easy striking distance of the Philippines, Borneo, Malaya, the Dutch Indies, Thailand and Burma.

In 1941 Japan continued on her way of aggression. A boundary dispute between Thailand and French Indo-China gave her the opportunity to come forward as mediator. On the French she imposed acceptance of proposals for the cessation of territory to Thailand. Thus, she made Thailand her debtor and extracted further concessions from France. The occupation of key points in South Indo-China followed.

At the same time the Japanese Press suggested that Great Britain had aggressive designs on Thailand. Oddly enough reports were then current that it was Japan that was pressing for permission to use Thai bases. Furthermore, Thailand had accorded recognition to the puppet state of Manchukuo, and also entered into an agreement for the export of rice to Japan.

There was no doubt now about the tendencies of Japan's policy. Her only failure had been an abortive attempt to involve the Dutch East Indies in a trade, shipping and immigration agreement that would have virtually placed her in economic control of her neighbour. But her successes in Indo-China and Thailand induced Great Britain and America to act. They denounced their Commercial Treaties with Japan and at the end of July 1941 froze all Japanese assets in their territories. The practical effect of these measures was to paralyse Japanese foreign trade. Restrictions in respect of the export to Japan of oil, wool, and scrap-iron had already been imposed. Japan now had a clear warning that further aggression would not be tolerated.

CHAPTER 3

Negotiations followed. Whilst they were still in progress in Washington the Japanese on Sunday morning, December 7th, 1941, attacked the American naval base of Pearl Harbour in Hawaii. The next day, December 8th, Great Britain and America declared war. For many decades India had regarded her Eastern and North-Eastern frontiers with equanimity. It was the North-West frontier that must be watched with constant vigilance, and defence schemes and the training and disposition of troops were all made with this object. But on the East, beyond Burma, there lay no militarily powerful neighbours. China did not threaten, and the only trouble makers were primitive tribes dwelling in remote areas and incapable of anything more than petty annoyance. So secure did Burma seem that no overland line of communications was established between the province and the rest of India. The linking up of the Burma and Assam railway systems and the construction of a road had been discussed from time to time but there were always other and more pressing projects to be carried out. Trade did not require such a link and military necessity did not appear to demand it. The question was last considered in 1938 and then dropped on the grounds that the time had not come for considering it seriously.

In accordance with this view the Regular Forces maintained in Burma were small. Prior to Separation the Burma District formed part of the Indian Command. District Headquarters, located in the hill station of Maymyo, the Government summer capital, approximated to that of a lower scale Division. The Command was usually held by a General Officer whose last post it was to be before retirement, and the District came to be regarded as a safe place for 'duds'.

In the District which covered Burma and the Andaman Islands were stationed an Indian Mountain Battery, a Company of Sappers and Miners, two Battalions of British Infantry, and three, sometimes four, Battalions of the Burma Rifles. These last were, of course, a part of the Indian Army. There were also a few ancillary and administrative units. Apart from these regular troops there were certain units of the Auxiliary Force, India, and of the Indian Territorial Force.

Units were grouped into two areas, the Rangoon Brigade Area covering Lower Burma and the Andaman Islands, and the Maymyo Infantry Brigade Area comprising Upper Burma. This latter area was directly under the command of District Headquarters and had no separate Brigade Staff.

The primary duty of these forces was the maintenance of internal security and frontier watch and ward. There were also available for these duties nine Battalions of the Burma Military Police, a semi-civil organisation, not subject to military control but under the command of the Inspector General of Police, Burma.

In spite of the growing threat of Japanese aggression the strength of the forces in Burma had remained more or less constant over a long period prior to 1937, save for the temporary reinforcements that were made to cope with the rebellion that broke out in December 1930. With the restoration of order these additional troops were withdrawn.

Not the least of many important changes brought about by separation from India was the disappearance of the Burma District. By Sections 4 and 7 of the Government of Burma Act, 1935, control of all the armed forces of the Crown in Burma was vested in the Governor. For the purposes of administering these forces and dealing with the other subjects directly controlled by the Governor a Defence Department was created.

There thus came into being a small independent military command. It was carved out of the much larger Indian organisation and was necessarily deprived of many of the advantages possessed by the Indian Army. Its justification was the intention to establish Burma as a self-governing country independent of India, but from the military point of view the change was attended by obvious disadvantages. Furthermore, in the event of serious external aggression it was evident that the Army in Burma could not stand alone. It would be employed in delaying the invader until assistance arrived from other sources.

The severance from India resulted in the transfer of the Burma Rifles to the Army in Burma. It was intended that two British Battalions should continue to be maintained in the country mainly for internal security purposes, but that the Indian Army units should all ultimately be withdrawn. The two Indian Infantry Battalions did leave. To replace them the Training Battalion of the Burma Rifles was converted into an active Battalion, each Battalion thereafter training its own recruits. The Mountain Battery and the Company of Sappers and Miners remained on loan from India, but on the raising of the first company of Burma Sappers and Miners the Indian Company was withdrawn early in 1940.

The Auxiliary Force and Territorial units were embodied in the newly created Burma Auxiliary Force and Burma Territorial Force respectively. These units were:

Rangoon Field Brigade R.A. Burma Auxiliary Force.
(Armament, one Battery of four 18 pdr. guns)

Tenasserim Battalion, Burma Auxiliary Force.
(Headquarters and two Rifle Companies)

CHAPTER 3

Rangoon Battalion, Burma Auxiliary Force.
(Headquarters, and three Rifle Companies, and an Armoured Car Section)

Upper Burma Battalion, Burma Auxiliary Force.
(Headquarters, and two Rifle Companies)

Burma Railways Battalion, Burma Auxiliary Force.
(Headquarters, and four Rifle Companies composed entirely of railway personnel. The duties of the unit were the maintenance and protection of the railway system.)

11th Battalion Burma Rifles, Burma Territorial Force.
(The composition of this unit was Burmese and Karens)

Rangoon University Training Corps, Burma Territorial Force.

Separation effected an important change in the Burma Military Police. Six of its Battalions became the Burma Frontier Force. This body was administered by the Defence Department although it was not within the command of the G.O.C. Burma. It was placed under the Inspector General of the Burma Frontier Force. The three remaining Battalions together with the civil police were administered by the Home Department in charge of the Home Minister, an elected member of the Legislature, and responsible for the subjects of Law and Order. This force of police was under the Inspector General of Police.

With the general demand for the Burmanisation of all Government services there was included the demand for a greater proportion of Burmese in the Armed Forces. The word Burmese is here employed in contradistinction to Burman which includes all the indigenous races of Burma. The Burmese had no recent military traditions, had showed no desire in the past to serve in the Army, and were temperamentally unsuited to the discipline of a military career. The Regular Battalions of the Burma Rifles had been recruited from the indigenous tribes, the Chins and Kachins of the hills, and the Karens. The personnel of the Military Police (and later the Frontier Force) was largely Indian in composition. The Auxiliary Force was originally confined to Europeans, Anglo-Burmans, and Anglo-Indians. At the time of Separation in 1937 the Burmese element in the Army was therefore very small and mainly to be found in the Territorial Battalion of the Burma Rifles.

The Chins and Kachins were a potentially good military type, but their numbers were limited. The Karens were numerically larger, but qualitatively were not uniform. The Burmese formed the largest potential recruiting reserve, and to meet the political demand it was decided to give them increased representation in the Army. Burmese Class Companies were formed in three of the Regular Battalions of the Burma Rifles, and recruiting for the Burma Sappers and Miners was confined to Burmese. Incidentally this unit had first been raised during the First World War but, possibly short sightedly, had been later disbanded.

The scheme to enlist Burmese was accepted by the Military Authorities without enthusiasm. Political leaders who had pressed for it took little real interest in it. Finally, in the event, the scheme was adopted too late. When the Burma Army came to be tested its Burmese element consisted of young and inexperienced soldiers with similarly inexperienced Burmese N.C.Os. and G.C.Os.

The situation in the Far East and the peril of an outbreak of war in Europe led to a review of the measures for the defence of Burma. Early in 1938 an Inter Service Conference was held in Rangoon and certain recommendations were then made. These were considered by the Committee of Imperial Defence which advised the Secretary of State for Burma on them. As a result, plans were made for Anti-Aircraft Defence of Rangoon, the oil-fields areas, the oil refineries at Syriam near Rangoon, and other strategic points. Landing Grounds were to be protected. An examination battery of two 6" guns was to be installed at Dry Tree Point near the mouth of the Rangoon river. The desirability of proceeding with Air Raid Precautions was also generally agreed, but the protection of the civil population was rightly regarded as a matter for the Home Department of the Burma Government. The danger from aerial attack had always been clearly visualised by the Military Authorities. In this as in other matters the Ministry displayed a complete disregard for realities and no substantial measures for the protection of the general population were taken until the middle of 1941. It was then much too late to make up for lost time.

Early in 1939 the Governor approved the formation of another Territorial Battalion, 12th Battalion Burma Rifles. This too, was to be composed of Burmese and Karens. About the same time, it was decided to raise a Burma Army Signals unit. Later this unit was much enlarged to provide for the needs of the expanded Army.

On the outbreak of war with Germany in September 1939 Burma, together with other parts of the Empire, took certain protective measures and began to expand her forces. In the two years that followed and as Japanese intentions clarified this expansion was speeded up. There were, however, many limiting factors. Defence expenditure had been rigidly restricted. This was the initial reason

CHAPTER 3

for an over-worked staff, poor armament, and absence of adequate administrative services. Then, the recruiting reserve was small, particularly for the officer class. Arms, equipment and instructors in the country were inadequate for a rapidly growing force. The urgent demands of the Armies in Great Britain and in the active theatres of war naturally had preference, and the result was that this inadequacy was never fully remedied. Until the end of 1940 the supply of modern equipment for Burma had been entirely negligible. Lastly, the attitude taken up by most Burmese politicians who had minimised the gravity of the situation and claimed that Burma was not concerned with the war did nothing to assist the flow of recruits.

In September 1939 the Rangoon Field Brigade had been embodied and with its 18 pdr. guns manned the Examination Battery at Dry Tree Point. Later, when the 6" guns intended for the Battery arrived from England, the 18 pdr. guns were withdrawn and were then used to provide the armament of 5 Field Battery R.A., B.A.F., a permanently embodied battery of the Field Brigade the establishment of which was enlarged. The Field Brigade personnel continued to man the Examination Battery.

The Burma Frontier Force at once took over the defence of the landing grounds on the Singapore air reinforcing route, and a detachment of the Rangoon Battalion, B.A.F. was embodied for guard duties at Rangoon and Syriam. The formation of Garrison Companies for the carrying out of these and other guard duties had been visualised in 1938. The plan was at once put in hand, and these companies were eventually formed into two administrative Battalions, 1 (Oilfields) Garrison Battalion, and 2 (Rangoon) Garrison Battalion. Their personnel was obtained from ex-regular soldiers and also from substandard recruits, i.e. men who had not attained the physical standard or minimum age limit for regular soldiers. As these recruits grew up or developed physically a potential reserve for regulars was formed. New companies were raised by 'milking' existing companies whilst each company also trained a certain number of recruits to complete its strength. Class platoons were maintained in the Garrison Companies.

The main portion of the fighting troops of the Army in Burma consisted of the two British Infantry Battalions in the country with the Burma Rifles and the Burma Frontier Force and Military Police. Except in the case of the British units a very considerable expansion was made in 1940 and 1941. The quality of these troops was not without effect on the campaign which opened in December 1941. It is necessary therefore to discuss these units in some detail.

The two British Battalions were the 1st Battalion the Gloucestershire Regiment and the 2nd Battalion King's Own Yorkshire Light Infantry.

Both units had been in Burma for some time and had been largely drawn upon to provide not only the necessary British framework for newly formed units and services in Burma, but also experienced officers and other ranks for service in the United Kingdom and in India. Good men thus lost were not replaced. The result was that both were very weak, and neither could produce more than two full companies on parade.

The strength of the Burma Rifles was doubled. The new Battalions were:

5th Battalion Burma Rifles.	Raised from existing Regular Battalions by a process of 'milking': Each had a Burmese Company.
6th Battalion Burma Rifles.	
7th Battalion Burma Rifles.	Raised from the Civil and Military Police. It had a composition of Gurkhas, Sikhs, Punjabi Mussalmans and Burmans.
8th Battalion Burma Rifles.	Composed of Sikh and Punjabi Mussalman volunteers from the Burma Frontier Force.
9th Battalion Burma Rifles.	A holding unit with an establishment of some two thousand designed for the holding and training of recruits who passed out of the 10th Battalion Burma Rifles.
10th Battalion Burma Rifles.	A training unit located at Maymyo with an establishment of about two thousand five hundred and raised to replace the Training Battalion.
13th (Shan States Battalion) Burma Rifles.	These two units were Territorial Battalions raised in the Shan States and recruited Shans. They were officered by Shans,
14th (Shan States Battalion) Burma Rifles.	Karens and Burmese.

CHAPTER 3

Even when the Burma Rifles formed a part of the Indian Army no unit had had the experience of duty on the North West Frontier. After Separation no Regular Burma unit was required to serve abroad, but the standard of training was analogous to that of Indian units. Brigade training was carried out to the full extent of funds, equipment and facilities available. Yet the general conditions of service were not the best training for a rigorous campaign and the enlistment of Burmese and Shans, brought about by political considerations, no doubt resulted in a lowering of the efficiency and fighting value of the units concerned. It cannot in fact be denied that the pre-war units through no fault of their own were not of the first quality, and that the expansion carried out only served to lower the existing standard.

The post-Separation position regarding British officers also warranted criticism. The majority of officers were seconded from the British, and Indian Armies for a four-year tour of duty with the Burma Rifles. The system was similar to that employed in the King's African Rifles, but there were certain fundamental differences. In Africa a cadre of British Non-Commissioned Officers was employed. In Burma there was no such cadre and British officers dealt direct with Burman officers and men. Again, in Africa instruction, training and leading were all done in English. In Burma before Separation from India the official language was Hindustani, foreign alike to officers and men. After Separation English was adopted. The British officer if he was to identify himself with his men was also required to master not one, but two or three languages. Consequently, it was only towards the end of his four years with a Battalion that he began to be of any real value as a regimental officer. After 1939 the majority of the younger officers bearing Emergency Commissions had been previously employed in civil occupations in Burma. These officers were of exceptionally good quality and many possessed experience of conditions in the jungle and a knowledge of local languages. The few remaining Regular officers had a very heavy responsibility to carry when fighting began. On the other hand, Governor's Commissioned Officers (the equivalent of the Viceroy's Commissioned Officers in India) and Non-Commissioned Officers were generally inexperienced, some of the former having had not more than two years' service.

The Burma Military Police and, after Separation, also the Burma Frontier Force, earned a well-deserved reputation for the part they played in the settlement of internal disorders and in frontier watch and ward duties. Within the limits of the purposes for which they were raised they were reasonably efficient bodies. They were never intended to be used as Regular Troops, or to fight against a first-class enemy.

From 1937 the remaining three Battalions of Military Police became in effect armed civil police. Detachments were stationed at the Headquarters of every District in Burma and came under the command of the District Civil Police Officers.

The Frontier Force carried out frontier duties, provided escorts and guards to Civil Departments, and reinforced the Military Police for internal security. In 1939 five of the six Battalions of this force were known after the areas in which they were stationed. These were Myitkyina, ??, Northern Shan State, Southern Shan States, and Chin Hills. The remaining reserve Battalion was stationed at Pyawbwe.

Neither the Burma Frontier Force nor the Burma Military Police had a reserve.

Each Battalion had a Headquarters Wing, Training Company, and a varying number of Rifle Companies. There were no mortars, and automatic weapons were restricted to one Lewis Gun per Company. British officers were few. Each Battalion had a Commandant and one or two Assistant Commandants. Some important isolated posts were also in charge of Assistant Commandants.

Neither body had its own medical service, being dependent on the Civil Hospitals. There was no supply system other than that of reliance upon local contractors.

Prior to 1937 all recruitment had been done in India, but upon Separation the Indian Government imposed certain restrictions. This tended to lower the standard of recruits and led to the enlistment of a certain number of Burma-born Gurkhas. These were below the standard type. Many men in the Military Police and Frontier Force extended their service with the object of qualifying for a pension at the end of fifteen years, and this raised the average age much above that of men serving in the Regular Units of the Army.

The Burma Frontier Force had taken over in 1939 the protective duties on the aerodromes of the Singapore air route. But additional Aerodromes and Landing Grounds were built on the Eastern Frontier, and R.A.F. dumps came into being. These all required protection. So, too, did the vast quantity of stores that had accumulated at the China base at Lashio. For these purposes were raised thirty-nine additional platoons of the Territorial Battalions of the Burma Rifles, the Burma Frontier Force and Armed Civil Police. In 1940 the Kokine Battalion of the Frontier Force was formed to carry out these special duties.

CHAPTER 3

In the following year it was decided to raise mobile units from within the Frontier Force to carry out specific outpost work. There were at first four of such units known as F.F.1, F.F.2, F.F.3, and F.F.4. Later their number was increased. Their role was that of harassing and delaying an enemy advance until regular troops could be brought up. They had some motor transport, and F.F.2, operating in Tenasserim and the Mergui Archipelago, was supplied with native craft fitted with motors. Each F.F. unit generally consisted of Headquarters, two troops of Mounted Infantry, and three infantry columns each of about one hundred men. Their fire power was increased by allotting to each column five Thompson sub-machine carbines and one mortar. In addition, each platoon was given a light machine-gun. These new weapons were not available until after the war with Japan had broken out and units were required to employ them in action before they had time to learn the efficient use of them. F.F.5 and the mobile units subsequently raised were very hurriedly formed and incompletely equipped. Officers and men had no opportunity of becoming acquainted before going into action. These factors all affected efficiency.

The formation of these new units, and the drafting of personnel, including officers, to them and to the 7th and 8th Battalions of the Burma Rifles caused a very considerable lowering in efficiency in existing Battalions. All Regular Assistant Commandants were posted to newly raised units as were the best of the Governor's Commissioned Officers and other ranks.

Shortly before the end of 1941 and after the outbreak of war with Japan the F.F. units were placed under the operational control of the Army, but for other purposes they remained under their own Inspector General. Early in 1942, during the progress of the campaign, the whole of the Burma Frontier Force and later the Burma Military Police came under Army control for operations whilst remaining for other purposes subject to their Inspectors General. By that time the Inspector General Burma Frontier Force, Brigadier Roughton, had been placed in charge of the Central Area of Burma with Headquarters at Yenangyaung, and the importance of this office rendered it almost impossible for him to discharge his duties as Inspector General. Burma Frontier Force units were unaccustomed to working under Army administration and were very lost without their Inspector General. They consequently found it difficult to get decisions on important problems and those up-country were often completely out of touch with what was happening in Burma itself.

The recruiting field for the Auxiliary Force was much enlarged by the issue of a Governor's Ordinance making eligible for service all

British subjects in Burma. This opened the force to Burmese and other indigenous races and also Indians settled in Burma.

An Army in Burma Reserve of Officers was formed, partly by the transfer to it of officers resident in Burma who were on the Army in India Reserve of officers and partly by the acceptance of new entrants. Before the end of 1939 the first of a series of officer's training courses had begun in Maymyo.

In the same year the Burma Chamber of Commerce, had voluntarily complied a register of all male Europeans in Burma, and in November 1940, as a result of the insistence of the European community itself, the National Service (European British Subjects) Act, Burma, with certain exceptions made service obligatory for all European British Subjects of military age. Many of these employed in public utility undertakings and essential war industries or were otherwise not available. Yet upon the final evacuation of Burma in 1942 the Army in Burma Reserve of Officers had increased to a strength of over nine hundred. In addition, about one hundred and fifty gentlemen had received Emergency Commissions. Of all these the very great majority were European British Subjects who had been resident in Burma.

Europeans called up for service together with suitable volunteers of the indigenous races underwent three months training in a militia company. Selected men then did a further two months course of officers training before being commissioned. The demand for officers was heavy owing to the creation of many new units and the difficulty of obtaining replacements of officers recalled to India. The original number of trained Regular Officers in Burma had been small and, relatively speaking, this position did not improve.

After the entry of Japan into the War the demand for Junior Staff Officers, Officers for Supply and Transport, and other services and posts increased enormously. Many gentlemen were then commissioned direct from civil life and placed in appointments for which they were suited by training and experience.

Originally the Burma Army Service Corps had no Mechanised Transport Sections, but eventually provision was made for twenty-nine such sections. Much of the personnel was taken from the Burma Rifles. After Japan had entered the war additional Auxiliary Transport Units were formed by taking over fleets of civilian lorries, notably in Lashio and elsewhere in the Shan States. Numerous miscellaneous Burma Army Service Corps units were also required and accordingly raised.

It was necessary to expand or raise on a considerable scale the Burma Military Engineering Service, the Burma Corps of Clerks, Medical,

CHAPTER 3

Ordnance, Provost and other ancillary and administrative units. In 1941 it had become clear that in the event of a campaign in Burma the Government Posts and Telegraph Department would have to be militarised. This was actually carried out early in 1942.

The Army controlled the Observer Corps formed to man a series of posts throughout the country to give warning of enemy air raids. The location of these posts was largely dictated by the existing telephone and telegraph systems to which they were linked. As far as possible the whole eastern frontier was covered. A somewhat similar system of coast watchers was also organised.

For defence against aerial attack a new Auxiliary Force unit, 1 Heavy Anti-Aircraft Regiment, was raised in 1941. It was armed with 8" and light Bofors anti-aircraft guns. These only arrived after the outbreak of war with Japan. Prior to the formation of this unit an Anti-Aircraft Light Machine-Gun Battery of the Burma Auxiliary Force had been formed. It was disbanded when the Anti-Aircraft Regiment was raised.

After the outbreak of war in 1939 the formation known as the Maymyo Infantry Brigade Area was divided, the Maymyo Infantry Brigade with its own Headquarters being formed. This assumed command of the Regular Infantry Battalions in the old Brigade Areas, the remaining units being grouped under a new Upper Burma Area.

When the attitude of Japan became more menacing the Maymyo Infantry Brigade was moved into the Southern Shan States for the defence of the eastern frontier. Later the units were regrouped under the Southern Shan Area and 1 Burma Brigade Group. The latter, commanded by Brigadier G.A.L. Farwell, M.C., comprised the 2nd Battalion The King's Own Yorkshire Light Infantry, the 1st Battalion Burma Rifles, and the 5th Battalion Burma Rifles.

Further south, in Tenasserim, additional troops were also made available for frontier defence. Some of the newly raised Burma Rifles Battalions were employed for this purpose. There was first formed the Tenasserim Brigade Area and then, in addition, 2 Burma Brigade Group. This was commanded by Brigadier A.J.H. Bourke and included the 2nd, 4th, 6th, and 9th Battalions of the Burma Rifles. Later, in December 1941, two companies of the 3rd Battalion Burma Rifles were moved to Mergui and came under command of 2 Burma Brigade. The Tenasserim Brigade Area was also commanded by Brigadier Bourke and, after the formation of 2 Burma Brigade, this comprised little more than the Tenasserim Battalion, R.A.F.

In April 1941 the 13 Indian Infantry Brigade Group (Brigadier A.C. Curtis, M.C.) landed in Burma, the first reinforcements to enter the country. The Infantry units were the 1st Battalion 5th Punjab Regiment, 2nd Battalion 7th Rajput Regiment, and the 1st Battalion 18th Royal Garhwal Rifles. These were stationed in Mandalay and later in the Shan States since it was considered that the main body of any invading force would enter the country by the Chiang Rai-Kengtung road.

The three Brigade Groups (1 Burma Brigade, 2 Burma Brigade and 18 Infantry Brigade) intended for the active defence of the frontier were then formed into 1 Burma Division in July 1941. Divisional Headquarters were at Toungoo midway between the Tenasserim and Shan States areas and considerably removed from both of them. It would have been well-nigh impossible to have maintained operational control of either area from Toungoo, but the creation of a Divisional Headquarters relieved an over-worked Army Headquarters of some of its functions. The Division was commanded by Major General J. Bruce-Scott, M.C.

In November 1941, the first elements of the 16th Indian Infantry Brigade Group arrived and were moved to Mandalay. This was under the direct command of Army Headquarters. Brigadier J.K. Jones was in command and its Infantry Battalions were the 1st Royal Battalion 9th Jat Regiment, the 4th Battalion 12th Frontier Force Regiment and the 1st Battalion 7th Gurkha Rifles. These were the last troops to enter the country before the Japanese invasion of Burma, and it will be noted that the greater part of our available forces were now disposed to cover the Shan States. Several other formations were still directly controlled by Army Headquarters. The Location Statement for December 1st 1941 (Appendix A) and the skeleton Order of Battle for December 8th 1941 (Appendix B) give details of their composition and dispositions.

Was the Army in Burma ready for war in December 1941? Undoubtedly considerable expansion had taken place within the last two years and many new units and services had been created. But expansion of itself does not imply readiness, and in this case it implied weakness. The policy was sound provided first class troops were found from elsewhere to bear the brunt of the fighting and the Burma Army was regarded as second line or Lines of Communications troops. As first line troops or administrative units with active formations they were subject to a strain they were unfitted to bear. There were many factors that made for unpreparedness. Some of these lay within Burma itself, others were of a nature that could not be remedied locally.

Lieut.-General D.K. McLeod, C.B., D.S.O., who was in command had been in Burma some years and in the normal course would have proceeded to leave early in 1942 prior to retirement. He had made great endeavours in spite of a very limited staff and resources to prepare the country for war. But the staff was totally inadequate and a few overworked staff officers were struggling to compete with problems quite beyond their powers. There was no intelligence staff worthy of the name. Owing to the policy adopted by His Majesty's Government no proper arrangements existed for external intelligence and as a result there was usually complete ignorance of what was happening in Thailand. The possibility that Burma might be invaded and the necessity of 'leaving behind' a suitable intelligence organisation had not been considered.

Army Headquarters was at the same time a War Office, a General Headquarters, a Corps Headquarters, and a Lines of Communication Headquarters, this last owing to the absence of any lines of communication staff. Army Headquarters, as such, had responsibilities which covered exactly the same field as General Headquarters in India. It was therefore impossible for the G.O.C. with his vast responsibilities to keep detailed operational control of the forces in the field.

The whole conduct of military administration was complicated by Army Headquarters having to deal with numerous civil departments and agencies ignorant of how quickly events move in war and thus unable to realise the necessity of unified control well ahead of any likely emergency. There was no plan for the militarisation of railways and inland water transport. This matter does not appear to have received prior consideration either by the Army or the Defence Department.

The nucleus of Base and Administrative element of Lines of Communication units as it existed consisted of locally raised units partially trained and very weak in Governor's Commissioned Officers and N.C.Os. they naturally had few trained reserves.

The recruiting reserve was insufficient and casualties could never adequately be replaced. The 'milking' of all Regular units had necessarily lowered the general standard of efficiency. The system whereby administrative control of Frontier Force units remained vested in an independent Inspector General was unsound. Reference has already been made to these matters.

The problems of equipment and transport vehicles were also serious. The urgent requirements of the Armies in Great Britain and the active theatres of war naturally had preference, but the result was a shortage in Burma. Ordnance had no real reserve of small arms. Thompson sub-machine carbines, mortar ammunition, grenades, and anti-tank mines were particularly lacking. The total target of twenty-four heavy and sixty-eight light guns for anti-aircraft units was never attained. There was a general shortage of web-equipment, steel helmets, and numerous other items. Transport was not up to full scale, and arrangements for supplies were largely carried out by means of requisitioned vehicles.

To sum up, in the words employed by Lieut.-General Hutton in his despatch, 'The force, such as it was, was quite unprepared for war'.

Brief mention must now be made of the other armed forces available in the country.

A small organisation known as the Supply Base (Burma) had been set up by the War Office for the conduct of operations in China in the event of war with Japan. It was intended to maintain guerilla companies and also Bomber squadrons of the R.A.F. in China. These were to be supplied by several motor transport companies operating along the Burma Road. A training school and depot for the guerilla companies was established at Maymyo under the name of the Bush Warfare School. Several companies were trained and sent to China.

The course of actual operations largely frustrated the objects of the Supply Base and it was closed before the end of December 1941, but the remaining personnel of the Bush Warfare School rendered good service in Burma in Commando units.

Air attack being regarded as the main danger to Burma it was intended that a considerable force of aircraft should be maintained in the country. In fact, there were very few. India almost denuded of modern aircraft, had nothing with which to reinforce Burma.

Early in 1941 one squadron of Blenheim Bombers was stationed at Mingaladon, the airfield on the outskirts of Rangoon, and a small Royal Air Force command was set up. In the course of 1941, the aircraft of the Blenheim squadron were flown to Malaya and were not returned. When war broke out with Japan the only effective R.A.F. unit in the country was No. 67 Squadron with some sixteen Buffalo aircraft. New operational airfields were under construction at Heho and Namsang in the Shan States and at Toungoo. Those in the Tenasserim area were extended, and satellites to the main airfields were built.

Intended for service in China was an air force known as the American Volunteer Group with a personnel composed of American subjects. It was formed in Toungoo in 1941 and comprised pilots, ground staff, hospital, and administrative unit. It was equipped with P.40 (Tomahawk) aircraft. The aerodrome at Magwe had also been placed at its disposal. Members of the A.V.G. were to play an important part in the air defence of Burma.

The Burma Volunteer Air Unit was a training organisation stationed at Mingaladon. Selected volunteers from Burma were trained by two R.A.F. officers attached to the unit as instructors. Two Moth type aircraft were used. On the completion of their course with the unit members were sent to India for advanced training.

The air garrison of Burma and the operations undertaken by it are discussed in detail in a subsequent chapter.

The Burma Royal Naval Volunteer Reserve had been raised in Burma in 1940. Officers were British and Burman, and the ratings were almost wholly Burman. It maintained an examination service at the mouth of the Rangoon river, carried out mine-sweeping, and furnished a Mergui Archipelago patrol operating in a few armed launches. It had personnel of about fifty officers and six hundred ratings. Operations in which it was concerned are mentioned in the course of the narrative.

Shortly after the outbreak of war with Japan, Captain J.I. Hallet, D.S.O., R.N., was appointed N.O.I.C. Rangoon. Later, Commodore C.M. Graham assumed the appointment of Commodore, Burma Coast.

It needs to be mentioned that India had no responsibility for the defence of Burma but, being well aware of the weakness of its forces in numbers, armament and quality, it frequently represented the need for reinforcements and the advantages of giving the Commander-in-Chief, India the task if placing Burma in a proper state of defence. This had been urged in many telegrams from no less than three successive Commanders-in-Chief, and also personally during a visit to the War office by the C.G.S., India (Lieut.-General Hutton) in October 1940 and by General Wavell during a similar visit in October 1941. The state of unpreparedness of Burma was also strongly represented by various Senior Staff Officers from India and elsewhere who visited the country in 1940 and 1941. In December 1941 it was stressed by the G.O.C. Burma (Lieut.-General D.K. McLeod) and repeated by General Wavell after his visit to Rangoon on December 22nd in that year. From the time of his arrival as Governor of Burma in May 1941 Sir Reginald Dorman-Smith made frequent comments on the subject.

India was, however, herself engaged in the vast expansion which, begun a year too late, was to bring her forces from some two hundred thousand to nearly two million in just over two years. She was almost as short as Burma herself of all modern munitions of war and motor transport. She was also under very strong pressure to send the maximum number of troops and administrative services to the Middle East, Malaya, Iraq and Persia where they were most urgently required.

Nevertheless, India initiated action regarding reinforcements for Burma, and the second Infantry Brigade to arrive, if not the first, was despatched entirely on the initiative of G.H.Q. India. Administrative units could only be made available at the expense of the Middle East and elsewhere if so decided by the War Office. Consequently, Burma was advised to raise as many of such units as she could from available indigenous material.

Here it is convenient to consider briefly the enemy forces employed in Burma during the Campaign.

The normal Japanese Infantry Division then had an effective fighting strength of about sixteen thousand men. It comprised three Infantry Regiments each of three Battalions, and had a Field or a Mountain Artillery Regiment of three Batteries each of three Troops. Each Troop had four 75 mm. guns. There were also a Cavalry Regiment, an Engineer Regiment, and other ancillary and administrative troops.

An Infantry Regiment (strength about three thousand men) besides its three Battalions consisted of a Regimental Gun Company with four 75 mm. guns, possibly an Anti-Tank Company with four 37 mm. guns, and a Signal Company. In addition, each Battalion had two 70 mm. 'Battalion' guns, and a Machine-Gun Company with eight machine-guns. Rifle Companies of a Battalion were armed with light machine-guns and 2" grenade dischargers. A Japanese rifle company was always, both in fire and bayonet power, a 50% stronger organisation than our own rifle company.

In Burma the Japanese employed their 18th, 33rd, 55th and 58th Divisions. Of these the first to enter the country was the 55th Division. This was closely followed by the 53rd Division, this being an excellent fighting formation of experienced and well-trained troops. The 55th Division was less seasoned, but was well led.

These two Divisions, each with two Infantry Regiments only, carried on the campaign until the end of March 1942. They entered Burma from Thailand. Both were present at the battle of the Sittang Bridge in late February 1942. In March the 55th Division struck north along the Sittang valley towards Toungoo and Mandalay, whilst the 33rd Division opposed the Imperial Forces concentrated in the Irrawaddy valley further west.

Early in April the 18th and 56th Divisions landed in Rangoon. So, too, did the third Regiment of the 33rd Division. One Battalion or more of this Regiment joined the Division in the Irrawaddy valley, whilst one Battalion eventually occupied Akyab in the Arakan area.

The 18th Division would appear to have been employed against the Chinese Army and the Imperial Forces then holding the line south of Mandalay between the Irrawaddy and the Shan foothills. The 56th Division in motor transport and well supported by tanks moved from Toungoo through Karenni and the Southern Shan States on Lashio.

CHAPTER 3

Ultimately part of this Division took Bhamo and Myitkyina. This advance had a decisive effect on the operations in Burma.

In the last stages of the campaign the 18th Division remained in the Mandalay-Taunggyi area, whilst the 23rd and 56th Divisions thrust north along the west and east banks of the Irrawaddy. Part of the 33rd Division also moved up the Chindwin river to intercept the withdrawal of the Imperial Forces to India.

In addition to the Divisional formations mentioned, the Japanese had in Burma medium artillery, possibly as much as a Regiment of Tanks, Anti-Tank Artillery, various Signals and Wireless, and Motor Transport units. There were also Hospitals and Lines of Communication units.

The Japanese were assisted by the Thai Army and the Burma Independence Army. Although Burmese were present at a number of engagements neither the Thais nor the Burmese participated to any marked extent in the actual fighting. However, they were no doubt of assistance in releasing Japanese troops from routine duties, thus substantially reducing the numbers that would otherwise have been required by the Japanese for their campaign in Burma.

Chapter 4

Appreciations of a possible Japanese attack on Burma – View of Singapore Defence Conference – View of Burma Army – Dispositions made in accordance with these views – Reconsideration of situation after outbreak of war with Japan – Changes of Command affecting Burma – The Reinforcement problem.

As already indicated the danger of a land attack on Burma by an external enemy was long regarded as remote. Until 1939 this was the view taken by the Committee of Imperial Defence. In that year, however, the possibility of Japanese action in Thailand was visualised and the altered situation considered. The danger of air attack was the main concern of the Army in Burma. Major General D.K. McLeod, then G.O.C., Burma Army, in a letter to the Deputy Chief of the General Staff, India, said: "On the Siamese (Thai) border there is not much scope for a larger force (than raiding parties) to attack Burma by land....Myawaddy: This is the only practicable route for a force of any size – say a brigade. The objective would be Moulmein. But I do not regard the land threat very seriously – air attack by Japan from Siamese aerodromes is the big danger." This letter was written in 1939 before the outbreak of war with Germany.

In November 1940 the Far Eastern Command was created, Air Chief Marshal Sir Robert Brooke-Popham, G.V.C.O., K.C.B., C.M.G., D.S.O., A.F.C., being Commander-in-Chief, Burma, previously directly under the War Office, came under operational control of the new command. In the previous month there had been held at Singapore a Defence Conference. This had been specifically assembled to consider defence requirements in the Far East in view of a possible Japanese attack. The position of Burma was examined.

CHAPTER 4

The Conference decided that the immediate threat to Burma and Eastern India would be:

(a) Air attack on the oil refineries and docks at Rangoon, and possibly on vulnerable points in Eastern India.
(b) Land, seaborne, and air attack, including airborne troops, on Tenasserim to capture and/or destroy aerodromes on the Singapore air route.

The Conference also agreed that attacks on the remainder of Burma's eastern territory would probably in the first place be limited to raids, and that an attack from Chiang Rai into the Southern Shan States was a feasible proposition for a large force against which defence measures must be taken.

When war with Japan became imminent the G.O.C. Burma was instructed by the C.-in-C. Far East, that his first duty was to maintain the Imperial air route to Singapore by providing local protection for the various landing grounds in the south of Burma. His next duty was the safeguarding of the Burma Road and communications with China. At that time, it was not anticipated that Singapore would fall to the enemy or that command of the seas in the Far East would be lost. The Japanese although active in French Indo-China had made no move against Thailand. The Burma Road could be cut by means of an attack on the Shan States through Indo-China.

The possibility of a Japanese advance through Thailand could certainly not be ruled out. It was necessary, therefore, for the Burma Command to consider the probable weight and direction of such an attack.

Communications between Burma and Thailand were very bad. Only one motor road existed. Much of the frontier country was mountainous and densely covered with jungle, and an invader would also be faced with the formidable natural obstacle of the Salween. Few tracks crossed the frontier and, in most places, the dense forests traversed by these would compel an invader to confine himself strictly to the tracks.

The one existing motor road was that from Thazi through Kengtung and Tachileik to Chiang Rai. One of its southern feeder roads from a point about sixty miles east of Taunggyi ran south-east to Mongpan, forty miles from the frontier. Tracks linked Mongpan with the road system centered on the Thai towns of Chiangmai and Mae Hong Son.

Between Chiangmai and Chiang Rai and the Burma frontier the Thais were improving their communications which were now comparatively good. This area, therefore, appeared to offer the best line of advance to an invader. Against this were the facts that such an advance would not immediately threaten any vital point in Burma, and would give the defence ample ground for manoeuvre and the fighting of delaying actions. The road passed through country very suited for this. Such an advance, too, would necessitate the maintenance by the invader of very long lines of communication. Thazi where, presumably, the main road and railway would be cut was considerably more than two hundred and fifty miles west of Tachileik on the frontier. Finally, the securing of Thazi by the enemy would still leave the defenders of Burma covering their main base of Rangoon and with extensive communications behind them.

From Mae Hong Son on the Me Pai river, a tributary of the Salween, existed two possible lines of approach. One was down the Me Pai river itself, the other by tracks across the Salween which joined the Toungoo-Bawlake-Taunggyi road running through the Karenni States. The country was most difficult.

Further south were the Tenasserim routes, the easiest being that through the frontier village of Myawaddy. The Dawna Hills although precipitous and densely covered with forest were of no great depth, and less than twenty miles to the west of Myawaddy an invader would emerge into level and comparatively easy country. A successful advance here must constitute an immediate threat to Rangoon, and the immobilisation or fall of that city would strangle the whole defence of Burma. In addition, the moral effect of a blow at the heart of Burma would be far greater than an attack through the distant Shan State of Kengtung.

Road and rail communications in Thailand indicated Chiang Rai and Chiangmai in the north and Raheng in the west of Thailand as likely concentration areas and advance bases for an attack. This confirmed the two danger points as the Thazi-Kengtung-Tachileik road and the Myawaddy route.

It was estimated that the Japanese might be able to employ up to eight Divisions in Thailand, but that owing to the maintenance difficulties it was unlikely that more than two Divisions would e used against Burma. It was also estimated that these Divisions could be supported by eight Bomber and four Fighter Squadrons of aircraft.

Having regard to the better communications existing both in the Southern Shan States and opposite them on the Thai side of the frontier it seemed that the main thrust must be through Kengtung and Mongpan towards Thazi. Recent experience in Europe and Africa had shown dependence of modern armies on motor transport. Hence the

CHAPTER 4

G.O.C. Burma, with the full approval of the C.-in-C. Far East, decided that the threat of invasion was the more serious in the north. At the same time subsidiary advance could be made through Tenasserim. The enemy might be able to maintain two Brigades on the Raheng-Myawaddy-Kawkareik route; whilst subsidiary land threats to Tavoy, Mergui, and Victoria Point could be expected combined with sea operations based on Renong, the Thai port close to Victoria Point. Owing to its isolated position there was no intention to hold Victoria Point if it was seriously attacked by an invader.

Upon this appreciation of the situation two Brigade Groups (1 Burma Brigade and 13 Brigade) had been moved into the Southern Shan States. F.F.3 and F.F.4 were also in this area. F.F.5 of approximately one hundred men covered Karenni. 2 Burma Brigade with F.F.2 had been given the task of covering the Tenasserim Frontier. Both Tavoy and Mergui as well as the Moulmein area with the important landing grounds at these places were to be strongly held.

Internal Security was considered to be a real problem. In the event of a heavy enemy threat the loyalty of the local population was in doubt. It was necessary therefore to maintain a substantial force to deal with such a situation. Approximately one Brigade including the 1st Battalion the Gloucestershire Regiment and the Rangoon Battalion Burma Auxiliary Force was to be retained in Rangoon, whilst in Central Burma there were available some units of the Burma Frontier Force and the Burma Rifles.

The general plan of defence against a superior invading force was delaying action and, finally, the holding at all costs of the line of the Salween.

Liaison had been established with the Chinese and arrangements made that one Regiment of Chinese troops was to be moved close to the Burma frontier early in December 1941. This force would then be available for the defence of the Southern Shan States in the event of operations there.

In accordance with this plan lines of communication to the frontier were organised, the main base being Rangoon where all supplies entered the country. All units were originally supplied with Ordnance Equipment from the small Arsenal at Rangoon, but on the approach of war and on the assumption that the main thrust would come through the Shan States administrative plans for the location of Supply Depots, Ordnance and other services were made accordingly. The Tenasserim front was regarded as subsidiary.

Examining this appreciation of the situation in the light of subsequent events it is clear that undue weight was attached to the supposed advantages of an attack through the Southern Shan States. The only argument in its favour was the existence of the road from Tachileik to Thazi. Otherwise, everything pointed to the greater benefits of the Myawaddy route. Undoubtedly the Japanese ability to overcome natural obstacles and the mobility of his forces was, as elsewhere, underestimated. Standards normally considered requisite for the movement of British troops would appear to have been applied. Yet the transport needs of the Japanese Army had been intentionally reduced much below this, and it was wrong to assess the possible weight of an attack through Kawkareik at no more than two brigades.

This mistake was realised as soon as the Japanese attack on Malaya opened in December 1941. The extreme rapidity with which comparatively large bodies of troops moved through difficult country led to a complete reconsideration of the situation in Burma. It then became apparent that the danger of an advance in strength through Myawaddy had not been properly appreciated. Tenasserim was now seen as the main battleground.

To repair the error was not easy. The main strength of the small forces available had to be shifted hundreds of miles to Tenasserim in the south, and communications and supplies built up to meet the altered plan. It also became necessary to visualise an early situation when Rangoon as the door to Burma might be closed by enemy action.

Tavoy and Mergui presented difficult problems. Whilst we held Malaya the airfields at these places required protection. They were not only essential to the air reinforcement of Malaya but also afforded most valuable bases from which attacks could be carried out on the Lines of Communication of Japanese forces operating in Malaya. The distance from Rangoon to Singapore was too far for modern bombers, even without a bombload, to attempt safely without refuelling. At that time no Flying Fortress aircraft were available. Yet the isolated position of these airfields, their proximity to the frontier, and the lack of communications with them complicated the task. The total naval forces available were limited to a few motor launches of the B.R.N.V.R., and to country craft manned by native crews who would be unreliable in the presence of the enemy. The single road linking Mergui, Tavoy and Ye and running close to the frontier would very easily be cut by an invading force. Eventually it was decided that in the case of a serious threat the Mergui garrison would be evacuated to Tavoy which could then be held. A stop across one track leading in from Thailand would enable the Tavoy force, if necessary, to withdraw on Moulmein.

CHAPTER 4

There is no doubt that if Japan had been in a position to launch an immediate major attack on Burma in December 1941 her success would have been speedy and the fall of Rangoon must have rapidly ensued. But there was to be no immediate serious attack and the respite that was gained gave time for a certain amount of regrouping of forces, the entry into Burma of Chinese troops, and the landing of reinforcements. As a result, the enemy was delayed in Burma until the break of the monsoon and this enabled India by a narrow margin to stave off the invasion that would almost certainly have taken place if Burma had been overrun as rapidly as Malaya. This made little difference to the final outcome of the campaign in Burma itself, but it did have a definite bearing on the general conduct of the war in the Far East.

During the campaign that followed upon the declaration of war against Japan on December 8th the British forces in Burma were subject to several changes in command. It was unfortunate that the necessity for these was not foreseen and that some of them at least were not carried out earlier. On December 15th Burma, including its air defence, came under the Command of the Commander-in-Chief, India. The post was then held by His Excellency Sir Archibald P. Wavell, G.C.B., C.M.G., M.C., A.D.C. In the following month when General Wavell assumed supreme command of the South West Pacific (ABADACOM) Burma was transferred to that command for operational purposes. Administratively it remained under India. After the occupation of Java by the Japanese, General Wavell returned to the Indian Command. Shortly before this, on February 22nd, Burma had been again placed under the operational control of the Indian Command, General Sir Alan F. Hartley, K.C.S.I., C.B., D.S.O., then being Commander-in-Chief.

On December 27th 1941 Lieut.-General T.J. Hutton, C.B., M.C., succeeded Lieut.-General D.K. McLeod in the command of the Army in Burma. In February 1942 in view of the proposed great expansion of the forces in Burma the British War Cabinet decided to place Lieut.-General Sir Harold Alexander, K.C.B., C.S.I., M.C., in command, Lieut.-General Hutton remaining as Chief of the General Staff. Early in April Lieut.-General Alexander was promoted to the rank of 'General'. He had assumed command on March 5th 1942.

The disadvantages of these frequent changes and the division between Command and Administration will be appreciated. Even worse was the enormous distance separating Burma from General Wavell's Headquarters in Java. Although he made several somewhat risky visits to Burma by air both the High Command and the

Command in Burma itself suffered from lack of mutual understanding, and up-to-date information. This was not improved by the extreme difficulty in maintaining satisfactory Signal Communications. It now seems clear that Burma should have been placed under India as soon as the Japanese threat became obvious, and should have remained under that command. That this was not done appears to have been mainly due to an incorrect appreciation of the effect that air operations might have on the course of the campaign in Malaya.

Before passing on to a consideration of the actual operations conducted in Burma it is necessary to refer to the reinforcement problem. This was acute.

On his appointment to the command of the Army in Burma Lieut.-General Hutton had been directed by the Commander-in-Chief to organise the military resources of the country so that ultimately a maximum force of four Divisions supported by fifteen squadrons R.A.F. (including forces already in Burma) could be maintained and operated. That the Army must be substantially reinforced was evident. But reinforcements could only be obtained at once from India which in the period December 1941-February 1942 was faced simultaneously with the problem of strengthening the Malayan front where Japanese were pressing forward in a vigorous offensive. The Japanese were also engaged in the Philippines and in the North-East Islands of the Netherlands Archipelago. With this wide dispersal of their forces it was considered unlikely that they would immediately undertake another major land offensive in Burma.

This was not the view held and pressed by Lieut.-General Hutton and the Governor of Burma, Sir Reginald Dorman-Smith. To them it was evident that the holding of Burma was of the greatest importance. It involved the maintenance of the Burma Road and continued contact with the Chinese. It was vital to the defence of India and meant the preservation of a base from which a force could be built up for the ultimate counter-offensive. These considerations must have been apparent to the Japanese.

The Japanese were reported to have at least three Divisions in Thailand, two in the south and one in the north. There was also the Thai Army to be considered. The prompt capitulation of Thailand had placed it at the disposal of the invaders. Its fighting value was exceedingly doubtful but it consisted of some twenty-six infantry battalions, several regiments of artillery, some cavalry, and had tanks numbering well over a hundred. It could not, therefore, be disregarded and could be usefully employed by the Japanese on garrison and similar duties. There was no

CHAPTER 4

reason, too, why the Japanese should not bring into Thailand further troops of their own for use in an invasion.

The needs of Malaya were deemed to be of primary and urgent importance, and the largest stream of reinforcements flowed to Singapore even to within a few days of the fall of that fortress on February 15th. Very considerable numbers of Indian troops had already been sent overseas to the Middle East, East Africa, and quite recently to Iraq and Persia. The defence of India and the building up of the defences of Ceylon against a possible Japanese attack had now to be considered. In India there was not only a shortage of trained personnel, but also of arms, equipment, and motor transport. All these factors necessarily affected and restricted the supply of reinforcements for Burma. A heavy risk had to be taken somewhere, and in view of Japanese commitments elsewhere those responsible considered Burma to be in no immediate danger.

It seems evident that if some part of the reinforcements sent to Malaya had been landed promptly in Rangoon events in Burma would have taken a very different course. The line of the Sittang at least, and possibly that of the Salween, could have been long maintained. The implications of a serious delay imposed on the enemy at either point are great.

The first reinforcement to arrive was 23 Garrison Company. This went to Akyab in December 1941 for the defence of the airfield and port. Later, in January 1942, it was relieved by the 14th Battalion 7th Rajput Regiment. In Rangoon the first reinforcements to arrive were 8 Indian Heavy Anti-Aircraft Battery (less two sections), and 3 Indian Light Anti-Aircraft Battery. These embarked on the last day of 1941 and at once took up duties at airfields and other vital points around Rangoon and Moulmein.

In mid-December 17 Indian Division had been selected for service in Burma. It was commanded by Major General J.G. Smyth, V.C., M.C. Eventually two Brigade Groups went to Malaya, and only Divisional Headquarters and 48 Indian Brigade Group were sent to Burma. 46 Brigade arrived towards the end of January. It was at once moved to the area Thaton-Martaban. Divisional Headquarters had arrived early in the month and was established in Moulmein. All troops in the Tenasserim area came under its command at midnight on January 5th/6th.

17 Division was made up of young troops and had been originally destined for Iraq where it was to complete its training. It was not really fit for immediate active service and had no experience in jungle warfare. The Infantry Battalions of 46 Brigade (Brigadier R. Ekin) were

the 7th Battalion 10th Baluch Regiment, the 3rd Battalion 7th Gurkha Rifles and the 5th Battalion 17th Dogra Regiment.

Towards the end of December 48 Indian Infantry Brigade Group of 19 Indian Division was earmarked for Burma. It was commanded by Brigadier N. Hugh-Jones, M.C., and its Infantry units were the 1st Battalion 3rd Q.A.O. Gurkha Rifles, the 1st Battalion 4th P.W.O. Gurkha Rifles, and the 2nd Battalion 5th Royal Gurkha Rifles, F.F. When it arrived in Rangoon on January 31st it was transferred immediately to the area of 17 Division.

Three unallotted British Battalions were also allocated to Burma. These were the 1st Battalion the West Yorkshire Regiment, the 1st Battalion the Cameronians, and the 2nd Battalion the Duke of Wellington's Regiment. The first named Battalion landed in Burma at the end of January; the other two Battalions in the course of February. Early in March the 1st Battalion the Royal Inniskilling Fusiliers was flown into Burma to the Magwe airfield. Rangoon had fallen.

Headquarters Army in Burma had been informed that 14 Indian Division (less one Brigade Group) 63 Indian Brigade Group, two East African Brigades, not then in India and which had done excellent work in the Italian Campaign, and 7 Australian Division would be available in due course. One East African Brigade had been promised for January, the other for March. Of all these only 63 Brigade group arrived. The convoy bringing in these troops reached Rangoon on March 3rd and the brigade, consisting of partly trained troops, was just in time to participate without its transport in the final stages of the battle for the port. It was commanded by Brigadier J. Wickham and was composed of the 1st Battalion 11 Sikh Regiment, the 2nd Battalion 13th Frontier Force Rifles and the 1st Battalion 10th Gurkha Rifles.

14 Indian Division had not been due to arrive until April, and the African Brigades were diverted elsewhere. The Australian Division, withdrawn from the Middle East, could have been landed in Rangoon at the end of February. However, the Australian Government considered its return to Australia to be essential and accordingly the proposal to utilise it in Burma was negatived. In addition, the Governor of Burma had been informed that a British Division there on the high seas could be available for employment in Burma. This, presumably, was 18 Division which landed in Singapore just before the fall of that stronghold.

In addition to the Anti-Aircraft Batteries already mentioned the following Artillery reinforcements were landed before the evacuation of Rangoon: 8 Anti-Aircraft Battery R.A., 2 Indian Anti-Tank regiment, 1 Indian Field Regiment, Headquarters 29 Mountain Regiment, 15 and

CHAPTER 4

28 Mountain Batteries. There were also sent a few Engineer, Supply and Transport, Medical and other units.

On February 6th General Wavell visited the Salween front. On seeing the country, he considered that parts of Lower Burma during the dry weather would provide good going for tanks which could operate across the flat sun-baked paddy lands. He therefore proposed to divert to Rangoon 7 Armoured Brigade Group then intended for service in Java. The Brigade was equipped with General Stuart tanks, its regiments being the 7th Queen's Own Hussars and the 2nd Battalion Royal Tank Regiment. In the group were also 414 Battery R.H.A. and 'A' Battery, 95 Anti-Tank Regiment, R.A. Brigadier J.H. Anstice, D.S.O. was in command. The Brigade landed in Rangoon on February 21st and was destined to render stalwart service.

With the evacuation of Rangoon, the entry of reinforcements almost entirely ceased. They could then only be brought in by air or through the very difficult overland route from Manipur Road in Assam via Imphal and Tamu to Kalewa on the Chindwin river. In fact, no reinforcements entered Burma by this route.

The Imperial Forces in Burma were largely assisted by the entry of Chinese troops. One Regiment entered Burma in December 1941 and later the Chinese V, VI, and LXVI Armies were also brought into the country. These troops eventually undertook the defence of the Shan States, Karenni, and the Sittang Valley fronts and played an important part in the campaign. The circumstances attending their entry and employment are detailed in subsequent chapters.

Chapter 5

Opening of the Campaign in December 1941 – Early Operations – F.F.2 raid on Prachuab Girikhan – Japanese occupation of Victoria Point and Bokpyin – F.F.2 attack on Bokpyin – Other Operations in Tenasserim, Karenni, and in the Shan States – Internal conditions in Burma – Air raids on Rangoon and their serious results – Civil Defence in Burma.

The campaign opened quietly. On November 30th Army Headquarters warned all formations under its command of the threatened invasion of Thailand by the Japanese. Accordingly, precautionary defensive measures were at once put into force. Full signal security was instituted. Orders were issued for the obstruction of landing grounds. In Tenasserim preparations were made to carry out a raid into Thailand by F.F.2 with the object of disabling the Thai-Malaya railway in the neighbourhood of Prachuab Girikhan. Patrol activities increased.

On December 8th general mobilisation of the Army in Burma was ordered. In effect the Army was as far as possible already mobilised, and little more than some of the Auxiliary Force units were affected.

Up to this date contact with the Thais along the frontier had been friendly. British, Indian, and Chinese refugees who had already entered Burma through Myawaddy from Bangkok, reported that they had received kindness and assistance from the Thais, and this continued even after the Japanese obtained control of their country. On the other hand, Thai officials, both civil and military, were inclined to be suspicious of British intentions. In their case Japanese influences had been at work. Whatever may have been the feelings of the people at large the Thai rulers were certainly not prepared to incur the anger of Japan if, in fact, they were not in secret agreement with her. This was demonstrated by the feebleness with which the invaders were resisted. Opposition lasted less than forty-eight hours, and on December 9th opposition ceased. The Japanese entered Thailand

CHAPTER 5

both through Indo-China and by sea. They now had at their disposal the numerous airfields of Thailand, assembly areas for overland attacks on Malaya and Burma, and a very useful railway system which included the important Bangkok-Malaya route. They also obtained control of the Thai Army. Europeans who had been resident in Thailand generally expressed the opinion that if the British had anticipated the Japanese invasion and themselves entered the country they would have been welcomed and actively supported in opposing the Japanese. Subsequently the invaders held out as a bait to their somewhat reluctant allies the prospect of recovering Tenasserim which once had been a province of Thailand.

The first offensive action by the enemy was an air-raid on the Tavoy aerodrome on December 11th. Bombs were dropped and the airfield was machine-gunned. The petrol dump was destroyed but casualties were very slight.

Next day the enemy crossed the frontier in the extreme south of Tenasserim and occupied the village of Marang. Victoria Point suffered an air raid and it was reported that the Japanese were concentrating motor boats at Namchoot. Accordingly, the small Burma Frontier Force garrison at Victoria Point prepared to carry out demolitions at once and to evacuate the Port by sea. The enemy had moved down the Pakchan [Kraburi] river from Marang to Maliwun twenty miles from Victoria Point. He was reported to be using eight motor boats. On December 13th, after Japanese aircraft had heavily bombed and machine-gunned the town and aerodrome, destruction of the Wireless Station, stores and landing ground installations were carried out and the garrison withdrew in accordance with instructions. The withdrawal was covered by a motor launch of the B.R.N.V.R. The Civil Sub-Divisional Officer who had received no orders to leave remained at his post and was captured by the Japanese when they entered the town on December 15th.

Subsequent reports from this area indicated that the Japanese were in some force in Renong and that they were well equipped with out-board motors for use with country crafts.

On December 13th Mergui was raided twice by enemy aircraft. Both airfield and town were attacked. R.A.F. buildings, Power Station, and a petrol dump were destroyed, whilst Telegraph and other communications were damaged. A few military personnel and civilians were killed and the raid resulted in the almost general evacuation of the town by the population. In consequence there was a serious labour shortage, a feature subsequently common after air raids on other towns in Burma.

At dusk on December 12th two columns of F.F.2 led by Captain Stephenson crossed the Thai frontier by way of the Maw Daung Pass to put plan 'Yacht' into operation. This raid into Thailand was the only offensive operation of its kind undertaken during the campaign and accordingly some details of it are warranted.

Plan 'Yacht' for the cutting of the Bangkok-Malaya railway south of Prachuab Girikhan had been drawn up the previous October. It was intended that two bridges near the villages of Heng Hin and Hwa Don respectively should be destroyed by columns of F.F.2.

Officially no reconnaissance across the frontier had been permissible before the outbreak of war with Japan none of our patrols was able to penetrate as far as the railway. The plan had been worked out on quarter inch maps issued some thirty years previously. There were no guides. To add to difficulties, it was essential that the operation be carried out in the hours of darkness.

F.F.2 had been in the frontier area of Mergui for several months. It had lived in the jungle throughout the previous monsoon which is heavy in the district. Transport problems caused a shortage of rations, and many men were further debilitated by malaria.

On December 12th when orders to put 'Yacht' into operation were received another column of F.F.2 under Captain J.O.W. Edwards was already in Thailand near Prachuab Girikhan. At that town the Japanese were in occupation of the aerodrome and were busy disembarking troops. These facts were reported by Captain Edwards to F.F.2 Headquarters by wireless.

Moving through dense jungle in the dark, the 'Yacht' columns soon lost direction and were compelled to halt. The two wireless sets that were carried almost at once went out of action, and thereafter the only means of communicating with the supporting force at the head of the Maw Daung Pass was by runners. The columns had no transport. All weapons, ammunition, explosives, and rations were carried by the men. Rations comprised no more than a few packets of biscuits and tea.

As soon as it was sufficiently light on the morning of December 13th 'Yacht' force continued its march through uninhabited country. In the afternoon the sound of firing was heard from the north-east and stragglers from Captain Edwards' columns were met. They reported that their column had been attacked.

Captain Stephenson decided to go on. He did not know that as a result of the attack on Captain Edwards' columns the Japanese had obtained full information of his own movements. They had captured a wireless set with Captain Edwards and with it a message, just deciphered, giving details of the movements of 'Yacht' force. By 1700 hours that evening hostile aircraft were searching the jungle for the raiding columns.

CHAPTER 5

Marching south by compass Captain Stephenson made for a river marked on his map. The railway bridge near Hwa Don crossed the river. After several hours of marching the river had not been reached, and Captain Stephenson then struck east for the railway. This was soon encountered, but no bridges could be found, either to the north or south.

On the morning of December 14th enemy patrols were active, many men of 'Yacht' force were exhausted through hunger and some men were ill with fever. There was nothing for it but to withdraw to the Maw Daung Pass.

Subsequent consultation of up-to-date maps showed that the Hwa Don river marked on Captain Stephenson's map was a tidal creek. Much of it after the making of the early maps was reclaimed and converted into paddy land. Across this land 'Yacht' force had marched and thus, inadvertently, went many miles too far to the south.

Having established themselves at Victoria Point the Japanese proceeded to move up the coast by sea; and on December 19th a party of about eighty occupied Bokpyin, a village one hundred miles to the north. There was a landing ground near the village. Accurate information of enemy movements was difficult to obtain, but on December 22nd when it was verified that Bokpyin was in enemy hands F.F.2 was ordered to take offensive action. A Naval patrol was also ordered to be carried out in the Bokpyin area.

The Japanese had occupied the Police Station, which designed as a blockhouse, was in a strong position on the top of a hill. They had also fortified and held the Court House and jetty. A detachment of F.F.2 under command of Major S.W.A. Love proceeded by sea from Mergui and landed in the vicinity of Bokpyin. On December 26th an attempt was made to carry the Police Station and Court House by storm. Major Love had a mortar but no ammunition with him and decided to go on with the attack without waiting for the arrival of mortar ammunition. Its absence led to the failure of the assault on the objectives. Captain E. Booker and two men reached the Police Station under heavy fire but could not force an entry. They were compelled to withdraw after disposing of some of the enemy outside the building. At the Court House machine-gun fire held up the attacking platoon. Falling back to the jungle on the outskirts of the village our force re-organised for fresh attacks. It now found itself under fire from the rear as well as from the village. Major Love was killed. Shortly afterwards all ammunition became exhausted and the force withdrew to its left flank through dense jungle. Its total casualties were three killed and four badly wounded.

A further attack was then ordered to be made by the 2nd Battalion Burma Rifles, and a company was sent down to Bokpyin on December 29th. A Naval inshore motor-boat patrol also approached the village. However, on December 28th M.L.1101 under Lieutenant Penman,

R.R.N.V.R. had entered the Bokpyin creek and effectively shelled the jetty where the enemy were said to have posted some machine-guns. The Japanese officer in command of these posts was killed, and on the following day the whole enemy force retired overland across the Thai frontier. Bokpyin was later occupied without opposition by the company of the 2nd Battalion Burma Rifles.

In the Kawkareik area there had been some firing across the frontier by Thai posts. On December 13th a patrol of the 4th Battalion Burma Rifles, the Battalion stationed in the Kawkareik area, entered Thai territory and had a brush with a police out-post. But at this period, it was to our advantage to allay panic on the frontier since we required information of the intentions of the enemy. It was learnt that the Mesohd-Raheng road was being improved and that both Japanese and Thai troops were moving to this area. The Thais were constructing posts along the frontier. Returning spies stated that they had overheard Japanese officers discussing plans for the invasion of the Tavoy district about the middle of January.

All indications now pointed to the opening of an early enemy offensive on this front. Major operations in Lower Burma and through the passes from Thailand could only be carried out during the dry season. There was therefore a definite time limit for the launching of an attack if it was to be carried through before the onset of the south-west monsoon in May.

To strengthen our forces in Tenasserim, 16 Brigade, then concentrating in Mandalay, was ordered into the area. On December 19th the 1st Battalion 7th Gurkha Rifles arrived in Martaban. The other two battalions of the brigade were to move from Mandalay in January.

Particularly during the earlier phases of the campaign frequent changes in the composition of our Brigades were made. It is unnecessary and would be tedious to catalogue all these changes. Those of an important nature will be detailed from time to time.

In Karenni the small F.F.5 force was now strengthened by the transfer to the area of the 1st Battalion 18th Royal Garhwal Rifles. The district was most malarial and our troops on patrol and in outposts suffered severely from fever.

On the Southern Shan States front December passed very quietly. There were reports that some bodies of troops were being moved north through Thailand, but it was not very clear whether these troops were Thai or Japanese. In any event it was to be expected that the enemy would strengthen the frontier posts. There was no definite evidence of Japanese troops in the area.

Of greater importance were the earlier reports that heavy guns and tanks were being moved north on the main Bangkok-Chiangmai Railway

CHAPTER 5

and had arrived at Lopburi, and that the railway bridges on the line were being strengthened up to Pitsamloke. The Lampang-Chiang Rai road was reported to be closed in places and a bridge was believed to be under construction over the Namhok river near Waw-Pakok. The Namhok flows into the Mekong at the junction of the Burma-Thai-Indo-China frontier.

Our patrols were active and there were some very minor frontier encounters. At Tachileik on December 22nd one of our patrols crossed the frontier and engaged some Thai troops who were dispersed by our fire. No Japanese were met.

In accordance with arrangements previously made one Regiment of the Chinese 93rd Division moved across our frontier to take over the defence of the Mekong river west of the road Kengtung-Mongpayak. The remainder of the Division was at Puerh in China.

The internal situation in Burma during this opening phase of the campaign was quiet. The action of the British Government in detaining the Premier U Saw, naturally created a certain amount of excited comment, but had no repercussions. The arrest of about three hundred known Fifth Columnists and malcontents acted as a check to seditious activity. The bombing of Tavoy, Mergui, and, later, Rangoon came as a rude shock to many who had believed that Japan was entirely disinterested in her often-proclaimed friendship for the people of Burma.

Rangoon was raided by enemy aircraft on December 23rd and 25th. On each occasion material damage was slight and the raiders sustained very heavy losses. But the first raid was accompanied by numerous civilian casualties, about two thousand people being killed. The great majority of these casualties were amongst persons who neglected to take cover. As a result, there was a large exodus from Rangoon. In particular the lower-class Indians who provided by far the greatest part of the labour fled. Work in the Port was almost at a standstill for some time, and the handling of important cargoes and munitions was seriously delayed. Ships could not be unloaded. This held up the arrival of other ships. The evacuation included practically the whole of the bazar population, and many domestic servants and menials. Hospitals found it impossible to keep sufficient staffs to maintain essential services.

For a period in January the position improved somewhat; but rumours of further impending air attacks and, so it is said by Burma Government representatives, of an intention that the military would take over the city led to a further flight of many of the labourers who had returned. The Japanese had brought about the almost complete paralysis of the Port of Rangoon at a time when it was essential that it should function in the most effective manner. There is no doubt that although the air raids of December 23rd and 25th achieved little in the way of material damage they had far reaching effects and were the most important incidents in the early phase of the campaign.

The organisation of civil defence in Burma had not been undertaken seriously until a very late stage. Sir Reginald Dorman-Smith had assumed the office of Governor of Burma in May 1941 and at once endeavoured to initiate a vigorous policy. He secured the appointment of an expert Civil Defence Commissioner but it was not until November 1941 that his advice that air raid shelters should be erected was accepted. Work was then begun on surface shelters; underground shelters being declared unsuitable by reason of the nature of the subsoil.

In Rangoon surface shelters for the accommodation of only twenty-five thousand of the population had been erected. Well-constructed buildings could also afford protection to about seventy-five thousand people.

Work on other branches of Civil Defence began equally late and the Civil Defence Commissioner found himself faced with an almost impossible task. In Rangoon the fire service was totally inadequate only peacetime medical arrangements existed, no equipment, vehicles, or trained parties existed for rescue operations, nothing had been done to ensure the feeding, clothing, or housing of the homeless, and no arrangements existed for the training of instructors or personnel.

Within the short time that remained the Civil Defence Commissioner and his staff achieved as much as was humanly possible with the material and personnel at their disposal, but in Rangoon and throughout Burma the essential element of morale was almost wholly absent. The Government had given the people no lead, and it was not to be expected that the majority of Indians and Burmans would readily remain in areas subject to aerial attack. No strong ties of loyalty bound them to the British, they were not martially inclined, and they were certainly not prepared to die for a cause which many even barely understood.

The position in Rangoon was complicated by an evacuation scheme that contemplated the removal of one fifth of the population, the non-essential elements, to camps outside the city. But no machinery existed for determining who were essential and who were not. By what process of reasoning it was believed officially that those required to work in essential occupations were likely to remain while at the same time others whose services could be dispensed with were pressed to leave 'dangerous areas' was difficult to discover. In the result essential and non-essential persons fled together. The camps round Rangoon were not used. The Burmans went into the villages or jungle, whilst the intended destination of most of the Indians was India.

Chapter 6

Detailed appreciation of the military situation by Lieut.-General Hutton – Events in Tenasserim in January 1942 – Signs of an early Japanese advance – The evacuation of Mergui – Japanese attack on and capture of Tavoy – Advance of Japanese 55th Division on Kawkareik – Operations in that area – Withdrawal of 16 Brigade.

Early in January Lieut.-Genera Hutton prepared a detailed appreciation of the general situation in Burma and considered the steps necessary to meet a Japanese attack. The appreciation is too lengthy to reproduce but it was a remarkably accurate forecast of events. It clearly set out the advantages to the enemy of an advance through Tenasserim, and visualised the possible strength, mobility, and tactical methods of an invading force. It stressed the Japanese methods of deployment on a wide front and their bold enveloping movement, their awareness of the advantages of air superiority and the early seizure of airfields, and their habit of supporting an advance by outflanking landings from the sea whenever possible. The necessity to the Japanese of carrying out an invasion before the onset of the monsoon was set out.

Lieut.-General Hutton also saw the advantage of utilising with promptitude and to the full the Chinese V and VI Armies which had been offered to us. This would permit the concentration of the British forces in Tenasserim. At the same time, he appreciated the danger of endeavouring to hold the whole of the Shan States east of the Salween and Tenasserim as far south as Mergui. He said:

"By holding right forward to Loimwe we expose our L of C Loimwe-Taunggyi to infiltration by …… columns moving north-west from Chiang Rai and Chianmai.

"Similarly in the south by holding the whole of the Tenasserim peninsular south to Mergui we should use up troops in small packets out of supporting distance of one another.

"With our present weakness in troops we must endeavour to concentrate as great a strength as possible at the really vital areas.

"These would appear to be as follows:

Martaban-Bilin, Ywathit-Bawlake, Mongpan, Takaw.

"By denying these four areas we virtually deny every practicable route into Burma from Thailand."

But local military considerations alone do not always prevail. It was essential to gain time for the arrival of reinforcements and this could hardly be furthered by abandoning large areas of difficult country without fighting. So long as Malaya held it was desirable to maintain the aerodromes of the reinforcement route, and the effective use of such fighter aircraft as might be available in Burma was dependent in retaining the warning system established in Tenasserim. Furthermore, Rangoon was very vulnerable and with enemy aircraft based on Tenasserim aerodromes the port might become almost unusable.

In the north it would have suited the Burma Command to withdraw behind the Salween, but this would have left the Chinese Regiment on the line of the Mekong unsupported on its right flank. It would also have left Yunnan open to invasion. This, therefore, would not have helped the Chinese who were themselves prepared to relieve the troops already deployed east of the Salween. Actually, the withdrawal of these troops began early in the campaign and only a thin covering screen was left. However, shortage of transport and the long distances to be traversed made the withdrawal a protracted and tedious business. Some of our troops had to march for three weeks before being picked up by motor transport.

We therefore did not give up any portion of the Shan States, nor did we concentrate behind the Salween in the Martaban-Bilin area. In Tenasserim in the opening phases of the campaign we did use up troops as they arrived in small packets. There was in fact no alternative. In the Shan States when the Japanese thrust occurred in April it did not come through Thailand but from Karenni. But the wide dispersal of the Chinese VI Army over the areas east of the Salween and its inability to concentrate a striking force in the threatened sector had a decisive bearing on the campaign.

Until the beginning of April 1942 there was little activity in the Shan States or Karenni. The minor operations in these areas over this period

CHAPTER 6

are described subsequently. It was on Tenasserim and later on Central Burma that interest was focused.

In Tenasserim the first fortnight of January was a period of increasing tension. Enemy aircraft were active, particularly in the areas about Moulmein and Tavoy. Moulmein town and aerodrome, Martaban and its ferry and railway installations, and the landing stage at Kyondo on the Haungtharaw river were all attacked and bombed. Tavoy also suffered on several occasions, and enemy reconnaissance aircraft paid particular attention to the Tavoy-Myitta road. On January 13th one of these reconnaissance aircraft was shot down by a Buffalo fighter from the Tavoy airfield.

This activity suggested early advances by the enemy against Moulmein and Tavoy. There was other information to the same effect. It was reliably reported that there was a concentration of five thousand Japanese troops in and around Meshod where four hundred mules had arrived. Coolies were improving the Meshod-Raheng road which was much used. In Raheng over sixty barges had assembled. On reconnaissance flights the R.A.F. could observe no troop concentrations, but the jungle-covered country made concealment easy. We were soon to learn, too, that the Japanese made it a practice to lie up under cover by day and to carry out their movements by night. In the neighbourhood of Myawaddy Thai outposts began to show a greater zeal, and there were interchanges of shots across the frontiers and patrol encounters.

On January 8th, Headquarters and one company of the 1st Battalion 7th Gurkha Rifles moved up from Moulmein to the Kawkareik position which until then had been held by the 4th Battalion Burma Rifles alone. Another company of the 1st Battalion 7th Gurkha Rifles went forward beyond Kyain-Seikkyi to watch the track through the Three Pagodas Pass south-east of Moulmein.

Tavoy was garrisoned by the 6th Battalion Burma Rifles, and patrols were covering the trans-frontier tracks. Early in the month a small party of Japanese had been observed near Sinbyudaing on the Tenasserim river. Sinbyudaing was then reported to be occupied by three hundred of the enemy, and later it was learnt that they had been there since January 8th. Sinbyudaing was connected with Myitta by a track and the enemy began to repair this. A company of Burma Rifles was then sent forward to Kyaukmedaung on the Myitta road and platoon posts were established at Myitta and north of it at Sainpyon. Meanwhile the two companies of the 3rd Battalion Burma Rifles in Mergui received orders to be in readiness to reinforce the Tavoy garrison at short notice.

This, briefly, was the position in the Moulmein and Tavoy areas on January 14th. Major General Smyth whose arrival had been delayed by illness from which he never fully recovered, was deprived of the opportunity to reconnoitre the Tenasserim area in any detail and to prepare plans for its defence.

Further south, in the Mergui district the enemy appeared to be infiltrating cautiously northwards. On January 2nd the Naval Office reported the presence of a Japanese patrol at Hangapru and a few days later small parties of the enemy were between Karathuri and Victoria Point. F.F.2 which had the area under observation reported on January 16th that bodies of Japanese were advancing along the Lenya river, and from Bangsap Anyiac, and through the Maw Daung Pass, from Prachuab Girikhan. Hostile Burmans armed with rifles and a light machine-gun were near Karathuri. This was the first instance of Burmans actively joining hands with the invaders.

On January 17th the Mergui garrison was reduced. The two companies of the 3rd Battalion Burma Rifles were moved by sea and road to Tavoy where the situation was rapidly developing. If Tavoy fell Mergui would become dangerously isolated. Consequently, on January 18th Army Headquarters directed 17 Division to concentrate all its available strength on Moulmein, Kawkareik, and Tavoy. The Mergui garrison was to be moved to Tavoy, and all tin and wolfram mines in the area were to be immobilised. Mergui aerodrome was to be demolished and all stores destroyed. Later in the day this order was modified to the extent that no further troops should be put into Tavoy unless communications with that place could be left open. General Smyth thereupon directed the Mergui garrison to withdraw by sea avoiding Tavoy which was now seriously threatened.

There were not sufficient sea-going vessels in Mergui for the evacuation of all military and civil personnel. On January 20th the S.S. Harvey Adamson sailed for Rangoon with some civil evacuees and part of the garrison. Meanwhile demolitions were carried out and all local power-craft and lighters were collected for evacuation purposes. On the following day the remainder of the garrison and evacuees, with the exception of a small rear demolition party, left for Tenasserim Island to await the arrival of another steamer. Having completed demolitions at Mergui the rear party on January 22nd rejoined the main body at Tenasserim Island, and early next morning S.S. Heinrich Jessen sailed thence for Rangoon with the remaining troops and civilians. All craft that could not proceed to Rangoon were destroyed. M.Ls. 1100 and 1104 of the B.R.N.V.R. which had covered the evacuation of Mergui

CHAPTER 6

made a search for and found some military and civil stragglers and took them aboard. They then carried out further destruction of craft and also of the secret fuel dumps on the islands.

It is now necessary to return to events at Tavoy. On January 15th a force of Japanese was within three miles of Myitta and our post there was reinforced. That evening the enemy attacked, and for some time the small force of two platoons checked all attempts to advance. However, the enemy eventually worked round the post and our troops withdrew.

Our main position was now on the hills astride the road to Tavoy near Milestone 25 west of Kyaukmedaung. The country was very broken and covered with dense jungle thus lending itself to the infiltration tactics so regularly employed by the Japanese. On January 16th Kyaukmedaung was found out to have been occupied by the Japanese, but they were reported to be moving through the hills to the south. Next day the position at Milestone 25 was held by two companies, one of the 3rd Battalion Burma Rifles and another of the 6th Battalion Burma Rifles. A third company of the 6th Battalion Burma Rifles held a flank position to the south-west at Yebyutaung.

At about 2330 hours that night the Japanese attacked out troops at Milestone 25. The attack was made in two parts, frontally along the road and also across the hills from the northern flank. The flank advance was directed on detachment Headquarters. It succeeded, and the detachment transport was captured. The least that can be said is that most of our troops appear to have melted away. A number later collected at the Hermingyi tin mine several miles north of the road and made their way to Moulmein as, later, did some of the garrison of Tavoy town.

It should here be mentioned that the 6th Battalion Burma Rifles had been newly raised. It had no opportunity of carrying out higher training in any form. In the absence of any definitely appointed commanders the action of the three companies concerned in the operation was probably not too well planned or directed.

During the next two days much useful information was forwarded to Tavoy regarding the movements of Japanese troops by managers and employees remaining at the mines in the neighbourhood. Some of these mines were connected by telephone with Tavoy, and messages were sent through after the Japanese had passed on. Many mine employees were members of the Tenasserim Battalion, B.A.F. and they carried out road and mine demolitions and also employed harassing tactics against the enemy. Some of them then returned to our lines through the jungle or by country boats long after the other troops had left.

Orders were issued to establish a perimeter defence for Tavoy, but with the remaining troops at his disposal the Commander could do little. On the morning of January 19th at about 0730 hours the enemy attacked the town and airfield from the north-east. In spite of a spirited resistance the remnants of the 6th Battalion Burma Rifles, a detachment of 5 Field Battery R.A., B.A.F., and the small Burma Frontier Force detachment were soon overrun. The town was in the hands of the Japanese by midday. Shortly afterwards enemy aircraft landed on the airfield.

The Japanese 55th Division had carried out these operations in south Tenasserim. It was now to be engaged in further operations consisting of an advance on Moulmein through Kawkareik and the Three Pagodas Pass.

Our small force in the Kawkareik-Myawaddy area occupied positions designed to cover the road from Meshod in Thailand to Kawkareik through the Dawna Range, and also the tracks in the neighbourhood of this main road. Kawkareik itself lies in the flat country to the west of the mountains and in a direct line is only about twenty miles from Meshod, but the intervening country is very broken and densely forested. The frontier itself was formed by the Thaungyin river, not a very serious obstacle particularly having regard to the fact that we were not in sufficient strength to keep it under close observation. Of the tracks the most important were one from the frontier village of Palu, south of Myawaddy, by which Kawkareik could be entered without the use of the road; and another from Payataung, north of Myawaddy, giving access to a pass through the hills at Kyaw Ko Ko to Nabu, a village on the western plain.

From Kawkareik the normal method of communication with Moulmein was by the steamer route from Kyondo. There was also a track motorable in dry season, which crossed the Haungtharaw river by ferry at Kyain. This Kyain is not to be confused with Kyain Seikkyi mentioned elsewhere in this chapter. The track through Kyain was used for bringing motor transport into the area.

The Kawkareik sector had been held by the 4th Battalion Burma Rifles (Lieut.-Colonel Abernethy) since November 1941, but it was evident that a single Battalion could not adequately cover the great stretch of difficult country that had to be protected. Nor, indeed, could the additional troops moved into the area in January 1942 do more than attempt to impose some delay on any large formation of the enemy advancing across the frontier. These additional Battalions were the 1st Battalion 7th Gurkha Rifles which arrived on January 9th,

CHAPTER 6

and the 1st Royal Battalion 9th Jat Regiment, (less one company and one platoon) sent forward on January 16th. These Battalions together with the 4th Battalion Burma Rifles now constituted 16 Brigade, Headquarters of which had been established on the main road near Milestone 23, about six miles forward of Kawkareik.

16 Brigade had existed in name in India for some months. None of its three Indian Battalions had been with it longer than six weeks before landing in Rangoon. Although Regular Battalions they had been heavily 'milked', and two of them received very large drafts of recruits just before leaving India. No Brigade training had been carried out, and the Brigade Signal Section was picked up en route to the port of embarkation. Most of the young soldiers were not even reasonably efficient with automatic weapons, and only the N.C.Os. and a few of the old soldiers were acquainted with the No.36 Grenade. Many junior officers had not fired a pistol course. It had been hoped that training would be completed in Burma.

From the middle of January enemy reconnaissance and bombing aircraft were very active. The landing stage at Kyondo was destroyed; and positions on the main road were attacked daily. Our casualties from these raids were few. The Brigade Intelligence Officer, Lieut. Raymond Hall, who had been in civil employment in the district and knew it well, had organised a local intelligence service which now reported the concentration by the Japanese of stores and men for a general advance. It was evident that a large-scale attack was imminent.

The Brigade front, as the crow flies, was about twenty miles; on the ground it was much more. On the arrival of the 7th Gurkha Rifles it was the intention of Brigadier J.K. Jones to hold the front with the two fresh Battalions, and to bring the 4th Battalion Burma Rifles into reserve at Milestone 20 with one of its companies at Nabu. The Burma Rifles had been much depleted by malaria and many men still on duty were far from fit. The fighting strength of the brigade in the area was about seventeen hundred men.

On arrival, the 1st Battalion 7th Gurkha Rifles took over certain of the forward positions, whilst one company had been previously detached for duty some sixty miles to the south where it was covering the trans-frontier track leading to Kyain Seikkyi from the Three Pagodas Pass. This company was to be relieved by a company of the 1st Royal Battalion 9th Jat Regiment, which was proceeding to Kyain Seikkyi direct from Moulmein.

The main position was near the summit of the Dawna Hills about Milestone 35 on the main road. Forward of this position was a company strong point somewhat east of Milestone 51, with a detached platoon post in Myawaddy itself.

South of the road one company held positions at Kwingale, Atet, Mekane, and Ale Mekane. From this later village a motor truck patrol was maintained along the track to Palu. North of the road a company watched the frontier in the Mepale-Tichara area and covered the track through the Kyawko Pass. Another company was at Nabu where the track debouched on the plain east of the hills.

When the relief of forward positions began, the Battalions were disposed as follows:

1st Royal Battalion 9th Jat Regiment, less two companies and one platoon, in the area of Milestone 17. One company of the Battalion had just relieved a company of the 1st Battalion 7th Gurkha Rifles in the Kwingale positions.

1st Battalion 7th Gurkha Rifles, less three companies, on the Milestone 35 position with one company Burma Rifles under command. One company of the Battalion was holding the Milestone 51 strong point, whilst the company from Kwingale was preparing to relieve the Burma Rifles company at Milestone 35 on the following day.

4th Battalion Burma Rifles, less three companies, at Milestone 19. The remaining three companies were at Habu, Milestone 35, and in the Mepale area.

It will be observed that the Brigade was widely dispersed and that the only line of easy communication was the main road. Many of the posts were without wireless equipment and could only make contact with their respective Headquarters by runner.

The Japanese crossed the frontier in strength early on January 20th at Palu, Myawaddy, and at points north of the Mepale river. At about 0500 hours the Gurkha Rifles Platoon at Myawaddy was surprised. Hearing firing the Platoon Commander went forward with his reserve section to investigate. In the village he met a party of men who were taken to be the local police. An electric torch was flashed upon the Gurkhas, and a moment later the section had been shot down by a burst of automatic gun fire. At the same time the rest of the Gurkha Rifles forward company was attacked in its strong point near Milestone 51. It was completely surrounded but held out for some hours. It then fought its way through the enemy and with all its transport mules carried out a compass march to the Salween river. A barge was found and the company embarked on this, floating downstream to Martaban to rejoin its Battalion some days later.

CHAPTER 6

News of the attack was received at Battalion Headquarters and the Commander, Lieut.-Colonel B.G.H. White, together with the Brigade Intelligence Officer went forward from Thingannyinaung having first made contact with the Gurkha Rifles company from Kwingale. With this company, a few men of the 9th Jat Regiment, and a platoon of Burma Rifles, they then advanced to Milestone 47 where they were ambushed by the enemy. Lieutenant Hall was killed. Believing that his company at Milestone 51 had now been wiped out Lieut.-Colonel White reported this fact to the Brigade Commander who ordered him to fall back to Milestone 35 and to cover the forward road demolitions that were being blown by the Sappers.

Information of the attack had been given to 2/Lt. Balls of the 9th Jat Regiment at the Ale Mekane post, and he at once took out a patrol of twenty men in two trucks along the Palu track. About ten miles out the patrol met a strong enemy column headed by five mounted officers and accompanied by elephants carrying mortars. The first burst of light automatic gun fire from the patrol accounted for at least three of the mounted officers. Successive defensive positions were then taken up by the patrol to delay the advance whilst information was sent back to Ale Mekane. After inflicting causalities on the enemy, the patrol retired on Ale Mekane where, after a further engagement, 2/Lt. Balls and a few of his men withdrew to the main road to join Lieut.-Colonel White. The remaining men retired on Kwingale and there with the rest of the company were ordered by their Commander to scatter in the jungle. They made their way into Kawkareik along the Koko Chaung track.

There was no communication with the Burma Rifles company in the Tichara-Mepale area and the position there was not known. The day closed with Headquarters and one company of the 1st Battalion 7th Gurkha Rifles and two companies of the 4th Battalion Burma Rifles holding the Milestone 35 position. Here, our troops had been heavily dive-bombed by hostile aircraft all day.

Owing to the evacuation of the Kwingale positions the right flank of the Brigade was open. Accordingly, the remainder of the Battalion of the 9th Jat Regiment was moved by the Brigadier during the evening to positions immediately east of Kawkareik through Tadangu and Myohaung, covering the tracks emerging from Kwingale. Strong patrols were to be maintained forward along these tracks.

Headquarters of the 4th Battalion Burma Rifles and one company of the 1st Battalion 7th Gurkha Rifles were that night in position about Milestone 18 on the main road.

Before dawn on January 21st Kawkareik was evacuated by the Sub-Divisional Officer and all civil officials save the telegraph staff.

This remained at the request of the Brigade Commander. Almost the entire population left the town. This was a wise precaution as at 1100 hours that morning Kawkareik was heavily bombed by a large formation of enemy aircraft.

Our troops at Milestone 35 were in contact with the enemy whose patrols attempted to work round the northern flank of the position. Japanese aircraft were active in bombing forward areas, about 1600 hours Lieut.-Colonel White informed the Brigade Commander that he was convinced that if he continued to hold the position at Milestone 35, he would be cut off by the following morning.

Shortly afterwards the Jats reported the loss of an officers patrol sent out along the Koko Chaung track down which the Japanese were advancing. They further reported that the enemy was entering the plain about three miles south of Myohaung.

Army Headquarters had issued orders to 17 Division that the Brigade was not to become so involved as to render withdrawal impossible. At the same time, it was not to give up more ground than necessary and was to occupy an intermediate position. These orders had been communicated verbally to the Commander of 16 Brigade.

The Commander was faced with a difficult decision. His force was fighting in dense jungle country, and there was no doubt that many young soldiers in the Brigade were shaken by their first experience of war. One unit, at least, could not be relied upon at that time. In the open plain west of Kawkareik there was no position that could be safely maintained for long. Moving on a wide front and in superior numbers the enemy could easily by-pass any position held by us. Having regard to these factors and the reports he had received, Brigadier Jones decided to withdraw his force during the night of January 21st/22nd. Orders for the withdrawal were issued. An intermediate defensive position was to be taken up at Milestone 12 west of Kawkareik where some delay could be imposed on an enemy advance. The 1st Royal Battalion 9th Jat Regiment was to cover the withdrawal of other units from the forward positions on the main road. It would continue to hold Kawkareik until the movement was completed.

The mechanised transport of the Brigade with such stores as could be carried and with an escort was to be evacuated to Moulmein by the fair-weather track via the Kyain ferry. This ferry was very primitive and was operated by local boatmen. Kit and stores that could not be removed were to be abandoned and destroyed.

That evening the transport column moved off for the Kyain ferry. Only one vehicle at a time could be carried across the river. Arriving at the further bank the ferry boat was not properly tied up and when

CHAPTER 6

the first truck drove off, the moorings gave way. The truck slipped into the water completely blocking the landing place. This prevented the further use of the ferry and closed the only outlet for motor transport. The result was that before the final withdrawal of 16 Brigade from Kyondo all vehicles had to be destroyed.

Shortly before 1800 hours the firing of dumps of kit and surplus ammunition by the Jats at the camp originally occupied by them near Milestone 17 led to a report that the enemy was advancing. Some of the Gurkha Rifles company in position at Milestone 18 withdrew. It is on record that the effects of fighting in the jungle combined with exhaustion and ignorance of the country were very marked on the inexperienced soldiers engaged in these operations. Light and shade on trees and undergrowth were taken to be movements of hostile men. Bullock carts were reported as tanks, and stumps of trees became guns. There is no doubt that there was considerable confusion in certain units of the Brigade during the night of January 21st/22nd.

The withdrawal from the position at Milestone 35 began at dusk. Demolitions were blown. The enemy did not follow up our troops as they left. When these had passed through the position at Milestone 18 the force there proceeded to carry out demolitions and destroy dumps. Animal transport was sent ahead, and Headquarters of the 4th Battalion Burma Rifles together with the attached company of the 7th Gurkha Rifles followed in motor lorries.

In Kawkareik itself the 1st Royal Battalion 9th Jat Regiment was now withdrawing protected by small covering parties. A sudden outburst of firing created a certain amount of panic and accelerated the withdrawal. The entry into the town of the animal transport from the Milestone 18 position added to the confusion. The mules were fired on as they passed through Kawkareik. Carrying with them mortars, Bren guns, and other equipment they bolted back into the jungle. The incident was reported to Lieut.-Colonel Abernethy who had halted his motor transport short of the town. The firing in the town continued and also broke out from the direction of Milestone 12 beyond Hlaing-Wa village. No contact could be made with the 9th Jat Regiment. Lieut.-Colonel Abernethy then took the motor transport some way back along the road, debussed, destroyed vehicles and stores that could not be carried, and took his force across country towards Kyondo.

The defensive position at Milestone 12 was manned by elements of the 1st Battalion 7th Gurkha Rifles. This was held until 1300 hours prior to which the bridge near the position was blown. The covering troops then fell back.

Meanwhile the 1st Royal Battalion 9th Jat Regiment had withdrawn on Kyondo where a bridgehead was to be established. Here further confusion was occasioned for some time by the firing of a few shots which gave rise to a report that the Japanese were in the village. The Jat company detailed to cover the river crossing failed in its duty and withdrew without orders. The remaining motor transport and surplus stores were then destroyed and the force eventually crossed the river to Thayettaw in small boats. The crossing was completed on the evening of January 22nd.

Nowhere had the Japanese pushed home their attack. It is possible that if 16 Brigade had stood on its positions it might have been overwhelmed, since it was later estimated from information that became available that about two thousand five hundred enemy troops were engaged in the initial attack. However, there is little doubt on the whole that a Brigade of seasoned troops could in fact have retained its positions for the time being.

On January 23rd and 24th the main force marched across country down the left bank of the Gyaing river without further contact with the enemy. It was eventually picked up by steamers which carried it to Martaban. On January 25th it went into a rest camp twelve miles from Martaban, and here was joined by Lieut.-Colonel Abernethy's force which en route had been augmented by the Burma Rifles company from Nabu. The Brigade was now without transport and had lost most of its equipment including mortars, Bren guns, and Thompson sub-machine carbines. It was considerably disorganised. There was still no news of the Burma Rifles company in the Tichara-Mepale area, but this rejoined some days later.

The exploits of this company relieve the somewhat dismal picture of the Kawkareik operations, when it had encountered a superior force advancing from Thailand, after a sharp engagement it drove back the Japanese. On the following day identifications and important papers were obtained from an enemy patrol that was destroyed. Unfortunately, these papers and identifications were all lost when the truck carrying them to Battalion Headquarters ran into the enemy at Thingannyinaung. The company continued to dominate the Tichara-Mepale area and was in contact with the enemy until January 23rd when the Company Commander, who had no wireless equipment, suspected that something was wrong as he was receiving no communications form the Battalion Headquarters. In fact, orders to withdraw had been sent to him on January 21st but never reached him.

CHAPTER 6

According to a previously arranged plan the company now fell back slowly to Kyawko where it remained on January 24th covering the pass through the hills. Next day it retired on Nabu to find that village unoccupied and burnt out by hostile Burmans. Two engagements were fought with guerilla bands. The company then marched to Paan on the Salween across two unbridged rivers. It eventually rejoined 16 Brigade with mules, equipment and reserve ammunition complete, after having killed thirty of the enemy without loss to itself.

The Kawkareik operations in which only a small number of casualties were sustained were not very creditable to those engaged in them. There were isolated instances of gallantry and coolness one of which has just been mentioned. The company of the 1st Battalion 7th Gurkha Rifles posted in the strong point at Milestone 51 also did especially good work. It is only fair to add that the Commanders and units concerned completely rehabilitated themselves by their subsequent achievements.

Chapter 7

The Japanese advance on Moulmein – Operations leading up to the attack on that town on January 30th 1942 – The defence of Moulmein – British withdrawal on January 31st, 1942.

In view of the disorganised state of the troops withdrawn from Kawkareik and the fact that the enemy was believed to be in considerable strength the Commander of 17 Division represented to Army Headquarters the view that his division should be moved back to the area Bilin-Kyaikto-Sittang. Here all approaches converged and a counter-attack could be launched. Lieut.-General Hutton thought a withdrawal on this scale to be unjustified and considered that Moulmein should be held to delay an enemy advance as much as possible. At the same time, he did not intend to allow the isolation of a force there. The town was difficult to defend without a far larger force than was available. At least two Infantry Brigades were required to hold a secure perimeter. The nearest point of contact was Martaban, two and a half miles distant, on the opposite bank of the swift flowing Salween.

Lieut.-General Hutton decided, therefore, that whilst Moulmein should be defended the main defensive line must be that of the river itself. Behind this, forces could be assembled for the taking of the offensive when adequate reinforcements arrived.

A certain amount of confusion was caused by an alteration in policy. On January 24th orders were issued to 17 Division that the G.O.C. did not intend to leave a Brigade isolated in Moulmein and that plans should be made to evacuate if it became necessary. Touch with the enemy was to be regained and a delaying action fought to cover withdrawal of stores, animals, and motor transport. Owing to the poor communications across the river and the considerable quantity of stores which, very unwisely, had been dumped in Moulmein, this was likely to take a considerable time. This withdrawal was begun, but after the visit of General Wavell

CHAPTER 7

to Burma on January 25th a decision to retain Moulmein was made. The withdrawal of surplus stores was to continue. 17 Division was informed that the 2nd Battalion King's Own Yorkshire Light Infantry would, if time permitted, be moved up to reinforce Moulmein. This fact much heartened the troops there.

By January 25th Headquarters 16 Brigade was established at Martaban with the 1st Battalion 7th Gurkha Rifles, less two companies one of which was still missing after the Kawkareik action, two companies of the 4th Battalion Burma Rifles, and the 1st Royal Battalion 9th Jat Regiment. 46 Brigade had been ordered up to the area about Bilin. It was without its transport which did not arrive in Burma until January 30th.

The defence of Moulmein had been entrusted to 2 Burma Brigade which for this purpose consisted of 12 Mountain Battery, 'C' Troop, 3 Indian Light Anti-Aircraft Battery, one section 60 Field Company Sappers and miners, the 4th Battalion 12th Frontier Force Regiment, the 3rd Battalion Burma Rifles (less two companies), the 7th and 8th Battalions Burma Rifles, and the necessary supply and medical units. There was also a detachment of the Kokine Battalion, Burma Frontier Force, protecting the aerodrome. This detachment consisted of five platoons, one being a machine-gun platoon.

Divisional Headquarters moved from Moulmein to Kyaikto on January 24th, and surplus stores were then back-loaded across the river as rapidly as possible. Refugees from Tavoy and stragglers from Kawkareik and Tavoy actions were passing through the town, which itself was being evacuated by the civil population. Only some of the disaffected elements remained, and looters became active in the bazars and other deserted quarters. Control of the town was therefore assumed by the Military authorities and looters were shot.

Close contact with the enemy had been lost after the withdrawal from Kawkareik. The Japanese did not press forward and it was evident that they were bringing in additional troops and probably fanning out on a wider front in the more open country west of Kawkareik. A patrol of the 7th Battalion 10th Baluch Regiment reported their presence near Paan on January 24th, and two days later a large party with pack artillery was located at Kyain Seikkyi. This party must have entered Burma through the Three Pagodas Pass and was following up the company of the 1st Battalion 7th Gurkha Rifles withdrawing from Kyain Seikkyi.

A company of the 4th Battalion 12th Frontier Force Regiment was in contact with a Japanese and a Thai force estimated at a strength of one Battalion at Chaungnakwa on January 28th. Our troops were subjected to heavy mortar and small arms fire and extricated themselves with difficulty. Next day the enemy was in Peinnegon and Kado. At 0400 hours on January 30th another company of the Frontier Force Regiment at Mudon, fourteen miles south of Moulmein, was attacked by a superior force. The Japanese were mounted and employed light machine-guns and mortars, and infantry guns. The company withdrew after losing four of its three-ton lorries. Cut off from Moulmein it crossed the Salween river in country craft and rejoined its Battalions at Kyaikto on February 2nd. During the same night our posts along the river front in Moulmein frequently fired on suspicious looking craft.

Lying on the east bank of the Salween just below its confluence with the Gyaing and Ataran rivers, Moulmein is a very long and narrow town. For much of its length its eastern side is bounded by a sharp ridge. The Ridge dominates and tactically is the key of the town. It is surmounted by three pagodas. The largest is at the northern end and has several monastery buildings round it. There is a smaller pagoda in the centre of the Ridge and a third, again with monasteries, towards the southern end. East of the Ridge the country is flat until it reaches the Ataran river. Much of the country is paddy land with patches of jungle. South of the town the country is more broken. Here are rubber plantations and much jungle. Through this area runs the main road to Mudon and Amherst. On the west and north the town is bounded by the river.

The perimeter of about eleven and a half miles was held by the three Battalions of Burma Rifles, the 4th Battalion 12th Frontier Force Regiment being in reserve about Point 183, near the bungalow which housed Brigade Headquarters. The 7th Battalion Burma Rifles held the south end of the town about the railway jetty, and the whole of the west and north river fronts to a point near the Kyaikpane Jetty. Thence the line cut across country to Hmyawlin on the Ataran river, followed that river south to Ngante and turned south-west along the road to the Zegyo quarter of Moulmein. The whole of this sector from near Kyaikpane Jetty up to a point midway between Ngante village and Zegyo was held by the 3rd Battalion Burma Rifles. The gap between the 3rd Battalion Burma Rifles and the left flank of the 7th Battalion Burma Rifles at the south of the town was filled by the 8th Battalion Burma Rifles. To the south-east and outside the perimeter was the aerodrome. No efforts were made to put Moulmein in a state of defence during the period before operations began. Once our troops became engaged it was too late to do anything really effective, but the Army Commander after a rapid reconnaissance had given orders for defences to be put in hand.

The Army Commander had directed Brigadier Ekin to take control of operations in Moulmein. Brigadier Ekin arrived there at midday on January 30th when the attack on the town had already begun.

It opened at about 0720 hours with a typical Japanese attempt at a surprise. Four of our own lorries with drivers in civilian clothes approached Zegyo along the road from Mudon. They were travelling fast and were filled with Japanese soldiers. At that moment 'D' company and one platoon of 'A' company of the 8th Battalion Burma Rifles had just begun to move down the road to deal with an enemy force reported to be near the aerodrome. The road block in the perimeter defence line was open. The Japanese in the leading lorry opened fire, but our own troops on the road and at the post covering it, immediately replied. The vehicles were brought to a halt, and our first burst of Bren gun fire killed at least thirteen Japanese in the leading lorry. The Japanese sustained further severe casualties as they hurriedly debussed.

A heavy attack on the 8th Battalion Burma Rifles and on the left flank of the 7th Battalion Burma Rifles now rapidly developed. The Japanese from the lorries joined up with others who were on the road to the aerodrome and attempted to work round the left flank of the 8th Battalion Burma Rifles. Our forward platoons suffered considerably from grenades and small arms fire but maintained their positions. A section of 12 Mountain Battery gave them excellent support and inflicted many losses on the enemy. Later the attack died away, but sniping of our positions on this sector continued.

On the east the enemy crossed the Ataran during the morning and penetrated the positions of the 3rd Battalion Burma Rifles to occupy both Hmyawlin and Ngante. Again, the Mountain Battery did good work engaging an enemy battery near Ngante. At least one gun was destroyed and the battery silenced. At 1300 hours Brigadier Ekin ordered the 3rd Battalion Burma Rifles to withdraw to a shortened line east of and covering the Ridge and Zegyo. At the same time the 4th Battalion 12th Frontier Force Regiment (less one company in Brigade Reserve) was ordered to occupy the Ridge. Later that day when the position on the Ridge was serious the reserve company rejoined the Battalion.

The detachment of the Kokine Battalion on the aerodrome was fighting an isolated action. It was first attacked by a small party of the enemy at about 0730 hours. This attack was beaten off. Later a heavier attack developed. The detachment was in communication with Brigade Headquarters and asked for artillery support. This was accurately given by the Mountain Battery. Thus assisted, the detachment put up a splendid resistance against superior forces throughout the day although at about 1630 hours a hill feature dominating the aerodrome was captured by the Japanese. From this hill heavy mortar and gun fire supported further attacks. As darkness fell the enemy began to close in round the aerodrome.

About 1730 hours the posts along the Ridge were heavily engaged by the enemy at close quarters. There was no sign of the 3rd Battalion Burma Rifles which was supposed to be holding a line east of and covering the Ridge. The situation now appeared to be critical, but the 4th Battalion 12th Frontier Force Regiment repulsed all attempts to dislodge it and was well supported by its own mortars and the guns of the Mountain Battery. As darkness fell heavy gun and mortar fire was directed against the Ridge and the southern front of the perimeter. At this time, too, Brigade Headquarters was informed that hostile craft were coming down the Salween from the direction of Kado.

Headquarters of the 8th Battalion Burma Rifles had been located that day in a bungalow on the south end of the Ridge. It was in a prominent position and the considerable movement round the house must have been seen by the enemy. As a result, the bungalow was shelled with extreme accuracy at about 1830 hours and after some casualties had been sustained Battalion Headquarters moved to ales conspicuous position.

In order to shorten and strengthen the perimeter and, if possible, to counter any penetration into the town under cover of night, Brigadier Ekin at 2300 hours withdrew the troops on the southern face of the perimeter. They fell back about one thousand yards to an east and west line joining the south of the Ridge with the river front. The enemy followed up the withdrawal and on this sector our positions were engaged all night with small arms, automatic, and cracker gun fire. The aerodrome detachment was ordered to make its way back as best it could through the positions of the 8th Battalion Burma Rifles. Many of the detachment came in safely.

Throughout the night the Japanese were in contact with our troops on the Ridge and frequent assaults were beaten off, the 4th Battalion 12th Frontier Force Regiment maintaining its positions intact. In the sector of its left-hand company were now also Headquarters and such men as remained of the 3rd Battalion Burma Rifles.

CHAPTER 7

During the evening of January 30th Brigade Headquarters had moved from the Ridge to the P.W.D. bungalow in Salween Park. This was given particular attention by the enemy who directed fire on it. Early next morning it was attacked by a small party of Japanese who had infiltrated through the defences. Headquarters therefore moved to the Telephone Exchange near the Mission Street Jetty. Barely had it been established there when large fires broke out in buildings along the river front close by. Fifth Columnists appeared to have a good knowledge of the movements of Headquarters.

The Bofors guns of the Anti-Aircraft Battery had been stationed in the northern area of the town to cover the jetties and the Ridge. In the early hours of January 31st these guns were over-run by parties of the enemy. These had landed from the river near the Timber Yard at the north end of the town. When challenged they gave the correct password and posing as Burmans or mingling with withdrawing Burmese troops entered the gun positions. The gunners were taken by surprise and some were bayonetted. There was a fierce hand-to-hand encounter, but the survivors of the gunners were compelled to withdraw abandoning their guns. However, they were able to remove the breech locks of two guns.

Divisional Headquarters at Kyaikto was in continuous telephonic touch with Moulmein and was kept closely informed of events. Early on January 31st Brigadier Ekin gave General Smyth an appreciation of the situation. It had been reported that a large number of men, mostly Burmans, were streaming down to the jetties. These men had been at once ordered back to their units, but the incident pointed to a break in the morale of certain units. This fact combined with the landing on the northern front and the repeated attacks against the Ridge, led Brigadier Ekin to consider the situation as extremely serious. He now had no reserve, and doubted very much if the force in Moulmein could hold the town against renewed attacks from three sides during the coming day.

Here it is significant to note that when it was known that the 2nd Battalion King's Own Yorkshire Light Infantry was not arriving as a reinforcement there had been a general drop in morale, particularly among the Burman troops. The Battalion was now available, but events had moved too quickly. The Battalion was weak and one of the only two British Battalions in Burma. There was no guarantee that its dispatch across the Salween would enable Moulmein to be held, and the possibility of withdrawing it after it was committed was equally remote.

The situation did not improve and the Brigadier was satisfied that the town could not be held much longer. He decided to withdraw his troops across the river and telephoned his decision to the Divisional Commander who concurred. He asked for air support during the withdrawal operations. General Smyth said that he would endeavour to obtain support from the R.A.F. Orders for a withdrawal to begin at 0800 hours were then issued.

Meanwhile at about 0600 hours the enemy had attacked from the Timber Yard area. The 7th Battalion Burma Rifles in spite of a counter-attack was forced back to a line about the Jail and Police lines. Other Japanese troops were infiltrating across the Ridge through the environs of the pagoda above the jail. Here a dawn attack penetrated the defences of the 3rd Battalion Burma Rifles at one point, a machine-gun post being overrun after heavy fighting. The Commander, Subedar Maru Gam, although wounded accounted for four of the enemy with his dah. On the south, at the other extremity of the perimeter, also at about 0600 hours an attack was made along the whole front. Some of the enemy suddenly appeared in Salween Park, but an immediate bayonet charge by Headquarters Company of the 8th Battalion Burma Rifles was entirely successful and cleared the Park of Japanese.

The plan for withdrawal was simply conceived. The 'box' of the diminishing perimeter was to be kept closed, units maintaining touch as they fell back on the jetties. 12 Mountain Battery and the 4th Battalion 12th Frontier Force Regiment were to form a bridgehead covering the Post Office, Maingay Street, and Mission Street Jetties at each of which five river steamers were berthed to take off the troops.

Each unit was detailed to withdraw on a particular jetty or jetties, and embarkation was controlled by specially appointed officers. Wounded, together with Medical and Supply units, had been evacuated as soon as the decision to withdraw was made.

At 0800 hours the troops holding the perimeter began to fall back. Rear parties were followed up by the enemy, not at first in great strength. Street fighting took place both in the north and south quarters of the town, but the enemy was held off and suffered many casualties. Then, however, the Japanese began to close in on the Post Office Jetty and embarkation there was seriously held up. Counter-attacks to clear the approaches were launched by parties of 60 Field Company and the 7th Battalion Burma Rifles.

Of the many acts of gallantry carried out that morning two deserve special mention. Major J.G.L. Hume, R.A., Commanding 12 Mountain Battery, on arrival at his embarkation jetty was informed that one section of the Battery was missing. At once he set out with a small party of his own men and some of the 12th Frontier Force Regiment, forced his way

CHAPTER 7

through the enemy to the gun position, and brought both guns back. The Battery thus saved all its guns.

Second Lieutenant Mehar Dass of the Anti-Aircraft Battery learnt that the Japanese had left no sentries on the Bofors guns they had captured. Organising a party from Troop Headquarters he succeeded in bringing to the Post Office Jetty the gun that had not been disabled by its crew. Here he made every endeavour to load the gun on a steamer but was unable to do so. Then under fire he went ashore from the last vessel at the jetty to disable the gun and assist survivors. He was not seen again, but long after the close of the campaign was reported to be a prisoner of war.

By 1000 hours the 4th Battalion 12th Frontier Force Regiment had withdrawn to within a few yards of the Maingay Street and Mission Street Jetties. The Power House and the Telephone Exchange had been destroyed, and all vehicles used to bring arms and vital equipment to the steamers had been put out of action. Brigadier Ekin then ordered the final evacuation, Brigade Headquarters together with the rearguard leaving on the last steamer from Mission Street Jetty. As the vessel left, the enemy gained the jetty and a brisk exchange of fire took place.

Fighting still continued round the Post Office Jetty. Many who could not embark on the steamers had to leave on improvised rafts or by swimming, and eventually nearly all who had been left behind escaped in this manner.

The Japanese were now in position on the Ridge. Their Artillery and machine-guns opened accurate fire on the steamers going up the river, and one of the smaller vessels was sunk by shell fire. Large formations of hostile bombing aircraft had been overhead during the period of evacuation but, fortunately, they persisted in bombing Martaban and not Moulmein. No R.A.F. cover had been provided.

On arrival of the steamers at Martaban every encouragement and threat was used to induce their local civilian crews to return to the Post Office Jetty to take off personnel remaining there. It was also known that a party of our troops was isolated at the Kaladan Jetty north of the embarkation area. However, the crews refused to take their ships back to Moulmein. They had been highly tried and were, of course, not subject to military discipline.

Our casualties during the operations on January 30th and 31st amounted to six hundred and seventeen, a considerable proportion being missing, and approximately three fourths of the Moulmein force was evacuated. It was several days, however, before all the stragglers eventually came in from these and the previous operations. The four

Bofors guns were lost. Heavy casualties were inflicted on the Japanese at Zegyo, on the Ridge, and during the final withdrawal. Before the action finished it is estimated that a whole Japanese Division was engaged. This was identified as the 55th Division which had also been at Kawkareik and at Bokpyin and Tavoy.

The problem of Moulmein had not been easy. Once the enemy reached its outskirts in force it was really indefensible with less than two Brigades. No prepared defence existed. The earlier appreciations of the probable direction of an enemy advance and the changes in command no doubt accounted for this omission. Poor communication, dependent on locally manned craft which could be brought under close range fire from outside the perimeter, would have rendered the retention of the town as a bridgehead almost impossible. Furthermore, the retention of Moulmein would not have blocked the enemy's advance. There was another route via Paan which for an enemy not dependent on motor transport was in many ways preferable. If, of our small forces available, the greater part had been isolated in Moulmein it is probable that they would have been cut off and destroyed, and that the occupation of Rangoon by the enemy would have been carried out considerably earlier than it was. The evacuation was subsequently approved by General Wavell as the only course open.

Chapter 8

Operations on the west bank of the Salween river – Defence of and withdrawal from Martaban – Attack on the 7th Battalion 10th Baluch Regiment at Kuzeik – Decision to withdraw to the Bilin river – Evacuation of Thaton on February 15th, 1942.

Before the withdrawal from Moulmein the line of the Salween river continued to be held by 16 Brigade now considerably strengthened. With Brigade Headquarters at Thaton its area of responsibility was defined as Kamamaung-Paan-Martaban-Thaton-Duyinzeik.

The Division was required to cover a most extensive and difficult track of country extending from the Salween north-east of Papun to the Sittang river on the west and the coastline on the south. Martaban in a direct line is more than fifty-five miles distant from Kamamaung. The country being very broken and jungle clad increased the problems of defence. Along the coast is a flat and narrow belt much intersected by tidal creeks and streams. This area and some of the flat lands bordering the Salween and its tributaries the Donthami and Yunzalin is given to the cultivation of rice. Apart from the coastal belt and the riverine tracts the country is rugged and jungle clad and becomes increasingly broken and mountainous towards the north. At the foot of the hills are extensive rubber plantations and in 1942, about Hninpale, large areas were also planted with sugar cane.

On the Salween were several ferries between Martaban and Dagwin, east of Papun. Tracks and roads led east from these and consequently the ferries required careful watching. So too, did many estuaries and creeks along the coast. The Japanese were known to be in possession of many rafts, river craft and launches. They were, therefore, well able to attempt coastal landings behind our lines.

46 Brigade was responsible for the area immediately behind 16 Brigade. It was required to watch the coast approaches south-west of

Thaton and also the long stretch of the Salween between Kamamaung to the point above Dagwin where it formed the frontier with Thailand. The 2nd Battalion Burma Rifles, recently withdrawn from Mergui, was allotted the task of protecting this northern flank and as stationed in the area of Papun-Dagwin. The Battalion remained in this area until the remainder of 17 Division had withdrawn beyond the Sittang on February 23rd.

Behind 46 Brigade were 2 Burma Brigade and 48 Brigade. This latter arrived in the Divisional area on February 7th. The tasks of these Brigades were to cover the Sittang and Bilin rivers and their estuaries, and to protect the Sittang railway bridge at Mokpalin. This bridge was the only one across the Sittang south of Toungoo and formed the sole and vital connecting link with the road and rail system to the west.

Whilst holding the Salween line 16 Brigade was made up as follows:

5 Mountain Battery.
2nd Battalion The King's Own Yorkshire Light Infantry.
1st Royal Battalion 9th Jat Regiment.
7th Battalion 10th Baluch Regiment.
1st Battalion 7th Gurkha Rifles.
3rd Battalion 7th Gurkha Rifles.
4th Battalion Burma Rifles.
8th Battalion Burma Rifles.

The 2nd Battalion King's Own Yorkshire Light Infantry had recently arrived from the Shan States. The 7th Battalion 10th Baluch Regiment and 3rd Battalion 7th Gurkha Rifles had been detached from 46 Brigade.

The ferries at Shwegun and Kamamaung were watched by the 4th Battalion Burma Rifles which also maintained patrols along stretches of the Salween and Donthami rivers. Later a company of the 8th Battalion Burma Rifles took over the post at Kamamaung. The detachments at this place and at Shwegun remained in position upon our withdrawal from the Salween further south and came under command of the 2nd Battalion Burma Rifles at Papun.

At first the Martaban area was strongly covered by the 7th Battalion 10th Baluch Regiment, the 1st Royal Battalion 9th Jat Regiment, the 3rd Battalion 7th Gurkha Rifles and the 8th Battalion Burma Rifles together with a section of 5 Mountain Battery. Within a few days,

CHAPTER 8

however, this force was thinned out. Only the 3rd Battalion 7th Gurkha Rifles supported by a company of The King's Own Yorkshire Light Infantry remained. Patrolling of the river bank, the coastline, and between rear and forward positions was regularly carried out.

It will be appreciated that several of the above-mentioned Battalions which had been engaged in the previous fighting were very weak and disorganised, and had lost much transport, arms, and equipment which could not be replaced. In normal circumstances they would have been withdrawn to refit.

The enemy was not slow in testing our positions and paid particular attention to Martaban. It was frequently bombed by aircraft and shelled by guns from the vicinity of Battery Point, the north-west corner of Moulmein. Later the Japanese established mortars on a small island in mid-river south of Martaban and from that position shelled the railway.

On February 2nd, before daylight, a landing was attempted from about fifty small rafts. A company of the Baluch Regiment successfully repulsed the attempt. The same afternoon Japanese were observed landing on Kawkami island east of Martaban.

We carried out certain demolitions, and apparently in the belief that we had withdrawn, the enemy sent across another landing party. The boast as they approached the foreshore were sunk by fire from the 1st Royal Battalion 9th Jat Regiment.

The water front was not wired. The river was tidal, and mud flats and shallow water between some small islands and the mainland made wading ashore possible. Thus, attempts by the enemy to land at night or during the early morning fog were by no means easy to observe or prevent. The Japanese were also astute in their attempts to gain points from which to cross the river. What appeared to be derelict river steamers moved up and down stream with the tide, and sometimes drifted in a curious manner on to mud banks. From Observation Posts on the hills it was noted that these vessels were propelled by sampans on their further side. When sufficiently hidden from view at ground level by the height of the banks these steamers were unloaded. It was in this manner that the Japanese established themselves on the island from which their mortars shelled the railway.

Our own mortars were not idle when they found possible targets and an excellent piece of work was carried out by the mortars of the 3rd Battalion 7th Gurkha Rifles. Firing at extreme range they sank a river steamer that appeared off Me Kyun Island.

For some days after the evacuation of Moulmein officers and men contrived to cross the river at Martaban to rejoin our forces. They came singly or in small parties and some were dressed in Burmese clothes. One British officer crossed by swimming from island to island.

Further up the river the Japanese were also active. On February 3rd they advanced on Paan. After a brisk fight with the Gurkha platoon in position there, they occupied the village and then proceeded to shell our main position at Kuzeik on the west bank of the Salween.

The R.A.F. gave our forward troops support and attacked the enemy with good effect. Kawkami Island was bombed and much confusion caused amongst the enemy there. Paan was also attacked and a direct hit made on the Japanese Headquarters in the village. Large fires were caused in Moulmein.

During this period a visit by the Commander-in-Chief, General Wavell, accompanied by Lieut.-General Hutton did much to hearten the personnel of the Division. General Wavell visited 16 Brigade, 46 Brigade and 2 Burma Brigade. It was on this occasion after observing the nature of the country that he decided to divert 7 Armoured Brigade from Java to Burma.

The relief of 16 Brigade by 46 Brigade had been arranged for February 8th/9th, but owing to the limited number of troops available it was not possible to relieve all units in the forward areas. It was intended that on relief the composition and dispositions of 46 Brigade should be as follows:

Thaton:
Brigade Headquarters.
12 Mountain Battery (less one section).
60 Field Company Sappers and Miners.
2nd Battalion King's Own Yorkshire Light Infantry (less one company).
Two companies 1st Battalion 9th Jat Regiment.
Armoured Car Section, Rangoon Battalion B.A.F.

Duyinzeik:
5th Battalion 17th Dogra Regiment.
4th Battalion Burma Rifles – also patrolling to the Salween.

Paan (Kuzeik):
7th Battalion 10th Baluch Regiment.
One Section 12 Mountain Battery.

Martaban:
One company 2nd Battalion King's Own Yorkshire Light Infantry.
3rd Battalion 7th Gurkha Rifles.

CHAPTER 8

In the meantime, small parties of the enemy were infiltrating across the river. Some were dressed in Burmese clothes, and one such party of three Japanese in disguise was intercepted by a civil Sub-Inspector of Police and his patrol of villagers. The Japanese were shot and on their bodies were found maps and papers indicating that the enemy was to cross the Salween in force at one or more points between Shwegun and Kado. On the whole, however, it was very difficult to deal with these enemy parties owing to the enclosed country and the long distances involved. No information was forthcoming from the local inhabitants. Later intelligence received on February 8th indicated the likely crossing points of the enemy as Paan, Mizan, Shwegun, and Kamamaung.

Whilst the relief of 16 Brigade was taking place Paan, Thaton, and Martaban were all heavily bombed by enemy aircraft, and on the morning of February 9th it seemed evident at Headquarters in Thaton that the Japanese were west of Martaban in some strength and by-passing our positions.

The force at Martaban was in an isolated salient and with the concurrence of Major General Smyth, Brigadier Ekin proposed to withdraw it before it was cut off. Accordingly, at 0900 hours on February 9th 2/Lieut. G.H. Jolliffe the Liaison Officer of the 3rd Battalion 7th Gurkha Rifles at Brigade Headquarters was sent to Martaban with orders for the withdrawal of the force. Firing had been reported at Milestone 10 on the Martaban road and 2/Lieut. Jolliffe was accompanied by two armoured cars of the Rangoon Battalion B.A.F. and four carriers of the 5th Battalion 17th Dogra Regiment.

A few miles south of Paung at Milestone 8 on the main road the party encountered an enemy road block. The two armoured cars were put out of action and Lieut. Jolliffe was fatally wounded. Only two carriers passed through the block, and these did not get back to Thaton. The other two carriers with the casualties returned to Thaton. Many of the enemy encountered near the block were in Burmese dress.

Next day, February 10th, a strong column including one company of The King's Own Yorkshire Light Infantry and six carriers set out along the Martaban road to find the missing carriers and to dispose of the enemy at Milestone 8 it came under heavy fire and could not get beyond the block.

The position at Martaban was that on the morning of February 9th the telephone line to Thaton had been cut and no wireless communication with Brigade Headquarters could be established, messages being repeatedly used. As a result, a strong officers patrol of the 3rd Battalion

7th Gurkha Rifles was sent out along the road to Thaton to investigate. It met the enemy near the road block at Milestone 8 and only one man made his way back to Martaban at 1530 hours. Captain Stourton who led the patrol was killed.

Meanwhile Observation Posts near the town were busy reporting landings from boats, barges, and a small steamer on the coast west of the town; whilst two officers of the 3rd Battalion 7th Gurkha Rifles reconnoitring along the road to Kwegyangyi and Thebyugon north of Martaban found another enemy block about seven miles out of town. 2/Lieut. Carver, one of these officers, was then ordered to attack this block with two companies. A bayonet charge dislodged the Japanese who were driven into the hills to the west of the road. A small gun, a mortar, and numerous other arms abandoned by the enemy were taken.

At about 1800 hours Lieut.-Colonel H.A. Stevenson (commanding the 3rd Battalion 7th Gurkha Rifles) and Major Haughton, commanding The King's Own Yorkshire Light Infantry company, from a point in the hills about four miles out of Martaban, observed a large body of at least one thousand of the enemy moving north across the flat coastal belt west of the town. These troops were making for the road block at Milestone 8 on the Thaton road and the hills to the west of it. There was practically nothing between them and Thaton some thirty-seven miles distant.

It now seemed clear that the enemy had by-passed Martaban and was also in a position to attack it from the north-west. No good purpose could be served by holding the town any longer and as he could not establish contact with Brigade Headquarters Lieut.-Colonel Stevenson decided to withdraw his force. Detaching 'D' Company of his Battalion to cover the Thaton road and a pass through the hills he destroyed all motor transport and after nightfall took his force along the road to Thebyugon, passing the now deserted block on that road. At the end of the road the force struck across country and after an exhausting march of over fifty miles through marshes, muddy fields, and waterless hilly jungle reached Thaton on February 11th. 'D' Company had been ordered to rejoin the main body by way of the pass. It misinterpreted its orders and made direct for Thaton by the hills north of the main road. The enemy had placed a cordon across the hills and the company had to fight its way through this, but the greater part of it eventually rejoined the Battalion.

It was not until February 13th that boats were reported to be moving between Moulmein and Martaban. Consequently, our defence of the latter place had for several days denied to the enemy its use and direct

CHAPTER 8

access to the main road. The question may well be asked whether it would not have been possible with the troops available to have held the line of the Salween longer. This would have accorded with the orders issued by the Army Commander but Major General Smyth was throughout in favour of an early withdrawal to the Bilin river.

The 1st Battalion 7th Gurkha Rifles at Kuzeik had been relieved by the 7th Battalion 10th Baluch Regiment (Lt.-Colonel C.J. Dyer) on February 8th. The relief was interrupted by bombing attacks from enemy aircraft and by mortar and infantry gun fire from Paan. Both our Battalions suffered casualties, the Gurkhas in particular losing heavily. There can be little doubt that the enemy was acquainted with the movements of our troops. The telephone line between Battalion and Brigade Headquarters was frequently cut either by Burmans or Japanese in native dress.

The position occupied was a saucer of open paddy land just north of Kuzeik village. It adjoined the river and was skirted on its southern side by the road to Duyinzeik. It was roughly circular in shape and with a diameter of some six hundred yards. The edges of the saucer were on higher ground and surrounded by close jungle with considerable undergrowth. Fields of fire were very limited. The eastern side of the position was on the river bank and also along this as on the southern side ran the road to Duyinzeik. Battalion Headquarters lay in the centre of the position. 'A' Company held the river bank, 'D' Company the northern face, 'B' Company the eastern face, and 'C' Company held the southern face of the perimeter along the Duyinzeik road. Mortars and machine-gun sections were in the area occupied by 'A' Company, one machine-gun section also being with 'B' Company. The Companies in the Battalion positions were considerably depleted in strength as patrols were constantly maintained along the river bank to Pagat on the south and Mikayin on the north.

The role of the Battalion was to prevent a crossing of the river in the Paan area. If necessary, the 5th Battalion 17th Dogra Regiment at Duyinzeik would render support, and it maintained contact with the Kuzeik position by means of a road patrol.

On February 9th one section of 12 Mountain Battery was placed under command of Lieut.-Colonel Dyer, and the same evening it shelled the town of Paan. The Battalion mortars were also employed on this task.

Late on the night of February 10th 'B' Company set out on patrol to Pagat to relieve 'A' Company.

The Japanese appear to have been crossing the river that night in force under cover of darkness. One platoon of 'A' Company and another platoon of 'B' Company were attacked and overrun near

Pagat. The remainder of 'B' Company advancing on that village was shadowed along its route, its positions being signalled by the tapping of bamboos. At about 0200 hours contact was made with the enemy estimated at a strength of about one company. Light machine-gun and rapid rifle fire drove the enemy back and heavy fighting ensued when the Japanese attempted to surround the patrol. This then withdrew on the main position at Kuzeik which was attacked at about 0430 hours. The Japanese were easily driven off.

For two hours that morning twenty-seven enemy aircraft carried out dive-bombing attacks on the Battalion. Only one casualty resulted owing to the excellent protection afforded by slit trenches.

During the day small parties of the enemy were observed crossing the river north of Paan, and that evening patrols reported the advance from Pagat towards Kuzeik of a strong force of about one Battalion. Lieut.-Colonel Dyer had sent back by a patrol a written situation report to the Officer Commanding the 5th Battalion 17th Dogra Regiment stating that he expected to be attacked by the enemy in strength that night and suggesting that he be reinforced as soon as possible. He also asked that Brigade Headquarters be informed of the situation since wireless communication had ceased. There were then five platoons of the Battalion out on patrol and these took no part in the subsequent action. They were cut off from the Battalion. In addition, the strength of 'A' and 'B' Companies had been greatly reduced by casualties.

At 1630 hours a small enemy force attacked the Kuzeik position from the south along the river bank. A counter-attack by 'C' Company resulted in the withdrawal of the Japanese.

A section of 'C' Company was now posted one mile from the Battalion position down the Duyinzeik road with orders to make contact with the 5th Battalion 17th Dogra Regiment which was expected to arrive shortly. It is not clear whether Lieut.-Colonel Dyer's written report was ever received by this Battalion, but no steps were in fact taken to reinforce our troops at Kuzeik.

At 0045 hours on February 12th this section on the Duyinzeik road saw a large body of troops advancing down the road from the west. Believing them to be reinforcements from Duyinzeik the Lance Naik in command of the section halted the leading troops whereupon heavy fire was at once opened on the section. It replied with light machine-gun fire and the Japanese, about a Battalion in strength, were compelled to deploy.

A quarter of an hour later the main Battalion positions were attacked from the west and south-west, the brunt of the first attack falling

CHAPTER 8

on 'C' Company. Later, attacks were also directed against 'B' and 'D' Companies from the north-west.

The enemy used cat calls and shouted and chattered incessantly. The cat calls had a psychological effect on the defenders and helped the enemy to maintain both morale and direction. The defence responded with Dogra and Mianwali war cries which both upset the enemy and encouraged our own men. Simultaneously the Japanese employed tracer ammunition and Chinese crackers to draw fire and locate the positions of our automatic weapons.

The attacks were made in waves, each wave consisting of several parties of ten or fifteen men. These were armed with swords, bayonets, and grenades and were supported by automatic weapons. Each party advanced in short rushes, the men lying prone after every advance.

As the enemy approached our positions counter-attacks were launched with bayonets and dahs, the Japanese being killed or driven back.

Between 0200 hours and 0700 hours 'C' Company counter-attacked in this manner every half hour, the company commander, Captain Siri Kanth Korla, personally leading no less than six attacks himself.

A whole Japanese Regiment was engaged and numerical superiority soon began to have effect. Infiltrating between 'B' and 'D' Companies the enemy surrounded the 'B' Company position.

This company, consisting of only about thirty-five men, fought on gallantly; but the enemy was now able to attack Battalion Headquarters in the centre of the position.

The Pioneer Platoon counter-attacked and succeeded in forcing back the Japanese and filling the gap between 'B' and 'C' Companies. Then the enemy again broke through the left flank of 'D' Company and once more attacked Battalion Headquarters. Hand to hand fighting followed and the Japanese were driven off. Officers, signallers, and mess servants restored the line.

Mortars and guns of the Mountain Battery had been firing on pre-arranged targets outside the perimeter. The guns of the Mountain Battery were in position near Battalion Headquarters. 'A' Company and the machine-guns in that sector had successfully prevented the enemy from breaking through from the north and south along the river bank.

It was now nearly 0500 hours and although the position was serious it was felt that the Battalion would be able to hold on until the arrival of reinforcements. These were expected to arrive at first light although repeated attempts to establish wireless communication with Brigade Headquarters and out troops at Duyinzeik had failed.

The situation rapidly deteriorated. Pressing on from the south the Japanese captured most of the reserve ammunition of 'A' Company. 'B' Company was completely overrun, the survivors only being overcome after fierce hand to hand fighting. 'C' Company was surrounded and had little ammunition left. Captain Korla with Jemadar Anant Ram fought his way through to 'A' Company, collected two boxes of ammunition, and again fought his way back to his company.

At first light, 0630 hours, the sounds of fighting had almost ceased except in the 'C' Company area. Battalion Headquarters and a part of 'A' Company still remained a fighting force, but 'D' Company had also been overrun. A Japanese officer from the slight ridge that had formed the 'B' Company position then called on the survivors to surrender. He was answered by bursts of machine-gun fire and fighting continued. Enemy mortars opened fire with accuracy and effect, and infantry guns from Paan shelled the river front positions.

The remaining personnel of Battalion Headquarters and 'A' Company now formed up for a counter-attack on the 'C' Company position where it was hoped that some men might still be holding out. Coming under mortar and small arms fire the counter-attack was launched across the open paddy fields. Major P.O. Dunn and 2/Lieut. G.L. Holden led about thirty other ranks. Casualties were severe but the objective was reached, the enemy withdrawing. Heavy fire from automatic weapons now disintegrated this small remnant of the Battalion, and by 0800 hours all organised resistance had ceased. The section of guns of the Mountain Battery had been lost.

Of those of the Baluch Regiment actually present in the Kuzeik position during the Japanese attack five officers, three Viceroy's commissioned officers, and sixty-five other ranks succeeded in re-joining 46 Brigade. Lieut.-Colonel Dyer and six other officers were reported missing. Of the officers who rejoined, Major Dunn and Captain Korla had been taken prisoner but escaped. For his gallantry and leadership during the operations Captain Korla was made a Companion of the Distinguished Service Order.

It was not until 1100 hours of the morning of February 11th that the 5th Battalion 17th Dogra Regiment moved from Duyinzeik to the support of the 7th Battalion 10th Baluch Regiment. This was on orders from Brigade Headquarters which that morning had received a wireless message that the force at Kuzeik was heavily engaged.

The 5th Battalion 17th Dogra Regiment advanced to a point some six miles short of Kuzeik. It then met stragglers who gave the impression that all was well. The Battalion consequently returned to Duyinzeik

CHAPTER 8

where only a small garrison had been left to defend the important ferry crossing.

The remnants of the 7th Battalion 10th Baluch Regiment were withdrawn to Kyaikto to reorganise and were there joined by a few much needed first reinforcements. Young and untried, the Battalion had acquitted itself magnificently. By far the greater part of it had stood fast under all attacks. Although it had suffered heavily it had also exacted very heavy payment from the Japanese.

The crossing of the Salween in strength by the enemy and the extinction of our force at Kuzeik necessitated the reorganisation of our defences. To replace the 7th Battalion 10th Baluch Regiment and to meet the new threat to Duyinzeik, the 1st Battalion 7th Gurkha Rifles was sent forward from Bilin to assist in covering the Donthami about the ferry area. To the right of this force the 4th Battalion Burma Rifles now continued the line through Singyon, Zemathwe and south-west to the pass through the hills about three miles from that village. One company of the 2nd Battalion King's Own Yorkshire Light Infantry held the area about Yinnyein. The remainder of this Battalion with the 3rd Battalion 7th Gurkha Rifles defended Thaton, whilst the two companies of the 1st Royal Battalion 9th Jat Regiment rejoined their Battalion at Bilin.

During this period Thaton and Duyinzeik were subjected to frequent air bombing attacks and a great part of Thaton was destroyed by fire. Fifth Columnists, usually in the guise of Buddhist priests, were most active. They signalled to the enemy from the wooded heights above Thaton and also started fires in various parts of the town. The King's Own Yorkshire Light Infantry effectively cleared areas of the town of these priests, but all efforts to capture the signallers failed. It is of interest to note that Fifth Columnists employed the same tactics in several other places later in the campaign.

In spite of negative reports from our patrols working in the enclosed country east of the Donthami the Japanese opened a sudden and heavy bombardment of Duyinzeik and the ferry on the afternoon of February 13th. This lasted about forty-five minutes but was not followed by any infantry attack. This bombardment and the previous aerial bombings much disorganised the 5th Battalion 17th Dogra Regiment.

At the same time the detached company of The King's Own Yorkshire Light Infantry at Yinnyein was attacked by a small force on which casualties were inflicted. After blowing up the road and railway bridges across the Yinnyein river the company withdrew to Thaton. It was not followed up.

The Commander of 46 Brigade now reported to Divisional Headquarters that there appeared to be no substantial enemy threat from the south and that the attack on Duyinzeik was probably a feint to distract attention whilst a crossing of the Donthami was made further north with a view to cutting the Brigade line of withdrawal. However, the Brigade was ordered to fight on the line Thaton-Duyinzeik.

Next day, February 14th, the Army Commander was at Divisional headquarters and the situation was reviewed. In reply to a telephonic enquiry from Major General Smyth, Brigadier Ekin replied that he was more strongly than ever of the opinion that the Japanese had by-passed the Thaton position and were moving round his left flank. Subsequent events proved this view to be correct and that the Japanese 33rd Division had crossed the Salween at Paan or above it and was advancing north-west on tracks east of the line Martaban-Thaton-Kyaikto.

At 1730 hours that evening Divisional Headquarters issued orders to 46 Brigade to withdraw to Kyaikto at once, Thaton to have been completely evacuated by first light next morning. Demolition of as many wooden bridges as possible along the road south of the Bilin river was to be carried out. At the same time 16 Brigade was ordered to hold a strong defensive position behind the Bilin river from approximately Leikkon to Payaseik. This was a line that the Divisional Commander was confident he could maintain against the enemy. 48 Brigade was to act as Divisional reserve and to be prepared to hold a defensive line from Taungzun behind the Thebyu river.

Shortly after 2000 hours that night very heavy firing broke out round Thaton on the west, north and east. It was undoubtedly the work of Fifth Columnists, probably supported by small parties of the enemy since coloured tracer ammunition was employed. It had a most disquieting effect on the young soldiers of 46 Brigade who imagined that the line of withdrawal had been cut. Many drivers of motor transport temporarily deserted their vehicles.

Nevertheless, the withdrawal was made in accordance with the plan, and its arrangements within the brief time available, constituted a good piece of staff work. Scattered units and detachments spread over ten miles of jungle country had to be assembled and the movement of some four hundred vehicles along a single road detailed in time to ensure the evacuation of Thaton before first light.

During the hours of daylight on February 15th the Thaton force halted under cover in the Kinmungyon-Theinzeik area protected by the 1st Battalion 3rd Gurkha Rifles which had been sent forward for

CHAPTER 8

that duty. The 5th Battalion 17th Dogra Regiment and the 1st Battalion 7th Gurkha Rifles, withdrawing independently from Duyinzeik by jungle paths via Methawbo-Thegon-Chnungsauk and so to the main road, also halted. That evening the Brigade continued its march, dropping the 5th Battalion 17th Dogra regiment at Milestone 58 on the main road to provide a forward outpost line and patrols to cover the main Bilin position of 16 Brigade. On crossing the Bilin river the 2nd Battalion King's Own Yorkshire Light Infantry and the 1st Battalion 7th Gurkha Rifles also joined 16 Brigade, whilst the remainder of 46 Brigade continued to Kyaikto to man the defences of that place.

It may be questioned whether the line of the river Salween was not given up too easily. Martaban certainly formed a difficult salient but, if sufficient troops were available, it should have been possible to counter-attack any enemy who succeeded in getting across and drive them into the river. Unfortunately, 48 Brigade, the only fresh troops available, did not arrive in the area till 7th February and it is doubtful whether the Brigade could have been employed in time to restore the situation at Martaban. General Smyth was particularly anxious to keep these troops in reserve until they had had the opportunity to acquire some knowledge of local conditions and then to use them in a decisive counter-attack role. The fact that they subsequently did so well was no doubt due to the fact that they were not, like some other units, thrown straight into the battle immediately on arrival.

There is also no doubt that the morale of a number of the other units in the area had been considerably shaken as a result of the operations at Kawkareik and Moulmein and there had been serious losses of equipment and vehicles. The net losses in men had not however been heavy, but many had been cut off or were missing for periods up to 14 days and had suffered considerable hardships. Once the enemy succeeded in infiltrating in rear of the Martaban position, nothing but vigorous offensive measures would have restored the situation. The alternative as the withdrawal decided upon by the Divisional Commander.

It must be remembered that at this time the Japanese tactics of infiltration and encirclement were not as well understood by the troops as they were afterwards. General Smyth realised this and felt that his young and inexperienced troops would be at a disadvantage when fighting in the jungle. Hence his desire to occupy the Bilin river position where there was a definite line and more open country where his troops could be relied upon to show to the best advantage.

The withdrawal from the Thaton-Duyinzeik area which was in thick jungle and could hardly be called a position was due to similar considerations.

If the enemy had not brought up another division it is possible that General Smyth's arguments would have been proved to be right but the river Bilin itself was a very ineffective obstacle and the left flank was always liable to be turned, as eventually it was, by a movement through the jungle.

Finally, it must be observed that in operations of this nature a considerable degree of latitude must of necessity be left to the Commander on the spot in interpreting the orders and instructions of the higher Command. An Army Commander, situated of necessity in Rangoon, could hardly control the operations in any detail and it may be noted that the necessity for the early provision of a Corps Commander and staff was strongly pressed by the Army Commander at this time. Meanwhile, Brigadier Cowan, who subsequently assumed command of 17th Division, was placed at General Smyth's disposal to strengthen his staff.

Chapter 9

British dispositions on the Bilin river line – Operations on that line – Heavy enemy attacks held – The Japanese infiltrate round both flanks and carry out coastal landings – Withdrawal of 17 Division to Kyaikto.

Major General Smyth reported to Army Headquarters his withdrawal to the Bilin river. He was confident that he could hold this line and check a further advance by the enemy. Any withdrawal west of the Bilin would inevitably endanger the communications between Rangoon and the north of Burma, since the Sittang river, the next defensible line of importance, was no great distance from the road and rail links between Rangoon and Mandalay.

Most units of the Burma Rifles and certain Indian Army Battalions were no longer fit for further fighting without rest and reorganisation. If the enemy could be halted it was hoped, as soon as reinforcements were available, to withdraw these tired units west of the Sittang.

On his visit to the front on February 5th General Wavell had stressed the importance of allowing the enemy no further advance. He was anxious, too, that a forward movement should be initiated as soon as it became possible to do this.

Whilst the main Bilin position was being manned certain moves were carried out to protect the area to the north of 17 Division. The 2nd Battalion Burma Rifles still covered Papun, but 2 Burma Brigade was now ordered to Nyaunglebin to ensure that the line of the Sittang should be patrolled and, if possible, prepared for defence. River crossings were to be watched, and the important railway bridge across the Sittang near Mokpalin, now boarded over for traffic, was to be safeguarded. At this time 2 Burma Brigade comprised the weakened 3rd and 7th Battalions of the Burma Rifles. The former Battalion was stationed at Mokpalin.

That these steps were necessary was indicated by a report on February 16th that a large enemy force had crossed the Salween at Yinbaing above Kamamaung. The company of the 8th Battalion Burma Rifles at Kamamaung sent out a patrol and established contact with the enemy (later identified as Thais) whose strength was estimated as eight hundred. The enemy had been endeavouring to collect bullock carts near Mepli west of the Salween, and action was taken to prevent thus.

The Bilin line to be defended by 17 Division was in country presenting certain difficulties for the limited number of troops available. The river itself was not a very formidable obstacle. It was fordable in many places. Save for the coastal belt the country was hilly and covered with considerable patches of dense jungle. There were also extensive rubber plantations.

16 Brigade (Brigadier J.K. Jones) was entrusted with the defence, and it was ordered to take up a position from Leikkon on the river estuary to Payaseik on the north with a detached company further north at Yinon. The line of the river near Payaseik was found to be unsuitable, and it was decided to prolong the position from Bilin to include the village of Danyingon, Point 313, and Paya. For this operation the Brigade had under its command the following units:

5 Mountain Battery.
12 Mountain Battery.
One Section 5th Field Brigade, B.A.F. (2 x 18 pdrs in an anti-tank role).
One Section Armoured Cars, Rangoon Battalion, B.A.F.
2nd Battalion The King's Own Yorkshire Light Infantry.
1st Royal Battalion 9th Jat Regiment.
1st Battalion 7th Gurkha Rifles.
5th Battalion 17th Dogra Regiment.
8th Battalion Burma Rifles – less one company at Kamamaung.

On the right the 1st Royal Battalion 9th Jat Regiment held a three-mile front from Shwele up to and including the road bridge across the river just south of Bilin village. South of Shwele, towards Leikkon, the front was covered by patrols. Bilin village was held by the 8th Battalion Burma Rifles with one company forward on high ground east of the river astride the main road where a block was established. North of Bilin the line was to be continued by the 2nd Battalion of The King's Own Yorkshire Light Infantry covering the villages of Danyingon and Paya. A detached company of the Battalion was to be further north at Yinon.

CHAPTER 9

To cover the preparations of the main defensive positions, the 5th Battalion 17th Dogra Regiment occupied outpost positions three miles east of the river and maintained patrols down the Thaton road. These outpost positions were occupied early on February 16th when the Battalion arrived from Thaton with 46 Brigade.

The flanks of the Bilin position were protected by columns of F.F.2. One column was responsible for watching the area north and forward of the left flank, whilst on the right another column protected the coastal belt and supported several coast watching posts established by the Burma Military Police.

The 1st Battalion 7th Gurkha Rifles acted as Brigade Reserve. Behind the main position 48 Brigade was in Divisional Reserve astride the main road east and west of the Thebyu Chaung.

46 Brigade manned the defences in the vicinity of Kyaikto which held 17 Division Headquarters. Of this Brigade the 4th Battalion 12th Frontier Force Regiment had one company guarding the approaches along the Sittang estuary against a possible sea attack. The 3rd Battalion 7th Gurkha Rifles, the 7th Battalion 10th Baluch Regiment, and the 4th Battalion Burma Rifles (less one company) had been brought back for rest and reorganisation and were not at that time fit for an active role.

The Japanese followed up our withdrawal from Thaton very closely. They were advancing in two columns; 55th Division by the main road, 33rd Division by the jungle tracks north-east of it. The intention of the enemy would appear to have been to fight frontally with 55th Division whilst 33rd Division by-passed the British position and moved directly on the vital Sittang bridge. During the march of 46 Brigade from Thaton elements of the Japanese 33rd Division must have been in close proximity to our column comprising the Battalions of the 17th Dogra Regiment and 7th Gurkha Rifles. The Japanese reached the Bilin river simultaneously with 46 Brigade.

The 2nd Battalion The King's Own Yorkshire Light Infantry moving into its position on the morning of February 16th came into contact with parties of the enemy in Danyingon village. The Japanese did not suspect that they were near our own troops and one party was surprised when washing round a village well. The men fled, but there were considerable numbers of the enemy close by and an action soon developed. That day repeated attempts were made by The King's Own Yorkshire Light Infantry to clear the village. 'D' Company of the Battalion suffered heavily in carrying out these attacks but could not dislodge the Japanese. Eventually a line was established along the main road south and west of Danyingon.

One Company of The King's Own Yorkshire Light Infantry was sent to Yinon in motor transport under escort of three tracked carriers of the Battalion. These were the only carriers in the Brigade and they continued to maintain contact with the Yinon company.

On the southern part of the front the day passed quietly. There was some firing by Dogra patrols, and here the Japanese were obviously feeling their way forward.

The morning of February 17th opened with heavy fighting on the northern flank. At about 0800 hours the 1st Battalion 7th Guhka Rifles attacked Danyingon village still held by the enemy. The country round the village was thick with jungle and this made the attack difficult. The Battalion had recently carried out the cross-country march from Duyinzeik and was by no means fresh. Yet, in this its first attack in jungle country, it went forward with great determination. One company advanced on the village from the north, two more companies from the west. The Gurkhas made two charges and there was heavy hand-to-hand fighting. Battle cries were used by us for the first time and a tremendous shout went up as our own troops closed with the enemy. The Battalion worked through the village; but some pockets of resistance were left, and another company was moved further round the north flank to deal with these. However, the enemy continued to maintain a hold on the village and was also in possession of Point 313 dominating it from the north-west.

The Brigade Reserve had been used up, but with Point 313 remaining in enemy hands it was necessary to cover the tracks running south of the main road between Paya and Danyingon. A platoon of The King's Own Yorkshire Light Infantry was brought into Brigade Reserve and together with Brigade Headquarters protected the track leading to Chaungbya through a gap in the hills. From Point 313 the Japanese commanded the main road, the only line of communication for wheeled transport, and also covered the out-flanking movement of their own troops round the village of Paya.

The Divisional Commander now ordered 48 Brigade to send forward the 1st Battalion 4th P.W.O. Gurkha Rifles. This Battalion was fresh and had not yet been in action. It was at once hurried forward in motor transport and that afternoon carried out a further attack on Danyingon and Point 313. On the right the advance was made into open paddy land, but the left company had to work through dense jungle.

CHAPTER 9

Supported by the guns of 5 Mountain Battery and its own mortars and those of the 2nd Battalion The King's Own Yorkshire Light Infantry, the Battalion made considerable progress and eventually reached a line about six hundred yards from the road. Here it dug in on the left of the 2nd Battalion King's Own Yorkshire Light Infantry. Point 313, itself jungle-clad but surrounded by paddy fields, lay further to the left and was independently attacked by a third company. It was taken without trouble. For the next two days we continued to hold this hill. A Forward Observation Officer was posted on it, and enemy columns by-passing our position to the north were severely handled by our guns. So, too, were parties of the enemy on the east side of the river where in places their movements could be observed.

With the 1st Battalion 4th P.W.O. Gurkha Rifles established on Point 313 and in the southern portion of Danyingon, the 1st Battalion 7th Gurkha Rifles was withdrawn south of the main road. Here it occupied a hill on the left flank and maintained contact with our troops on Point 313.

The heavy fighting on the Danyingon sector left 16 Brigade without reserves, and at 1300 hours the 5th Battalion 17th Dogra Regiment was ordered to withdraw across the Bilin river by the road bridge and to take up a position in reserve behind the 1st Royal Battalion 9th Jat Regiment. The withdrawal began at 1415 hours when the Battalion was in contact with the enemy who was now pressing forward on the axis of the road and railway from Thaton.

The Japanese attacked at once. Getting astride the road between the Battalion and the bridge they captured some trucks. The line of withdrawal for the Dogra Regiment was altered to the demolished railway bridge and a ford below it. Accurate and heavy mortar fire was opened by the Japanese. The Battalion which had a large percentage of young and untrained soldiers disintegrated and crossed the river in disorder. The Battalion Commander was then left with some thirty-five men. At the same time the forward company of the 8th Battalion Burma Rifles east of the river was overrun by the enemy.

At 1700 hours when all forward troops were across the river the road bridge was blown under the orders of Lieut.-Colonel Godley commanding the 1st Battalion 9th Jat Regiment.

Meanwhile enemy pressure increased on the northern sector. For about three quarters of an hour small arms and mortar fire covered the area of the road about Danyingon. It then died down without further development.

It had now become apparent that a single Brigade Headquarters could not control the extended jungle-broken front. This was particularly so in view of the new thrust south of Bilin. Accordingly, Brigadier Hugh-Jones, 48 Brigade, was ordered to go forward to Bilin to assume command of the right sector. He took with him the 2nd Battalion, 5th Royal Gurkha Rifles, F.F.

The Japanese continued their pressure on the south and soon after darkness fell crossed the river opposite Bilin, and entered the village. A gap was thus caused in the forward positions of the 6th Battalion Burma Rifles which extended as far as the left of the positions held by the Jats. Of the Burma Rifles there remained Battalion Headquarters and three platoons in rear positions. As soon as the 5th Royal Gurkha Rifles arrived Brigadier Hugh-Jones at once employed a company to reinforce the Burma Rifles.

On the right flank, near the mouth of the river, the Jats had maintained patrols throughout February 17th. They failed to make contact either with F.F.2 or the enemy.

During February 18th there was further severe fighting on the northern sector. Carriers proceeding to Yinon ran into a road block about half a mile south of Paya. Unable to clear the block they disengaged after inflicting casualties on the enemy. They were sent out again with a platoon of The King's Own Yorkshire Light Infantry. An engagement lasting a couple of hours ensued. Both sides sustained casualties, but our small force was unable to overcome the resistance around the block. There were no troops available for a larger scale attack, and the company at Yinon was cut off.

In this operation tracked carriers of The King's Own Yorkshire Light Infantry and wheeled carriers of the 1st Battalion 4th P.W.O. Gurkha Rifles were engaged. The superiority of the tracked carrier operating in country where movement off roads is difficult was very marked.

The strength of the Japanese was increasing and it was evident that the northern flank of our position was being enveloped. Parties of the enemy were moving through the gap between Yinon and Paya, and a large body of Japanese was reported to be moving west from Paya.

Danyingon was again the scene of activity. The 1st Battalion 4th P.W.O. Gurkha Rifles carried out extensive patrolling, one platoon working forward to the river bank at Pogon. Here casualties were inflicted on the enemy whilst he was crossing the river. In the afternoon the Gurkha platoon at Pogon was forced to withdraw under heavy light machine-gun and mortar fire.

CHAPTER 9

In the Bilin area two companies of the 2nd Battalion 5th Royal Gurkha Rifles, F.F. had that morning restored the situation. Supported by the Battalion mortars and 12 Mountain Battery an attack on the village met no opposition. The gap between the Gurkha Rifles and the Jats was closed. The 8th Battalion Burma Rifles now held positions north and in front of Bilin village.

On the front of the Jat Regiment there was little activity and one company was withdrawn to increase 48 Brigade Reserve then consisting of a single company of the 5th Royal Gurkha Rifles, F.F. During the day a Japanese ambulance was observed to drive up to the demolished road bridge. From it descended two officers who proceeded to carry out a reconnaissance of the bridge. Unfortunately, our troops refrained from firing on the ambulance.

On this and the previous day the R.A.F. gave out troops excellent support and the bombing of villages east of the Bilin river broke up at least one attack as it was about to develop. Stretcher bearers could be plainly observed carrying away casualties.

In the evening a body of the enemy landed west of the river estuary near Kawadut and a company of the 5th Royal Gurkha Rifles, F.F., was sent to Zothok to counter this new threat.

Japanese patrols were active that night on the west bank of the river and frequently employed sound effects such as crackers and 'marriage' bombs to create confusion. These were not without result. At about 2000 hours the reserve company of the Jat Regiment left 48 Brigade Headquarters to rejoin its unit, and whilst in the area of the 5th Royal Gurkha Rifles, F.F., this company thought it had been ambushed and exchanged fire with some of our own troops. Both parties sustained casualties and the Jat Company was unable to rejoin its Battalion until the following morning.

There was also considerable patrol activity by the enemy after dark on the northern sector. Tracer ammunition and grenades were freely employed whilst rear positions of Battalions came under mortar fire. Chinese crackers exploded in areas as far back as Battalion Headquarters. In reply to these attacks our own troops opened up heavy and unnecessary fire which took some time to stop. Much ammunition was wasted and our positions disclosed to the enemy. Our guns and mortars fired on probable enemy positions.

The Divisional Commander had received definite orders that he was not to withdraw from the Bilin position without the permission of Army Headquarters. The danger on the northern flank appeared to be very serious and he decided, therefore, that a risk must be taken about a possible coastal attack on Kyaikto. The only remaining Battalion fit for an active role was the 4th Battalion 12th Frontier Force Regiment. This Battalion, less the company watching the coast near Kyaikto, was accordingly directed to prevent further infiltration on the left flank of 16 Brigade and to counter the advance from Paya. On the night of February 18th/19th it went forward in motor transport to Alugale village and then marched to Paingdawe.

On the morning of February 19th heavy fighting continued on the northern sector. On the extreme left of our position the 4th Battalion 12th Frontier Force Regiment swept the hills from the direction of Paingdawe towards Paya. It arrived here about 1245 hours, and attacked the jungle covered hills dominating the village from the north west. The attack went in with determination, the men firing from the hip and using the bayonet. Despite a heavy mortar barrage from the neighbouring hills our troops took the hill. They then held on under continuous mortar fire which was followed by Japanese counter-attacks. Owing to the dense jungle only the two forward platoons were able to get into close contact with the enemy. After heavy fighting in which the enemy repeatedly made assaults, the Battalion was ordered to withdraw. It had sustained over fifty casualties. Taking up a position at Chaungbya it became the reserve for 16 Brigade.

Elsewhere on the front of 16 Brigade there were patrol encounters throughout the day and occasional mortar fire by the enemy. Our guns continued to find good targets; the fire effect being observed from Point 313.

Although the enemy was now well established along the whole front our positions from Bilin to the south were not heavily attacked on February 19th, the danger here being from coastal infiltration.

At first light a carrier patrol of the 2nd Battalion 5th Royal Gurkha Rifles, F.F., was sent out from Brigade Headquarters to make contact with the company sent to Zothok on the previous evening. It did not find the company at the appointed rendezvous, and on the return journey just south of Taungale it was fired on by Japanese and men dressed as Burmans. Accordingly, on the arrival of the patrol at Brigade Headquarters a second company of the Battalion was sent out. This second company encountered the enemy at Anaingpun. The main street of the village was cleared, but parties of the enemy still held out in Anaingpun.

Meanwhile the Jat Regiment had reported the enemy to be in position on Hill 302, north-east of Taungale. This appeared to be an enemy strongpoint. Only a weak company of the Jats was available for

CHAPTER 9

an attack, and as this was clearly insufficient it was decided to deal effectively with the position on the following morning. Companies of the 5th Gurkha Rifles, F.F., and the Jat Regiment would then attack Hill 302 with artillery and air support.

The Gurkha Company sent towards Zothok on the previous evening was also in action on February 19th. In the afternoon when approaching Taungzun railway station from the south-east it came under fire from the jungle north of the railway line. There was a sharp engagement and all Japanese who came out into the open were shot down. After losing eight men the enemy withdrew and, despite a long search our men were unable to regain contact. In the evening the company returned to Brigade Headquarters.

It is significant that at Taungzun signal cables had been deliberately tampered with as early as February 15th. The work had been done by persons with expert knowledge. That the local population was friendly towards the invader was to be markedly demonstrated on February 20th.

The Army Commander visited 17 Division during the morning of February 19th. The Divisional Commander reported to him that his troops were rapidly becoming exhausted, that he now had no reserves, and practically nothing to cover his important communications with the Sittang bridge. Consequently, it seemed to Lieut.-General Hutton, that there was a grave risk of not being able to disengage his troops unless a further withdrawal was ordered. The enemy was in rear of the right flank and firmly in position opposite the centre of our position; and there was every indication that he was bringing up strong forces against the left. Air reconnaissance that day had indicated that he was being reinforced. There was also the possibility that he was moving west through Paya and north of it. Further back lay the strong Sittang river line where open paddy land would provide a more easily defended position. In view of the anticipated arrival of reinforcements, especially tanks, it was clearly inadvisable to fight it out against greatly superior numbers, on the Bilin position. Subsequent events established that had a withdrawal been further delayed the Division would have been entirely cut off and practically destroyed. Reinforcements, if they could have entered the country at all, would not have been able to make contact with the Division.

Consequently Lieut.-General Hutton now told the Divisional Commander to make all necessary preparation for withdrawal, and to judge for himself when the necessity for this step had arisen. The bottleneck of the Sittang bridge and the difficulties attending its defence made it essential that the withdrawal should not be too long delayed.

The evening of February 19th found both bridges still closely engaged but holding their ground everywhere. On the left the 1st Battalion 4th P.W.O. Gurkha Rifles had withdrawn after dark to newly prepared forward defence lines sited in low ground some two hundred yards behind their original positions. These latter lent themselves to assault at close range during the hours of darkness, and were in fact attacked by the Japanese at 2330 hours. Silhouetted on rising ground the enemy presented excellent targets and came under severe punishing fire before withdrawing.

Orders for a general withdrawal were issued that night. 48 Brigade was to cover the withdrawal and at the Thebyu Chaung was to be reconstituted to comprise the original units of the Brigade as follows:

12 Mountain Battery.
1st Battalion 3rd Q.A.O. Gurkha Rifles.
1st Battalion 4th P.W.O. Gurkha Rifles.
2nd Battalion 5th Royal Gurkha Rifles, F.F.

Meanwhile all remaining troops, including 46 Brigade, were to take up a position behind the Kadat Chaung just west of Kyaikto. No steps were taken at this stage to strengthen the Sittang bridgehead.

In the dark 16 Brigade broke contact with the enemy. The first position to be vacated was Point 313 at 0430 hours. There was a heavy mist from the river, but the withdrawal was carried out well and in complete silence. The Brigade was clear of its positions by first light. After concentrating in the Bilin rubber estate it marched back to Kyaikto.

On the right sector the 8th Battalion Burma Rifles was withdrawn during the night, and the positions of the 2nd Battalion 5th Royal Gurkha Rifles, F.F., was adjusted to cover the withdrawal of the Jats. The Gurkhas were then to act as rearguard to 16 Brigade.

In the early hours of February 20th, the right and centre of the Jats were penetrated, and Battalion Headquarters was surrounded at a distance of about one thousand yards. As far as was known the enemy still occupied Hill 302. This situation was reported by the Battalion to Brigade Headquarters. It was decided that the Battalion must await daylight when it could break out with artillery and air support. This had already been arranged against Hill 302 for 1200 hours. Since orders for a general withdrawal had been received very late from Divisional Headquarters it was impracticable to change the timing for air support. The Brigade Commander therefore considered that the withdrawal of the Jats should be at the hour originally fixed for the attack.

CHAPTER 9

Owing to the failure of the wireless, the orders concerning this withdrawal sent to the 1st Royal Battalion 9th Jat Regiment were not received. The Battalion had then been withdrawn into a defensible position in scrub jungle with fair fields of fire. At 0900 hours a party of the enemy crossed the Bilin river by the railway bridge and was surprised at very close range by mortar and automatic fire. It was compelled to withdraw after sustaining casualties. At 1130 hours, shortly after wireless communication had been re-established, orders to withdraw were received by the Jats from Brigade Headquarters. Following this, at 1200 hours, our aircraft bombed the area of Hill 302. The Battalion then rejoined the rest of the Brigade near the Bilin rubber estate. Late that night our troops arrived in the Kyaikto area, the withdrawal being covered by units of 48 Brigade.

Orders to withdraw were dropped by aircraft on the detached company of The King's Own Yorkshire Light Infantry at Yinon on the afternoon of February 18th. The company had not been worried by the enemy save for a brief attack by a solitary Japanese aeroplane.

Proceeding cross-country towards Kyaikto the company encountered a small force of Japanese on the morning of February 19th. In the engagement that followed both sides suffered casualties, but the Japanese withdrew hurriedly. Continuing towards the Thebyu Chaung the company found numerous indications that enemy troops had already passed along the jungle tracks ahead of it.

All troops that had fought on the Bilin river were very tired, and some units had had fairly severe casualties. There is no doubt that they were in urgent need of a period of rest. Yet at Kyaikto 17 Division was still in a precarious position and one that did not enjoy even the moderate protection afforded by the Bilin river.

Chapter 10

Operations carried out by 17 Division on February 21st, 22nd and 23rd, 1942 – The withdrawal from Kyaikto – Japanese attacks on the Sittang bridgehead and on our force east of the river – Battle of the Sittang – Withdrawal of 17 Division across the Sittang.

Before proceeding to an account of the operations covering the important three days beginning with February 21st it is necessary to consider the general situation as it was then known, and also the nature of the country between Kyaikto and the Sittang river.

By 1600 hours of February 20th a large enemy coastal column with elephants had reached Kyeinphan, a village less than eight miles from Kyaikto. This column had been welcomed by the villagers of Taungzun and Kawkadut with flags and rejoicing. From various reports it was now fairly certain, too, that considerable parties of the enemy were north of Kyaikto where tracks led down to the Sittang river in close proximity to the railway bridge just north of Mokpalin. In addition, there was the fact that the Japanese had engaged us with large forces on the Bilin positions. Everything indicated continued enemy pressure and the danger of holding on east of the Sittang in difficult country with the bottleneck of the bridge behind us.

The road that had served as the main line of communication for the Division stopped at Kyaikto. Between that place and the Sittang bridge sixteen miles distant it had been demarcated; but all that actually existed was a rough earth track with badly built up sides, already much cut up by the heavy motor traffic that had passed over it. It was many inches deep in dust. This track (hereafter called the main road) skirted the eastern boundary of the extensive Boyagyi rubber estate and ran north-west through dense jungle country to Mokpalin village and the Sittang railway bridge.

CHAPTER 10

The railway, running south of the main road, afforded an additional approach for marching troops. Tracks connected the many villages along the line. The main road and railway met near Mokpalin Station and for some distance continued north in close proximity. The railway line then turned westward for the bridge, whilst the road proceeded north and approached the river in a wide sweep from the north-east. Here, between it and the railway, was high ground. That part of the ridge near the river was known as Pagoda Hill, whilst its eastern extremity was called Buddha Hill. A prominent pagoda and a great image of Buddha on the ridge gave rise to these names.

The railway emerged on to the bridge by way of a cutting through the bluff overlooking the river. The bridge itself, over five hundred yards long was, as already related, decked over with planks to take road traffic. Immediately above the bridge a ferry service of three power-driven vessels had been provided.

The river itself was a formidable obstacle even to the most expert swimmer. Below and above the bridge it widened rapidly, the current was swift, and the stream was subject to a strong tidal bore.

Between the bridge and the quarries east of Mokpalin the country was hilly and covered with jungle and scrub. There were a few small patches of open paddy land. South of Mokpalin where the land adjoining the river was flat were large stretches of paddy fields.

Lieut.-General Hutton had telegraphed an appreciation of the situation to General Wavell on February 18th. He then visualised the necessity of withdrawing from the Bilin positions if the enemy maintained his pressure. He added, 'Probably the best that can be hoped for is that we shall be able to hold the line of the Sittang river, possibly with bridgeheads on the east bank.' This withdrawal was now in progress.

A Divisional conference had been held at Kyaikto on February 20th when the withdrawal was discussed. The Brigade Commanders present strongly supported a suggestion that unwanted transport, numbering hundreds of vehicles, should be sent across the river as early as possible and that Brigades should only retain the minimum of transport for first line requirements. The suggestion was not accepted, although Army Headquarters had already ordered that all transport should be sent across the Sittang at an early stage.

It should be noted that rations, petrol, and other supplies would appear to have been sent up to units in motor transport whilst dumps of these stores established along the railway were being withdrawn by train.

The Divisional Commanders plan for the withdrawal was for 48 Brigade to move back first and to cross the bridge, going into Divisional Reserve about Abya. It was to pass through 46 Brigade which was already at Kyaikto. 46 Brigade could have reached the Sittang first and there been employed to secure the bridgehead for the Division.

On February 21st the leading Battalion of 48 Brigade was only to go as far as the Quarries two miles east of Mokpalin. The remining two Battalions were to halt on positions some four and seven miles further back along the main road. The whole Division was intended to cross the bridge on February 22nd.

On February 21st 16 Brigade and 48 Brigade were to march no further than the Boyagyi rubber estate about three miles north-west of Kyaikto. 46 Brigade as rearguard would hold defensive positions on the line of the Kadat Chaung just east of the rubber estate.

The use of the railway line and of tracks near it for marching infantry does not appear to have been considered except as a route for the flank-guard.

In view of the serious threat to Kyaikto and the line of retirement of the Division, the 2nd Battalion Duke of Wellington's Regiment (less one company) joined 46 Brigade at Kyaikto on February 20th. The remaining company had been detached for duty at the Sittang bridge by orders of Army Headquarters. 17 Division had been ordered to send back the rest of the Battalion to hold the bridgehead as early as possible. These instructions were not carried out.

The vital north flank of the Division was covered by two columns of F.F.2. On February 21st these were on a line from Kyaikto through Kinmun Sakan to a point some five miles north of the latter place. Their orders were to remain on this line until 1430 hours on February 22nd and then to withdraw towards Mokpalin covering the area to the north of it.

That the enemy was pressing forward was demonstrated by a raid on Kyaikto at 0600 hours on February 21st. The perimeter defences within which stood 17 Division Headquarters were attacked. Using coloured tracer ammunition, uttering war cries, and making much noise the Japanese and probably some fifth Columnists succeeded in creating confusion in the darkness. This led to indiscriminate firing by certain units, and for a time the position appeared somewhat precarious. The uncontrolled fire caused some casualties amongst our own troops. Otherwise the raid achieved little, and at first light the enemy retired.

Later that morning the Divisional Commander and his advanced Headquarters left Kyaikto for the Mokpalin Quarries. The remains of the 7th Battalion 10th Baluch Regiment had been sent there on the previous

CHAPTER 10

day to afford protection to dumps and Rear Headquarters of the Division. On the evening of February 21st 46 Brigade Headquarters and the 1st Battalion 4th P.W.O. Gurkha Rifles also arrived at the Quarries. Four miles down the main road was the 2nd Battalion 5th Royal Gurkha Rifles, F.F., and three miles behind it was the 1st Battalion 3rd Q.A.O. Gurkha Rifles.

To strengthen the bridgehead defence, still only consisting of the weak 3rd Battalion Burma Rifles and one company of the 2nd Battalion Duke of Wellington's Regiment, the Divisional Commander had ordered the 4th Battalion 12th Frontier Force Regiment to Mokpalin. This Battalion arrived at the Sittang bridge that night. Little appears to have been affected by the troops already in position to prepare the bridgehead for defence. Admittedly the ground was jungle covered and difficult, but something could have been done to improve matters.

The Gurkha Battalion at the Quarries was intended to cross the river early on February 23rd to take up anti-parachutist duties on the west bank. Consequently, additional troops from 48 Brigade available in an emergency for the bridgehead defences, were that night still several miles from these positions and could not, in the ordinary course of events, arrive there much in advance of the other two Brigades.

In the early afternoon of February 21st 46 Brigade, as rear-guard to the Division, withdrew from Kyaikto. The positions on the Kadat Chaung were manned. The road bridge over this Chaung was narrow and ill-constructed, many of the Burmese inhabitants of Kyaikto were now evacuating the town, and the passage of our troops was seriously hampered by slow moving bullock carts.

The day was one of extreme heat. Thick dust, raised in dense clouds along the unfinished main road by transport and marching troops, accentuated by a shortage of water added to the trials of our men. Enemy aircraft were active. They bombed Kyaikto.

In the afternoon and evening our columns on the main road and troops in the Boyagyi estate were repeatedly bombed and machine-gunned by relays of aircraft. Vehicles including ambulances evacuating casualties were ditched or destroyed; mules got out of control and vanished with their loads into the dense jungle; heavy casualties were caused. The equipment lost or damaged included many wireless sets. 48 Brigade Signals Sector had only one set in working order at the end of the day; the Section itself had sustained numerous casualties. Morale throughout the Division was seriously affected, and the disorganisation created by these attacks was not without effect on the events of the following day.

Some, at least, of the attacks were made by our own aircraft, both R.A.F. and A.V.G. Reconnaissance machines had reported a very long column of enemy transport, estimated at three hundred vehicles, moving through Kyaikto to Kinmun Sakan. The total available strength of the R.A.F. and A.V.G. on the Rangoon Aerodromes was employed to deal with this column. By some error which has never been explained the wrong targets were included in the attacks with the result that our own forces suffered. Aircraft with A.V.G. markings were in action as far west as the Mokpalin Quarries.

In the course of the afternoon the two columns of F.F.2 on the line Kyaikto-Kinmun Sakan made contact and were heavily engaged with the enemy. They were out of touch with one another and with 17 Division. Breaking off their actions with some difficulty they fell back towards the Sittang by jungle tracks north of the main road. No information of these operations was received by 17 Division, the lack of knowledge being attended by the most serious consequences. Next day, February 22nd, these columns of F.F.2 were again in action with bodies of Japanese who were between them and the river.

The Commanders of the two rear Brigades on the evening of February 21st agreed upon the necessity of withdrawing from the Boyagyi estate area towards the Sittang as speedily as was permitted by the situation on the road ahead of them. They had received no definite marching times and were bound to conform to the movements of 48 Brigade. A night march was therefore out of the question. However, it was arranged that save for essential vehicles the motor transport of both Brigades should be sent on ahead escorted by carriers. Machine-guns, mortars, and reserve small arms ammunition would be in these vehicles. Motor transport was to be clear of the starting point by 0500 hours next morning, 16 Brigade was to march at 0515 hours, and 46 Brigade was to follow it immediately. In 46 Brigade it was arranged that units were to march with no tactical gaps between Battalions or Companies. This formation was adopted to ensure mutual support in the event of an attack on the column in the thick jungle country.

At about 0100 hours on February 22nd the two rear Brigades received an immediate cipher message from Divisional Headquarters warning them that a strong enemy force was probably moving round the northern flank and suggesting that Brigades should move towards the river as early as possible. It was then too late to alter timings. Meanwhile, some of our outposts on the line of the Kadat Chaung were in contact with enemy patrols.

CHAPTER 10

During the night the Divisional motor transport began to move across the Sittang bridge. Very early, Divisional Headquarters marched form the Mokpalin Quarries, followed at 0400 hours by the 1st Battalion 4th P.W.O. Gurkha Rifles. 48 Brigade Headquarters marched half an hour later.

Shortly before this, all traffic across the bridge had been held up by the overturning of a lorry. This entirely closed the bridge for about three hours and the forward movement did not start again until 0630 hours. The approach to the bridge and the road through Mokpalin and beyond it, were now packed with a long line of halted vehicles. To add to the congestion the transport of the two rear Brigades was arriving, and the block was extended far east of Mokpalin. North of the bridge the ferry was being employed for the transport of mules across the river.

There appears to have been no traffic control along the road. Vehicles forced their way into the column in any order. Shortage of motor transport owing to previous losses resulted in overloading. This caused delays whilst articles that had fallen off lorries were picked up. The road itself was pitted with bomb craters, dangerous traps in the dark. An unfinished embankment across a water course had not been blocked nor the diversion marked, and here, too, was much delay. Vehicles that had driven on to the embankment had to be backed into the crowded stream of traffic. There were many ditched vehicles. Amongst these were ambulances still carrying casualties. Parties were detailed to render unusable, vehicles that could not be extricated.

An officer who was present describes the traffic situation east of Mokpalin, "Vehicles of all sorts including carriers and of many different units were all mixed up together. They were head to tail in a defile and in many cases had double banked on the road."

The 1st Battalion 4th P.W.O. Gurkha Rifles crossed the bridge before first light. It was followed by Divisional Headquarters and Headquarters 48 Brigade. Soon afterwards at about 0830 hours, and as the 7th Battalion 10th Baluch Regiment was marching through the railway cutting immediately east of the bridge, the enemy from concealed jungle positions to the north-east of the bridgehead put in a heavy attack. The one and a half companies of the 3rd Battalion Burma Rifles holding that sector of the perimeter gave way at once, and the attack went through almost to the end of the bridge itself. The 7th Battalion 10th Baluch Regiment came under mortar fire from the direction of the bridge. An Advanced Dressing Station north of the bridge was overrun. The A.D.M.S., D.A.D.M.S. and all medical personnel were taken prisoner. Motor transport drivers, men standing by with mules, and some of the bridgehead troops panicked and made a rush for the bridge.

Two companies of the 4th Battalion 12th Frontier Force Regiment at once counter-attacked, and retook the original positions on the north and northeast of the perimeter at the cost of about fifty casualties. For his gallantry and leadership on this occasion Captain S.H.F.J. Manekshaw gained an immediate award of the Military Cross. The Battalion was supported by the weak 7th Battalion 10th Baluch Regiment which now joined the bridgehead troops.

At about 1000 hours the Commander of 48 Brigade, Brigadier N. Hugh-Jones, took command of all troops holding the bridgehead.

'D' Company, 2nd Battalion Duke of Wellington's Regiment, then on the west bank, was ordered across the river and took up a position on Bungalow Hill on the south-east of the bridgehead perimeter. This Hill was already held by the remnants of a company of the 3rd Battalion Burma Rifles.

In view of the situation at the bridgehead the C.R.E., 17 Division gave orders for the destruction of about three hundred sampans collected on the west bank of the river. He further ordered the destruction of the power-driven ferry vessels, if they could not be manned. Accordingly, all these craft were destroyed by the Engineers in the course of the day.

Simultaneously with their assault on the bridgehead the Japanese attacked the column of transport massed along the road through Mokpalin. When they first appeared here the only troops to oppose them were the small baggage guards with the vehicles. At this stage vigorous action by the Japanese might well have secured for them the whole area of Mokpalin, and the eastern approaches along the main road and railway.

Lieut.-Colonel R.T. Cameron of the 2nd Battalion 5th Royal Gurkha Rifles, F.F., had entered Mokpalin ahead of his Battalion. Learning of the attack he determined to sweep the right flank of the road and to picquet it until the transport had crossed the bridge. He was ignorant of the situation at the bridgehead.

The Battalion deployed, and at once came under fire at close range from a temple on the knoll on the eastern outskirts of the village, and from a house to the west of the temple. The opening burst of enemy fire stampeded the mules of the Mortar Platoon. Only a single 3" mortar was saved; the 2" mortars had already been sent across the bridge. Two attacks were made on the enemy positions, but were halted with heavy casualties. A third assault followed and overcame the Japanese resistance. A 'blitz' party then went on to clear the enemy from a long double row of bamboo huts north of the temple.

CHAPTER 10

The advance of the Battalion was continued to the area of the Railway Station. In the Goods Yard snipers had established themselves, but hurriedly withdrew when a further advance was made.

Without artillery support and with but the single mortar which was without sights, two companies of the Battalion proceeded to advance along the east of the main road against Buddha Hill. The ground was covered with thick scrub jungle and contact was difficult to maintain. The two companies lost touch with one another.

In the low ground south of Buddha Hill, the left company came under intense mortar fire, suffered heavily, and was withdrawn to the higher ground further south. The right company was out of contact with the Battalion.

It had been thought that the 7th Battalion 10th Baluch Regiment was on the west of the main road. When this flank was found to be devoid of troops, a third company was moved forward to prolong the line astride the road and to the west of it. The Battalion had been in action without any support against superior enemy forces for about three hours, but by its determination it had cleared the Japanese from Mokpalin.

At this juncture the leading company of the 1st Battalion 3rd Q.A.O. Gurkha Rifles, commanded by Lieut.-Colonel Ballinger, arrived at the Railway Station. Our artillery also began to enter the village. The 1st Battalion 3rd Q.A.O. Gurkha Rifles was now to assume the main role and to bear the brunt of the battle. On this and the following day all units in Mokpalin were severely tried by the bitter fighting that continued incessantly, but a special tribute must be paid to these two Gurkha Battalions, the first to be engaged, the 2nd Battalion 5th Royal Gurkha Rifles, F.F., and the 1st Battalion 3rd Q.A.O. Gurkha Rifles. This latter Battalion when it mustered west of the Sittang two days later numbered just over a hundred of all ranks.

The Commanding officers of the two Battalions conferred. It was agreed that the 3rd Gurkha Rifles should attack Buddha and Pagoda Hills, on both of which the enemy was believed to be in position. The attack was to be supported by our guns in the village. The 5th Royal Gurkha Rifles, now reorganising, would hold the eastern outskirts of Mokpalin, the left forward company remaining in position west of the main road and facing Buddha Hill.

This plan was drawn up without any knowledge of the situation at the bridgehead with which there was no communication. The Japanese were on and forward of Buddha Hill. It was not unreasonable to suppose that they also held the whole of Pagoda Hill, more particularly as there was a report that they had secured the bridge. This being so, the plan proposed was proper. On the other hand, if the true state of affairs had been known it would have been a comparatively easy matter to establish contact with our bridgehead troops on Bungalow Hill and to co-ordinate an attack that would have cleared the way to the river. It might have been necessary to abandon the transport, but our troops could certainly have crossed the Sittang by the bridge.

In the early afternoon, at about 1400 hours (there is some disagreement as to the exact time) the Batteries grouped near Mokpalin Station put down an intensive concentration on Pagoda and Buddha Hills. Part of this fire fell on our bridgehead troops and resulted in their withdrawal by order of Brigadier Hugh-Jones.

Two companies ('B' and 'C') of the 3rd Gurkha Rifles attacked astride the road. Crossing the low ground at the foot of the hills they were soon in contact with the enemy. 'Blitzing' as they went on, they killed many Japanese on the forward slopes. At the top of the ridge stronger opposition was encountered. Much confused fighting followed, but 'C' Company established itself on Buddha Hill, and eastwards across the main road. On the left, 'B' Company had encountered a strong enemy post on the forward slope. The attack of 'B' Company swung rather too far to the west, direction was lost in the dense jungle, and finally two platoons under Captain Macrae entered our deserted bridgehead positions. Here they reorganised and manned the vacant posts on Pagoda Hill. They were out of touch with 'C' Company.

The Japanese determined to prevent a breakthrough to the bridge, filled the gap between the two companies and worked round the east flank of 'C' Company. They flung in reinforcements.

Lieut.-Colonel Ballinger ordered 'D' Company to clear up the situation and to link up 'B' and 'C' Companies. The ridge was again attacked. In its advance 'D' Company met more of the enemy, killed them, and joined 'C' Company on Buddha Hill.

Shortly after this Lieut.-Colonel Ballinger decided to go forward to 'B' Company with his Command Post. He and his party encountered some Japanese who raised their hands in surrender. As the Commanding officer went to meet them, they threw themselves on the ground, and fire was opened on Lieut.-Colonel Ballinger and his men from both flanks. The majority of the Command Post including Lieut.-Colonel Ballinger were killed.

There were now no British officers left with 'C' and 'D' Companies, but they were gallantly commanded by their Gurkha officers. Clinging

CHAPTER 10

resolutely to their ground on Buddha Hill, and in spite of severe losses, they repelled the repeated attempts of the enemy to dislodge them.

The Battalion Reserve consisted of Headquarters Company and a single platoon of 'A' Company; the other platoons having been sent forward. This small reserve was in position covering the main road on the outskirts of Mokpalin north of the Railway Station. Contact with the forward companies had been lost, and the remnants of the Battalion were commanded by Major Bradford. As evening approached, they became heavily engaged with the enemy.

It is now necessary to return to the bridgehead. As already related, part of the artillery concentration laid down by our guns at 1400 hours on Pagoda Hill fell on the bridgehead positions. At the same time these posts came under mortar fire from the enemy. Casualties were suffered by the 4th Battalion 12th Frontier Force Rifles. The Battalion together with the other covering troops was accordingly withdrawn to the west bank of the river.

Two hours later the bridgehead was occupied, the original force being accompanied by the 1st Battalion 4th P.W.O. Gurkha Rifles. This reoccupation took place just after the platoons of 'B' Company of the 1st Battalion 3rd Q.A.O. Gurkha Rifles gained Pagoda Hill. The northern, or left, sector of the defences was held by the 12th Frontier Force Rifles, the centre by the 4th Gurkha Rifles, and the right (Bungalow Hill) by the company of the Duke of Wellington's Regiment with some men of the 3rd Burma Rifles. The platoons of the 3rd Gurkha Rifles remained on Pagoda Hill.

Heavy fire was maintained on our bridgehead posts by the enemy throughout the day and into the night; but stragglers from all the units concerned in the fighting to the south-east in Mokpalin village came in, many under cover of darkness. One complete company of the 3rd Battalion 7th Gurkha Rifles made its way in, about 1645 hours, by keeping under cover of the river bank south of the bridge.

It will have been noted that the fighting in the morning and afternoon of February 22nd covered three distinct areas about Mokpalin. These were the bridgehead positions, Buddha Hill, and the village itself. Meanwhile 46 Brigade was engaged in an entirely separate battle some miles to the east.

This Brigade had marched from the Boyagyi rubber estate immediately behind 16 Brigade. The order of march was 3rd Battalion 7th Gurkha Rifles, 46 Brigade Headquarters, 5th Battalion 17th Dogra Regiment, 2nd Battalion Duke of wellington's Regiment. This last-named Battalion was delayed in starting through the non-appearance of its 'B' Company which had been attached to the 4th Battalion Burma rifles. This company took no part in the subsequent operations and its movements are chronicled later. The 4th Battalion Burma Rifles, acting as a flank guard, marched to Mokpalin along the railway.

During the march of 46 Brigade the sound of firing was heard ahead, and this presumably was from the fighting near the river. At about 0930 hours the Brigade was halted just short of the Meyon Chaung to wait for the 2nd Battalion Duke of Wellington's Regiment. 16 Brigade did not conform to this halt and a gap of nearly a mile developed between the two Brigades.

Concealed in the dense jungle on the eastern flank, the Japanese seized this opportunity to take up positions astride the road and to erect a block. When the road trace had originally been cut the cleared brushwood was thrown back upon the edges of the jungle. This now proved an obstacle on each side of the road and afforded additional protection to the enemy. Very shortly after 46 Brigade had resumed its march the 3rd Battalion 7th Gurkha Rifles encountered the block. Our troops at once came under heavy fire from small arms and mortars. Lieut.-Colonel H.A. Stevenson, commanding the Battalion, ordered two of his companies to attack the enemy from the left flank, and a forward movement through the jungle was initiated. Soon the whole Battalion was involved. The block was not taken although some of the attacking force on the extreme left worked round and beyond it.

The enemy was in considerable force and fresh attacks developed on 46 Brigade Headquarters and the 5th Battalion 17th Dogra Regiment. Finally, the 2nd Battalion Duke of Wellington's Regiment also came under short range heavy fire, the Japanese employing a number of light automatics and small mortars. The latter were used against any targets on the road itself. Fighting was at close quarters and most confused, and both sides suffered very severe casualties. Direction was difficult to maintain in the thick jungle, companies and smaller units rapidly separated, and men of all three Battalions became mixed. The Brigade, however, maintained its hold on the road although Japanese attacks came right through on to it. But little progress towards Mokpalin could be made.

After about an hour of this confused fighting Brigadier Ekin decided to sweep the jungle on the west of the road. A column of about five hundred rifles was collected and under command of Brigadier Ekin advanced through the jungle, clearing it of the enemy. The remnants of the Brigade followed, a carrier on the road covering the right flank.

After moving forward for some two miles the column became split and contact was lost between the various parts. Brigadier Ekin with

CHAPTER 10

some three hundred men eventually after nightfall reached the railway at Tawgon south of Mokpalin. The main body continued along the road and joined 16 Brigade which had now halted near the Quarries and close picquetted the road. Maintaining this close picquetting, and followed up at short range by the enemy, 16 Brigade and the remaining troops of 46 Brigade entered Mokpalin during the course of the afternoon and evening.

The 4th Battalion Burma Rifles had marched in along the railway without incident. On this route, too, the enemy was advancing. A body of twelve hundred Japanese was seen marching down the railway by 'B' Company 2nd Battalion Duke of Wellington's Regiment. This company, after failing to make contact with its Battalion, had sought to enter Mokpalin along the railway. It found the enemy ahead of it. Turning east it then made a detour out of the battle area, and late on the night of February 24th crossed the Sittang at a ferry several miles above the bridge.

When Brigadier J.K. Jones (16 Brigade) entered Mokpalin in the late afternoon he found the 2nd Battalion 5th Royal Gurkha Rifles, F.F., engaged with the Japanese who were trying to break through on the east out of the jungle to the main road just south of the Station. Contact had been lost with the greater part of the 3rd Gurkha Rifles, but what remained under Major Bradford was in position astride the main road north of the Station. Small arms, mortar, and artillery fire was heavy. The 8th Battalion Burma Rifles (16 Brigade) now took up the defence of the southern outskirts of the village. Here the Japanese were advancing along the line of the railway.

Brigadier Jones ascertained the situation and assumed command of all troops in the area. Less than an hour of daylight remained. Accordingly, the Brigadier decided to form a rough perimeter for the night, the positions on the east and south being maintained. In places there were gaps, and not all adjoining units were in contact.

Astride the main road and railway some four hundred yards south of the Station the 8th Battalion Burma Rifles held the line. On its right the 2nd Battalion King's Own Yorkshire Light Infantry continued the defence along the Bund and towards the river. Next in line along the river face was the 4th Battalion Burma Rifles. The 1st Royal Battalion 9th Jat Regiment held the high ground south-east of Bungalow Hill, and the remnants of the 1st Battalion 3rd Q.A.O. Gurkha Rifles were across the main road and railway north of the Station. On the east of the main road the perimeter was maintained by the 2nd Battalion 5th Royal Gurkha Rifles, F.F. Along the railway, near the Station, the 1st Battalion

7th Gurkha Rifles was in local reserve. In Brigade reserve were the two companies of the Duke of Wellington's Regiment. These were near Brigade Headquarters which had been established in a building close to the Bund at a point almost due west of the Station.

Stragglers, formed parties that had lost touch with the main bodies of their units, and the remnants of the 5th Battalion 17th Dogra Regiment and the 3rd Battalion 7th Gurkha Rifles were also within the perimeter. The last-named units were in position in the southern sector held by the 8th Battalion Burma Rifles.

The battle continued to be general on the north, east, and south. On the east our troops were pressed back towards the railway station. Enemy artillery and mortar fire from time to time set alight vehicles in the long line of crowded transport.

Our own guns grouped to the south and west of the Station were continuously in action, often engaging targets at short ranges and over open sights. They must have caused heavy losses to the enemy. The artillery units in action were 5 Field Battery R.A., B.A.F., 5, 12, (one section), 15 and 28 Mountain Batteries of 28 Mountain Regiment, I.A.

Enemy aircraft took no part in the operations on February 22nd, probably owing to the confused nature of the situation and the difficulty of distinguishing between the opposing forces. On February 21st the Army Commander had flown to Lashio to interview the Generalissimo on his way back from India. Returning on the evening of the 22nd he found the situation on the Sittang to be already serious.

That night enemy pressure was maintained. Both sides kept up heavy small arms and artillery fire, the Japanese employing much tracer ammunition. Our troops sought to improve their positions, and slit trenches were dug. On Buddha Hill 'C' and 'D' Companies of the 3rd Gurkha Rifles were continuously engaged throughout the night. In the early hours of the morning they had exhausted their ammunition. At about 0500 hours they were finally overrun, only a few men being able to fight their way back into Mokpalin. In this, its first action in the campaign, the Battalion was most gallantly upholding its fine Regimental traditions.

One of the main problems facing our force in Mokpalin was the lack of medical facilities, only Regimental Aid Posts being available. Medical Officers did splendid work. They laboured without rest to cope with the incessant stream of casualties.

Brigadier Jones had not been able to make a detailed reconnaissance before dark, but during the night and after a further examination of the ground another attack towards the bridge was planned. The Brigade

CHAPTER 10

reserve with the 1st Battalion 7th Gurkha Rifles (less one company) was to assault Buddha and Pagoda Hills as soon as possible after first light. The advance would be covered by the Jats from their position on the high ground south-east of Bungalow Hill. Having made contact with the bridgehead and cleared the main road and railway, the assaulting troops would maintain their positions until casualties were evacuated and such transport as could be moved had crossed the bridge. There was still no wireless communication with our force about the bridge or on the west bank of the river, and in consequence no information of this plan could be sent to Headquarters 17 Division.

Meanwhile, at the bridgehead itself the situation appeared to be deteriorating. It was not known how our troops in Mokpalin were faring, and the enemy was making repeated attempts to infiltrate to the bridge. The defence held its ground, but the Japanese established a machine-gun on the railway line. This brought fire to bear down the whole length of the bridge. Efforts to dislodge this gun failed. Confused fighting was in progress, and Brigadier Hugh-Jones was doubtful if the bridge could be held against a dawn attack. The 4th Battalion 12th Frontier Force Regiment had suffered considerable casualties and was somewhat shaken. So, too, was what remained of the 3rd Battalion Burma Rifles.

If the bridge fell intact into Japanese hands a complete disaster must have resulted. We had few troops available on the west bank on the river and the road to Rangoon would have been open to the enemy. Brigadier Hugh-Jones to whom the responsibility for blowing the bridge was delegated was faced with the making of a most difficult decision. To destroy the bridge meant the abandoning of our force still fighting desperately about Mokpalin; to delay its destruction might well have involved an even greater catastrophe.

Brigadier Hugh-Jones consulted the Divisional Commander by telephone and as a result decided that the right course was to blow the bridge before daylight. Accordingly, the covering troops were withdrawn. At 0330 hours on the morning of February 23rd the bridge was destroyed.

The sound of the tremendous explosions had a remarkable effect. All firing ceased and for a brief period complete silence reigned over the battlefield. Then the Japanese broke into excited shouts and chatter. The feelings of our own troops on the east bank of the river can well be imagined. The alternatives facing them were grim. On the previous day practically all the available craft had been broken up or sunk.

Half an hour after the destruction of the bridge a wireless message, the first since the beginning of the action, was received from Headquarters 17 Division. It was from 'Punch' to 'Jonah', i.e. from Brigadier Cowan B.G.S. 17 Division to Brigadier J.K. Jones. The message in clear referred to, 'Friends waiting to welcome you at the East gate'. Obviously sent off before the blowing of the bridge the message was heartening as it indicated that the force on the west bank of the river was ready to give whatever co-operation was possible.

Not long after dawn Brigadier Ekin accompanied by 2/Lieut. J.B. Goudge and a Gurkha orderly entered Mokpalin from the south. This party had had an adventurous night. The presence of Brigadier Ekin's column at Tawgon had been revealed to the enemy by a Burmese hpongyi and the position it had just vacated was heavily attacked. In the darkness the column became split up and Brigadier Ekin lost touch with it. One party under Major G.W.S. Burton (Brigade Major, 46 Brigade) withdrew to the east. Four days later it crossed the river several miles above the bridge. Another party under Lieut.-Colonel H.B. Owen, commanding the 2nd Battalion Duke of Wellington's Regiment, and consisting mainly of men of his own Battalion swam the river and landed near the village of Kayinnizu. Here the body of Lieut.-Colonel Owen was later found in a hut. He had been murdered, presumably by Burmese.

The bridge having been destroyed it was necessary to consider the situation. Brigadier Jones decided to maintain his positions round Mokpalin during the day of February 23rd. Casualties were to be evacuated by raft, and troops thinned out. Complete withdrawal would be effected before first light on February 24th. All men who could be spared would be employed in building rafts. No men were to cross the river until ordered to do so. The plan was communicated to Unit Commanders at 0930 hours.

A V.C.O. of the Jats volunteered to swim the river carrying details of this plan to Divisional Headquarters. However, a small boat was discovered and the V.C.O. crossed the river in this, safely delivering his message.

Since first light heavy fighting had been in progress. Shortly after 0730 hours the position of the 3rd Gurkha Rifles on the perimeter was attacked with determination. The Japanese were thrown back with severe loss, the Battalion mortars firing with great accuracy. Of this repulse of the enemy the Unit War Diary says: "This was the hardest single blow the Battalion gave the Japanese at the Sittang."

CHAPTER 10

A small single engine Japanese aircraft audaciously flying at a height of only sixty feet or so, carried out a reconnaissance of Mokpalin. Immediately afterwards, at 1000 hours, infantry guns and mortars shelled our main artillery positions near the Railway Station. Horses and mules stampeded; ammunition exploded; some men made their way to the river and began to swim across. No efforts by officers could restrain them. Fighting flared up on the east and south. With the exception of the 4th Battalion Burma Rifles, which broke, all troops in position on the perimeter held their ground. The attempts of the Japanese infantry to advance were repulsed. After three quarters of an hour the attacks died away.

On repeating its reconnaissance flight, the small Japanese aircraft, for the appearance of which our troops were prepared, was shot down. Its fall was greeted by loud cheers.

As many men as could be spared from the defence were set to work building rafts from the bamboos and timbers of huts and buildings, and in collecting petrol tins, water bottles, and other buoyant articles. A matter that caused grave anxiety to all commanders was the evacuation of the wounded which began at once. Many of the slightly wounded swam the river, more serious cases were taken across on rafts. But in spite of every effort of doctors and others it is feared that the vast majority had to be left on the battlefield.

At 1115 hours a formation of about twenty-seven Japanese bombing aircraft made an attack on our positions and on the massed transport along the main road. The bombing caused considerable damage. More gun ammunition and vehicles were set alight, houses and the surrounding jungle began to burn, and there were a number of casualties. Enemy mortar fire increased. Sniping and small arms fire continued against our troops south of the Railway Station.

Brigadier Jones visited units and was satisfied that some troops were now in no condition to hold out much longer. To attempt to maintain our positions until nightfall might lead to disintegration. Under the circumstance's orders for a general withdrawal at 1400 hours were issued. These orders did not reach some posts with which it was impossible to get into touch.

Defensive positions were withdrawn towards the river bank, but fighting still continued from isolated posts south of the Railway Station and east of the main road. The Japanese did not follow up the withdrawal and it is probable that after the severe casualties they had sustained they were in no mood to do so.

The remains of Mokpalin village and other buildings were fired. So, too, were vehicles. These conflagrations and the burning ammunition dumps made a protective barrier for our retiring troops.

Guns were dismantled, the breach mechanisms and sights being thrown into wells or the river. Machine-guns and mortars were similarly treated. Many men cast their rifles into the Sittang.

The scene on the river bank which was protected by a cliff has been described by a senior officer. "Here was chaos and confusion; hundreds of men throwing down their arms, equipment and clothing and taking to the water ..... It is only fair to emphasise the conditions under which these men had been fighting. 17 Division had now been fighting almost day and night for five weeks continuously in most difficult country against a superior and far better trained enemy. They were exhausted after their non-stop efforts since the recent battle of Bilin river, and now they were attacked by two Japanese Divisions, and their only line of withdrawal, the Sittang bridge, had been destroyed ..... As we crossed, the river was a mass of bobbing heads. We were attacked form the air and sniped at from the opposite bank. Although it was a disastrous situation there were many stout hearts and parties shouted to each other egging on others to swim faster with jokes about the boat race! Some took their arms with them on rafts."

Certain units maintained their cohesion to the last until men received the order to enter the water and to make their way across the river. Sections endeavoured to keep together, the men helping one another. Many men in their attempt to swim the river were drowned; others who could not face the ordeal walked back into the jungle and, if not captured, contrived to cross the Sittang further north.

There were magnificent acts of devotion and bravery. Swimmers assisted non-swimmers, and men swam across the river two or three times to bring in the wounded. Each journey entailed the passage of the swift flowing stream well-nigh a mile wide.

Our guns on the west bank of the Sittang rendered what support was possible and succeeded in keeping down enemy machine-gun fire.

'C' Company of the 2nd Battalion Duke of Wellington's Regiment had been attached that morning to the 1st Battalion 3rd Q.A.O. Gurkha Rifles on the north-east of the perimeter. It withdrew towards the bridge to find that the enemy had vacated his positions near it. There was only a gap of about twenty yards in the broken span of the bridge. Major Robinson, Corporal Fox, and Lance-Corporal Roebuck swam the river and returned with ropes to construct a life line. They then remained in the river and encouraged non-swimmers of their own company and at least three hundred Gurkhas and other troops to cross by means of the ropes. Throughout the hours of daylight, the bridge was under fire, but these gallant men continued in their work of assisting others.

Orders to withdraw had not reached our troops on the sector south of the Railway Station. Here were the 8th Battalion Burma Rifles, two companies of the 2nd Battalion King's Own Yorkshire Light Infantry, some men of the 3rd Battalion Gurkha Rifles, and the remnants of the 5th Battalion 17th Dogra Regiment. Japanese mortar and light machine-gun fire was heavy and accurate, whilst the enemy infantry endeavoured to work its way forward. Our troops held on to their positions, and their gallant defence undoubtedly assisted the general evacuation of the force. At 1930 hours when it was evident that a general withdrawal had been affected Lieut.-Colonel Bowers, of the 8th Battalion Burma Rifles and in command of the sector, ordered a retirement to the river. This was not followed up by the Japanese. Of this phase of the action the Commander 16 Brigade said, "The 2nd Battalion King's Own Yorkshire Light Infantry and the 8th Battalion Burma Rifles in particular fought stubbornly to the last and ..... enabled many of their comrades to cross the river successfully."

Lieut.-Colonel H.R. Power, commanding the 5th Battalion 17th Dogra Regiment, decided not to attempt a night crossing of the river and took his Battalion back to the railway line in an endeavour to work north. Numerous Japanese patrols were encountered, and consequently the Battalion withdrew to the river bank where it found a body of some three hundred men of the 3rd Gurkha Rifles and other units. Next morning parties of these men began to swim the river, but the rest were located by a Japanese patrol. Lieut.-Colonel Power then ordered any remaining men who could swim to cross the river and collect boats. Major Terry, second in command of the 5th Battalion 17th Dogra Regiment, and some others swam the river and were returning with boats when Lieut.-Colonel Power and his party were surrounded and captured. This disposed of the last formed body of our troops that remained in Mokpalin.

During the withdrawal of our forward Brigades across the Sittang the west bank of the river was held by the 4th Battalion 18th Frontier Force Regiment and the 1st Battalion 4th P.W.O. Gurkha Rifles.

Men crossing the river generally arrived without arms and often without clothing. As a fighting force 17 Division had ceased for the time being to exist. Nearly all its guns, ammunition, and transport had been lost together with by far the greater part of its mortars, automatic weapons, and rifles. The table in Appendix C shows the state of Battalions of the Division on the evening of February 24th.

It was essential for the Division to reorganise, but it gained only a very brief respite for this. 7 Armoured Brigade had just landed in Rangoon, and to this Brigade had been added two newly arrived Battalions of British infantry. Covered by this Brigade 17 Division withdrew to Pegu on February 24th. Here a partial re-arming and re-equipment was carried out. 46 Infantry Brigade was broken up. Stragglers were collected at Pegu, but many continued to rejoin the Division for some weeks after the battle.

There is no doubt that the Sittang battle was nothing less than a disaster. The stubborn resistance put up by 17 Division had prevented the capture intact of the Sittang railway bridge, and the heavy losses suffered by the enemy temporarily halted his advance. At the same time our own losses were so severe that the holding of the Sittang line was rendered quite impossible and the Japanese advance across the river could not be long delayed.

Two Japanese Divisions had been engaged in the battle. 55th Division followed up our retiring forces along the main road and railway; 33rd Division, moving from Paan along jungle tracks north-east of Thaton, Bilin, and Kyaikto, was no doubt intended to cut off and annihilate these forces east of the Sittang. It had launched the attack on the bridgehead and also ambushed 46 Brigade. Yet the Japanese Command would appear to have overlooked the advantages of an outflanking move across the river by way of the Mokkamaw ferry six miles above the bridge. Such an additional advance may well have destroyed 17 Division.

The enemy had the assistance of local guides. Many of our stragglers reported that they had found the tracks used by Japanese to be carefully marked by paper arrows. This is only one instance of the thorough methods employed by the Japanese in jungle fighting. Against their Divisions specially trained in this particular form of warfare we had been compelled to employ troops inferior in numbers, without any specialised training, and in many cases even with their general training incomplete.

Chapter 11

Operations in the Pegu area between February 26th and March 8th, 1942 – The Japanese attack on Pegu – Establishment of a road block south of Pegu – Decision to withdraw our troops from Pegu – British withdrawal from Pegu and successful attack on the road block.

7 Armoured Brigade landed in Rangoon on February 21st and within twenty-seven hours of the commencement of disembarkation a Squadron of the 2nd Royal Tank Regiment had been sent to Pegu. Having regard to the difficulties under which the work of unloading was being carried out at Rangoon this was a remarkable achievement.

As tanks could not cross the canal bridge at Waw, Lieut.-Colonel Hutton decided to concentrate and organise 17 Division in the Pegu area. The Division now consisted of 16 and 48 Brigades; 46 Brigade having been broken up. To obtain units of reasonable proportions it had been necessary to amalgamate many Battalions, although in the majority of cases this amalgamation proved to be only a temporary measure. Reinforcements that had not taken part in the Sittang battle and returning stragglers made it possible to reconstitute some Battalions.

Apart from 7 Armoured Brigade there were now available the 1st Battalion the Cameronians and the 1st Battalion the West Yorkshire Regiment. Both had recently arrived in Burma, and the latter Battalion had been part of what was known as the Pegu Force. This was formed on February 18th and also comprised F.F.6 and detachments of Burma Military Police. Its duty had been to protect the coastline west of the Sittang. In co-operation with the force an armoured train was maintained on the Pegu-Thongwa branch of the railway.

Further east, covering the coast near the mouth of the Rangoon river, was a similar force. This was made up of a company of the 1st Battalion the Gloucestershire Regiment, F.F.7, and detachments of Burma Military Police.

The 1st Battalion the Cameronians became support Battalion to 7 Armoured Brigade, and with the 2nd Battalion Royal Tank Regiment covered Pegu on the north-east on the line Payagyi-Waw. Further south, with Headquarters at Thanatpin, the 1st Battalion the West Yorkshire Regiment performed similar outpost duties and with the 7th Queen's Own Hussars was responsible for this area south of Pegu. Along the front motor patrols were sent out for considerable distances.

For some days after our withdrawal across the Sittang the main duty devolving upon the forward Battalions was the protection of stragglers and the vast number of Indian refugees streaming north out of the battle zone. Hostile Burmans were active and many were armed with British weapons. They attacked unarmed stragglers, robbed and murdered Indian refugees, spied upon the movements and dispositions of our troops, and indulged in promiscuous sniping. The 1st Battalion the Cameronians dealt with many of these disaffected elements. The civil administration had ceased to function in the district and the almost complete absence of civil liaison officers made it difficult to deal adequately with suspects.

On February 27th it was evident that the Japanese had crossed the Sittang. Their movements indicated a westward infiltration through the thirty-mile gap between 17 Division about Pegu and 2 Burma Brigade of 1 Burma Division holding the area immediately south of Nyaunglebin. 1 Burma Division on relief by the Chinese VI Army had moved out of the Shan States and was now concentrating to cover Karenni and the Sittang Valley sector, south of Toungoo.

In the early hours of February 27th, a patrol of the Cameronians was attacked by Japanese some miles north of Payagyi. The attack was made whilst the patrol was talking to an apparently friendly Burman. The same day Japanese cyclists were observed, but it was not possible to establish contact with them.

On the same day, too, 'A' Squadron of the 2nd Battalion Royal Tank Regiment supported by a company of the Cameronians entered Tazon, twelve miles north of Pyagyi, and cleared it of a force of hostile Burmans. Fourteen were killed and six captured, and it was now established for the first time that the Japanese had raised and armed and organised a Burmese force known as the Burma Independence Army. The tanks then went on to clear of Burmans, the village of Sinchidaing, eight miles south-east of Tazon.

To counter the danger of Japanese infiltration through the Pegu Yomas a Squadron of the 7th Queen's Own Hussars and a company of the 1st Battalion the West Yorkshire Regiment were sent to Tharrawaddy on

CHAPTER 11

the Rangoon-Prome road. In this area the civil authorities anticipated serious unrest, and there were dumps of supplies at that time entirely unguarded. It was also considered advisable to move Headquarters of 17 Division to Hlegu, midway between Rangoon and Pegu. On March 1st 16 Brigade moved into a harbour near Hlegu.

The G.O.C.-in-C. was now of the opinion that with the forces available, the line of withdrawal from Rangoon could not be covered for more than a brief period in event of an enemy attack. The question was, therefore, whether it was desirable to prejudice the blowing of demolitions and the evacuation of essential civil personnel, administrative units, etc., by hanging on sufficiently long to enable 63 Brigade, a young and only partially trained formation, to arrive. The G.O.C. was of the opinion that it was not, and both the Air and Naval opinion was against it especially in view of the risks involved in bringing a convoy into Rangoon at that stage. While, therefore, this recommendation was referred to India, all preparations were proceeded with for blowing the demolition.

Owing to General Wavell being on the way from Java to India, a reply was not received for several days. The civil authorities and the other services were naturally pressing for an early decision and on February 27th, therefore, a telegram was despatched saying that if no instructions to the contrary were received on the following day, it was proposed to carry on with the evacuation and demolitions. Meanwhile, however, a reply was received which indicated that if possible, no action should be taken until General Wavell who was coming straight on to Burma arrived.

General Wavell arrived in Magwe on March 1st and was met by the Governor of Burma, Lieut.-General Hutton, and Air Vice Marshal Stevenson. After discussion, General Wavell issued instructions that Rangoon should be held as long as possible and at least as long as was necessary to enable 63 Brigade and other reinforcements available immediately to be landed. General Wavell considered that even if Rangoon had to be evacuated the largest possible force would be required to establish a line across the lower Irrawaddy valley and to link up with the Chinese who were to take over the defence of the areas to the east.

After the meeting General Wavell accompanied Lieut.-General Hutton on a visit to the front and spent some time at Headquarters of 17 Division. He saw several units in the area.

On February 28th in anticipation of a general withdrawal our troops in Payagyi and Waw had fallen back on Pegu. Next day, upon the decision to maintain our ground, they were pushed forward again. By this time the Japanese had occupied Waw, and on March 2nd a Squadron of tanks patrolling on the west of the canal north of Waw came under shell fire. Two tanks were knocked out. That afternoon an attack by a company of the Cameronians supported by artillery was made on Waw, but the Japanese were in considerable strength and were not dislodged.

On March 3rd there was further fighting near Waw and at Pyinbon where the enemy had put down a road block. As was so often the case this block was erected to protect the flank of a force by-passing our positions. On March 4th another block was established just south of Pyuntaza. Here elements of 2 Burma Brigade were in action. Between these two blocks the Japanese were moving across the Rangoon-Mandalay road into the Pegu Yomas with the object of out-flanking Pegu and taking Rangoon. Through the gap between Pyuntaza and Pyinbon went columns with tanks and guns. They marched by night.

The block at Pyinbon was first encountered by a carrier patrol of the Cameronians. Subsequently, when a Squadron of the 2nd Battalion Royal Tank Regiment reconnoitred Pyinbon, two tanks were damaged by shell fire. The enemy then began to advance south towards Payagale and Payagyi.

From Waw the Japanese also pushed forward south-west along the railway to Kyaikhla, and on the morning of March 3rd were established in a patch of jungle near that village. A company of the Cameronians attacked from the direction of Naungpattaya. It was supported by artillery and a Squadron of the 2nd Battalion Royal Tank Regiment. The only covered approach to the enemy position was by way of a nullah. This was found to be filled with water and commanded by Japanese machine-guns. The Cameronians could make no progress and were extricated with some difficulty.

Next day the Japanese infiltrated round two companies of the Cameronians at Naungpattaya and these were withdrawn to Shanywagyi. At Payagyi the enemy attacked at first light. Although repulsed by the Cameronian company there, the Japanese succeeded in establishing themselves in the town. It was decided to eject them by means of an attack supported by bombing aircraft, artillery, and a Squadron of tanks.

Our bombing aircraft failed to appear and accordingly the attack was cancelled, but a troop of the 7th Queen's Own Hussars went through the town without opposition. Patrols of the Cameronians followed and encountered parties of Japanese who were dealt with in hand to hand fighting. Payagyi was then fired.

CHAPTER 11

On March 5th the enemy held the road from Waw to Payagyi, and it seemed that an out-flanking movement on Pegu from the north-west was in progress. At 0130 hours a patrol of the 1st Battalion the West Yorkshire Regiment which had relieved the 1st Battalion the Cameronians was ambushed south of Payagyi, and it was later found that a road block had been set up in Payagyi itself. A patrol of the 2nd Battalion Royal Tank Regiment moving north of Pegu on the west bank of the Pegu river came under fire from an anti-tank gun. The patrol was forced to turn back. During the morning vehicles on the road between Pegu and Rangoon were fired at from several positions. Later the enemy established a block on this road, but this was cleared with little difficulty by tanks of the Royal Tank Regiment. This was, however, clear indication that the Japanese were now well behind our forces in Pegu.

It was on this day that an enemy tank was encountered for the first time. Coming within range of a troop of the 7th Queen's Own Hussars near Shanywagyi it was at once destroyed. It was a small two-man tank and appeared to be similar to the Italian CV/43 model. Supported by a company of Cameronians the tanks then cleared the enemy from the vicinity of Shanwagyi, and patrolled the area immediately south of Payagyi. In the afternoon the R.A.F. bombed Waw and left it in flames.

On the morning of March 5th, General Hutton proceeded to Headquarters of 17 Division at Hlegu with the intention of visiting the troops holding Pegu, but by that time the road was cut and he was unable to proceed. After consultations with General Cowan, who had just assumed command of the Division, he issued orders to withdraw 48 Brigade to Hlegu and 16 Brigade to Taukkyan across roads. This was necessitated as much by the situation at Pegu as by the fact that an enemy column, believed to include tanks, had already passed through Paunggyi, north of Hlegu, making for the Prome road which might, it appeared, be cut in the near future. The withdrawal of the force in a fit state to continue the defence of the oil fields, and the evacuation of the administrative units, demolition parties, and essential civilians from Rangoon was obviously seriously threatened.

However, while Lieut.-General Hutton was still at Headquarters of 17 Division General Alexander arrived in Rangoon to assume command of the Army in Burma and at once visited Headquarters of 17 Division at Hlegu. Here he met Leiut.-General Hutton who was to remain in Burma as Chief of the General Staff.

As related in the next Chapter, General Alexander decided against a withdrawal and was of the opinion that it might still be possible to effect a junction between 17 Division and 1 Burma Division. This would prevent any further Japanese infiltration through the Pegu Yomas. Consequently, General Alexander ordered 17 Division and 7 Armoured Brigade to carry out offensive operations in the area of Waw and at the same time directed 1 Burma Division to advance south from Nyaunglebin. To support 17 Division there was available 63 Brigade which had just arrived at Rangoon from India. A reconnaissance party consisting of the Brigade Commander (Brigadier Wickham) and Battalion Commanders arrived in Pegu that evening. However, events were now moving too fast to permit of any attempt at further offensive action in this area. Our force in Pegu was already in considerable danger of being cut off.

At about 1600 hours enemy aircraft bombed the road bridges over the railway and river in Pegu. They did no damage to the bridges but started large fires which spread until half the town was ablaze.

The situation in Pegu that night was that an early attack by the enemy was expected. 48 Brigade had taken up defensive positions about the town on the east side of the Pegu river.

The composite Battalion made up off the 1st Battalion 3rd Q.A.O. Gurkha Rifles and the 2nd Battalion 5th Royal Gurkha Rifles, F.F. held the north face of the perimeter eastwards from the railway bridge across the Pegu river. On the east face was the 1st Battalion 4th P.W.O. Gurkha Rifles. The defence was then continued on the south of the town back to the river by the combined 1st and 3rd Battalions of the 7th Gurkha Rifles.

That evening Headquarters 7 Armoured Brigade with the 2nd Battalion Royal Tank Regiment withdrew from Pegu to Hlegu. The 7th Queen's Own Hussars, 414 Battery R.H.A., and attached British infantry were left in support of 48 Brigade. These troops were directly under command of 17 Division. They were disposed in the following manner:

The 7th Queen's Own Hussars with 'D' Troop, 414 Battery R.H.A. and a company of the 1st Battalion the West Yorkshire Regiment leaguered for the night east of the Pegu river and immediately north of the town. 'E' troop of 414 Battery R.H.A. was in harbour astride the main road about one and a half miles south of Pegu.

Headquarters and the remaining two companies (B and D) of the 1st Battalion West Yorkshire Regiment covered the north-western area of Pegu. 'B' Company was posted north of and astride the junction of the main railway line with the Moulmein branch line. These railways afforded the enemy possible ways of approach. 'D' Company was disposed in the area of the gigantic reclining image of Buddha west of the railway.

CHAPTER 11

Two companies of the 1st Battalion the Cameronians were in Shanywagyi. These were ordered to withdraw to Pegu at 0700 hours on March 6th. The other two companies were in Pegu west of the river, one of them covering the road bridge across the river, the other protecting the long and important road bridge across the railway just south of the station.

There was a heavy mist on the morning of March 6th. At first light 'B' Company of the 1st Battalion the West Yorkshire Regiment in its position astride the railway heard troops marching towards it along the main line. Fire was held until the Japanese column was less than one hundred yards away and then our troops opened fire with devastating effect. The enemy, estimated at a strength of one thousand, scattered and reformed on the flanks of 'B' Company which fell back. Advancing, the Japanese occupied the Railway Station and the jungle fringing the western outskirts of the town. Here they came into contact with 'D' Company of the Battalion. This company was completely surrounded but maintained its positions until ordered to fall back south of the railway station at 1600 hours that afternoon.

The enemy penetrated to houses commanding at short range the road bridge over the river. The companies of the Cameronians returning from Shanywagyi with a company of the 7th Gurkha Rifles in Brigade reserve were employed to attack westward astride the road. They succeeded in restoring the situation in this neighbourhood.

Meanwhile the West Yorkshire Regiment had attempted to retake the Railway Station, but before this was done it was found necessary to eject the enemy from the jungle to the north-west. An attack with bayonets was not successful. The enemy was then driven from the jungle by mortar fire.

The main weight of the Japanese attack shifted further west and infiltration began into the area held by the Cameronians south of the station. A counter attack drove the enemy back for some distance, and relieved the situation. But the Japanese were in considerable force and hostile activity continued. Corporal Sayle of the Cameronians distinguished himself by stalking two machine-gun positions, destroying the crews, and returning with their flag. For a time, Headquarters of the Cameronians and of the West Yorkshire Regiment were each threatened by parties of the enemy and came under fire. In each case, however, energetic action resulted in the destruction or retreat of the Japanese who had worked forward.

In the early morning 'B' Troop, 414 Battery R.H.A. in its harbour south of Pegu was shelled by mortars. A number of casualties were sustained before the troop was withdrawn into Pegu town. From positions here at ranges of sixteen hundred to eighteen hundred yards it very effectively fired upon bodies of the enemy throughout the day.

The main road to Rangoon was again cut by the enemy who established a block in Kyaikpun village. Here, around the village and bordering the road on each side, was jungle. 63 Brigade had been ordered to Pegu to reinforce our troops there, but at about 0930 hours it was halted south of the road block and took up positions near the road junction at Intagaw. Tanks of the 2nd Battalion Royal Tank Regiment forced their way through the block and went on to Pegu to bring out Brigadier Wickham and unit Commanders of 63 Brigade. The tanks then returned escorting two carriers in which were Brigadier Wickham and his reconnaissance party. The tanks got through the block with some difficulty, but Japanese posted in trees overlooking the road sniped and bombed the carriers and killed and wounded everyone in them. One carrier driven by Lieut. Hawkins of the first Battalion 4th P.W.O. Gurkha Rifles who was himself wounded succeeded in returning to Pegu. A section of the carriers of the 1st Battalion the Cameronians was also ambushed at the road block and further casualties were sustained.

At about 1200 hours an attack was launched from the main road northwards to clear the Railway Station. It was carried out by three companies. On the right a company of the 7th Gurkha Rifles moved up the west bank of the river, in the centre was a company of the Cameronians, and on the left a company of the West Yorkshire Regiment. The attack was supported by mortars and 'E' Troop, 414 Battery, R.H.A.

The Station and its northern outskirts were won, but a further advance was held up. As parties of the enemy streamed out of the town, they afforded excellent targets for the mortars and machine-guns of the 2nd Battalion 5th Royal Gurkha Rifles, F.F. The guns of 414 Battery also did good execution amongst the retiring Japanese.

It was decided to consolidate the positions gained. A company of the 1st Battalion 4th P.W.O. Gurkha Rifles relieved the company of the 7th Gurkha Rifles which had been fighting all day and was exhausted. The positions of the composite 2nd Battalion 5th Royal Gurkha Rifles, F.F. east of the river were adjusted to link up with the new positions on the west bank.

West of the company of the 4th Gurkha Rifles, the West Yorkshire Regiment continued the line facing north and west. On its left the Cameronians faced west and then continued the line south to the river, thus completing the perimeter.

That afternoon hostile aircraft bombed Headquarters 48 Brigade. A direct hit was scored on the Mess building. One of the officers of 63

CHAPTER 11

Brigade reconnaissance party was killed, and the Commander 23 Field Ambulance (Lieut.-Colonel O'Neill, I.M.S.) who had been visiting his detachment at the Advanced Dressing Station was severely wounded. So, too, was the Brigade Orderly Officer.

Heavy hand to hand fighting continued all day in the western portions of Pegu and on its outskirts. All ranks displayed great gallantry, and the positions taken up by us after the recapture of the Railway Station, were maintained.

North of Pegu the force under command of the 7th Queen's Own Hussars was involved in a separate action. At first light the tanks had advanced towards Payagyi but soon came under shell fire from anti-tank guns. Two tanks were hit. The enemy guns appear to have been man-handled into forward positions as neither mules nor motor transport were visible. As the early morning mist cleared the guns of 'D' Troop 414 Battery, R.H.A. speedily engaged the enemy, and the company of the West Yorkshire Regiment held the position whilst the tanks withdrew. Under cover of an artillery concentration this company then attacked with the bayonet. A large number of Japanese were killed and four guns were captured. With co-operation from the tanks the infantry went on to clear the enemy from a patch of jungle. It was established that sixty casualties were inflicted on the Japanese without loss to our own infantry.

Later in the day three enemy tanks were sighted. These were attacked by the 7th Queen's Own Hussars and were destroyed by 37 mm gun fire at a range of twelve hundred yards. The Japanese tanks appeared to be similar in appearance to our own, but their armour must have been thin and of poor quality.

At 1540 hours the 7th Queen's Own Hussars were ordered to concentrate in the northern part of Pegu to rejoin 7 Armoured Brigade at Hlegu.

At 2000 hours Brigadier Hugh-Jones also received orders to withdraw his Brigade from Pegu. At first it was intended to carry out the evacuation of the town that night, and the 7th Queen's Own Hussars moved out at about 2030 hours.

Immediately south of the town the road was impassable owing to an enormous forest fire, but the tanks found a diversion and regained the road about a mile north of the road block. This was covered by a gun and machine-guns, and the tanks were unable to force it. The 7th Queen's Own Hussars and attached troops subsequently leaguered in open paddy fields on the east of the road. Here 'D' Troop of 414 Battery, R.H.A. was rejoined by 'E' Troop of the Battery.

There were wounded and motor transport to be got out of Pegu, and Brigadier Hugh-Jones decided that the block must be attacked in daylight as soon as the ground mist had cleared. The plan of withdrawal was to have all troops and transport west of the Pegu river before first light. The road bridges over the river and railway were to be blown after the last vehicle had left the town. The 7th Gurkha Rifles were to move out first followed by the transport which would be protected by all carriers of the Brigade supplemented at a few points by picquets of the 7th Gurkha Rifles. These picquets were to be relieved by troops of the main body as they came up. The rest of 48 Brigade was to follow in the order 1st Battalion 4th P.W.O. Gurkha Rifles (less one company), Brigade Headquarters, detachment 23 Field Ambulance, composite 2nd Battalion 5th Royal Gurkha Rifles, F.F. On arrival at the harbour of the 7th Queen's Own Hussars the column was to halt and motor transport was to close up. It was the intention to force the block in conjunction with the 7th Queen's Own Hussars and supported by the fire of 414 Battery, R.H.A. The rearguard under Lieut.-Colonel Marindin (West Yorkshire Regiment) was to be formed by the 1st Battalion the West Yorkshire Regiment with one company of the 1st Battalion 4th P.W.O. Gurkha Rifles, and the 1st Battalion the Cameronians. The rearguard was to hold positions facing east on the western outskirts of Pegu until the road block had been broken.

The initial phase of the withdrawal was carried out according to plan and without interference by the enemy. The early morning ground mist rendered observation difficult. Forward defence lines were evacuated by 0445 hours and all transport crossed the river safely. The road bridges over the river and railway were blown at first light. Immediately afterwards the companies of the West Yorkshire Regiment and of the 4th P.W.O. Gurkha Rifles holding rearguard positions in the area of the railway station came under fire. At about the same time the Japanese opened mortar and machine-gun fire upon the whole length of our column. The fire came mainly from the west of the road from gardens and plantations fringing it. At one point the enemy mounted a light machine-gun on the top of an ambulance containing wounded officers and fired right down the column of transport.

Snipers at close range, from trees and a house top, were particularly active and caused several casualties, mostly amongst officers. Captain Woodhouse, 8th Punjab Regiment, Staff Captain of the Brigade but officiating as Brigade Major, was killed instantaneously. Lieut.-Colonel R.T. Cameron, commanding the composite 2nd Battalion 5th Royal Gurkha Rifles, F.F. was wounded but remained in command of

CHAPTER 11

his Battalion. The Brigade Ordnance Warrant Officer (W.O. Walters, I.A.O.C.) was wounded through the arm, but subsequently drove an ammunition wagon to Divisional Headquarters at Taukkyan where he was again wounded and had to be evacuated. About the same time Lieut. Flack, 4th P.W.O. Gurkha Rifles and attached to Brigade Headquarters, and Captain Grieve, 5th Royal Gurkha Rifles, F.F. were also wounded. Captain Grieve remained on duty.

Later another Japanese attack developed from the north-east. In places along the column there was hand to hand fighting. The 2nd Battalion 5th Royal Gurkha Rifles attacking from the south attempted to dislodge the enemy but could not do so.

The 1st Battalion 4th P.W.O. Gurkha Rifles was then ordered to attack from the east of the road. Gallantly led by Lieut.-Colonel Lentaigne the Battalion charged the enemy and wiped out at least one company. The Japanese put up little or no resistance and in close range fighting were no match for the Gurkhas who sustained small loss. Approximately eighty Japanese corpses were counted on the ground. One 37 mm gun and four light machine-guns were captured.

The attack on our column by the enemy delayed our own attack on the road block. Mortar and small arms fire had knocked out and set some of our motor transport alight. For the purpose of protection this transport had been double banked on the road. It now became difficult to extricate vehicles.

At 0810 hours an intensive barrage was put down by our guns on the road block and the enemy in position near it. The Japanese were present in considerable numbers with mortars, anti-tank guns, and light machine-guns. The bombardment was very successful, and after some delay caused by the congestion of transport on the road the tanks of the 7th Queen's Own Hussars stormed the road block and forced a way through. In this operation they were stoutly supported by 'A' Company of the 1st Battalion the West Yorkshire Regiment. This infantry company engaged the enemy with its grenades. It suffered heavily from Japanese snipers concealed in trees. 2/Lt. A.R. Davis was killed and the Company Commander Captain Francis and most of the N.C.Os. were wounded. One tank was lost. The crew were unhurt, and casualties to personnel of tanks were very light. The guns and the tanks, together with the transport of the 7th Queen's Own Hussars and the supporting company of infantry, passed through the block. A small portion of 48 Brigade transport followed, but owing to the road being packed with damaged and abandoned vehicles the rest of the transport could not get through immediately. This gave the Japanese the opportunity to reoccupy the road block. The advance guard of the composite Battalion of the 7th Gurkha Rifles was held up. During this period Lieut.-Colonel B.G. White, commanding the Battalion, was killed by a sniper concealed in a tree. This sniper must have been in position for a considerable time in close proximity to our troops.

There was now no artillery available for support and an encircling movement against the block was initiated. The 1st Battalion 4th P.W.O. Gurkha Rifles with one company of the 7th Gurkha Rifles attacked it from the west of the road, whilst the 2nd Battalion 5th Royal Gurkha Rifles, F.F. advanced against the block from the east flank.

This movement was partially successful, the troops on the east missing their objective and passing beyond it. Subsequently they made their way to Hlegu where they rejoined the remainder of 17 Division. On the right, or west, of the road part of the attacking force also lost direction in the jungle and went beyond the block. However, one company of the 4th P.W.O. Gurkha Rifles together with the company of the 7th Gurkha Rifles cleared the enemy from the immediate vicinity of the block, capturing five machine-guns and killing their crews. One of these crews was in position in a culvert under the road.

A further attack by one company of the West Yorkshire Regiment and another of the Cameronians, brought up from the rearguard, then succeeded in overcoming the remaining opposition. On the site of the block a 75 mm gun was captured. Within fifteen yards of the gun were a wrecked tank, an overturned carrier, and several other vehicles that had been destroyed by it. An officer who was present says that the road for four or five miles beyond the block was a "an appalling shambles of dead men, and derelict vehicles of all kinds."

It was now 1530 hours and the Brigade Commander decided that he must send the transport along the road and take the risk of its encountering further Japanese opposition beyond the block. Captain J. Mahoney of the Cameronians had previously twice gone through the block in a carrier and on the second occasion reported that there was no longer any real opposition along the road. Accordingly, the transport column moved off escorted by carriers. The journey to Hlegu was completed safely.

Prior to the final attack on the block by the companies of the West Yorkshire Regiment and the Cameronians the rearguard had been involved in heavy fighting. The companies of the West Yorkshire Regiment and the 4th P.W.O. Gurkha Rifles holding the Railway Station area were surrounded by the enemy but eventually broke through to the south along the railway. Here, too, where companies of the Cameronians and West Yorkshire Regiment were in position, there had

CHAPTER 11

been considerable enemy pressure. The Japanese entered Pegu from the east and west, and then attempted to advance south. This movement had been broken up by machine-gun fire.

After the transport column had gone down the road towards Hlegu 48 Brigade prepared to move in hollow square formation across the open paddy fields towards the railway line. Some machine-gun fire was maintained by the enemy from the direction of Pegu, and a Japanese pack battery appeared about seven hundred yards to the east and came into action with one gun. This was silenced by mortar and machine-gun fire.

The enemy did not follow up the withdrawal. Moving along the line of the railway the Brigade halted just north of Tawa at about 2100 hours, the Brigade marched again at 2200 hours, and at 0430 hours reached Intagaw where a three hours halt was made. The men were much exhausted and the Brigade Commander was anxious that at Hlegu food should be ready and transport available to lift the most footsore. There was, however, no means of communicating with Divisional Headquarters.

Lieut. Darby, the Cameronians, although there was every reason the believe that large numbers of the enemy were between Intagaw and Hlegu, at once volunteered to go forward with a message. He arrived at Hlegu without incident. As a result, a cooked meal and transport awaited 48 Brigade when it entered Hlegu at 1300 hours on March 8th.

Meanwhile, as stated in the next Chapter, Rangoon had been evacuated and the whole British force was withdrawing north. This withdrawal, begun on the previous day, was temporarily delayed by a road block put down by the Japanese across the Prome road just north of Taukkyan. When 48 Brigade arrived in Hlegu the road had been cleared and the Brigade, less transport required for rearguard duties, was moved in motor transport to Taikkyi.

Chapter 12

Situation in Rangoon during January and February 1942 – Labour shortage – Evacuation of non-essential population – Outbreak of lawlessness and looting – Decision of General Alexander to withdraw from Rangoon – Demolitions – The final withdrawal from the city – The Japanese establish a road block north of Taukkyan on the Prome road – Operations in the Taukkyan area on March 7th and 8th.

The normal life of Rangoon ceased after the Japanese air raid on December 23rd 1941. The second raid, on Christmas Day, served to hasten the flight of Indian labourers and others who still wavered. The exodus from the city was not general at first but, as previously stated, was very marked amongst the classes whose work was essential for the continued working of the port.

During January 1942 when the A.V.G. and R.A.F. so effectively protected the city against further attack there was some return of labour, but the Japanese capture of Tavoy and the advance through Kawkareik persuaded large numbers of people that they would be safer in India or Upper Burma. By the middle of February, a very large proportion of the population of Rangoon had left the city.

It was vital to keep the port open and working. Reinforcements and military stores were coming in, and there was also a vast accumulation of Lease/Lend material awaiting transport to China. The flight of labour seriously interfered with the handling of much of this material, and the working of transportation services for military purposes was most precarious throughout the period prior to the fall of Rangoon. Military units for essential work of this kind were only available on a very limited scale.

It was necessary, too, to maintain in action as long as possible the Syriam and other oil refineries near Rangoon, although the removal of certain plant from the refineries to the Yenangyaung oil fields had

CHAPTER 12

ensured the continued output of a very considerable quantity of petrol in the event of the loss of Rangoon.

The necessity of maintaining the functions of the port affected the arrangements for the evacuation of the city. This was planned to be carried out in three stages, during the first of which all non-essential persons would be encouraged to depart leaving only those required to run essential services. In the second stage all civilians not required for essential services would be evacuated; whilst the last stage contemplated the carrying out of demolitions and the final withdrawal of remaining military and civilian personnel under special transport arrangements.

Voluntary evacuation began after the bombing of Rangoon, and many essential workers then left the city. There was no effective method of preventing this. At the same time large numbers of other persons left by road, rail and ship, and military transports returning to India were also utilized for evacuation purposes. In the light of subsequent events this undoubtedly saved many people from the perils and hardships of the overland routes. Many thousands of Indians set out on foot for Prome, and thence across the waterless Arakan Yomas to Taungup intending to proceed to Chittagong by country craft. Others went to Upper Burma, preferring to follow the Chindwin routes to Assam. On the Taungup route lack of food, water and medical attention soon caused suffering and many deaths, mostly from cholera and exhaustion. Cholera also appeared south of Prome, and a serious epidemic was anticipated.

Indians who fled not only from Rangoon but from other towns were not content to seek safety in rural areas. With their fellow countrymen who had settled on the land in Burma they believed that their only safety lay in returning to India. They feared that upon a general British withdrawal they would receive harsh treatment form the Burmese. It was this fear that set scores of thousands of Indians on the long trail to India. Subsequent events were to prove that these misgivings were often not ill-founded. In many parts of the country attacks were made on these unfortunate people. Many were maltreated and deprived of their few valuables. Murder and mutilation were not uncommon. There were, however, frequent instances of kindness and assistance by Burmans to Indian refugees.

The first stage of the evacuation of civilians was marked by the order to remove within 72 hours all motor transport not marked with an E Label. This was put into effect on February 20th after the withdrawal of 17th Division behind the line of the Sittang. The decision was reached after consultation between the Governor, His Excellency Sir Reginald Dorman-Smith and the combined Commanders. The withdrawal to the Sittang endangered both the road to Mandalay and the railway to that city. The railway had already almost ceased to function owing to defections amongst the subordinate staff. There was cholera and danger of civil unrest on the road to Prome. It was decided at the same time to close down the Syriam and other oil refineries to ensure timely removal of all skilled personnel beyond the risk of capture, and to enable comprehensive preparations for demolitions of all oil installations to be completed.

At this time the Rangoon Garrison carried out a multiplicity of duties over a very widespread area. These duties included internal security, aerodrome and anti-aircraft defence, manning of the Examination Battery at Dry Tree Point, protection of Syriam and other refineries, and the guarding of the approaches from the coast. Brigadier B.B. Leslie, M.C., was in command of Rangoon Fortress and the garrison now comprised:

1 Heavy Anti-Aircraft regiment, B.A.F. (with one Light Anti-Aircraft Battery).
Rangoon Field Brigade, R.A., B.A.F.
Detachment Royal Engineers.
Detachment Burma Sappers and Miners.
Detachment Royal Marines (Force 'Viper').
1st Battalion the Gloucestershire Regiment.
12th Battalion Burma Rifles.
One Company 1st Royal Battalion 9th Jat Regiment.
Headquarters, 2 Garrison Battalion.
4 Garrison Company.
23 Garrison Company.
One Company Kokine Battalion, Burma Frontier Force.
F.F.4.
Burma Military Police.

The Royal Marine Detachment had recently arrived from Ceylon. It acquired a small fleet of launches and was employed on river patrol work. Later in the campaign it was destined to carry out similar duties on the Irrawaddy. Commanded by Major Johnston, R.M., the detachment consisted of five officers and one hundred and two other ranks. All had volunteered for special service.

Within a day or two Rangoon became almost a deserted city although essential services were maintained and the port remained open. Convoys of military transports still came in. With the approach of the enemy to the Sittang the Observer Corps warning system

CHAPTER 12

became curtailed to such an extent that the greater part of the R.A.F. was withdrawn to Magwe and Akyab, leaving only a fighter force at the newly prepared strip 'Highland Queen' north of Rangoon. This withdrawal based no doubt on sound operational grounds, was naturally disheartening to the troops and resulted in some unfair criticism of the R.A.F. But at this time our air force had so enforced its supremacy over the Rangoon area that the Japanese made no attempts to attack the city or port from the air, and their aircraft did not interfere at all with the arrival of convoys or final demolitions before we left.

On February 21st Rear Headquarters of the Army left for Maymyo. Thereafter only an Advanced Headquarters, reduced to a minimum in numbers, remained in Rangoon.

Even before the general evacuation there had been a certain amount of looting and after February 20th both looting and arson were rife for a period. The general evacuation left unprotected property in every part of the city. This attracted such of the local population as remained and the Burmans from surrounding villages. The position was aggravated by the action of the civil authorities in opening the doors of the jails and the lunatic asylum and releasing the inmates. This was due mainly to the defection of the staffs, and the inmates made use of their freedom in a manner to be expected. On the waterfront warehouses were being rifled by soldiers, sailors, and coolies.

The majority of the Rangoon Police had been evacuated; so, too, had the greater part of the Burma Military Police and the Fire Brigade. To cope with the general lawlessness five hundred of the Military Police and part of the Fire Brigade were brought back to the city and Major Walton, of the Gloucestershire Regiment, was appointed Military Commandant. A system of patrols by troops and Burma Military Police was instituted. The 12th Battalion Burma Rifles first employed on this duty proved extremely weak in dealing with looters, many of whom were fellow Burmans. In some instances, too, men of the Burma Rifles were themselves looters. Later, detachments of the 1st Battalion the Gloucestershire Regiment restored order. In many cases looters were shot. Others, both soldiers and civilians, were punished by caning and being set to work at the docks where labour was scarce. Disorder was thus put down in the centre of the city but continued in the suburbs where many houses evacuated by Europeans were ransacked. Burmese women took part in the looting.

Motor launch patrols of the B.R.N.V.R. had been operating about the mouth of the Rangoon river eastward to the south of Amherst. Ships of the R.I.N. (*Hindustan*, *Ratnagiri* and *Indus*) were patrolling further out to sea.

On the afternoon of March 4th R.A.F. reconnaissance aircraft reported eight river type of craft moving west from the mouth of the Salween, and our sea patrols were on watch for these vessels. One of these, a power-driven sampan, was intercepted early next day by M.L.s 1100 and 1103 and H.M.I.S. *Hindustan* off the mouth of the Rangoon river. The sampan contained fifty-five men of the Burma Independence Army and a Japanese officer. Much to the disappointment of our crews and of the Japanese officer, the Burmese promptly hoisted the white flag and hurriedly surrendered.

Seven other power-driven sampans were later sighted but could not be intercepted and were able to land their occupants who now formed a force that threatened Syriam. The captured Burmese were taken into Rangoon and on interrogation stated that they were the first flight of a seaborne expedition. It is believed on the evacuation of Rangoon these men were released but under what circumstances is not very clear. At this stage it would have been difficult to transfer them to Upper Burma. There was not time to put them on trial as traitors.

As already related General Alexander arrived in Rangoon on March 5th. On his way to Burma he had met General Wavell in Calcutta. The Commander-in-Chief, having just returned from a visit to Rangoon and the Sittang Front, gave General Alexander a resume of the position in Burma and a directive to the following effect:

"The retention of Rangoon was a matter of vital importance to our position in the Far East, and every effort must be made to hold it. If, however, that was not possible the British force must not be allowed to be cut off but must be withdrawn from the Rangoon area for the defence of Upper Burma. This must be held as long as possible in order to safeguard the oil fields at Yenangyaung, keep contact with the Chinese, and protect the construction of the road from Assam to Burma."

Arriving in Rangoon at midday on March 5th General Alexander was at once faced with the very grave question whether in view of his instructions he should endeavour to hold on to Rangoon any longer and thereby run the risk of allowing his force to be cut off and of leaving the whole of Northern Burma and the oil fields open to the enemy. Rangoon, it should be noted, was quite indefensible and any force that was cut off there was not likely to survive more than a few days. The remnants of 17 Division with 7 Armoured Brigade were engaged in the Pegu-Waw area. 63 Brigade was in process of disembarking and assembling at Hlawga sixteen miles north of Rangoon. Its transport was still on-board ship. There was a gap of some thirty miles between the left flank

CHAPTER 12

of 17 Division and the foremost elements of 1 Burma Division south of Nyaunglebin. It was known that Japanese columns had infiltrated through this gap into the Pegu Yomas.

Not satisfied that Rangoon could not be held General Alexander went at once to Headquarters of 17 Division at Hlegu where he met Lieut.-General Hutton and Major-General Cowan. The latter had a few days previously taken over command of 17 Division. After studying the situation General Alexander, as already detailed, ordered 17 Division to carry out offensive operations at Waw. But this did not prove to be possible; since the Japanese were already closing in on Pegu from the west and a wider encircling movement threatened to isolate our force there.

Meanwhile the general situation elsewhere had also deteriorated. There was further confirmation from the R.A.F. of reports by Burma Frontier Force patrols that a force of two thousand Japanese had passed through Paunggyi, in the Pegu Yomas, about thirty miles north of Ilegu and was moving south-west. Light tanks had been observed. On March 6th there were reports that the Japanese were only a few miles from the road and railway at Prome.

Bassein had been evacuated by the civil authorities who had destroyed the stocks of coal there. The only troops in the area consisted of a Garrison Company which had been detailed to protect the aerodrome. It was now therefore practically open to the enemy, and as communications were cut it was impossible to obtain any information about the situation. Control generally of the Delta districts had ceased. Disorder there was rampant. Indians had been murdered and boats owned by them sunk. Rich Burmans were being plundered by their fellow countrymen.

In view of the situation General Alexander late on March 6th decided that the retention of Rangoon was quite impossible and that the right course was to carry out demolitions, evacuate the city, and regroup his forces northwards in the Irrawaddy valley. The order to put the Denial Scheme into operation was issued at 2359 hours that night. All demolitions were to be begun simultaneously next day at 1400 hours.

The following morning, March 7th, General Alexander with Advanced Army Headquarters, administrative units, and all troops of the Garrison not required to cover demolitions moved out in motor transport along the Prome road. Advanced Army Headquarters was to proceed to Maymyo and there rejoin Rear Headquarters. Near Taukkyan, twenty-one miles north of the city, this force was compelled to halt. Ahead of it the enemy had established a road block. News of this situation was received by the demolition parties in Rangoon but this in no way interfered with their plans.

The demolition scheme had been drawn up long beforehand and rehearsals carried out. The important oil refinery and storage tank demolitions were under the general supervision of Mr. W.L. Forster (Production Manager, Shell Mex Ltd.) who had been specially sent to Burma for the purpose. A detachment of Sappers and other Military personnel commanded by Captain W.J. Scott, R.E., carried out the work at Syriam, Thilawa, Seikkyi and Rangoon. Acting employees of the companies concerned also took part.

Large number of vehicles and other supplies imported for China under Lease/Lend arrangements had already been destroyed by orders of a senior U.S. Army officer without reference to Army Headquarters. The loss of the vehicles was seriously felt later in the campaign.

Demolitions were carried out at the Rangoon Power Station, the Telegraph Office, Wireless Stations and Telephone Exchanges. The Telegraph and Telephone buildings were burnt. So, too, was the Mogul Guard, the Headquarters of the Rangoon Police.

From the Railway Workshops at Insein much machinery had been moved upcountry. The remainder was now destroyed. Locomotives were immobilised and the important railway bridge over the Pazundaung Creek was not very successfully blown. It was soon to be repaired by the enemy.

Next in importance after the oil demolitions was the attempted denial of the port to the enemy, but any measures taken could only be partially effective. Jetties and warehouses, many of them privately owned, extended over several miles of waterfront. No more could be done than to diminish seriously the capacity of the port.

The shipping berths with their storage sheds and other facilities which would have been of the greatest use to the enemy were completely destroyed by explosive charges and fire. Opposite three of the remining most useful berths, vessels were sunk. All wharf equipment including cranes was smashed or otherwise destroyed. Warehouses and all godowns containing stocks in the Port Commissioners custody were burnt. Many of the channel and mooring buoys were sunk by rifle fire. Dockyards, both Government and some privately owned, were immobilised; but demolitions were not very effective in all cases. Few large power-driven craft were left in the port, those that could not be removed being scuttled.

These steps could not serve to close the port. Many warehouses, wharves, and jetties remained. There were still available thousands of river craft ranging from paddy gigs, barges, and small launches to sampans. Numerous undamaged workshops were to be found in rice and timber mills and elsewhere. In the absence of the destroyed shore installations the most serious limitation was that of maximum lift dictated by the capacity of a ship's gear. Heavy motor transport, tanks, locomotives, and rolling stock could only be unloaded by ships specially fitted for the work. But the port still sufficed for the maintenance of several divisions, a force larger than the Japanese were likely to require un Burma.

In spite of the large quantities of valuable goods despatched to India by sea during January and February and the strenuous efforts to evacuate all military stores and lease-lend material for China to places in Northern Burma we were compelled to abandon in Rangoon very large stocks of various kinds including timber, coal, steel rails and bridging material.

All demolitions having been successfully carried out Garrison Headquarters with troops and civilian personnel concerned made their way to jetties and the railway where river steamers and trains were in readiness. Further down-stream a sea going convoy was waiting to sail for Calcutta with the parties evacuated by river.

The deserted city and oil refineries and shattered storage tanks along the river presented an awe-inspiring spectacle as huge columns of flame leapt skyward beneath a vast canopy of smoke. The last train drew out of Rangoon at 1930 hours, and the river steamers moved off from the jetties. Before dawn the first enemy patrols entered the empty streets.

On the evening of March 6th an advance guard for the move of the Rangoon Garrison had been formed at Taukkyan, north of Rangoon. This force under Lieut.-Colonel R.M.H. Tynte (The Cameronians) was made up as follows:

1 Field Battery, 1 Indian Field Regiment, I.A.
One Squadron 7th Queen's Own Hussars (already at Tharrawaddy).
One Company 2nd Battalion King's Own Yorkshire Light Infantry.

It was divided into an advance party which was to proceed to Prome at first light on March 7th, and a rear party consisting of tanks to move just ahead of the Rangoon Garrison. A detachment of the advance party was to be posted at Wanetchaung railway station and to rejoin the main body subsequently.

The advance party carried out its movements without incident and reached Tharrawaddy. The Rangoon Garrison, less troops covering demolitions in Rangoon, and led by Advanced Headquarters passed through Taukkyan at about 1100 hours. About a mile beyond that village it halted with the rear party of the advance guard at the fork made by the main road with the road running south-west to Hlawga railway station. Here information had been received that the Japanese were on the Prome road some five miles further north. At that point a carrier patrol had been destroyed by fire from an anti-tank gun placed behind the block.

Meanwhile this information had also been given to Headquarters 17 Division which at once ordered 7 Armoured Brigade to deal with the situation. A squadron of the 2nd Battalion Royal Tank Regiment was detailed for this duty, but the 7th Queen's Own Hussars arrived first. They were already on their way from Hlegu to Taukkyan where they were to leaguer. Two tanks of 'B' Squadron at once went up the road to the block. One of these tanks received a direct hit from a shell which did not penetrate but put its guns out of action.

The situation now appeared to be that the enemy had cut the road and was advancing round the west flank with the object of destroying our force near Taukkyan. The Japanese strength was judged to be one Battalion group with an additional force moving up. The area was accordingly put into a state of all-round defence with such troops as were then available. There were few combatant troops present and at this stage the defence could not have withstood any serious assault; but 63 Brigade near Hlegu had now been ordered to Taukkyan by 17 Division.

At 1500 hours an attack was launched against the road block. The available force then was:

7th Queen's Own Hussars – less one Squadron and two troops.
One Troop – 2nd Battalion Royal Tank Regiment.
One Company – 1st Battalion the Gloucestershire Regiment.
One Battery – 1st Indian Field Regiment, I.A.
One Section – 12 Mountain Battery.

The block was sited, as usual, on a stretch of road bordered on each side by close jungle. This was infested with snipers many of whom were posted in trees. These snipers were very active and conveyed the probably false impression that the position was held by large numbers of Japanese. The block was shelled, then attacked through the jungle by two platoons of the Gloucestershire Regiment supported by two carriers. These latter were knocked out by mortar and anti-tank gun fire, and the infantry advance was held up by snipers and machine-guns. Working its way forward, and dislodging the enemy with grenades, a patrol came within sixty yards of the anti-tank gun covering the block.

CHAPTER 12

A Japanese counter-attack then drove it back. By 1600 hours the attack had failed.

Two companies of the 2nd Battalion 13th Frontier Force Rifles (63 Brigade) had been stationed some distance back in Taukkyan village and were now brought forward to attack. They were shortly joined by the remainder of the Battalion from Hlegu. The two Taukkyan companies advanced against the block, and subsequently the whole Battalion was thrown into another attack. Both of these were unsuccessful, the Battalion sustaining substantial casualties. These amounted to twenty killed (including two British Officers) and about fifty wounded (including three British Officers).

It was now about 1730 hours and growing dark owing to the enormous pall of smoke above Rangoon and the burning oil refineries along the river. Further offensive action had to be postponed until the morning.

Advanced Army Headquarters, the Rangoon Garrison, and all other troops in the vicinity leaguered in a rubber plantation just beyond Milestone 22 at the road fork already mentioned. The perimeter was as far as possible guarded by tanks and infantry, and within it were crowded troops including every type of administrative unit and office staffs. In addition, there were a few civil officials and clerks and also one or two women who had disregarded the order to evacuate and had elected to remain with their men folk. Close by and on the road were many hundreds of vehicles. Throughout the night the area of the road block was kept under observation by infantry and a Squadron of the 2nd Battalion Royal Tank Regiment. There was considerable patrol activity, particularly on the west flank. Here an enemy machine-gun section was ambushed and annihilated by a patrol of the Gloucestershire Regiment.

After nightfall General Alexander issued orders for an attack at first light. Artillery fire was to be concentrated on the road block are which would then be charged by the tanks. They were to carry it at any cost. 63 Brigade was to attack astride the road and round the enemy's flanks.

It has been mentioned that the advance party of the Rangoon Garrison advance guard had proceeded to Tharrawaddy without incident. Here Lieut.-Colonel Tynte heard that the road behind him was cut. He then went back towards the block to make a reconnaissance and in carrying out this duty was mortally wounded.

Meanwhile the detachment at Wanetchaung remained in position. That night it withdrew north after encounters with hostile elements. Later that night there arrived at Wanetchaung the last train to leave Rangoon. This train was wrecked by enemy action at a bridge near

Wanetchaung station. The troops, Military Police, and civil personnel on the train were attacked by Japanese and hostile Burmans. They drove off the enemy, killing twenty of them, and during the morning of March 8th joined the main body of our troops.

Early on March 8th the situation of our force just north of Taukkyan was judged to be serious. The enemy appeared to be in a strong position astride the road. The troops of 17 Division, now withdrawing towards Taukkyan, were already tired by the recent heavy fighting near Pegu. The Division was also still very short of men, arms, and transport.

The attack opened at first light with an artillery concentration on the road block area. The 1st Battalion 10th Gurkha Rifles was to advance on the west of the road, the 1st Battalion 11th Sikh Regiment on the east, whilst the 2nd Battalion 13th Frontier Force Rifles moves as a reserve behind the tanks of the 7th Queen's Own Hussars.

The 1st Battalion 10th Gurkha Rifles had carried out a night march to the railway line which was its starting point for the attack. During the march it passed within two hundred yards of a line of bullock carts and animals proceeding along a jungle track in the opposite direction. This must have been part of an enemy force moving south towards Rangoon.

The Battalion advanced at first light through dense jungle towards the main road. A thick mist also hampered the keeping of direction, and the Battalion never reached its objective. It became very dispersed in the jungle. A great part of it did not rejoin the main body of our force for several days. Many of the men who did rejoin had been deprived of their arms by Burmans.

Whilst still at its assembly point in open country on the east of the road the 1st Battalion 11th Sikh Regiment was subjected to a severe bombing and machine-gun attack by low flying enemy aircraft. This caused considerable disorganisation amongst the many young soldiers of the Battalion who were experiencing for the first time the attentions of hostile aircraft. Incidentally this aerial attack was due to the action of the Battalion itself. It had reached its assembly point unobserved, but then disclosed its position by opening heavy fire on a couple of unsuspecting mounted Japanese who rode across its front at close range. Later a portion of the Battalion advanced unopposed on the road block.

Shortly before the 7th Queen's Own Hussars began their advance Major Bonham-Carter, commanding the squadron of the 2nd Battalion Royal Tank Regiment posted in the area of the block, had gone forward on foot and found the block undefended. The tanks now went down the road and through the block without opposition. The infantry then cleared the area of the few remaining snipers.

CHAPTER 12

At about 1030 hours our whole force began moving north. The road as far as Tharrawaddy was continuously patrolled by tanks whilst 16 Brigade close-picquetted the stretch in the immediate area of the block. The only opposition along the road itself was from the air, enemy bombing aircraft maintaining almost continuous activity. Headquarters of 17 Division which had moved to Taukkyan from Hlegu suffered heavily. Almost the entire strength of our anti-aircraft guns in Burma was in the Taukkyan area. One Japanese aircraft was brought down by a direct hit and other aircraft were probably disabled.

The 1st Battalion 11th Sikh Regiment holding a position north of the junction of the main and Wanetchaung roads was in contact with the enemy, including Burmese, throughout the day. Important documents, amongst them Code Books and Diaries, were captured, and it was established that we had here been in action against the Japanese 33rd Division.

At 1530 hours another force of the enemy moving in from the west endeavoured to place machine-guns in position near the road fork at Milestone 22. A troop of Hussars drove them off and the road was kept open. Similar attempts by enemy mortar detachments to shell the road from the direction of Hlawga were dealt with by the 1st Battalion the Gloucestershire Regiment.

Throughout the day and into the following night our force moved north from Taukkyan and Hlegu, one Squadron of the 2nd Battalion Royal Tank Regiment acting as rear guard. Shortly after 2300 hours the last of the marching infantry had passed through Haawbi, and the majority of the infantry battalions of 17 Division were assembled in open paddy land west of the village. They then carried out a further withdrawal across country towards Taikkyi, halting at dawn to disperse. Only emergency rations were available. Many of these troops had marched thirty miles in the last twenty-four hours, an outstanding feat under the trying conditions to which they had already been subjected. The rear guard now consisting of 7 Armoured Brigade leaguered near Myaungtanga.

On March 9th and 10th our force continued its withdrawal by motor transport and rail from Taikkyi to the Tharrawaddy area. Here intensive reorganisation and re-equipment were carried out. First reinforcements left behind by Brigades together with stragglers from the Sittang and more recent operations helped to swell numbers.

At Taukkyan the Japanese made one of their major mistakes in the campaign. Evidently the block had been established to protect the left flank of the Japanese 33rd Division crossing the Prome road with the object of entering Rangoon from the north-west. In its hurried dash for the city this force ignored the more important operation of cutting off the major portion of our troops in Burma, and, with them, Army Headquarters. That Rangoon had been given up must have been abundantly clear to the Japanese on the afternoon of March 7th. It is of course possible that they acted in the belief that a general British withdrawal by sea was in progress.

Although General Alexander's decision to defer the evacuation of Rangoon was very natural in the circumstances, there is no doubt that in consequence the whole force narrowly escaped destruction and that the demolition parties, etc., evacuated by sea were very fortunate in not being intercepted. The troops suffered seriously in casualties and losses of equipment, and their ability to continue operations for the defence of North Burma was considerably prejudiced. 63 Brigade in particular had undergone a serious trial for young and partially trained troops and did not recover easily.

Chapter 13

Effects of the loss of Rangoon – Regrouping of British forces in the Irrawaddy valley – Formation of Burcorps – Minor operations at Henzada and Letpadan – Japanese attacks on A.V.G. and R.A.F. at Magwe and the serious results thereof – Formation of a striking force to relieve pressure on Chinese V Army at Toungoo – Operations undertaken by the striking force at Padigon and Paungde – Enemy establish a road block at Shwedaung – Action at Shwedaung – Attack on our force at Padaung on the west bank of the Irrawaddy.

The loss of Rangoon had the most serious effect on the campaign. After the fall of that city the Army was fighting facing its former base and with no Lines of Communication behind it. Virtually cut off from outside assistance it could only be supplied with the very limited numbers of personnel and small quantities of stores which could be brought in by air.

Base and Lines of Communication installations and reserves of commodities had already been moved north of Rangoon, and this back-loading had to continue throughout the campaign. This placed enormous strain on the administrative machine and the transportation agencies. On the river steamers it was difficult to persuade native civilian crews to operate in forward areas. Civil heavy repair installations in the Rangoon area which could not be removed were lost altogether, and the maintenance of mechanical transport and equipment became a matter of great difficulty.

The destruction of the important oil refineries greatly reduced the output of petrol and lubricating oils. Large stocks of petrol and aviation spirit had been taken out of Rangoon, but when these had been consumed the Allied armies in Burma would be dependent on the largely improvised refining methods existing on the oilfields themselves.

The loss of the Rangoon aerodromes with their efficient warning system was soon to have grave consequences for the R.A.F. and A.V.G. The whole air situation in Burma was affected.

In December 1941, after the outbreak of war with Japan, the construction of a road linking Kalewa on the Chindwin river with Imphal in Assam had been undertaken. Work on this road was in progress both in Assam and in Burma. Very difficult country had to be traversed, and the work in Burma was hampered by shortage of materials of all kinds, the passage of innumerable refugees, and the difficulty of retaining a labour force. There was no prospect of the road being in a fit state for the purposes of maintaining an army for many months to come. Consequently, the retention of Upper Burma depended entirely upon the amount of force which the Japanese employed in this theatre of war. Having gained Rangoon, they were in a position to move very large numbers of troops by sea to Burma and to maintain them through Rangoon. It was unlikely that they would fail to make the most of their opportunities or give us time to complete the overland link with India. Under these circumstances the task of the Allies was to impose the maximum delay on the enemy and, in doing so, make him expend resources which might otherwise have been employed elsewhere.

In reorganising his forces General Alexander determined to concentrate all available British troops in the Irrawaddy valley. The Chinese V Army was to relieve 1 Burma Division now holding the Sittang valley sector. The Chinese were not willing to proceed south of Toungoo and, accordingly, General Alexander considered that the British concentration must take place in the Prome area. Territory to the south was therefore abandoned.

This resulted in the loss of an area seventy miles in depth in which there were large quantities of food, particularly rice. We were endeavouring to move these supplies which would be required by the Chinese. In Upper Burma there was little or no surplus production of rice.

The date of the concentration of the Imperial Forces necessarily depended on the moves of the Chinese V Army. These were governed by transport difficulties and the movement of the Chinese VI Army into the Shan States. This matter is discussed in detail in a subsequent chapter.

This regrouping of the Imperial Forces and the additional responsibilities placed on the Army Command by the arrival of the Chinese Expeditionary Force necessitated the immediate formation of a

CHAPTER 13

Corps Headquarters (Burcorps). On March 19th Lieut.-General W.J. Slim, M.C., arrived from India to command it. His B.G.S. was Brigadier H.L. Davies, D.S.O., M.C., who had until that time been employed in a similar capacity at Army Headquarters, and was now available owing to the appointment of Lieut.-General Hutton as C.G.S. Army in Burma.

Meanwhile 17 Division had been reforming in the area Thonse-Tharrawaddy-Letpadan. The 1st Battalion the Gloucestershire Regiment was formed into a Divisional reconnaissance unit. Fully motorised and provided with some light armoured vehicles, it was employed as a mobile screen well forward of the Division.

The 1st Battalion Royal Inniskilling Fusiliers, having been flown into the country from India, joined 17 Division on March 19th.

The Yomas Intelligence Service was also formed. This consisted of employees of the Forest Department and timber extracting firms and other persons well acquainted with the country. Better information of enemy movements was now obtained.

Here in the Irrawaddy valley the nature of the country had altered. On the east the Pegu Yomas were jungle-clad, but between the hills and the river were wide expanses of flat paddy lands. The villages themselves were often surrounded by small patches of jungle. Minor hill features were also not infrequently covered with scrub.

It should be observed that although at first sight the sun-baked paddy fields appeared to afford excellent opportunities for tank operations, they suffered from one serious drawback. The small earth bunds surrounding each field required tanks to slow down when crossing them. This rendered tanks particularly vulnerable to enemy fire.

During this period our forward elements kept the enemy under observation, but for about a week there was little activity. It was difficult to establish contact with the enemy who was also well served with information. The local people were friendly to him, and our withdrawals were regularly signalled by the lighting of bonfires in the villages evacuated. On March 13th 17 Division Headquarters withdrew from Tharrawaddy to Shwegon, two miles north-east of Okpo. In the following two days the Division concentrated in that area.

The detachment of Royal Marines had maintained patrols on the Irrawaddy in a flotilla of launches, and on March 17th one of these launches escorted a river steamer to Henzada then well behind the Japanese lines. On this steamer was a Commando force under Major J.M. Calvert. It was detailed to carry out certain demolitions along the river. These were effected. At Myanaung locomotives and rolling stock were destroyed. So, too, was a railway bridge. Boats on the river were sunk. At Henzada Major Calvert's landing party was surrounded, called upon to surrender, and attacked by a large force armed with machine-guns. A brisk engagement developed; heavy fire being directed on the enemy from our vessels. Mortar shells began to fall near the steamers, but the greater part of the landing party was taken off after it had fought its way back to the river. It was then found that some men were still ashore. The enemy held the river bank, but concentrated covering fire enabled the remaining party to get through to the foreshore where it was taken aboard the vessels. It is estimated that about a hundred casualties were inflicted on the enemy force which consisted mainly of Burmese. Our own casualties were five.

Two days later one company of the 1st Battalion the Gloucestershire Regiment was concerned in an equally successful minor operation at Letpadan. Information was received from F.F.2 that a Battalion of the enemy had entered the town at 0430 hours. An attack was accordingly planned for first light. One platoon moved down the road in motor transport from the north-east to attract the attention of the enemy. Debussing, it demonstrated against the eastern side of the town. Mortar fire was put down on the town, later shifting to cover the east and south exits. The remainder of the company attacked from the west. The Japanese were taken completely by surprise by this attack. A party occupying the school was annihilated by grenades and automatic gun fire. There was a panic, and the Japanese fled from the town pursued by our troops. Their casualties were very heavy. Our own were nine missing and one wounded.

By March 27th the Division had fallen back to the Prome area with Divisional Headquarters at Wettigan. Here, too, was 7 Armoured Brigade with one Regiment at Tamagauk. 63 Brigade was in Prome, 16 Brigade in the area Sinmizwe-Hmawza, and 48 Brigade was about Wettigan. The 1st Battalion the Gloucestershire Regiment was based on Paungde, covering the Divisional front. The left flank was protected by F.F. units whilst the Royal Marines River Patrol and a Commando watched the right. The Yomas Intelligence Service was also functioning along the whole front. Behind the Division the concentration of 1 Burma Division in the area Allanmyo-Kyaukpadaung-Dayindabo was proceeding. It had been relieved in the Toungoo area by the Chinese V Army.

General Alexander intended that the defence of the Irrawaddy valley should be based on the Brigade groups in Prome and Allanmyo. These towns were to be made defended localities stocked with supplies and ammunition for twenty-one days. If the enemy got round these places, as he obviously would, the garrisons were to remain and fight on. The remainder of Burcorps was to be mobile and prepared to act offensively.

CHAPTER 13

There were now frequent reports that the Japanese were being reinforced by substantial numbers of organised Thakins who had been formed into units of the Burma Independence Army. This particular district of Burma had always been a centre of disaffection and it was estimated that the Japanese here had a Burmese force of three or four thousand men co-operating with them. Recruiting for this force was proceeding actively.

On March 21st and 22nd the Japanese carried out a series of very heavy air raids on our aerodromes at Magwe and Akyab. The result of these raids was the almost complete elimination of our small air force in Burma. R.A.F. aircraft still capable of taking off were withdrawn to India and the ground parties retired by road to Loiwing in China north of Lashio, and thereafter the Allied Armies in Burma were almost entirely without air support. The Japanese were not slow to take advantage of this situation and, not surprisingly, the effect on the morale of our own troops was marked.

In addition, the Japanese began a series of heavy air bombing attacks on centres of communication in Central and Upper Burma. Such places as Prome, Meiktila, Mandalay, Thazi, Pyinmana, Maymyo, Lashio and Taunggyi were raided. The almost complete destruction by fire of many of these towns followed, and the moral effect upon the civil population was enormous. After a heavy raid on a town its people moved out en masse to the jungle. Many railway employees and crews of the Irrawaddy Flotilla Company left their posts. The Police force disintegrated, and power supplies broke down. The Posts and Telegraph service was affected to a lesser degree, many of the personnel remaining loyally at work. From the Military aspect this dislocation of public utility services was serious.

In an appreciation dated March 26th Lieut.-General Hutton set out the position in the following words:

"Many of the essential services of Burma have collapsed. Even at several hundred miles from the front services have already ceased to function, personnel have disappeared and orders are disobeyed or ignored. This applies to both superior as well as subordinate personnel, and even those who are permanently enrolled do not seem under any obligation to perform their duties. In the absence of any effective police forces, looting of trains, stations, and dumps is very prevalent. Cholera and other diseases are prevalent and likely to increase owing to the failure of the Medical and Hospital Services. The Civil A.R.P. organisation has almost entirely dispersed."

Towards the end of March General Alexander visited Chungking to discuss the military situation with the Generalissimo. The Chinese V Army was then heavily engaged round Toungoo and the Generalissimo therefore requested that to relieve pressure on it, offensive operations be initiated on the Irrawaddy front. A telegram ordering these operations was received by Burcorps from General Alexander early on the morning of March 26th.

17 Division was directed to carry out a local offensive. For this purpose, additional troops were placed at its disposal by Burcorps and the tasks of the striking force were defined as:

(a) To secure Okpo, establishing a lay-back at Zigon to watch the east flank.
(b) To destroy all enemy detachments encountered during the advance and to exploit any local success.
(c) To protect the west flank by securing Nyaungzaye.

The danger to the west flank was very real, reports having been received of a large mixed force of Burmans and Japanese with an estimated strength of over four thousand advancing up the west bank of the river from Henzada. This force had twenty rubber boats. It was expected to reach Tonbo on March 28th. A Commando under Lieut.-Colonel Musgrave was detailed to deal with it and moved by river steamer. Co-operating with the Commando was the Royal Marines River Patrol and a Burma Military Police detachment. This latter was already on the west bank of the river.

On March 28th the 1st Battalion the Gloucestershire Regiment was in contact with a column of the enemy at Paungde. Receiving information that the enemy had occupied the town the Battalion from a position just north of it at once moved forward to attack. Supported by mortars and machine-guns the advance made good progress, and very shortly there was fighting in the streets. Japanese snipers were active from houses and trees. Burmans actively supported the enemy. Clearing houses with grenades or burning them, our troops pushed through the town. An infantry gun attempting to come into action was at once knocked out by a mortar. Enemy mortars were similarly silenced.

At least one Japanese Battalion and two hundred armed Burmans were in the town. The Gloucesters were far ahead of 17 Division and could not expect support. Consequently, they were withdrawn before becoming too heavily involved. Their casualties were not light. They lost two officers killed and three wounded. Fifteen other ranks were killed and nine wounded. Some eighty of the enemy were killed.

For the initial phase of the proposed offensive our troops near Paungde were to be augmented by the striking force.

Brigadier Anstice of 7 Armoured Brigade was placed in command of this striking force. His orders were to attack Paungde on March 29th and to advance on Okpo the following day.

For the first phase (Paungde) the following troops were detailed:

414 Battery, R.H.A.
7th Queen's Own Hussars.
1st Battalion the Gloucestershire Regiment.
2nd Battalion The Duke of Wellington's Regiment.
1st Battalion The Cameronians.
One Company 1st Battalion West Yorkshire Regiment.
24 Field Company Sappers and Miners.

For the advance of Okpo, which was never carried out, additional troops were also to be employed. Strong lay-backs, each consisting of two Battalions, were to remain at Paungde and Zigon.

The 4th Battalion 12th Frontier Force Regiment and one Company of the 1st Battalion Royal Inniskilling Fusiliers together with Burma Police units were intended to provide protection at Shwedaung, Maudaing, Inma, and Nyaungzaye on the river flank. The 4th Battalion 12th Frontier Forced Regiment was to be posted in Shwedaung. As will be noted later it never entered the town. The Company of the 1st Battalion Royal Inniskilling Fusiliers watched the hill section of the road south-east of the village of Maudaing.

There was a shortage of motor transport and the forward movement of troops was carried out by a shuttling service of vehicles. This considerably delayed operations.

On the evening of March 28th, the 1st Battalion the Gloucestershire Regiment with a strength of only two Companies and a Headquarters Company was holding positions forward of Inma village which was at Milestone 154 on the Rangoon-Prome road. One company was at Wetpok (Milestone 148) whilst another was at Padigon on the railway line seven miles north-west of Paungde. Padigon and Wetpok were connected by a road branching north-east from the main road. Battalion Headquarters was at Inma. Here arrived that evening the 2nd Battalion the Duke of Wellington's Regiment, the leading unit of the striking force. This Battalion too, was much below strength. It consisted of two Companies and a Headquarters Company. It proceeded to send out two fighting and reconnaissance patrols. No.2 Company was to operate south from Padigon towards Paungde; No.1 Company was to patrol south-east from Wetpok to a point on the main road some two miles south of Paungde. These Companies were to make contact with the enemy. If possible, they were to drive him out of Paungde, but were to withdraw if opposed by much superior forces.

It was a moonlight night. The company reconnoitring from Padigon had a successful encounter with a Japanese Patrol near the railway bridge over the Wegyi Chaung. It then observed large bodies of Japanese troops north of Paungde, one of such bodies marching along the railway towards Padigon. A warning message was sent back to Padigon. Finding the Japanese on the outskirts of Paungde to be too strong to be dealt with, the Company made a detour north-east with the object of returning to Padigon.

The other Company reached the main road south of Paungde without incident before first light on March 29th. It was not far from the southern outskirts of the town.

Early that morning two distinct actions developed round Paungde and Padigon.

The Company of the 1st Battalion the Gloucestershire Regiment at Padigon was attacked from the east of the village by a Battalion of Japanese. The enemy appeared to be carrying out an outflanking movement northwards. Brigadier Anstice who had now established his Headquarters at Inma ordered one squadron of the 7th Queen's Own Hussars to move immediately to Padigon to contact our force there, and then to go on to Thegon to cut off the outflanking enemy column.

Three miles south of Padigon two tanks were knocked out by anti-tank guns on the road. Assisted by 414 Battery R.H.A. the enemy resistance was overcome by the 7th Queen's Own Hussars who then went forward. However, closer to Padigon a road block was encountered and anti-tank guns again opened heavy fire. The block was about one and a half miles south of Padigon where a long line of jungle-enclosed villages stretched east and west across the road.

Brigadier Anstice now ordered the 1st Battalion the Cameronians supported by a Company of the 1st Battalion the West Yorkshire Regiment, one troop of 414 Battery R.H.A., and a squadron of the 7th Queen's Own Hussars to attack the block.

The 1st Battalion the Cameronians (strength three companies and Headquarters Company) had arrived at Inma at about 0900 hours that morning. Passing through Shwedaung eight miles south of Prome about three quarters of an hour earlier it had received a report from a Burma Frontier Force Detachment that the Japanese were advancing on Shwedaung from the south-west. The significance of this advance was to become evident later in the day.

After a fifteen-minute artillery bombardment the Cameronians fought their way through the villages south of Padigon and cleared the road block. They then came under fire from snipers who had concealed themselves in village buildings. Many of these snipers were destroyed by the burning of the villages. A party of Japanese disguised as Burmans endeavoured to move round the left flank, but the Battalion machine-guns from a rear position dealt effectively with this group.

The tanks continued their advance. They met further road blocks and also came under artillery fire from Padigon, which appeared to be held by the enemy, and from positions south-east of it. This fire was ineffective and the Japanese guns were silenced by the troop of 414 Battery R.H.A.

At 1720 hours our force south of Padigon was ordered to withdraw on Inma.

In Padigon itself the Company of the Gloucestershire Regiment withstood a heavy attack early in the morning. At about 1000 hours it had been joined by No.2 Company of the Duke of Wellington's Regiment.

The village was now being attacked on the south-east, south, and south-west. Our troops were subjected to small arms and mortar fire, and the enemy began to work round further to the west.

Shortly after 1100 hours our force in Padigon withdrew north along a track on the western edge of the railway embankment. It then struck west with the object of gaining the main road some ten miles north-west of Inma. Arriving on the road at dusk it there made contact with the main body of the striking force then withdrawing towards Shwedaung.

The operations round Padigon had interfered very largely with the attack on Paungde, the first objective of the striking force. Although, on paper, three Infantry Battalions were available their actual strength did not exceed that of one and a half normal Battalions. The greater part of this force was employed about Padigon.

No.1 Company of the Duke of Wellington's Regiment south of Paungde was in position in a patch of jungle west of the main road and on the southern outskirts of the town. At about 0600 hours a body of about three hundred Japanese alighted from a column of motor vehicles and began to advance on the position. Fire was held until the Japanese had approached to within two hundred yards or so. It was then opened with excellent effect. Flanking movements from north and south were begun by the enemy, but the Company had no difficulty in maintaining its positions. It reported the situation to Battalion Headquarters asking for rations and further supplies of ammunition.

Tanks of the 7th Queen's Own Hussars made contact with the Company, and as Paungde itself did not appear to be heavily held by the enemy it was decided to attack the town with two platoons of the Headquarters Company of the 1st Battalion the Duke of Wellington's Regiment. 'C' Squadron of the 7th Queen's Own Hussars would be in support.

The attack made progress through the north-western part of the town but was then held up. The tanks destroyed some enemy transport and infantry, but the opposition was heavy. The Japanese were also largely reinforced by troops coming up the road from the south. Two of our tanks were hit, and our infantry sustained a number of casualties.

Our troops in Paungde and No.1 Company of the Duke of Wellington's regiment to the south of it had received orders that they were not to become so heavily involved as to render themselves liable to be cut off. Consequently, at 1530 hours when enemy pressure increased, No.1 Company began to withdraw. By this time Paungde was burning. Our troops in the town shortly afterwards began to fall back. The Duke of Wellington's Regiment had suffered some thirty casualties, including Captain Conningham who was killed, but it had punished the enemy severely. No.1 Company alone inflicted at least two hundred casualties on the Japanese.

Meanwhile, the Divisional Liaison Officer on his way back to Prome had found Shwedaung held by the enemy in considerable strength. He was compelled to return to Inma where he reported the situation to Brigadier Anstice who then, by wireless, asked Divisional Headquarters for orders. He was instructed to break out either by way of Shwedaung or Padigon, whichever was the easier. Since efforts to take Padigon had been unsuccessful Brigadier Anstice decided to fall back on Prome through Shwedaung. He therefore broke off the actions at Padigon and Paungde and concentrated his troops at Inma. At 1815 hours a force under Major Pereira, R.H.A. consisting of one troop 414 Battery R.H.A., one troop of the 7th Queen's Own Hussars, and two Companies of the 1st Battalion the Gloucestershire Regiment was sent on ahead to clear the road block at Shwedaung.

At that time, we were already engaged with the enemy at Shwedaung. The 4th Battalion 12th Frontier Force Regiment and the 2nd Battalion

CHAPTER 13

13th Frontier Force Rifles had been detailed by 17 Division to retake the town from the north. These Battalions were supported by a Battery of 1 Indian Field Regiment I.A. Attacking along both sides of the road the 4th Battalion 12th Frontier Force Regiment found itself strongly opposed. It gained the outskirts of the town but could get no further. About seventy prisoners, mostly members of the Burma Independence Army, a machine-gun, and several automatic weapons were taken. The Battalion was then reinforced by the 2nd Battalion 13th Frontier Force Rifles, but the enemy in Shwedaung held out. Our force eventually withdrew to a harbour about two miles to the north, and a further attack was planned for the following morning.

Shwedaung was a small town on the east bank of the Irrawaddy. Together with its adjoining villages it extended towards the east for more than two miles inland from the river. It also flanked the main road on both sides for more than a mile. Its southern outskirts were well fringed with trees and jungle growth. It was therefore an excellent position for the establishment of a block to prevent the passage of transport.

Major Pereira's force located a block about two miles south of Shwedaung at 1900 hours. This was only lightly held and was cleared by the tanks after it had been bombarded. A second block was then encountered just south of the town. This was strongly held with guns, mortars, and machine-guns.

Fire was again opened by the troop of 414 Battery R.H.A., after which the tanks went forward to investigate. The enemy remained active with machine-guns and mortars from the jungle on the sides of the road. The infantry endeavoured to clear this. Tanks succeeded in passing through the block with difficulty, but our infantry strength was not sufficient to sweep the enemy from the flanking jungle.

By this time Brigadier Anstice and the main body of the striking force had arrived. It was decided to attack the block again with one Company of the Gloucestershire Regiment and one Company of the West Yorkshire Regiment.

The attack, preceded by a bombardment by the whole of 414 Battery R.H.A., was made at 0200 hours on March 30th. Once again, the infantry could make no progress. Operations were then suspended until dawn.

Prior to the attack at 0200 hours two tanks had been hit. Lieutenant Patterson of the 7th Queen's Own Hussars was captured by the Japanese who tied him to the road block whilst it was being shelled by our guns. With his hands still fastened behind him this officer contrived to escape from his binding ropes and made his way back to his unit through the enemy lines.

At 0700 hours the attack on the block was resumed by the striking force. It was delayed for a short time by a heavy ground mist. There was then a fifteen-minute artillery concentration on the area of the block, 414 Battery R.H.A., being in action on the west of the road one thousand yards south of the block. The bombardment was followed by an infantry advance. The infantry force was commanded by Lieut.-Colonel P.C. Marindin, M.C. (West Yorkshire Regiment). The 1st Battalion the Cameronians attacked north along the east of the main road, and the company of the West Yorkshire Regiment with a company of the Gloucestershire Regiment advanced on its west. The 2nd Battalion the Duke of Wellington's Regiment was in reserve. Tanks of the 7th Queen's Own Hussars lent support. The object of the attack was to sweep through Shwedaung clearing away all opposition and thus enabling the transport to pass through.

The Cameronians encountered considerable opposition near the road, but the company on the right flank entered the village with some difficulty.

On the west of the road our advance was at once held up. The company of the West Yorkshire Regiment on the outer flank came under fire from the left rear where the Japanese were concealed in tree-girt villages. These were dealt with by tanks, and a company of the 1st Battalion Duke of Wellington's Regiment went in to sweep a patch of jungle five hundred yards west of the road. From this point fire had been directed on our guns. Here close range and confused fighting ensued. There were enemy snipers posted in trees and our troops were also subject to mortar and machine-gun fire. Nevertheless, they cleared the jungle, inflicting heavy casualties on the enemy and destroying two machine-guns. Our attack on the extreme west flank now went forward, and a part of the company of the West Yorkshire Regiment fought its way through the town to its northern outskirts.

Round the road block there was very bitter fighting in which tanks and troops of all three leading Battalions took part. The Japanese had a strong point in a rice mill on the western side of the road close to the block. From this heavy machine-gun fire was directed on our force which was now at close range. Grenades were freely employed.

Anti-tank guns, mortars, and Molotov cocktail bombs were used against our tanks, but by 1030 hours the block was in our hands. The enemy had fallen back towards the centre of the town. Our troops followed up, but the main road was not close-picquetted.

Our transport column then began to move forward and to pass through the site of the block. It was soon brought to a halt as a second block had been established towards the north of the town. Mortar fire wrecked some of the vehicles and set others on fire. In places vehicles were nose to tail and double banked on the road, and this added to the difficulty of extricating the transport. Diversions down side roads were found, but here too, blocks were created by burning or overturned vehicles. Close fighting continued.

On the south of the town a rearguard composed of the Duke of Wellington's Regiment (less one company) and a squadron of the 7th Queen's Own Hussars held covering positions. During the afternoon they were joined by a body of about two hundred Burma Military Police under Lieutenant R. Saunders which had marched in from the south. Save for those immediately controlled by Lieutenant Saunders the greater part of these men disappeared in the course of the action.

Japanese reconnaissance aircraft were overhead all the morning and indulged in some fruitless machine-gunning of transport. In the afternoon, at about 1500 hours, Japanese bomber aircraft began a series of heavy and accurate attacks on the massed columns of vehicles and also on our rearguard south of Shwedaung. These attacks continued at intervals for a couple of hours and resulted in casualties and the destruction of much transport. Shwedaung was now on fire.

The tanks, with considerable loss, were able to force a passage for themselves and for 414 Battery R.H.A., which succeeded in getting through the town with the loss of two guns. It had become evident, however, that there was little prospect of the unarmoured vehicles passing through the enemy safely.

Meanwhile the rearguard squadron of tanks reported to Brigadier Anstice that it was in contact with a column of enemy advancing from the south. All our available troops were engaged.

The 4th Battalion 12th Frontier Force Regiment, the 2nd Battalion 13th Frontier Force Rifles and one Squadron of the 2nd Battalion Royal Tank Regiment, had attacked Shwedaung from the north during the day, but again could not progress beyond the edge of the town. The Battery of 1 Indian Field Regiment supporting this attack fired on parties of the enemy crossing the river from the west bank. From this direction the enemy received substantial reinforcements during the action.

A further attempt was made to extricate the transport in the town. Tanks found a new diversion and some vehicles were taken out on this route, but the greater part of the unarmoured vehicles could not be saved. Opposition continued to be heavy and grenades and machine-gun fire were still employed by the enemy.

At about 1800 hours orders were issued to abandon the transport. All troops remaining in Shwedaung were to proceed north on foot. The remnants from all infantry units then withdrew under fire. A few more vehicles were taken out of the town.

That night the striking force retired towards the area of Prome where units concerned re-organised.

Captain C.W. Elphick, Medical Officer of the Cameronians, found himself alone with his staff, his wounded, and a handful of drivers in the south end of Shwedaung. Puzzled by the sudden silence, he went forward to find the town abandoned by our troops. All wounded were promptly loaded on to vehicles. A burning truck blocking the road was then rammed and cleared, and the small column made its way out of the town under machine-gun fire.

Next morning 1 Indian Field Regiment from north of Shwedaung subjected the town to harassing fire and also put out of action an infantry gun on the west bank of the river. The fire on Shwedaung was most effective, direct hits being obtained on motor vehicles in which Japanese troops were embussing.

During the operations of March 29th/30th a force consisting of one squadron of the 2nd Battalion Royal Tank Regiment, one Company of the 1st Battalion West Yorkshire Regiment, and the 1st Battalion 4th P.W.O. Gurkha Rifles occupied Sinmizwe on the railway south-east of Prome to counter any Japanese thrust from Padigon. No action developed here.

Although the enemy had been hard hit, our striking force lost heavily in transport, equipment, and personnel. Accurate casualty lists for the Burma Campaign have been difficult to compile, but for the actions on these two days it is possible to form a reasonable estimate of our losses.

The 7th Queen's own Hussars had many men wounded on its unarmoured vehicles. It lost ten tanks, eight of them on March 30th. 414 Battery R.H.A., had ten other ranks killed and six wounded. The 2nd Battalion Duke of Wellington's Regiment lost five officers (three killed, one wounded, and one missing) and one hundred and seventeen other ranks. The 1st Battalion the Royal Inniskilling Fusiliers had thirteen other ranks killed and four wounded. The 1st Battalion The Cameronians lost five officers (two killed) and sixty-four other ranks (twenty-six killed). The 1st Battalion West Yorkshire Regiment had one officer and eight other ranks killed and thirteen other ranks wounded or missing. The 1st Battalion the Gloucestershire Regiment lost two officers wounded and thirty-four other ranks killed, wounded or missing. The 4th Battalion

12th Frontier Force Regiment lost in killed one officer, two Viceroy's Commissioned Officers, and fifteen other ranks; in wounded two officers, three Viceroy's Commissioned Officers and forty other ranks. The 2nd Battalion 13th Frontier Force Rifles had one officer wounded, one other rank killed and twenty-three wounded. No figures for other units are available. Having regard to the fact that nearly every unit was by that time much below its proper strength the figures indicate a high percentage of losses.

During these operations we were engaged with the Japanese 33rd Division of which its 215 Regiment was encountered at Shwedaung. Here units of the Burma Independence Army took prominent part, and in particular opposed our attacks on the town from the north. They are reported to have fought with fanaticism and were killed in large numbers. These Burmese units had crossed the Irrawaddy having formed part of the enemy force marching up the west bank of the river from Henzada. Reference to this force was made earlier in this chapter.

On the night of March 28th/29th the Commando and Burma Military Police had been landed from the river near Padaung, and the following day Lieut.-Colonel Musgrave was ordered to defend Padaung with the object of preventing a crossing by the enemy to Shwedaung on the east bank. At this latter place fighting had already begun.

Two platoons and a Vickers gun section of the Royal Marines then accompanied Lieut.-Colonel Musgrave to Padaung from Sinde, a village five miles higher up the west bank of the river. This force moved into Padaung at dusk and was received by the villagers in a friendly manner. Supplies were sold to the troops and the Sub-Assistant Surgeon stationed in the village took a prominent part in greeting the force. This man is stated to have been an Anglo-Indian named Peters.

A defensive position was taken up round the compound of a bungalow near the river bank. Our patrols were already south of Padaung but additional patrols were sent out. A Commando detachment eight miles to the south reported that there were no enemy forces north of Tonbo, eighteen miles down the river.

At 0030 hours on the morning of March 30th a sudden attack was made on our positions round the bungalow, and in a short time a number of Japanese troops had entered the compound. Isolated parties of our men put up a stout resistance, but the attack was too heavy and too sudden to permit of any organised defence.

About half of the Commando eventually made its way back to our lines and so, too, did the greater part of the Burma Military Police. The Royal Marines losses were, one officer and thirty other ranks missing.

Apparently, the Japanese had arrived in Padaung ahead of the Commando and had then hidden in the houses of the villagers who gave our troops not the slightest hint of this fact.

As a result of this operation the Japanese found it possible during March 30th to reinforce from the west bank of the Irrawaddy their hard-pressed force in Shwedaung.

Following upon the action at Padaung the Japanese there were guilty of a cold-blooded atrocity. On the morning of March 30th, a dozen Commando and Royal Marine prisoners were lined up before a Battalion on parade. A section of the Battalion then charged the prisoners with fixed bayonets and proceeded to kill them. This fact was reported by one of the prisoners, a sergeant major who was able to break away and escaped after sustaining three bayonet wounds.

Chapter 14

Operations in the Shan States and Karenni in January and February 1942 – Relief of 1 Burma Division by Chinese VI Army – Concentration of 1 Burma Division south of Toungoo – Decision by Army Commander to release unreliable elements in Battalions of Burma Rifles – Our attacks on Pyuntaza and Shwegyin – Decision to withdraw 1 Burma Division to the Irrawaddy front on relief by Chinese V Army – Actions at Kyauktaga and Gonde.

Early in January the Chinese 227 Regiment had taken over the defence of the Mekong river east of the road Kengtung-Mongpayak. This reduced considerably the very long sector held by 1 Burma Division in the Shan States. But from our junction with the Chinese to the mouth of the Salween was a distance of some three hundred miles. Apart from 17 Division concentrated in Tenasserim we had only two Brigades of 1 Burma Division and a few F.F. units to cover this extensive front.

Although the enemy was not very active in the Shan States and Karenni during January and February the position gave rise to considerable anxiety. There were known to be numbers of Japanese as well as Thai troops in northern Thailand, and there were persistent reports of large enemy concentrations at Chiangmai and Chiangrai and indications of an early invasion. The road from Kemapyu on the Salween in Karenni to Toungoo was practically unguarded. Yet to meet the more threatening situation in Tenasserim troops had to be constantly withdrawn from the Shan States. Thus 1 Burma Division lost the 2nd Battalion King's Own Yorkshire Light Infantry, 5 Field Brigade, R.A., B.A.F., the Malerkotis Sappers and Miners and, later, the 1st Battalion Burma Rifles.

On January 19th the remainder of the Chinese 93rd Division was ordered to move into Kengtung, and later in the month General Wavell sanctioned the entry of 49th Division. Shortly afterwards it was agreed that 55th Division should also be employed. These three Divisions comprised the Chinese VI Army.

It was Lieut.-General Hutton's policy to concentrate as early as possible the whole of the available Imperial Forces in the south of Burma with the object of holding up the Japanese advance in the area where this presented the greatest threat to Rangoon and the communications with China. Accordingly, as the Chinese VI Army deployed, the remaining units of 1 Burma Division in the Shan States withdrew. 1 Burma Brigade moved south during February and early March. Additional units of 13 Brigade moved into Karenni in February and here 23 Mountain Battery, the 5th Battalion Burma Rifles, and the 5th Battalion 1st Punjab Regiment joined the 1st Battalion 18th Royal Garhwal Rifles.

The withdrawal of certain units from remote areas was not easy. Maintenance had been by mule and elephant transport, and when the Chinese forces took over there was the added difficulty of finding for them the correct items of supply. The line of communication previously considered incapable of maintaining more than two Brigades was now compelled to provide for two Chinese Divisions.

Both in the Shan States and Karenni, operations had been confined to minor encounters on the frontier, particularly in the neighbourhood of the Kengtung-Chiang Rai road. These actions were fought by F.F. Columns, the opposition being provided by Thai troops led by Japanese officers. Our men displayed a marked superiority over the enemy. On February 17th F.F.4 carried out a most successful surprise raid on the Thai outposts south of Pung Pahkyem. A Japanese officer and sixty enemy troops were killed without loss to ourselves. During this period a large patrol of the 1st Battalion 18th Royal Garhwal Rifles had also entered Thailand and reconnoitred the area of the Mae Hong Son airfield.

By the end of February 1 Burma Division was covering the Sittang valley south of Nyaunglebin with the very weak 2 Burma Brigade. This Brigade, after the defence of Moulmein, had been withdrawn to Kyaikto and in the middle of February became for a brief period a Lines of Communication formation. With Headquarters at Nyaunglebin it was then responsible for the protection of the Sittang river crossings from Shwegyin southwards. The 4th Battalion 12th Frontier Force Regiment had by that time reverted to 16 Brigade. When 1 Burma Division moved south 2 Burma Brigade rejoined it, having covered the concentration of the Division.

During this period the 1st Battalion Burma Rifles furnished the forward screen for 2 Burma Brigade. Covering Nyaunglebin it

CHAPTER 14

maintained contact by motor patrol with 7 Armoured Brigade to the south about Pegu.

It should here be note that 1 Burma Division only had one carrier platoon. This was made up of a few old tracked carriers originally issued for instructional purposes. This small unit had a mixed British, Indian, and Burman personnel and did valuable reconnaissance work until its carriers wore out and had to be abandoned. It also fought a very successful minor action under Lieutenant J. Wilson of The King's Own Yorkshire Light Infantry. Two enemy machine-guns and a mortar were destroyed.

North of 2 Burma Brigade on the main Rangoon-Mandalay road was 1 Burma Brigade about Pyu and Kyauktaga. 13 Brigade remained for the time being in Karenni covering Kemapyu and the important tin mines at Mawchi; but the 5th Battalion Burma Rifles and the 5th Battalion 1st Punjab Regiment were withdrawn for duty on the Sittang valley front. This left 13 Brigade with only one Battalion and one F.F. column.

East of 2 Burma Brigade at Papun on the upper Yunzalin river the 2nd Battalion Burma Rifles was watching the trans-frontier tracks converging at that point. On February 23rd, following upon the Sittang bridge battle, it received orders to retire from Papun and to join 1 Burma Division.

Events on the Tenasserim front were not without effect on the Burman troops in this Division. On February 26th Brigadier Bourke reported to 17 Division that men were deserting at the rate of twenty or so every night from each Battalion of 2 Burma Brigade. In some cases, arms and equipment were taken. Morale was so low even in units that had never fired a shot that no longer could he count on his Brigade to check an attack. At that time the Brigade consisted of the 1st and 7th Battalions of the Burma Rifles and the remnants of the 3rd Battalion. The first named Battalion had recently joined the Brigade but soon reverted to 1 Burma Brigade.

It is only fair to note here that officers who served with the Burma Rifles do not agree with Brigadier Bourke's views and regard the estimate of twenty desertions each night from Battalions in the Brigade as incorrect. They claim that the strength returns will support them in this and that numbers were fairly well maintained. Whilst agreeing that there were some desertions and that the men were depressed by our lack of success and by the streams of dejected troops of all classes and refugees passing through the covering positions, they also state that morale was still good, that the Brigade was keen to meet the enemy again and that a successful action would have removed any depression.

Certainly, all units were to prove in subsequent actions that there was plenty of fight left in them.

The above-mentioned report together with earlier events in the campaign led the Army Commander to authorise the release from Burma Rifles Battalions of all men considered unreliable. This and the shortage of trained recruits to replace battle casualties required a re-organisation of Battalions. The 3rd Battalion was broken up. The 9th and 10th Battalions were to be wasted out. The 6th Battalion became a Garrison Company of Karens.

It should also be noted that the Shans of the 13th and 14th Battalions Burma Rifles proved most unreliable, deserting in large numbers and often taking with them arms and ammunitions. On occasion officers went with deserters. These Battalions, however, were never actively engaged. They were recently raised Territorial Battalions. The majority of their officers were Shan Sawbwas (Chiefs).

Subsequently when 1 Burma Division had withdrawn to Toungoo the Karens of the 1st Battalion Burma Rifles consisting of a formed rifle company and a portion of Headquarters company were sent to strengthen the Karen Levies operating in their own hill country east of Toungoo. Early in April these Karens fought most gallantly against the very superior Japanese force advancing from Toungoo on Mawchi.

Whilst the Sittang bridge battle was being fought, other enemy forces were feeling their way north along the east bank of the river. They were a few miles south of Donzayit on February 23rd. Two days later they were at Kunzeik. Next day a mixed force of Japanese and Burmans was in Shwegyin from which we had previously withdrawn. The enemy then crossed the river, and on February 27th our patrols encountered a party of about one hundred on the Rangoon-Mandalay road about midway between the towns of Daiku and Pegu. On the same day another force of the enemy was astride the road and railway at Pyinbon, sixteen miles north of Pegu.

The wide gap between 2 Burma Brigade and 17 Division around Pegu was only covered by patrols which could not prevent infiltration by the enemy. Taking full advantage of this state of affairs and moving under cover of darkness Japanese tanks and columns crossed the main road. During the night of March 3rd/4th one such column passed through Daiku. Next morning the road was cut about one mile south of Pyuntaza at the Yenwe Chaung bridge where a patrol of the 1st Battalion Burma Rifles encountered a road block.

A Company of the Battalion succeeded in taking the block and the adjacent railway bridge, but was then forced to retire under heavy fire

CHAPTER 14

from machine-guns and mortars. The enemy force was a mixed one of Japanese and Burmans. Lieutenant Moir was killed and other casualties were twelve missing, believed killed, and eight wounded. Following this engagement during the early hours of March 5th a large body of the enemy with a long column of transport including mules, carts, and elephants, and with light guns passed through Pyuntaza travelling west. Touch between our two Divisions along the main road had now been lost.

The 1st Battalion Burma Rifles sent out patrols to reconnoitre the Japanese positions near Pyuntaza. Great enterprise was shown by Havildar Myaung Kyaw, a Burman, who disguised himself as a villager and thus entered the enemy lines where he helped to dig trenches. Having obtained valuable information, he returned to his Battalion.

Japanese infiltration and the attack from the west compelled our withdrawal from Pegu. The wider enemy encircling movement through the Pegu Yomas resulted in the fall of Rangoon on March 8th. The previous day 1 Burma Division had received orders to attack Shwegyin and Daiku, and to exploit any success southwards with the object of impeding infiltration round the north flank of 17 Division.

The attack was launched on March 11th. 1 Burma Brigade on the right was to secure Pyuntaza and Daiku, whilst 2 Burma Brigade (less one Battalion) took Madauk and Shwegyin. 27 Mountain Regiment I.A., was to support 1 Burma Brigade.

To ensure secrecy all forward movements of troops were made by night, the two Brigades concerned moving forward from Myaunglebin to their starting points for the attack during the hours of darkness on the night of March 10th/11th. By reason of the considerable Fifth Column activity in the district the Divisional Commander ordered that: "Ranks will only be told what they need to know when they need to know it in order to carry out their tasks."

On 1 Burma Brigade front it was intended that the 2nd Battalion 7th Rajput Regiment should take Pyuntaza and the road block south of the town. The 1st and 5th Battalions Burma Rifles were then to pass through to Daiku. The final objective.

The Rajputs moved out of Wingabaw village, where they had arrived earlier that night, at 0400 hours on March 11th. At first light 'C' and 'D' Companies advanced on Pyuntaza across the flat paddy lands. 'D' Company on the left was assisted by a section of carriers. Meanwhile, 'B' Company on the right flank advanced on the road block on the Yenwe Chaung bridge. The Infantry was supported by 2 Mountain Battery from Eywa village, the area south of the road block being shelled.

'C' and 'D' Companies secured Pyuntaza and then continued their advance towards the road block. The attack was now held up by extremely heavy machine-gun, mortar, and shell fire. Lieut.-Colonel A. Rea, commanding the Battalion, decided to throw in his reserve 'A' Company. The left section of the Mountain Battery had moved forward two thousand yards to support the second phase of the attack.

The enemy position round the road block was entered by 'A' Company, but an immediate counter attack by a much superior force compelled the company to fall back in some confusion. Information was received at Advanced Battalion Headquarters that the enemy was advancing round the left flank, and when it became obvious that the attack could not succeed without additional support Lieut.-Colonel Rea ordered the Battalion to withdraw from Pyuntaza.

During this withdrawal the right section of the Mountain Battery was attacked by a party of the enemy making much noise and armed with light machine-guns. At that time the Battery was without infantry protection, a Burmese Platoon of the 5th Battalion Burma Rifles acting as escort to the guns having deserted. There was a certain amount of disorder in the wagon lines but the guns were got away. The Battery casualties were one officer and over forty other ranks missing. Many of these latter appear to have deserted.

The 2nd Battalion 7th Rajput Regiment withdrew through the Battalions of Burma Rifles to concentrate at Tawpathi. The Battalion had suffered heavily, particularly 'B' Company. Its Commander, Captain Machia, was lost. Total casualties were killed eleven, wounded fourteen, and missing seventy-nine.

At the end of the day the line had been established on the Aleywa Chaung and was held by the two Battalions of Burma Rifles. These were in contact with enemy patrols and were not affected by the failure of our attack. Enemy reconnaissance aircraft had been active throughout the day.

The operations carried out by 2 Burma Brigade against Shwegyin and Madauk provided for the crossing of the Sittang river at Waing by the 5th Battalion 1st Punjab Regiment. The Battalion was then to be joined by F.F.3, already on the east bank of the river, for the attack on Shwegyin. The 7th Battalion Burma Rifles would secure Madauk. Both Shwegyin and Madauk were to be bombed by the R.A.F. for a period of half an hour immediately before the attacks were launched.

On March 10th the 7th Battalion Burma Rifles established a bridgehead at Waing, and at 0300 hours next morning the 5th Battalion 1st Punjab Regiment crossed the river on rafts constructed by the Divisional Engineers. The Battalion then marched five miles across rough country

CHAPTER 14

to the Shwegyin-Papun road where it was joined by F.F.3. Turning south the force moved slowly on Shwegyin, halting near the town at Milestone 2 at 0700 hours. It now waited for the bombing of the town. No aircraft appeared and it was decided to proceed with the attack.

The enemy was in position astride the road outside Shwegyin. The 5th Battalion 1st Punjab Regiment attacked with one Company on each side of the road and drove the enemy before it into the town. Here strong resistance was encountered, and two Mortar detachments went into action to support the advance. At the same time Lieut.-Colonel K.D. Marsland, commanding the Battalion, ordered one column of F.F.3 to work round the right flank. The advance soon continued, the Punjabis keeping excellent communication during the street fighting by their cries of "Sat Sri Akal" and "Ya Ali". Finally, the enemy fled across the Shwegyin Chaung at the south end of the town, many being killed in the stream by light machine-gun fire. By 1000 hours the town was free of the enemy of whom forty were captured and at least fifty had been killed. All of these appeared to be Burmans. They were dressed in civilian clothes, and were well armed with light machine-guns, Thompson sub-machine carbines, rifles, and grenades. Our casualties were four killed and seventeen wounded.

Madauk, to the west of Shwegyin, lies on both banks of the Sittang river. That portion of the village on the west bank was occupied by a company of the 7th Battalion Burma Rifles without opposition. It was then found that all boats had been removed to the opposite bank of the river. Major Kyadoe, (a Karen) the Company Commander, swam the river under fire from the enemy, secured a boat, and returned with it. Then, under strong covering fire, two platoons of the Company were ferried across the Sittang and dispersed the enemy on the east bank. Contact with the 5th Battalion 1st Punjab Regiment was established.

2 Burma Brigade now took up a line south of Madauk and the Shwegyin Chaung, and extensive forward patrolling was carried out. Next day 1 Burma Division issued an order that this line and that of the Aleywa Chaung on the west would be consolidated. But the Division was not destined to hold this position for long.

The Chinese V Army was now entering Burma to take the Sittang valley sector. General Alexander was concentrating the Imperial Forces in the Irrawaddy valley where he considered it necessary to have greater strength. This meant the transfer of 1 Burma Division from the Sittang sector as soon as its relief by the Chinese V Army could be arranged.

Although they could have done so, the Chinese were unwilling to take up a line south of Toungoo. It therefore became necessary to give up the extensive area we now held south of that town or, alternatively, to abandon the concentration along the Irrawaddy. This latter, General Alexander felt he could not afford to do. As a result, 1 Burma Division was ordered to fall back towards Toungoo whilst the Chinese V Army moved into position.

The first stage of the withdrawal was to the area Pyu-Bawgata-Myogyaung-Udo and the movement was completed without incident by the evening of March 15th. The front held by the Division was designed to cover the valley from the forest-clad hills of the Pegu Yomas on the west to those of Karenni east of the Sittang. Forward detachments continued to hold the Aleywa-Chaung-Shwegyin line thinly until the afternoon when enemy infiltration compelled their withdrawal.

Brigades were now warned that there would be a further withdrawal to the Toungoo area and thence to Prome where the newly formed Burcorps was to concentrate. 13 Brigade in Karenni would fall back by stages to Toungoo, leaving the Karen Levies to hold the area in front of the Chinese.

The withdrawal along the main road itself was followed up closely by the Japanese, and on March 17th an attack was launched against the 5th Battalion Burma Rifles in the centre of 1 Burma Brigade front. The Battalion was in position astride and to the east of the main road and railway just south of Kyauktaga. The country here is flat paddy land with an occasional village set amid trees.

At 1840 hours on the previous night seven lorries had driven along the main road to within two hundred yards of the Battalion posts. They were engaged by every Bren gun that could be brought to bear. Five lorries were disabled and heavy casualties inflicted. During the night the Japanese attempted to infiltrate through the 2nd Battalion 7th Rajput Regiment on the right of the line. Here were occasional bursts of uncontrolled fire in the dark. Nothing further happened until 0630 hours next morning when there was a brief attack on the right Company of the 5th Battalion Burma Rifles. This died away, but at 1150 hours there began heavy and accurate shelling of the centre company and Battalion Headquarters of the 5th Battalion Burma Rifles located on the southern outskirts of Kyauktaga town. It was estimated that mortars and two Mountain Batteries were employed, and the shelling continued intermittently all day.

About 1500 hours a large mixed force of Japanese and Burmans advanced against the centre forward Company on the sector immediately to the left of the railway, whilst a smaller force of Infantry and Cavalry moved against the left Company. The enemy did not press his attack seriously, but the Centre Company gave ground.

CHAPTER 14

Behind the Centre Company in a village in support, was the Burmese Company of the Battalion. Before this date it had become much depleted in numbers. The Company Commander now found that one of his Platoons had deserted en masse leaving him with only twenty-six men.

At 1700 hours the enemy attack developed again and infiltrated through the Centre Company to within a hundred yards of Battalion Headquarters. On the left the enemy had surrounded the remnants of the Burmese Company. This handful of men fought well and cut its way through the Japanese.

At 1745 hours the Battalion began to withdraw on orders from Brigade Headquarters. The Burmese Company lost two Governor's Commissioned Officers and fourteen other ranks killed, and a considerable number of men throughout the Battalion were missing.

Early next morning, March 18th, 1 Burma Brigade passed through the defensive position behind it taken up by 2 Burma Brigade. This position crossed the main road just south of Gonde, the central sector along the Kun Chaung being held by the 7th Battalion Burma Rifles. On the west the line was continued by the 2nd Battalion Burma Rifles whilst on the east was stationed the 5th Battalion 1st Punjab Regiment.

The last elements of 1 Burma Brigade had withdrawn at 0700 hours. At 1030 hours a Japanese column was observed marching up the main road. It was allowed to approach to within two hundred yards when 'C' Company of the 7th Battalion Burma Rifles opened fire. Our guns and mortars followed suit at once and very heavy casualties were inflicted on the enemy. The remnants of the column took cover in a piece of jungle to the east of the road. They were then shelled intermittently by mortars and artillery.

The enemy endeavoured to work round the east flank of our centre Battalion, and in the afternoon began to shell Gonde village. This was countered by our own guns and mortars which replied on each occasion when hostile artillery and mortar fire was opened. Meanwhile, the attempt of the enemy to advance on the east was met by a counter attack of the 7th Battalion Burma Rifles which maintained all its positions intact.

On the west of the main road the 2nd Battalion Burma Rifles observed two enemy tanks, but these appear to have taken no part in the operations. At 2000 hours the Brigade withdrew, and during this operation the 7th Battalion Burma Rifles was heavily shelled. Casualties were light owing to dispersion.

The units of the Imperial Forces now passed through the advanced posts of the Chinese 200th Division south of Pyu and along the Pyu river where the Chinese Divisional Cavalry were maintaining forward patrols. These were in contact with the enemy on March 19th.

Night marching combined with extensive patrolling and the reconnaissance and preparation of positions by day caused much exhaustion of the troops in 1 Burma Division during its withdrawal. Men fell asleep on their feet, and at halts during night marches it became necessary to keep a proportion of officers and men standing. Scanty hours of rest were often lost through preparation of positions which were soon abandoned. By the time that orders to withdraw had reached Battalions it was sometimes too late to recall distant patrols which were necessary in the absence of mobile troops or motor transport.

On March 20th the Chinese in Toungoo set fire to a large area of the town with the object of preparing a defensive position. The fire threatened the Railway Station and also Rear Headquarters of 1 Burma Division and the Supply Depot. Working parties were sent into the town by the Division and their strenuous efforts averted the danger. Surplus stores were cleared and the move of Divisional Rear Headquarters to Yedashe was expedited.

1 Burma Division withdrew to the area Yedashe-Kyungon preparatory to the move to the Irrawaddy front. This assembly was carried out on March the 21st, and next day units began to entrain for Taungdwingyi. The 5th Battalion Burma Rifles had been detailed to proceed to Prome by march route through the Pegu Yomas. With certain attached units the Battalion marched from Oktwin along the track to Paukkaung on March 22nd. Its orders were to deal with any enemy encountered in the Yomas where F.F.1 was acting as a covering force. F.F.1 had been operating independently for about three weeks and had shown considerable resource in living off the country. Owing to the failure of communications it had not been possible for 1 Burma Division to supply it.

On March 22nd, twenty minutes after the 5th Battalion Burma Rifles left Oktwin, a Japanese attack on the Chinese developed. Two days later whilst 33 Mountain Battery and F.F.3 were still at Kyungon the enemy carried out an outflanking movement round Toungoo and made an attack on the Kyungon landing ground. The Mountain Battery and F.F.3 became involved in the fight and put up a stubborn resistance. Eventually they were extricated and entrained next day for Taungdwingyi.

Meanwhile 1 Burma Division had received a modification of its original order to concentrate in the Prome area. Burcorps altered this to the area Dayindabo-Kyaukpadaung-Allanmyo-Thayetmyo immediately behind 17 Division.

Chapter 15

Entry into Burma of the Chinese Expeditionary Force – Organisation and equipment – Problems of Transport and Supply – Formation of Chinese Liaison Mission – Chinese system of Command – Operations until the end of March 1942.

When war with Japan became probable there was established in Burma the Supply Base to which reference has been made in an earlier chapter. This organisation was intended to maintain British forces in China where it was anticipated that in the event of war we would be in active conflict with the Japanese. Later, the possibility of a Japanese invasion of Burma was visualised and arrangements were then made for assistance to be rendered to us by China. The size of the force to be employed in Burma was somewhat conservatively fixed at one Regiment (227 Regiment of 93rd Division) since it was estimated that larger numbers could not be rationed by us in the Kengtung area where it was intended to employ these troops. Rations consisting mainly of rice were to be provided by Burma. The Chinese were always ready and willing to send a much larger force into Burma for its defence.

93rd Division was in Puerh in China and formed part of the Chinese VI Army which also included 49th and 55th Divisions. The Army was commanded by Lieut.-General Kan Li Chu. After the outbreak of war with Japan 227 Regiment moved direct into Kengtung from Puerh to take over the defence of the Mekong river sector, east of the Kengtung-Chiang Rai road. Regimental Headquarters was established at Mongyawng on January 1st 1942. After this date the Regiment was engaged with the enemy in patrol encounters on the frontier.

At that time 49th and 55th Divisions were stationed near Paoshan, but by January 14th, 49th Division was approaching Wanting to be held in reserve. Wanting was the Chinese frontier town on the Burma Road.

The Chinese anticipated that additional forces would be required to assist in the defence of Burma. They were anxious to render substantial aid, particularly in view of the importance to themselves of Rangoon and the Burma Road.

About December 23rd 1941 General Wavell who was then paying a visit to Rangoon had flown to Chungking to interview the Generalissimo. The latter was asked to allow the A.V.G. to continue in the defence of Rangoon and also to release some of the lease/lend equipment then in Rangoon for the use of the Burma Army. Although not then agreeing to the latter request the Generalissimo did so later. He did, however, offer both the V and VI Chinese Armies for the defence of Burma. In view of the subsequent allegations that this offer was refused it is desirable to state that the arrangements then made were as follows:

Of the VI Army the 93rd Division was accepted as a whole, and the 49th Division was to be moved close to the Burma Frontier at Wanting. The 55th Division was scattered and not as well organised as the others and was then to be left where it was.

The V Army was concentrating round Kunming and General Wavell asked that it should be retained in reserve in that area. Lieut.-General Hutton was informed of these arrangements.

When Lieut.-General Hutton assumed command of the Burma Army at the end of December 1941 it was laid down in his Directive that no additional Chinese troops beyond 93rd Division were to be brought into Burma without reference to the South West Pacific Command (Abdacom). In mid-January 1942 Lieut.-General Hutton visited Kengtung and examined the possibility of moving the remainder of 93rd Division into the Kengtung area. A few days later, on January 19th, when it was evident that the Japanese attack on Burma was developing in Tenasserim the move was ordered. This was done to release for service further south a portion of our own force then in the Shan States. Two days later General Wavell's permission to the entry of 49th Division was obtained. It was decided that this Division should enter Burma through Lashio and take over the sector east of the Salween about Takaw. At the same time 55th Division was to move to Wanting where it would remain in reserve and complete its training and equipment. This Division was weak in numbers and only partially trained. From now onwards Lashio formed the point of entry of all Chinese troops, and an ordnance dump was established there.

The Chinese were given their own area of operations. The Generalissimo, very wisely, had insisted on this and that his troops were not to be mixed with the British. As the Chinese took over the sectors

CHAPTER 15

in the Shan States the two Brigades of 1 Burma Division stationed there withdrew. At first it had been the intention of Lieut.-General Hutton to employ these Brigades in Karenni and south of Toungoo on the line of the Sittang. The Chinese then expressed their desire to place their V Army in Burma. This would enable the British to concentrate for the defence of Rangoon, and on January 31st Lieut.-General Hutton sent a personal telegram to General Wavell seeking his permission to make arrangements for the bringing of the Chinese V Army to Lashio. Here it would be readily available either for the defence of Burma or for offensive operations against Thailand.

Lieut.-General Hutton flew to Lashio on February 2nd to meet the Generalissimo. Unfortunately, his aircraft crashed at night on the way, and the G.O.C. did not escape without injury. However, next day he was able to confer with the Generalissimo then on his way to India. A most satisfactory discussion ensued when the Generalissimo accepted all proposals placed before him and in particular agreed to take over the Toungoo front with his V Army, then in readiness to enter Burma. This Army, commanded by General Tu Yu Ming, consisted of 22nd, 96th and 200th Divisions. These three Divisions were all partly mechanised. This Army had a number of lorries for the transport of personnel, some guns of the 105 mm howitzer type, anti-tank guns, some tanks of various kinds, a few old armoured cars, and about one hundred motor cycle combinations. It also had a small cavalry force. It was one of the best equipped and was regarded as one of the finest fighting formations in China.

The Generalissimo made it very clear that the whole of the Chinese forces in Burma would be entirely under General Hutton's command, and that any difficulties that might arise in this respect were to be reported to him personally.

On the same day the Chinese Minister for War issued orders for the move into Burma of the 49th and 55th Divisions of VI Army. Although agreed upon, these moves had not yet been carried out. The order of the Minister of War stated that 'H.Q. VI Army after moving into Burma will come under orders of G.O.C. Burma'. This was confirmed in the most definite manner by the Generalissimo, and it was only after the change in command in Burma that difficulties arose in this respect.

A few days later it was arranged that the VI Army should also take over the Karenni front and thus free the whole of 1 Burma Division for operations south of Toungoo. The 55th Division, originally intended to be in reserve at Loilem, was now to proceed to the Karenni sector. The two stronger Divisions of the Army would cover the routes from

Thailand through Kengtung and Mongpan respectively. These were regarded as the danger points. The Mongpan area was assigned to 49th Division, whilst 93rd Division held the left of the line covering the road Chiang Rai-Tachilek-Kengtung and the Mekong river front. The G.O.C. VI Army was reluctant to accept responsibility for Karenni. This extension of his front greatly dispersed his force and he decided to hold Karenni with one Regiment of 55th Division retaining the other two Regiments in Army Reserve.

It was not until the end of February that V Army began its advance into Burma. This had been delayed by the movement of the last elements of VI Army and the fact that a force entering Burma by Lashio could only proceed along the Burma Road, the capacity of which was limited. It had been estimated that the concentration of V Army at Wanting would take a minimum of twenty days. Consequently, when Rangoon fell early in March, only 200th Division of V Army had arrived in the country.

The position at that time was that the Chinese forces had taken over all sectors in the Shan States, were taking over in Karenni, and had also agreed to take over the Sittang valley sectors about Toungoo. On the Shan States and Karenni fronts the months of February and March passed with little incident, and in consequence the relief of the British was completed without interference by the enemy. There were occasional patrol encounters and engagements along the frontier and in one of them in mid-March, south of Mongtun, the Chinese inflicted one hundred casualties on Thai troops. At the end of the same month two companies attacked a mixed Japanese and Thai force of three hundred at Wan-Maklang on the frontier north-east of Chiang Rai. Heavy casualties were inflicted on the enemy and a mortar and heavy machine-guns were captured. The Chinese only had five casualties.

It is now necessary to digress and to consider briefly the organisation of the Chinese Armies, their system of command, and some of the difficulties involved in their co-operation with the British.

A Chinese Division was organised on the basis of three Regiments each consisting of three Battalions. The normal Regimental strength was about eighteen hundred, although there were considerable variations from this. For instance, 227 Regiment had been specially strengthened and when it entered Burma numbered two thousand five hundred. Divisional troops were approximately equal in strength to another Regiment. Rifles were only about two thousand five hundred to a Division, and there were also two hundred light machine-guns, thirty-six heavy machine-guns, and twelve mortars. These figures again must be taken as only approximate. Artillery was almost non-existent, the

CHAPTER 15

Divisions of VI Army possessing an average of six anti-tank guns and nothing else. Telephone equipment was fairly adequate but there were only about four wireless sets to a Division. There was practically no motor transport, each Division having only a staff car and a few trucks. It also had about two hundred mules. As has already been mentioned the equipment of V Army was on a somewhat higher scale which was exceptional.

The fire power of a Chinese Division was equivalent approximately to that of a British Brigade, and it will have been noted that the majority of the personnel were not armed with rifles. The surplus men were employed as carriers, for digging, and other duties. All were trained and were available to replace casualties.

Organised for warfare under conditions prevailing in China the Armies had no supply or administrative services. Matters of rationing and transport were regarded as the duty of the civil authorities of districts in which armies operated, and in China these authorities were always expected to make the necessary arrangements. Armies lived on the country and had at their disposal all its resources. Their officers had never studied the problems of railway transport and had no conception of timed or balanced railway running. They considered that as much rolling stock as possible should be produced and held indefinitely in readiness to be filled up as and when troops arrived. In China even quite junior commanders were accustomed to requisition trains and supplies by force.

In the absence of transport and administrative services the British, despite their own inadequate resources, were compelled to improvise an organisation. The work was shouldered by the staff of the newly created Chinese Liaison Mission which had not been intended for this purpose but for normal liaison between the two Allied forces. An officer of the Liaison Staff was attached to each Army, Division, and Regiment. There were also civil liaison representatives of the Burma Government. A special staff was maintained at Lashio.

The fact that the British Liaison Officers were largely employed on administrative duties, unavoidably thrust upon them, did little good to British prestige. The Chinese Commanders, except the best of them, made no secret of the fact that they regarded Administration as unworthy of the consideration of the fighting soldier.

The task of maintaining the Chinese troops in the field was no small one. The collection and distribution of rations in the Shan States area alone absorbed no less than three hundred lorries. The fact that the British eventually were able to move into Burma, feed, and maintain an army of some ninety-five thousand Chinese without the help of any regular administrative units at all was a remarkable example of successful improvisation. It was only rendered possible by the enormous quantity of indigenous foodstuffs available in the country.

It had been recommended by Lieut.-General Hutton that the Chief Liaison Officer should be Major General L.E. Dennys, M.C., then Military Attaché at Chungking. He was well known to and popular with the Chinese. The appointment was not made at once and subsequently his untimely death in an air accident was a serious blow to the cause of co-operation. He had taken a large part in making the earlier arrangements for the entry into Burma of the Chinese forces. His place was taken by Brigadier J.C. Martin, C.B.E., M.C.

The language difficulty could not be entirely overcome. Most British liaison officers could not speak Chinese, whilst many of the Chinese interpreters were young students who upon occasion caused much trouble. The position concerning the Burmese language was even worse, and the Chinese were often faced with an almost insoluble problem in dealing with the local people. Since they regarded the Burmese as definitely hostile this was peculiarly unfortunate.

Medical services were wholly inadequate. Medical officers were very few, and Battalions only had medical orderlies and field dressings. Drugs were very scarce. A number of British medical units which could ill be spared were placed at the service of the Chinese. There was in fact no possible alternative. Sterling service, too, was rendered by Dr. Seagrave of the Harper Memorial Medical unit, which had been asked by General Hutton to undertake this service with the Chinese. This was an American Missionary organisation and comprised a mobile unit with some half dozen doctors, including a lady, and about forty Karen nurses.

The Chinese system of command was unsatisfactory. It had been definitely laid down that the VI Army was to come under the command of General Hutton. When V Army arrived its commander, General Tu, was officially described as Acting Commander-in-Chief of the Chinese Expeditionary Force. He was regarded by General Alexander, then commanding the British, as subordinate to himself. On March 14th General J. Stilwell, of the United States Army, arrived in Burma in independent command of the Chinese force. General Stilwell had no signal communications and an inadequate staff entirely without the local knowledge necessary for the assumption of command.

Shortly afterwards, when General Alexander went to Chungking to pay his respects to the Generalissimo and to acquaint him with the

CHAPTER 15

military situation in Burma, the question of command was raised. The Generalissimo expressed his wish for unity of command and asked General Alexander to accept command of all his troops in Burma. General Stilwell readily agreed to serve under General Alexander and he and his staff of American officers rendered very loyal co-operation throughout the campaign.

Associated with General Stilwell was General Lo Cho Ying, designated as Commander-in-Chief of the Chinese Expeditionary Force. Orders issued by General Stilwell had to go out over the signature of General Lo.

There was also in Lashio the Chinese Mission headed by General Lin Wei, the personal representative of the Generalissimo. He defined his duties merely as those of observing and reporting. Disclaiming any title as a commander he exerted considerable influence. He had a forward liaison staff with British Army Headquarters at Maymyo, the senior Chinese liaison officer here being General Fisher T. Ho.

The Army Commanders exhibited considerable independence, and no orders of a major nature issued by Generals Alexander, Lo, or Stilwell could be carried out unless they had the sanction of the Generalissimo which was conveyed through General Lin's Mission. Such an arrangement was obviously quite unsuitable for modern war. Furthermore, the Chinese insisted on the direct issue of orders by a Commander himself. An order had to be given personally or signed by a Commander; the system of acting through a staff officer was not understood. Quick decisions for the employment of the Chinese forces were therefore well-nigh impossible to obtain. All this, together with the almost total lack of knowledge of staff duties amongst Chinese officers, lack of transport, and failure to make the best use of the railways and ill-treatment of the railway staff resulting in the desertion of subordinates, caused considerable delay in the execution of vital movements.

This delay was very marked in the deployment of V Army. On the fall of Rangoon, the early concentration of the weakened British force in the Irrawaddy valley became of great importance, but by mid-March only 200th Division was at Toungoo. It was the sole Chinese Division then available for the defence of the Sittang valley sector. Further, on his arrival in Burma, General Stilwell brought news that the advance of the army had been stopped on the orders of the Generalissimo, who at this time seemed anxious to concentrate his troops about Mandalay. General Stilwell himself ordered certain moves to take place and at once communicated with the Generalissimo. However, valuable time had been lost.

The Chinese were not prepared to stand on a line south of Toungoo although the taking up of a defensive position about the town itself had obvious disadvantages. It meant giving up considerable ground, and also that the airfield just north of Toungoo at Kyungon could not be employed. In addition, it endangered the Toungoo-Mawchi-Bawlake road, which, if uncovered, gave the enemy a good and direct line of approach to Karenni and the Shan States.

On March 19th, when the troops of 1 Burma Division passed through the cavalry screen of 200th Division about Pyu, 22nd Division was no further forward than Lashio whilst 96th Division was still in China. On that day Chinese cavalry were in action against the enemy in the vicinity of Pyu. The Japanese had followed fast on the heels of 1 Burma Division and an attack was launched on the Chinese by a party estimated to be four hundred and fifty strong. It was supported by armoured cars. The Chinese inflicted casualties and destroyed three of the armoured cars. Next day there was a further engagement when a force of six hundred Japanese crossed the Pyu river north of the town. Here the Chinese cavalry supported by an infantry company killed two hundred of the enemy at a loss of thirty to themselves. Later in the day the Japanese were reinforced and brought up some artillery.

Meanwhile the main body of 200th Division had been engaged in placing the area of Toungoo in a state of defence, and now the forward troops fell back. On March 21st and 22nd the Japanese 55th Division was in contact with the Chinese advanced positions about Oktwin, and began an attack on Toungoo. Two days later, when some units of 1 Burma Division were still at Kyungon pending their transfer by rail to the Irrawaddy front, the Japanese carried out an outflanking movement from the west and launched a surprise attack on the landing ground. 200th Division was now cut off in Toungoo. The leading Regiment of 22nd Division was then arriving at Pyinmana whilst its rear formation was in Lashio. 96th Division was approaching the Burma Frontier.

The force in Toungoo held on stubbornly, but the position was serious. Consequently, it was proposed to move across to the Toungoo sector two Regiments (less one Battalion) of the Chinese 55th Division from Karenni. Actually, only one Regiment (3 Regiment) was so transferred and was then retained in Thazi. This of course further weakened 55th Division in the Karenni area.

To relieve the situation in Toungoo, 22nd Division on March 28th attacked south from Yedashe. Advancing through jungle it encountered strong Japanese opposition, and although heavy casualties were inflicted on the enemy little progress was made. In Toungoo itself there was bitter fighting. The Japanese broke into the town from the

CHAPTER 15

north-west and the opposing forces fought hand to hand in the streets. An attack on General Tai's Headquarters was beaten off.

Unfortunately, the Chinese accounts of all operations undertaken by them in Burma are very meagre. Hence it is not possible to detail the gallant defence of Toungoo, nor to give full particulars of any subsequent actions fought by the Chinese.

A railway accident north of Pyinmana delayed the concentration of 96th Division whilst the Japanese round Toungoo were reinforced. Their aircraft subjected the Chinese positions to heavy bombing attacks, and to these there could be little reply. Fighter support was given to the Chinese by six Tomahawk aircraft of the A.V.G., the only force available. The recent heavy air attacks by the enemy on the Magwe airfield had destroyed the greater part of our air force in Burma. This was particularly unfortunate since the Chinese expected in Burma a reversal of the conditions prevailing in China where Japanese aircraft enjoyed complete mastery.

The Japanese at Kyungon had pushed north, and as there was now no prospect of relieving 200th Division it fought its way out of Toungoo on March 29th. Next day it established contact with 22nd Division which by a surprise attack from the west retook the Kyungon landing ground. 200th Division passed into reserve at Yezin, north of Pyinmana, whilst the line was re-established by 22nd Division south of Yedashe. The Chinese estimated their own casualties at three thousand, but the Japanese had not escaped lightly in the heavy fighting.

Before retiring from Toungoo the Chinese did not destroy the important bridge across the Sittang. Its demolition would have delayed an enemy advance on Mawchi and Bawlake.

There was a Chinese detachment at Mawchi. Between this place and Toungoo there were only some Karen Levies strengthened by the Karen personnel of the 1st Battalion the Burma Rifles. The Japanese at once began an advance on Mawchi.

On the road west of that town were some favourable defensive positions, but General Liang, Vice Commander 55th Division and commanding troops in Karenni, refused to move beyond Mawchi. His reasons were that Mawchi was his western boundary, and that he could not move into V Army area without instructions; furthermore, that his force was too small to hold both the Mawchi and Salween fronts. He maintained that an enemy advance across the Salween would cut off his force and leave open behind him the road to the Shan States.

Events in Toungoo, and subsequently in Karenni, were only second in importance in their effect on the course of the campaign to those on the River Sittang. There is no doubt that we could have maintained our hold on the area south of Toungoo at least as far as Pyu, and that the Chinese could have relieved us in force there. But for the Generalissimo's desire to concentrate round Mandalay, sufficient troops could have been moved up to ensure the retention of Toungoo. As long as Toungoo was held Karenni was in little danger since the approaches to it from the south or from Thailand across the Salween were very difficult.

However, with the loss of Toungoo, and with it the important bridge across the Sittang, Karenni was open to attack either from Mawchi or by a track leading north-east across the hills. The withdrawal of troops of the 55th Division from Karenni to Thazi when Toungoo was threatened was thoroughly unsound. It probably contributed substantially to the subsequent disaster on the Karenni front.

But for the decision of the Chinese not to stand on a line south of Toungoo vast quantities of rice available in the Sittang valley would have been removed. Their loss, like the loss of much of the rice in the Irrawaddy valley from the area below Prome, prejudiced the supply position of the Chinese Armies.

The Order of Battle and dispositions of the Chinese Expeditionary Force in Burma at the end of March 1942, together with later additions to the Force, will be found in Appendix D.

Chapter 16

The situation at Prome – Decision to evacuate the town – Dispositions of 17 Division in the area – Japanese attack on Prome on April 1st, 1942 – Our Withdrawal – Actions at Ainggyaungon and Hmawza – March to Dayindabo – Plan for the defence of the oilfields – Withdrawal of Burcorps to line Minhla-Taungdwingyi.

Following upon the action at Shwedaung and the loss of Toungoo by the Chinese V Army on March 29th it was felt that our continued occupation of Prome must be attended by considerable danger, and it was reported by the Corps Commander that the morale of the troops, following the recent actions, left a great deal to be desired. At the same time, it was very necessary that the large dumps of petrol, ammunition, and supplies that were in the town should be evacuated. On March 29th Army Headquarters informed Burcorps that it was essential to the continuance of operations in Burma that no stores should be abandoned in Prome.

Yet the back-loading of these stores was a matter of much difficulty. After the devastating attack on the Magwe airfield enemy aircraft made frequent raids on our road and river traffic between Prome and Allanmyo. Despite possible danger from Fifth Column activities and infiltration by the enemy we were forced into running night convoys on the road. This could not be done on the river which was abnormally low, thus making night navigation dangerous. Prome itself was bombed by Japanese aircraft and almost completely destroyed by fire.

Prome town was not easy to defend. It straggled for more than two miles along the east bank of the Irrawaddy and its outskirts were surrounded by dense scrub jungle. Particularly on the south it was dominated by similarly overgrown hill features. There were, however, certain areas which could have been defended in strength by concentrated Battalions, and from which vigorous action could have been taken against enemy forces by-passing them. The main road to Allanmyo left the town towards its southern extremity and ran nearly due east for over three miles before turning north. From the northern end of the town a subsidiary unmetalled road traversed jungle and reserved forest to join the main road at Dayindabo, seventeen miles distant from Prome.

A boom had been put across the Irrawaddy below Prome. This prevented any direct approach by river, but of course did not hinder the enemy from crossing the Irrawaddy from the west bank above the town.

On April 1st Generals Wavell and Alexander were at Burcorps Headquarters at Allanmyo where a conference took place that afternoon. General Wavell agreed that, in view of the difficulties of the country and the fatigue of the troops in 17 Division, consequent on the local offensive ending with the operations at Shwedaung, a withdrawal from Prome to the Allanmyo area should begin forthwith. This withdrawal might have to be continued even further north where the country was more open and more suitable for the operations of tanks.

A warning order was at once sent to 17 Division stating that a decision had been taken to regroup Burcorps in the general area Allanmyo-Kyaukpadaung-Bwetkyi Chaung-Thayetmyo. All possible stocks were to be back-loaded at once. When this order was received our force was in touch with the enemy immediately south of Prome.

After the striking force had disengaged itself at Shwedaung the Japanese took no immediate steps to follow up in strength, although small parties advanced towards Prome and Sinmizwe. Patrols were active and occasionally fired on our forward positions. On the west bank of the river the Japanese were opposite Prome on the night of March 30th/31st. The duty of preventing any advance in strength up the west bank of the Irrawaddy had now developed on 2 Burma Brigade of 1 Burma Division. The 2nd Battalion Burma Rifles with a Garrison Company was stationed at Thayetmyo with orders to patrol to the south.

On the morning of March 31st, an infantry gun from the west bank shelled the vessels of the Royal Marine Patrol off Prome. The patrol moved up river out of range, and our artillery silenced the enemy gun.

On April 1st our tank patrols south-east of Hmawza were in contact with small parties of the enemy, and some of these were successfully engaged by our artillery.

Prome itself was held by 63 Brigade now commanded by Brigadier A.E. Barlow, M.C. The river bank and the southern approaches to the

CHAPTER 16

town were protected by the 5th Battalion 17th Dogra Regiment. This Battalion was responsible for the defence of a block erected across the main road from Shwedaung. On the left the 1st Battalion 10th Gurkha Rifles continued the eastern defences up to and inclusive of the railway. The 1st Battalion 11th Sikh Regiment then held the line from a point north of the railway to the river north of Prome. The 2nd Battalion 13th Frontier Force Rifles was in Brigade reserve in the town itself. There was also available a force of some four hundred of the Rangoon Battalion, Burma Military Police, under Major H. Chappell. This Battalion was disposed in platoon posts guarding the foreshore, dumps, and 63 Brigade Headquarters in a building on the river bank. The remaining men were in defensive positions round the Police Lines in the north-east quarter of the town. 1 Field battery of 1 Indian Field Regiment and one section of 12 Mountain Battery were also stationed in Prome.

In the light of after events it is doubtful if the dispositions of 63 Brigade were the most effective that could have been made. The southern sector held by the 5th Battalion 17th Dogra Regiment was overlooked by the scrub-covered hill features already mentioned, whilst the area immediately behind the Battalion was closely built up. Consequently, any enemy infiltration at this point would increase enormously the task of the defence and open the town itself to an attacking force.

The area to the east of Prome, roughly on the line of the road to Paungdale, was held by 16 Brigade now comprising the 2nd Battalion Duke of Wellington's Regiment, the 1st Royal Battalion 9th Jat Regiment, the 7th Battalion 10th Baluch Regiment, and the 4th Battalion 12th Frontier Force Regiment. With 16 Brigade was 15 Mountain Battery.

The 1st Royal Battalion 9th Jat Regiment linked up on its right with the 1st Battalion 11th Sikh Regiment on the eastern perimeter of Prome. The line was continued to the east by the 7th Battalion 10th Baluch Regiment, and the 4th Battalion 12th Frontier Force Regiment. The 2nd Battalion Duke of Wellington's Regiment was in the area of Divisional Headquarters at the village of Nattalin. On the night of April 1st/2nd the 1st Battalion the Gloucestershire Regiment took up a position on the left of the 7th Battalion 10th Baluch Regiment.

To the left and somewhat forward of 16 Brigade was placed 48 Brigade about Hmawza. This Brigade now under command of Brigadier R.T. Cameron held the area demarcated by the ruined walls of the ancient city that once occupied the site. Here, on the extreme left, the 1st Battalion 4th P.W.O. Gurkha Rifles faced east astride the Prome-Paungdale road. On its right, facing south, was the combined Battalion 7th Gurkha Rifles; whilst further to the right the line was held by the 2nd Battalion 5th Royal Gurkha Rifles, F.F. The 1st Battalion Royal Inniskilling Fusiliers was in reserve, but left the area on the night of April 1st to join 1 Burma Division. 2 Field Battery of 1 Indian Regiment was in the Brigade area. The very weak 1st Battalion 3rd Q.A.O. Gurkha Rifles, just reformed, was not with the Brigade, but at Divisional Headquarters.

At Tamagauk, not far from Divisional Headquarters, was 7 Armoured Brigade with the 1st Battalion West Yorkshire Regiment, were maintaining patrols to the south-east of our front towards Sinmizwe, and also towards Wettigan. Near Paungdale we had a small force of infantry with the F.F.

A full Order of Battle for the Army in Burma as on April 1st 1942 set out in Appendix E gives further particulars of the units then with 17 Division.

On the evening of April 1st, before dusk, the enemy began to close in on Prome. Troops were brought up the main road in motor transport from the direction of Shwedaung, and an attack on the road block began at about 1900 hours. This soon developed into a general attack along the whole of the southern front held by the 5th Battalion 17th Dogra Regiment.

Further to the east where the line was held by 16 Brigade there was some firing. Our mortars shelled areas where the enemy had been observed at dusk, but here no attempt was made to advance against our positions.

Our artillery in Prome fired on the attacking Japanese infantry and on enemy transport. In some cases, the targets were so close to the Observation Post that it was impossible to observe fire by moonlight. The mortars of the 1st Battalion 10th Gurkha Rifles also engaged the enemy on the south of the town.

The first attack was held except in the road block area where parties of the enemy overran the block and infiltrated round the right flank near the river. By 2100 hours these had penetrated as far as Battalion Headquarters of the Dogra Regiment. 'C' Company of the 2nd Battalion 13th Frontier Force Rifles was sent forward to counter-attack. This movement, however, could make no headway owing to the impossibility of maintaining any cohesion amongst the streets and buildings in rear of the position originally held by the Dogra Regiment.

Infiltration into the town through the gap in our defences continued. Brigade Headquarters and our guns were threatened, at about midnight 12 Mountain Battery and 2 Field Battery of 1 Indian Field Regiment were ordered to withdraw from the town. The guns were got away very

CHAPTER 16

shortly before the enemy occupied their recent positions. Later, after the withdrawal of 63 Brigade, 2 Field Battery shelled the enemy in Prome from positions north-east of it.

Another attack developed at 2200 hours on the north-eastern sector held by the 1st Battalion 11th Sikh Regiment. The enemy here would appear to have crossed the river from the west bank of the Irrawaddy north of Prome. Battalion Headquarters was subjected to accurate machine-gun and mortar fire. The Japanese knowledge of our positions in this area indicated that these had been disclosed to them by Burmans.

The Battalion held its fire and waited for the enemy to advance. At one period the Japanese came up to the wire in front of our positions, but did not press home their attack and eventually withdrew.

No casualties were suffered by the Battalion, but 70 Field Company I.E. in the Battalion area were less fortunate. Several men and mules were hit by mortar fire.

Meanwhile in the south of Prome the situation had deteriorated, and efforts to restore it failed. The 5th Battalion 17th Dogra Regiment had fallen back towards the east. The area previously occupied by it was now in the hands of the Japanese who were working north along the river bank and through the centre of the town.

Brigadier Barlow, consequently decided to withdraw from Prome and to take up a position generally along the line of the road and railway on the east side of the town and in the area of 16 Brigade. This movement began at about 0100 hours on April 2nd.

It is not known what casualties the 5th Battalion 17th Dogra Regiment suffered, but the other Battalions of the brigade had not been heavily engaged and their total casualties appear to have been one other rank wounded.

The order to withdraw did not reach two platoons of the Burma Military Police at the north end of the foreshore, nor Major Chappell and his party in the Police Lines. The two platoons on the river bank were overrun by the enemy during the night, but the majority of the them fought their way north and rejoined our forces later. The party in the Police Lines remained in position until first light. Then, finding the town in enemy hands and all our other troops withdrawn, this body of men retired through the eastern outskirts of the town and went north, making contact with our main body some three hours later.

After the withdrawal of 63 Brigade the passage of troops and transport through Prome to the north had been observed by the Burma Military Police. This movement had not been interfered with as at that time it was believed that both troops and transport were our own. Later Major Chappell realised that this must have been a Japanese force. On re-joining 17 Division on the morning of April 2nd he at once reported this fact.

The Japanese column was thought to be heading for the unmetalled road to Dayindabo as the left prong of a pincer movement intended to encircle our forces around Prome. The Japanese troops comprising the right flank of the enemy advance were in action very early on April 2nd about Hmawza and at Ainggyaungon about six miles to the east.

The latter-named village was on the road from Sinmizwe to Paungdale where two troops of the 2nd Battalion Royal Tank Regiment with one company of the 1st Battalion 4th P.W.O. Gurkha Rifles had been posted to watch our left flank. Here, too, was F.F.2 at a strength of about one hundred and fifty.

On the night of April 1st/2nd the tanks were in Paungdale, but the remainder of our small flank-guard was in positions facing south-west astride the road near Ainggyaungon. At about 0300 hours an enemy column in very close formation approached from Sinmizwe. When it was one hundred yards away fire was opened on it and continued for some minutes. The Japanese were thrown into great confusion and must have suffered heavily.

Later, when the enemy began to mortar the flank-guard positions, our troops withdrew. At first light patrols observed seventy or eighty bullock carts being employed in the area of the action to evacuate enemy dead and wounded.

The Japanese advance against 48 Brigade in the Hmawza positions opened with a somewhat similar incident. A column came down the road from Paungdale. It was clearly visible in the bright moonlight. The troops were in packed together, talking and singing. The column was allowed to approach to a range of fifty yards before the 1st Battalion 4th P.W.O. Gurkha Rifles engaged it with all weapons. Here too, the close-range fire was devastating in effect. Machine-guns were employed in a swinging traverse as the enemy scattered into the stubble-covered paddy fields. The Gurkhas in the forward defence lines then worked outwards and bombed parties of men taking cover in ditches and behind bushes.

This incident occurred at 0030 hours. Half an hour later enemy infantry guns and mortars came into action, but their fire was generally wild. Their shells also proved ineffective and did little damage. The Battalion suffered very few casualties.

CHAPTER 16

The Battalion of the 7th Gurkha Rifles on the right of the position was also under shell fire but the enemy made no attempt to advance.

At about 0300 hours, following the withdrawal of 63 Brigade from Prome, 48 Brigade was ordered to break contact with the enemy and to withdraw to a position south of Tamagauk to cover the main road. The enemy did not immediately follow up this movement.

At this time the Divisional Commander considered it possible that the Japanese having broken into Prome would swing right on to our position to the east, and his dispositions were accordingly made to prevent an enveloping attack of this nature. Hence the general withdrawal towards Tamagauk. The possibility of a counter-attack by our own forces to regain Prome was not ruled out, but the launching of such an attack could not be carried out before the evening.

The initial stage of the withdrawal was covered by 7 Armoured Brigade and 16 Brigade, and through these there began to pass before first light the elements of 63 Brigade and 48 Brigade.

At about 0630 hours 16 Brigade also began to withdraw. The order to retire was not communicated to the 4th Battalion 12th Frontier Force Regiment until 1000 hours – this Battalion was in position north of the Hmawze ruins and had been under mortar fire for a couple of hours.

A defensive position was taken up south of the bridge across the Nawin Chanug. The line west of and astride the road was held by 48 Brigade and was continued further east by the 1st Royal Battalion 9th Jat Regiment. Three miles east of Tamagauk on the road to Wettigan was the 2nd Battalion Royal Tank Regiment with attached troops. It patrolled eastward from this point and our tanks were in contact with a column of Japanese cavalry.

On the east there was considerable enemy activity. This sector of the Nawin Chaung position was shelled. The enemy did not, however, at once attempt to follow up our troops along the main road. Later he began to shell the road, but no further action developed.

It was at about 1000 hours that Major-General Cowan received Major Chappell's report that a strong enemy column had moved north through Prome during the previous night. If this column was marching on Dayindabo with the object of cutting off 17 Division the position was a serious one.

The main road along which the Division must fall back on Allanmyo passed through some fifteen miles of reserved forest, ideal terrain for Japanese road block tactics. Caught between a block and a strong force following up behind it 17 Division might well have been destroyed. This would have left 1 Burma Division, then comprising two weak

Brigades and with practically no artillery, between the Japanese and the oilfields. These latter were not yet ready for destruction.

The Divisional Commander considered that it would be unwise to risk everything on a major battle when the Japanese were between his own force and 1 Burma Division, and that an immediate further withdrawal should take place. Lieut.-General Slim was consulted by wireless. An instant decision was necessary, and Lieut.-General Slim agreed that the proper course was for 17 Division to march at once for Dayindabo.

The hurried withdraw of 17 Division inevitable caused some confusion, but by 1130 hours the whole force was marching north with the object of harbouring round Dayindabo that night.

63 Brigade led, 16 Brigade marched on the east of the road, 49 Brigade on its west. The road itself was close picquetted to prevent the establishment of road blocks. On squadron of the 2nd Battalion Royal Tank Regiment acted as rearguard, whilst the remining tanks of the Battalion were interspersed between guns and vehicles and moved continuously up and down the road. On their northward journeys they ferried infantry.

April in Burma is the hottest month of the year, and 17 Division was now entering the most arid region of the country. The heat was intense, the route was dusty, and the march was a severe trial to the troops. Many men began the march exhausted and had had no water since the previous evening. Some Battalions were very short of water bottles, and north of Tamagauk was a stretch of waterless country where the road traversed teak-covered forest lands. In certain units, but by no means all, march discipline was not well maintained. The infrequent water-holes that were encountered on the line of march were surrounded by numerous stragglers who persisted in drinking from what were probably contaminated sources. Cholera was prevalent in the Prome area, having been spread by the numerous Indian refugees passing through on the way to India.

There was no air support, and towards evening bombing aircraft attacked our long column of troops. Considerable casualties were caused.

That night 17 Division was in the Dayindabo area. Contact with the enemy had been broken, and no attempt was now made by the Japanese to engage our forces. The Japanese column that had advanced through Prome the previous night had certainly not struck for Dayindabo.

The concentration of 1 Burma Division was still not entirely complete although it was accomplished very shortly afterwards. By the evening of April 2nd 1 Burma Brigade which, less the 5th Battalion Burma

CHAPTER 16

Rifles, had been in Shwebandaw was in position at Dayindabo and to the north of it. Next day 17 Division passed through this Brigade and marched on to the area of Allanmyo-Ywataung-Kyaukaadaung. It was again heavily attacked from the air on the line of march.

An Operation Instruction outlining the plan of further operations was issued by Burcorps on April 3rd. The intention was to deny to the enemy the main oilfields of Yenangyaung and Chauk, to cover Upper Burma, and to maintain touch with the Chinese V Army on the east.

Delaying positions were to be taken up on the Bwetkyi Chaung south of Allanmyo, on the Linban Chaung south of Sinbaungwe, and on the line Minhla-Taungdwingyi. The Corps would fight on the line of the Yin Chaung south of Magwe.

The defence of the river sector was entrusted to 1 Burma Division which would retain a Brigade group on the west bank of the Irrawaddy. 2 Burma Brigade already at Thayetmyo continued to carry out this role.

The defence of the Bwetkyi Chaung line was to be undertaken by 1 Burma Division; and the pause here was to be sufficient to cover the demolition of the small oilfields in the Thayetmyo area, and to allow for the backloading of stores and the resting of our troops. The successful evacuation of stores was now vital since our premature withdrawal from Prome had resulted in the loss of a substantial quantity of supplies.

17 Division would then hold the Linban Chaung whilst 1 Burma Division passed through it.

At Allanmyo the road turned north-east to Taungdwingyi away from the Irrawaddy. From Taungdwingyi it swung westward to rejoin the river at Magwe. It was necessary, therefore, for the Brigade of 1 Burma Division covering the east bank of the river to withdraw north to Migyaunge on a pack basis, whilst all wheeled transport of the Division together with the remaining Brigade made the long detour through Taungdwingyi. The Division would then be reunited on the Yin Chaung position about Tamo as 17 Division fell back towards Taungdwingyi.

Only such motor transport as was tactically required was to be retained in forward areas, and some Brigades were now placed entirely on a pack or bullock cart basis.

During April 4th 17 Division remained on the general line Ywataung-Kyaukpadaung and the troops obtained a much-needed rest. They were still very fatigued and it was considered desirable, therefore, to accelerate the withdrawal of the Division. Back-loading of stores and Administrative units continued whilst the line of the Bwetkyi Chaung was held by 1 Burma Division. South of it, at Nyaungbinzeik, a strong enemy column had been located. 48 Brigade and 7 Armoured Brigade, less one regiment, were formed into a Corps reserve.

Burcorps now proceeded to fall back rapidly to the north. On the night of April 5th/6th Allanmyo and Thayetmyo were evacuated. All stores and ammunition were got away and both towns were destroyed by fire. Demolitions on the oilfields had been carried out.

On the night of April 7th/8th we retired from the Linban Chaung position then held by 16 Brigade and the 2nd Battalion Royal Tank Regiment. Three vehicles alleged to be hostile tanks were encountered on the road near Nyaungbintha. These dispersed on being engaged by our own tanks, and the withdrawal continued without further incident.

By April 8th Burcorps was on the general line Minhla-Taungdwingyi. Enemy aircraft were active and carried our much bombing and machine-gunning of our forward areas. There was no contact with hostile ground forces.

Chapter 17

Defence of the line Minhla-Taungdwingyi – Failure of Chinese to assist in its defence – Operations in the areas of Kokkogwa and Alebo – The enemy take Migaungye – Result of this success and withdrawal of 1 Burma Division to line of the Yin Chaung – Action near Mingyun – Japanese attack on the Yin Chaung line – Withdrawal of 1 Burma Division to the Pin Chaung begun – Operations on west bank of the Irrawaddy – Decision to hold Taungdwingyi with 17 Division.

The stretch of front from Minhla to Taungdwingyi now held by Burcorps was over forty miles in length. In consequence, the defence was without depth.

With this fact in mind General Alexander had on April 4th requested General Tu, commanding Chinese V Army, to send one regiment to hold Taungdwingyi and thus enable Burcorps to form a reserve. General Tu informed General Alexander that he had already ordered one Battalion to Taungdwingyi. The fire power of a Chinese Battalion was, however, no more than that of a company of Imperial troops. A regiment was therefore promised.

After further consideration General Alexander decided that at least one Chinese Division was required if the line was to be maintained. When the Generalissimo was in Maymyo on April 6th he undertook to make a Division available for this purpose. In fact, only one Chinese Battalion ever reached the Taungdwingyi area and the failure to provide a Division had the most serious consequences. This matter is referred to again in Chapter 22. General Tu was responsible for this failure.

The Imperial Forces were now operating in the thinly populated dry zone of Burma. The country was very undulating, in places almost rugged. Watercourses bit sharply into hill features and, save for the main tributaries of the Irrawaddy, were dry in April.

The countryside presented a dusty, waterless appearance. Its thin vegetation and scanty patches of jungle were generally parched. Village cart tracks were rough, and at that season were heavy with loose sand or dust. Roads were even fewer than in Lower Burma.

The country between Taungdwingyi and the Irrawaddy was of this nature. Many of the bare hills were steep. The Yin Chaung, much shrunken, flowed between banks dropping sharply to the stream bed along which the vegetation was greener. The courses of feeder streams were marked by deep mullahs.

In an endeavour to improve communications Burcorps ordered the railway track between Taungdwingyi and Natmauk to be taken up. The permanent way was to be employed as a motor road. Working day and night Sappers effected this conversion. Intensive work was also done on the track from Natmauk to Ywamun, and along the two tracks linking that place with Zayetkon and Pyawbwe. They were made fit for heavy transport.

East of Taungdwingyi the forest-covered Pegu Yomas still separated our troops from the Chinese V Army which in mid-April was withdrawing upon Pyinmana. It intended to fight on a line covering this town.

The dispositions of Burcorps contemplated the secure protection of both its flanks and the formation of a striking force to deal offensively with the enemy. 17 Division, less 48 Brigade, was to hold Taungdwingyi which was put into a state of close all-round defence. The better to ensure these parts of the town were cleared by controlled burning, a necessary precaution as was proved later when enemy aircraft carried out bombing attacks. Elaborate works were constructed, barbed wire was put up, and booby traps prepared.

On the west bank of the Irrawaddy 2 Burma Brigade held Minhla and came directly under Corps control.

The centre of the line was held by the Corps Striking Force commanded by Major-General Bruce Scott. This force consisted of 1 Burma Division (less 2 Burma Brigade), 48 Brigade, and 7 Armoured Brigade.

Water supply dictated the areas to be occupied by the striking force. It was disposed as follows:

(a) 48 Infantry Brigade and 7 Armoured Brigade about Kokkogwa on the Yaume Chaung about ten miles west of Taungdwingyi.
(b) 13 Infantry Brigade in the area Thityagauk-Kyaungyatsan, eight miles west of Kokkogwa.
(c) 1 Burma Brigade about Migaungye on the Irrawaddy, ten miles south-west of Myaungyatsan.

CHAPTER 17

These three areas were linked by road.

The striking force was to reconnoitre the tracks leading into the area Inbingan-Alebo-Sannmagyi-Kandaw with a view to concentrating against enemy columns moving in that direction. It was also to be prepared to attack the flanks of any force advancing by the main road on Taungdwingyi or by the east bank of the river on Migyaungye. The Infantry Brigades would if necessary, operate along country tracks and move on a pack basis.

Along the whole Corps front an observation screen was established, the line for this being some eighteen miles to the south through Aleywa, Nyaungbintha, and along the Linban Chaung to the Irrawaddy. West of the river it continued through Zaunggyandaung and Linke. F.F. columns were allotted to formations for this purpose.

Patrol vessels on the Irrawaddy covered the river as far south as the mouth of the Linban Chaung.

On April 8th Corps Headquarters moved from Taungdwingyi to Magwe. By April 15th Headquarters had been transferred to Gwegyo on the road Yenangyaung-Meiktila.

Throughout April enemy aircraft continued to be active, and our troops and positions were frequently subjected to bombing and machine-gun attacks. Both General Alexander and the Corps Commander when on the road were involved in some of these attacks. Our own lack of air support was keenly felt by all ranks.

Before the operations on the Minhla-Taungdwingyi line are discussed in detail it is necessary to outline the development of the general situation at that time. The Japanese launched a direct thrust at the oilfields up the east bank of the river, ignoring the strongly defended area of Taungdwingyi. Their forces engaged us in a series of actions which satisfied Lieut.-General Slim that, without the aid of a Chinese Division, Burcorps could not continue to hold Taungdwingyi and at the same time cover the direct approach to the oilfields. But to have abandoned Taungdwingyi would have opened the right flank and rear of the Chinese V Army whose advanced troops were still south of Pyinmana. It would also have uncovered our own communications through Mandalay.

Consequently, Burcorps was ordered by General Alexander to hold Taungdwingyi at all costs. This order was received on the morning of April 13th. This resulted in the withdrawal to Taungdwingyi of 48 Brigade and the abandonment of the Kokkogwa position. On April 13th a Japanese force of about two thousand, having passed through our line, crossed the Yin Chaung. It marched towards the oilfields. Enemy pressure on 1 Burma Division south of Magwe continued, and a wide gap was caused between the two Divisions. Through this gap further hostile forces struck north.

Orders for the destruction of the Yenangyaung oilfields were issued on the night of April 14th. The necessary demolitions were extensive, requiring forty-eight hours for completion. They ended with the destruction of the Power House which was carried out when the Japanese were on the northern outskirts of Yenangyaung, and when 1 Burma Division was still several miles south of that place.

With this general picture in mind it is easier to follow the particular operations carried out by Burcorps during this phase of the campaign.

On April 10th a Burma Frontier Force Mounted Infantry column made contact with the enemy at Didokpin about twelve miles south of Thityagauk. Our patrol was ambushed and followed up by the enemy to the vicinity of Kanhla. The strength of the enemy was estimated at two companies.

The same day a patrol of the 7th Queen's Own Hussars with carriers of the 1st Battalion 10th Gurkha Rifles, moving south from Taungdwingyi to make contact with our observation screen, found a block near Nyaungbintha at Milestone 263 on the main road. This indicated that the Japanese were thrusting north by tracks to the west of Taungdwingyi, the block being intended to prevent an outflanking movement by us down the road.

Later, on the same day, three patrols of the 2nd Battalion 5th Royal Gurkha Rifles, F.F., sent out from the Kokkogwa position converged on Yagidaw village some seven miles to the south. In each case these patrols found in Yagidaw a large number of troops who were taken by some of our men to be part of the Chinese force expected in the area. Officers speaking English greeted our own officers in seemingly friendly fashion. The result was that the whole of one patrol and part of another were captured by the Japanese.

On the evening of April 11th patrols of 48 Brigade located and were in contact with the enemy at Yewe and Songon about two miles south of the Kokkogwa position. Our tanks burnt several villages to deny their use to the enemy. Further west, units of 13 Brigade had been in action.

That night the Japanese began an attack on 48 Brigade which was now heavily engaged with the enemy for almost two days.

The Brigade position was astride the main road and based on the adjoining villages of Yakaingzu-Kokkogwa south of the road. It also cut through the village of Thadodan north of the road. This latter village was too large to be held entirely. Between the two villages, in the centre

CHAPTER 17

of the position, the ground rose in a small plateau and here was 2 Field Battery, less one troop, of 1 Indian Field Regiment. The south-west corner of the position was entered by a bend of the Yaume Chaung. The stream bed was sandy and winding, with grass cover in places.

The western face of the perimeter was held by the combined Battalion 7th Gurkha Rifles with one detached company in a post on the road two miles to the west of Thadodan; the north by the 1st Battalion 4th P.W.O. Gurkha Rifles, F.F., with an attached company of the 1st Battalion 3rd Q.A.O. Gurkha Rifles. The remainder of this Battalion (Headquarters and one company) was in Taungdwingyi. The attached company of the 3rd Q.A.O. Gurkha Rifles held a post in Sonzu village, a mile south of the main position round Kokkogwa. A troop of the 2nd Battalion Royal Tank Regiment leaguered inside the perimeter, the remainder of 7 Armoured Brigade being in harbour at Wetchangan, two miles to the east. Throughout 48 Brigade there was a general lack of signalling equipment which handicapped inter-communication and thus hampered the defence.

Shortly after dark enemy patrols worked up to the listening posts on the south side of the perimeter, and there was other movement further to the west. Firing began to intensify at about midnight.

By 0130 hours on April 12th an attack in considerable strength had developed, the main effort being down the Yaume Chaung. Our automatic weapons and mortars opened fire on their night lines. Enemy mortars retaliated.

Our forward elements were driven in along the banks of the Chaung, hand grenades being freely used by both sides. The southern Battalion soon exhausted all its reserves, and Japanese armed with light automatic weapons penetrated Kokkogwa village as far as the Brigade Headquarters area. The only reinforcements available were the Brigade Employment Platoon, one platoon of the 7th Gurkha Rifles, and another of the 1st Battalion 4th P.W.O. Gurkha Rifles. These were rushed up.

Shortly before 0300 hours Captain Grieve, 5th Royal Gurkha Rifles, F.F., counter-attacked with his company, and in fierce hand to hand fighting partly restored the position. Our defenders on this sector rallied, and the Japanese were held. To add to the confused situation a thunderstorm was raging. At intervals the intense darkness was illuminated by flashes of lightning.

The Japanese now launched another violent attack on Thadodan village, held by one platoon of the 7th Gurkha Rifles. The detached company on the road to the west was recalled, but at the bridge across the Yaume Chaung it was heavily shelled and dispersed. The remnants of this company then counter-attacked Thadodan. They were met by light machine-gun fire and a shower of hand grenades from the eastern edge of the village. The fire was returned with effect, but the counter-attack failed with considerable loss. Advancing across the plateau east of Thadodan the Japanese reached our gun positions. They were flung back at the point of the bayonet. The guns were then swung round, Thadodan was shelled at point blank range, and the 7th Gurkha Rifles, re-organising, took up a new position on the western edge of the plateau.

By 0500 hours the situation had eased. It had been critical for some hours, and at Brigade Headquarters all officers stood by as a bombing squad ready to fight on any sector. They had been busy detonating bombs from the Brigade reserve.

Whilst the Japanese attack was in progress large numbers of motor vehicles were heard moving from east to west through Yewe village. A force was evidently by-passing 48 Brigade. Possibly it was the force afterwards reported to have crossed the Yin Chaung on April 13th and which appeared north of Yenangyaung on the evening of April 16th.

The company at Sonzu held out all night against a superior force, but at dawn it was attacked by enemy tanks and infantry. Without anti-tank rifles or 'Molotov cocktail' bombs it was overrun and dispersed. Some stragglers regained the main position.

At first light the 1st Battalion 4th P.W.O. Gurkha Rifles dealt with remaining snipers in Kokkogwa. Our tanks with fighting patrols of the 2nd Battalion 5th Gurkha Rifles, F.F., moved up the Yaume Chaung. They caught several parties of Japanese and found many of the enemy dead lying everywhere.

The Japanese were still in Thadodan, and large parties driven out by our infantry came under fire from the tanks. To dispose of the enemy finally in the village a company of the 1st Battalion 4th P.W.O. Gurkha Rifles was put into an attack with a squadron of the 2nd Battalion Royal Tank Regiment. At least two companies of the enemy broke out of Thadodan. One company was trapped in a nullah running into the Yaume Chaung. It was wiped out by our infantry and tanks. The other company scattered to the north and then came under fire from the tanks. Unfortunately, our own infantry casualties were not light, and two tanks were hit by artillery fire.

Wets of Thadodan, near Milestone 294, the Japanese had put down a road block. It was cleared without difficulty by the 2nd Battalion Royal Tank Regiment which then maintained a patrol to 13 Brigade at Thityagauk.

CHAPTER 17

By 1300 hours the situation had been fully restored. The perimeter was shortened as units had sustained severe casualties, but out troops felt that they could continue to hold their own. That evening the Commander of 48 Brigade reported that since he now only had seven infantry companies it was essential that he be reinforced by a fresh Battalion. The enemy still held positions north of Thadodan.

At about 0100 hours that night the enemy again attacked the southern sector. Firing became intense, but nowhere was our line broken and by 0330 hours the engagement was broken off by the Japanese.

On the morning of April 13th our fighting patrols were active. Captain Grieve with a patrol came upon the enemy in Yewe village and opened fire with automatic weapons. The Japanese scattered in great confusion. Captain Grieve burnt the village. Another patrol of the 2nd Battalion 5th Royal Gurkha Rifles, F.F., engaged a Japanese gun with a mortar and secured a direct hit. It then fired on an enemy platoon in Yewe. At Songon the Japanese were kept subdued by a patrol of the 1st Battalion 4th P.W.O. Gurkha Rifles.

Hostile aircraft made three attacks on our positions that day. Incendiary bombs set Kokkogwa alight, much mortar and other ammunition being destroyed. Casualties amongst men in the slit trenches were negligible.

The 1st Battalion 10th Gurkha Rifles arrived as a reinforcement just before dusk. One rifle company went into immediate reserve in each of the three perimeter sectors, the fourth company being held as Brigade reserve. The night passed quietly. Only enemy burial parties were abroad. Activity was shifting west and north.

For 1 Burma Brigade and 13 Brigade April 11th, 12th, and 13th had also been days of action. 1 Burma Division directed these two Brigades to destroy any enemy force found in the area Kanhla-Alebo. For this purpose, 1 Burma Brigade was to concentrate about Kandaw by first light on April 11th and to advance on Alebo. One Battalion was to hold the high ground about Kunon Taung. 13 Brigade with headquarters at Thityagauk was to maintain an observation line about Inbingan whilst one Battalion concentrated about Nyaungbingyi to attack south-west towards Alebo.

1 Burma Brigade had arrived in Migyaungye on April 9th, the 2nd Battalion 7th Rajput Regiment remaining south of that town with its 'C' Company at Sinbaungwe about fourteen miles downriver. Leaving this company of the Rajputs and F.F.5 to watch the river area, the Brigade concentrated at Kandaw at 0730 hours on April 11th. The 1st Battalion Burma Rifles had gone to the Kunon Taung position. The same evening the 5th Battalion Burma Rifles and the 2nd Battalion 7th Rajput Regiment

(less 'C' Company) were close to Alebo. Meanwhile 'C' Company of the Rajputs was in touch with a considerable force of the enemy advancing up the east bank of the Irrawaddy, and that night was on the line Minywa-Thabutkyaw.

That day, April 11th, the two Battalions of 13 Brigade were in contact with the enemy north of Alebo. The 1st Battalion 18th Royal Garhwal Rifles held a perimeter at Point 558 east of Powe. With it was 2 Mountain Battery. A force of fifteen hundred Japanese with animal transport was located by a dawn patrol in a village one and a half miles south of the position. An attack on this village was planned, but later cancelled by Brigade Headquarters.

The 1st Battalion Royal Inniskilling Fusiliers was in a position to the west of the 1st Battalion 18th Royal Garhwal Rifles south of Milestone 300 on the main road. Patrols were in contact with forward elements of the enemy. In these skirmishes the Battalion sustained several casualties.

A large force of the enemy was observed by the Royal Inniskilling Fusiliers to be moving west through Letpanwya, and on the evening of April 11th 'C' Company of the 2nd Battalion Royal Tank Regiment joined 13 Brigade. It arrived too late to take any action that day.

At 1930 hours that night the 5th Battalion Burma Rifles was ordered to clear Alebo. It did so in the dark, and, although making no contact with the enemy, discovered numerous signs of a very hurried flight. Considerable equipment had been abandoned. In officers' haversacks important papers were found.

The same night the Japanese attacked the southern sector of the perimeter held by the 1st Battalion 18th Royal Garhwal Rifles east of Powe. Employing Verey lights the enemy opened light automatic and rifle fire. Failing to penetrate this sector the attackers worked round to the western and northern sides of the position. Eventually at 0330 hours after continuing their efforts unsuccessfully for two and a half hours they withdrew. Dawn patrols found plenty of evidence of the recent attack, but were unable to establish any contact with the Japanese. It was not until considerably later in the day that another patrol found a force of Japanese in a position overlooking the main road. One company of the 1st Battalion 18th Royal Garhwal Rifles moved out of the main Battalion position in the afternoon and was posted west of Powe to cover the road.

The continued advance of the Japanese up the east bank of the river brought to a termination the operations of 1 Burma Brigade in the Alebo area. It was evident on the morning of April 12th that there was a considerable body of the enemy in the villages north of Alebo.

CHAPTER 17

It is not unlikely that portions of this force were by-passing our troops by night and moving further north across the main road. At the same time the threat to Migyaungye made it necessary to protect that area. Consequently, 1 Burma Brigade marched from the Alebo area for Kunon Taung about midday on April 12th. Orders had been sent direct from Divisional Headquarters to the 1st Battalion Burma Rifles to move from Kunon Taung to Migyaungye. These miscarried, and as a consequence the Battalion did not leave Kunon Taung until 0300 hours on April 13th. Migyaungye was at the same time only covered by 'C' Company of the 2nd Battalion 7th Rajput regiment and F.F.5.

Whilst 1 Burma Brigade was withdrawing to Kunon Taung on April 12th the units of 13 Brigade continued to be engaged with the enemy. The operations carried out on this day by the 1st Battalion 18th Royal Garhwal Rifles have already been detailed.

The 1st Battalion Royal Inniskilling Fusiliers on April 12th sent out a fighting patrol lifted on tanks to Alebo. Here there was a brisk engagement with the Japanese, and both sides sustained several casualties. Later the enemy tried to infiltrate into the Battalion position but all such attempts were beaten off with long range machine-gun and artillery fire.

On this day the 2nd Battalion King's Own Yorkshire Light Infantry which had been protecting the oilfields at Yenangyaung was ordered to move to Milestone 300 on the main road to reinforce 13 Brigade. It was relieved at Yenangyaung by the 1st Battalion the Gloucestershire Regiment. The latter Battalion then had a strength of two rifle companies. So short of arms were we by this time that the Battalion mortars and light machine-guns had to be made over to The King's Own Yorkshire Light Infantry.

The Japanese occupied Migyaungye on the night of April 12th/13th as a result of a surprise attack on the outposts. Approaching the forward positions, they called out that they were men of the Burma Rifles. The defences were then quickly overrun with little noise. The transport of the 1st and 5th Battalion Burma Rifles which had remained in Migyaungye and Headquarters of F.F.5 were entirely unaware of what had happened. However, the transport afterwards got out of the town.

The 1st Battalion Burma Rifles arrived on the outskirts of the town at 0600 hours, and the Commanding Officer, Lieut.-Colonel B. Ruffell, O.B.E., went forward to F.F.5 Headquarters to ascertain the situation. No sooner had he arrived at Headquarters than the Japanese attacked, and he with two Burma Frontier Force officers were captured. Subsequently Lieut.-Colonel Ruffell and one Frontier Force officer escaped, the third officer being killed. Simultaneously with this attack the 1st Battalion Burma Rifles, moving towards preliminary positions south of the town, was suddenly rushed by the Japanese. In the dark and confusion, it became split up. Lieut. Shan Lone, Captain Menon, and two platoons together with mortars, reserve ammunition, and medical equipment were captured, the enemy being believed to be Chinese.

Another part of the Battalion consisting mainly of 'A' Company was cut off from the main body. It stood its ground for some hours and eventually fought its way north, inflicting casualties on the enemy in the town and on patrols north of it.

The main body of the Battalion was assembled in a hollow square north of the road entering the town from the north-east. As it became light, heavy light machine-gun and mortar fire was opened on the square.

Lieut.-Colonel Ruffell re-joined the Battalion; and a bayonet charge cleared the enemy from broken ground south of the road. A further attack under Captain Ransford dislodged the enemy from the late F.F.5 Headquarters. Some prisoners were released and equipment, including a 3" mortar, recaptured. This mortar was effectively used against groups off Japanese concealed in buildings and compounds.

Ammunition was running low and the initial Japanese attack had considerably disorganised the Battalion. The enemy was now observed to be moving wide round the east flank and to the north. At about 1100 hours Lieut.-Colonel Ruffell accordingly withdrew his Battalion north-east. This movement was carried out in small parties under heavy mortar and machine-gun fire. Although causalities had been severe it was believed that enemy casualties were greater.

At Kunon Taung the 5th Battalion Burma Rifles was attacked soon after first light by small parties of the enemy. No serious effort was made to press home the advance although firing continued until 1100 hours.

Early in the afternoon 1 Burma Brigade withdrew north to Tebingan, and later to Milestone 309 on the Taungdwingyi-Magwe road.

The fact that the Japanese at Migyaungye were twice in one night mistaken for friendly troops may be of some significance. They were prompt to exploit the advantage gained. Always ready to avail themselves of disguise the Japanese were at this time making much use of bullock cart transport. In Burmese dress, or with the assistance of Burmans, they were able to infiltrate through our lines concealing arms, stores, and men in their carts.

The reverse at Migyaungye completely exposed our flank on the east bank of the Irrawaddy. The Corps Commander therefore decided to bring into Magwe from across the river the 7th Battalion Burma

CHAPTER 17

Rifles then with 2 Burma Brigade. The 1st Battalion the Cameronians and the Mounted Infantry detachment of the Burma Frontier Force both in Magwe were to be pushed forward towards Myingun, whilst as an immediate measure the very weak 2nd Battalion King's Own Yorkshire Light Infantry was to occupy that town. 1 Burma Brigade would eventually cover the sector. 13 Brigade was to move back to the Yin Chaung, after occupying a lay-back about Sainggya to assist the movement of 1 Burma Brigade.

In fact, the Cameronians and the Mounted Infantry detachment did not advance on Myingun, and the initial defence of that area devolved on the 2nd Battalion King's Own Yorkshire Light Infantry alone. On the evening of April 13th, it was ferried towards its destination by tanks of the 2nd Battalion Royal Tank Regiment, its transport proceeding independently. The Battalion formed a perimeter for the night north of Myingun. Burmans stated that a force of three hundred Japanese was in the vicinity.

7 Armoured Brigade, less 7th Queen's Own Hussars, had also been ordered to the Yin Chaung area. It was now evident that the Japanese were advancing direct upon the oilfields, and it was necessary to concentrate additional strength to meet this thrust. Moving out along the road from Kokkogwa the remaining squadrons of the 2nd Battalion Royal Tank Regiment came under accurate shell fire, but the guns of the 7th Queen's Own Hussars and of the artillery with 48 Brigade relieved the situation.

The decision to withdraw 13 Brigade to the north-west to Sainggya affected operations in the Alebo area where the Brigade continued to be actively engaged on April 13th. The withdrawal began at about 1900 hours, but prior to this the 1st Battalion 18th Royal Garhwal Rifles carried out a successful attack on a body of about two hundred Japanese with pack transport in a village south of the Battalion position.

The attack was carried out at 1430 hours, one company charging the village after a brief mortar bombardment. The Japanese were taken completely by surprise and fled in confusion. A single enemy mortar beyond the village fired on our troops and caused two casualties. On the other hand, the Japanese lost about fifty per cent of their men and animals. As our troops retired, they set fire to the village.

By April 14th a wide gap had developed between our two Divisions. That morning, to ensure the defence of the Taungdwingyi area, 48 Brigade withdrew on that place from Kokkogwa. The withdrawal was without incident although it was followed up at a distance by parties of hostile Burmans. From this time onwards 17 Division was supplied by the route Kyaukpadaung-Natmauk-Taungdwingyi, and 16 Brigade was moved to Natmauk.

Between Taungdwingyi and 13 Brigade was now a distance of some twenty-five miles, the road connecting Magwe and Taungdwingyi was cut, and parties of the enemy were observed near the Yin Chaung. Other parties, unobserved, had certainly penetrated further north. Early that morning the transport of the 2nd Battalion King's Own Yorkshire Light Infantry was ambushed at Toksan, two miles east of Myingun, and the Battalion was in action there.

Before news of this action was received 1 Burma Division issued an Operation Order for the occupation the same day of a defensive area about Magwe and Pado, but excluding the high ground about the two villages of Minywa. 1 Burma Brigade would hold the Yin Chaung about Pado with 13 Brigade on its left. 7 Armoured Brigade (less 7th Queen's Own Hussars) was to from part of the Divisional Reserve, being stationed west of Milestone 322 on the main road. Its primary duty was to attack to the north-east. The remainder of the reserve (Magforce) stationed in Magwe comprised 5 Mountain Battery, the 1st Battalion the Cameronians, and the 7th and 12th Battalions Burma Rifles.

It was intended by Burcorps to hold the Yin Chaung position as long as possible and to withdraw only under pressure. The intense heat which added to the exhaustion of the troops made a halt very desirable. Shortage of water in the area rendered it necessary that the next defensive line should be on the Pin Chaung north of Yenangyaung, over forty miles distant by road.

Throughout April 14th the 2nd Battalion King's Own Yorkshire Light Infantry was engaged with the enemy. It was still north of Myingun when its transport, which had not yet joined it, was ambushed. Since the transport contained all machine-guns, mortars and rations it was essential that it be recaptured, and Toksan was at once attacked by two companies from the north and west. Our troops drove the enemy out of the village, but when the transport was being extricated the Japanese rallied and counter-attacked in strength. They were temporarily held off by fire whilst some vehicles were driven out and collected in rear of the Battalion area, north-west of Toksan. Here a perimeter was formed. The wireless truck manned by Burman signallers endeavoured to contact Divisional Headquarters without result. It was then driven out of the perimeter without orders and was never seen again. Heavy firing was heard near Toksan and an officer's patrol was sent out to make contact with what was believed to be 1 Burma Brigade. This patrol did not return. As far as is known there were no British troops in Toksan.

Indian troops training in Mandalay on 23 September 1941, prior to the Japanese invasion of Burma. (Historic Military Press)

Indian artillery exercises in rugged Burmese countryside in late September 1941. (Historic Military Press)

A company of soldiers from the Burma Rifles 'marches out from the old fort of Mandalay' during September 1941. Originally formed in 1917 from Burmese, Karens, Kachins and Chins, with some Gurkhas, by the time of the Japanese invasion, the regiment consisted of fourteen battalions, including a holding battalion, a training battalion and four territorial battalions. (Historic Military Press)

A prelude to the Japanese conquest of Burma. Taken from wartime newsreel, this image depicts enemy soldiers landing on a beach during the invasion of Malaya, 8-9 December 1941. Note the ships of the invasion force in the background. (Critical Past)

An air raid shelter under construction in Rangoon during December 1941 or early January 1942. (Historic Military Press)

A poster in Rangoon that urged residents to enlist in the Auxiliary Fire Service. Despite the response to such appeals, the civil defence systems suffered badly when many of Rangoon's civilians fled the city in the face of the Japanese bombing. (Historic Military Press)

Residents of Rangoon, who fled the city in the face of Japanese bombing, 'rest on a roadside' during January 1942. Rangoon finally fell to Japanese troops on 31 January 1942. (Historic Military Press)

Burma under Japanese aerial attack. The original caption to this image states that 'there was no military objective in this happy Burmese village. The object of the savage Japanese bombing was to create panic and drive the native population on to the roads and into the jungle.' (Library of Congress)

Troops of Japanese Fifteenth Army on the border of Burma. Commanded by General Shojiro Iida, the men of this formation invaded the southern Burmese province of Tenasserim on 15 January 1942. (Historic Military Press)

An aerial reconnaissance photograph of the bridge over the Sittang River, known as the Sittang Bridge, which was destroyed in the face of the advancing Japanese on 23 February 1942.

Japanese horse transport passing through a Burmese village during their advance. (Historic Military Press)

A British soldier uses a sledgehammer 'against vital electrical equipment in a plant which furnished power to run 85 per cent of the oil fields in Burma. Smoke from burning oil rises in the background as [the] British carried out a "scorched earth" policy as the Japanese forced them back.' This picture was taken in Yenanguang oil field, the fighting for which lasted from 11 to 19 April 1942. (Historic Military Press)

Fires burn late into the night as the British 'scorched earth' policy is enacted at Yenanguang on or about 16 April 1942. The destruction wrought on the oil fields there during the retreat was so successful that according to one source it was at least a year before the Japanese were able to extract oil. (Historic Military Press)

British troops and native labourers prepare a road-block near the Burmese border with India in the face of the Japanese advance. (Historic Military Press)

A Japanese tank column crossing a river by means of a hastily constructed bridge built to replace one demolished by retreating British troops. (Historic Military Press)

Kachin tribesmen in action against the Japanese. The original wartime caption states: 'Here Kachins await the Japanese in dense jungle. Equipped with rifles and a machine-gun, Kachin fighters await the approach of Japanese soldiers along a jungle trail. They crouch beside a deep trap which they have dug in the trail and covered with leaves and bamboo roads.' (Historic Military Press)

CHAPTER 17

As soon as it was realised at Divisional Headquarters that the Battalion was unsupported and heavily threatened a mounted officers patrol was sent out from 2 Mountain Battery to recall it. This patrol met a liaison officer from the Battalion. It gave him the message. Returning to his Battalion this officer was thrown from his horse and severely injured, with the result that the message was not delivered.

Numerous Japanese and Burmese patrols moved round the Battalion position but put in no attack. At dusk they occupied the water point, closing in after dark. Knowing that it was our intention to hold the line of the Yin Chaung the Commanding Officer decided to move north under cover of night, and companies marched independently for the south bank of the Chaung. Here, near the village of Tatkon, between 0300 hours and first light the movement of numerous bullock carts was heard and it was found that the Battalion was still behind the Japanese. However, assisted by demonstrations by the 5th Battalion Burma Rifles and the 2nd Battalion 7th Rajput Regiment, all companies safely crossed the Chaung and the Battalion reassembled near 1 Burma Brigade Headquarters at Milestone 324. It then went on to Magwe to rest.

On the Yin Chaung position the right sector of 1 Burma Brigade was held by the 5th Battalion Burma Rifles disposed about Pado village. On the left, the 2nd Battalion 7th Rajput Regiment was in position covering the village of Zigyun. The 1st Battalion Burma Rifles was in reserve. Further to the north-east the line was continued by 13 Brigade covering the road into Magwe. This Brigade had now been joined by the 5th Battalion 1st Punjab Regiment from 2 Burma Brigade. This Battalion was in the sector adjoining 1 Burma Brigade.

Before first light on April 15th there was some spasmodic firing on the front of the 2nd Battalion 7th Rajput Regiment, but the day passed quietly. 1 Burma Division that day received a report that a force of two thousand of the enemy had crossed the Yin Chaung on April 13th. 7 Armoured Brigade was ordered to carry out a sweep to the north-east to locate these troops. This sweep was to be made on April 16th, but owing to the situation that arose it did not take place.

At about 0100 hours on April 16th an attack along the whole front of 1 Burma Brigade began. The Japanese employed their usual night tactics and sought by screaming, the use of tracer ammunition, and cracker gunfire to disorganise the defence and to compel it to disclose its positions. Two ambushes had been laid in the Yin Chaung by the 5th Battalion Burma Rifles. The Japanese walked into both of these in some force and suffered severely. This made them cautious; they then began to work round the right flank of the Battalion where the Karen

Company was in position. After holding its ground for some time this company gave way. Before it could be reformed the enemy infiltrated up to the position of the Battalion reserve. On the front of the left company of the Battalion the Japanese put in three bayonet charges. The first two were thrown back with loss, but the third penetrated the position. By this time the 5th Battalion Burma Rifles had largely disintegrated.

The attack on the 2nd Battalion 7th Rajput Regiment was launched at about the same time; the forward company being quickly overrun. At 0145 hours its remnants were withdrawn. The Japanese were now in occupation of Zigyun village, and there was a gap between the Battalion and the 5th Battalion Burma Rifles. The Japanese pressed round the left flank and by about 0600 hours the Battalion was practically surrounded. Shortly afterwards heavy mortar and machine-gun fire was directed on it from all sides. Lieut.-Colonel A. Rea, then out of touch with both flank Battalions and there being no sign of any assistance arriving, withdrew his men towards the main road.

The 5th Battalion Burma Rifles had already been withdrawn at 0600 hours, and the 1st Battalion Burma Rifles formed the rearguard to cover the considerably disorganised Brigade. It was joined by the 2nd Battalion King's Own Yorkshire Light Infantry now with a strength of about two hundred. This Battalion had been hurried out of Magwe. It took up a position south of Milestone 324 to cover the road and Brigade Headquarters and to permit the passage of our motor transport through Magwe on to the road for Yenangyaung. This transport together with covering troops came under brisk mortar fire from the enemy south of the road; but the road was held until the transport had been driven out of the danger zone.

1 Burma Brigade and 13 Brigade were then ordered to withdraw across country to the Magwe-Yenangyaung road, the movement being initiated about 0930 hours. In the earlier stages of this movement the rearmost troops of both Brigades were in contact with the enemy on whom casualties were inflicted. Later the withdrawal was not closely followed up. Headquarters of 1 Burma Division moved out of Magwe at midday, demolitions being carried out in the town immediately afterwards.

The 2nd Battalion Royal Tank Regiment supported by 414 Battery R.H.A. spent a busy day in covering Magwe and the withdrawal of the two Brigades to the Yenangyaung road. Two tanks were lost, but considerable numbers of the enemy were destroyed. A large column approaching Magwe was compelled to disperse. Eventually at 1800 hours, when our evacuation of Magwe was complete and our

CHAPTER 17

troops had gained the Yenangyaung road, the elements of 7 Armoured Brigade began their withdrawal to an area some five miles north of the Pin Chaung, beyond Yenangyaung. One squadron of the 2nd Battalion Royal Tank Regiment remained to protect 1 Burma Division.

Our withdrawal was harassed by low flying hostile aircraft. These subjected our troops to machine-gun and bombing attacks.

That evening 13 Brigade halted two miles south of the Kadaung Chaung whilst 1 Burma Brigade was two miles north of the Chaung. Magforce, acting as rearguard, covered the road junction near Milestone 348.

Both Battalions of 1 Burma Brigade engaged on the Yin Chaung had sustained fairly heavy casualties, and in each of them the number of missing was large. Some of the missing men later re-joined their units.

On the road between Magwe and Yenangyaung the Sappers and Miners of 1 Burma Division by most efficient work established dumps of water. These dumps were very essential, and in spite of them our troops on this day suffered from an acute shortage of water.

To meet the growing threat to the oilfields it had been intended to withdraw the whole of 2 Burma Brigade to the east bank of the Irrawaddy. The 5th Battalion 1st Punjab Regiment and 7th Battalion Burma Rifles did in fact cross the river, but the hurried evacuation of Magwe led to a cancellation of further moves. In withdrawing up the west bank 2 Burma Brigade had not been in serious contact with the enemy. Our troops had been warned to fire on all craft not flying the white Ensign, and on April 12th the 5th Battalion 1st Punjab Regiment opened fire on such a gunboat. This promptly ran up the white Ensign. The Battalion War Diary slyly adds that "a major of Royal Marines came ashore to parley". Luckily no casualties had been inflicted. On April 14th the 2nd Battalion Burma Rifles was shelled from the east bank of the river. It had some casualties and its mules were stampeded. Two days later the same Battalion was in action against enemy gunboat No. 209. This it compelled to withdraw downstream.

On April 16th 2 Burma Brigade withdrew from Minbu, opposite Magwe. On the night of April 16th/17th it was in the Sagu area. The Brigade was then composed of the 2nd and 8th Battalions Burma Rifles and F.F.8.

The same night 17 Division with the 7th Queen's Own Hussars, one troop of 414 Battery R.H.A., and one company of the 1st Battalion the West Yorkshire Regiment remained disposed about Taungdwingyi (48 and 63 Brigade) and Natmauk (16 Brigade). It was ordered by Lieut.-Colonel Slim to operate strongly from both these places against the right flank of the enemy following up 1 Burma Division. Lieut.-Colonel

Slim had been offered assistance by General Stilwell, and the Chinese 38th Division, then in Mandalay, was to co-operate in relieving enemy pressure. This help was offered by General Stilwell after General Tu, commanding the Chinese V Army, failed to make available the Division originally promised by the Generalissimo. The Chinese 38th Division, commanded by Major-General Sun, was the leading formation of the Chinese LXVI Army then entering Burma.

At the beginning of April, the enemy had received considerable seaborne reinforcements through the port of Rangoon. These were soon to add weight to the attacks on the Chinese V Army, and also enabled the Japanese to initiate a thrust through Karenni and then north from Mawchi against the widely dispersed Chinese VI Army.

Against the British forces the Japanese 33rd Division continued to operate during the earlier part of the month. It was assisted by a considerable number of Burmans who, if they did not participate in the fighting, served to release Japanese troops for actual combatant duties.

Of this phase of the campaign General Alexander in his Despatch has remarked that the operations "illustrate clearly the advantage which the initiative confers on a highly trained force which has the assistance of the local population in a country of great distances and poor communications. The successes which the Japanese gained cannot all be ascribed to their superior training and, at this time, superior morale".

Certainly, the enemy had remarkably accurate information about our dispositions, hit hard at us when it suited him, and left us groping for his main body as parties of his troops went through the gaps in our line.

We, on the other hand, were faced with a populace either hostile or persuaded into a policy of non-co-operation by fear of the advancing enemy. Combined with the total lack of air reconnaissance this made the obtaining of information most difficult. 1 Burma Division had no mounted reconnaissance unit and was therefore entirely dependent on its infantry patrols which, of necessity, could not come by or submit their information speedily.

Chapter 18

Denial Scheme for the Yenangyaung and Chauk oilfields – Orders issued for destruction of the oilfields – Japanese establish themselves on the Pin Chaung – Operations at Yenangyaung between April 16th and 21st – Withdrawal of 1 Burma Division from Yenangyaung – Operations by columns of 17 Division from Natmauk and Taungdwingyi – Plans for an offensive against the Japanese in the Yenangyaung area.

The heavy requirements of the Allied forces and essential services demanded the continued production of petrol until the last possible moment. At the same time, it was imperative that the use of the Yenangyaung, Chauk and adjacent oilfields and their very elaborate plant be denied to the enemy.

The denial schemes were carried out by Mr. W.L. Forster who had so thoroughly planned the destruction of the oil refineries in the neighbourhood of Rangoon. With Mr. Forster were again associated the staffs of the companies concerned, and in the work to be carried out the paramount object was the demolition of all vital installations. Private interests were in no way permitted to conflict with the larger issue.

Whilst the production of petrol still continued much preliminary demolition work was carried out on wells and plant not actually required. At the same time all preparations for final demolitions were made. Owing to the extensive nature of these final demolitions it was considered that at least forty-eight hours were required for their completion.

The Warden of the Oilfields received from the Commander of Burcorps the demolition signal for Yenangyaung and Chauk at 0100 hours on April 15th. The Power Station at Yenangyaung was excluded from the operation of the order.

The preliminary denial work already done, enabled Mr. Forster and his assistants to complete their task most expeditiously, and the evacuation of demolition parties from Yenangyaung was carried out on the afternoon of April 15th. Mr. Forster and a few of his assistants remained behind to deal with the Power Station. Around them was ample evidence of the thoroughness with which their labours had been done. The whole of the tank farm containing millions of gallons of crude oil was a vast sheet of fire rising many hundreds of feet; wells, plants and vital installations were burning everywhere, and the sky was darkened by a huge pall of smoke. Explosions resounded across the oilfields.

The work of destruction was entirely our own. Prior to the demolitions Japanese aircraft had carried out raids on April 11th and 12th, but they had carefully refrained from attacking any objectives that might later be of value to their own forces. The landing stages on the river had been bombed and so, too, was Twingon village just north of Yenangyaung. At this point the various roads through the oilfields converged on the one road giving access to the ford at the Pin Chaung. The enemy realised the importance of the crossing which was the single northern outlet for wheeled traffic from the area.

It has been suggested that Japanese aircraft undertook 'directional' bombing and that the fires so caused guided columns striking across country. This may account for the bombing of Twingon. Another possible instance of such directional bombing may have been the attack on Sittang village on February 21st. Later in the campaign, at the end of April, Alon village near Monywa was also bombed on the day preceding the unexpected attack on the latter place.

Another feature of this period in Yenangyaung was the burning of the town and village areas by saboteurs. It is significant, however, that no barrack buildings for oilfield employees were destroyed. This fact would seem to indicate that these fires were inspired by the enemy.

In Yenangyaung itself there still remained, as oilfield guard, Headquarters and one company of the depleted 1st Battalion the Gloucestershire Regiment. The Battalion was without automatic weapons or mortars. Its remaining rifle company was at Chauk. Beyond the Pin Chaung were certain Burma Frontier Force units and 8 Heavy Anti-Aircraft Battery, R.A. During the work of demolition our garrison in the area was therefore small, and by what a narrow margin of time the complete destruction of the oilfield had been safely effected was now to be proved.

CHAPTER 18

On the evening of April 16th when men of the Anti-Aircraft Battery were bathing in the Pin Chaung the gunner acting as their armed sentry was set upon by what was believed at that time to be a gang of dacoits. The gunner was killed. Local villagers were then rounded up by our troops. There was no suspicion that any Japanese were concerned in the incident, although there is now little doubt that they were responsible for the attack.

During the day Rear Headquarters of 1 Burma Division together with all motor transport that could be spared had crossed the Pin Chaung and came safely to its new area at Gwegyo. That night 7 Armoured Brigade passed north through the flaming desolation of Yenangyaung. Crossing the Pin Chaung its leading elements halted at 2300 hours to harbour for the night beside the main road some five miles beyond the Chaung. The greater part of the 2nd Battalion Royal Tank Regiment was then still on the road just north of the ford. Traffic was proceeding normally.

Without warning, fire from a light automatic weapon was opened on a station-wagon at a point about two miles beyond the Pin Chaung. The vehicle was set alight. A tank went forward to investigate, and as it approached the burning wagon it was hit by a shell or grenade and disabled. At the same time machine-gun fire opened on the rear of the column.

F.F.1, 3, and 4 were stationed close by, and F.F.4 was ordered to sweep the ground east of the road, the direction from which the hostile fire had come. Meanwhile the enemy set fire to the damaged tank. Some distance south of the obstruction there was forming a long line of stationary traffic. Throughout the night there were bursts of hostile light automatic and cracker fire. F.F.4 failed to establish contact with the enemy.

A section of 8 Heavy Anti-Aircraft Battery, R.A., in position near the ford, was surrounded by the enemy. Most of the gunners were unarmed, there being only a few rifles with the Battery, and were unable to offer any effective resistance. Later the majority of those captured made their escape and the guns were brought out by tanks.

During the night other bodies of the enemy were operating south of the Pin Chaung. Their patrols penetrated the northern portion of Yenangyaung itself, whilst a second road block was put down in Twingon village. Here, south of the Pin Chaung, upon the few men of the Gloucestershire Regiment fell the whole task of meeting the enemy thrust. They were attacked by the Japanese and compelled to fall back through the town.

The demolition of the Power House, begun at 2359 hours, was carried out successfully. The vital task of denying the important oilfield plant was thus completed with little time to spare.

A report of the situation at Yenangyaung first reached Headquarters of 1 Burma Division near the Kadaung Chaung at 0200 hours on April 17th. Orders for the following morning's march to Yenangyaung had already been issued, Magforce being detailed as Advance Guard. The time of departure for Headquarters was now put forward, and at first light Major-General Bruce-Scott left for the oilfields. Arriving there he was informed of the situation by Brigadier Roughton, Commander of the Central Area.

At first Major-General Bruce-Scott established his Headquarters at the Nyaunghla Stud Farm, but shortly moved to the road junction near Milestone 358. The only troops then available, the Divisional Employment Platoon and a company of Sappers and Miners, were put in to reinforce the weak company of the 1st Battalion the Gloucestershire Regiment covering the south of Yenangyaung. Nothing further could be done until the arrival of Magforce, and no offensive action could be taken before the Division had concentrated in the area that night. As soon as Magforce came up it took over the defensive line.

The Royal Marine river patrol had arrived the previous evening. It was now subjected to bombing and machine-gun attacks by enemy aircraft. The flotilla moved upstream, and as it did so, came under mortar fire from the town. It passed out of range without damage.

Meanwhile steps had been taken to attack the enemy north of the Pin Chaung at first light. From the north of the block the company of the West Yorkshire Regiment together with the half squadron of the 2nd Battalion Royal Tank Regiment then with Headquarters of 7 Armoured Brigade was to strike south, whilst the tanks and F.F. units on the other side of the block attacked from that direction.

The attack went in from both sides of the block as planned, and was supported from the north by 'E' Troop 414 Battery, R.H.A. One gun of 8 Heavy Anti-Aircraft Battery, R.A., also fired over open sights at parties of the enemy as they appeared.

Advancing south astride the road the company of the West Yorkshire Regiment cleared its way with grenades, and supported by mortar fire reached its objective. This was a ridge through which the road ran in a cutting. Owing to the unsuitability of the ground the tanks had been unable to take part in this advance.

From the south F.F.1 met opposition on both sides of the road. On the west a platoon of F.F.3 and tanks dealt with an enemy post, and an

CHAPTER 18

attack with tanks was then put in from the west across the road. The enemy fell back. F.F. units followed up to a line about eight hundred yards to the east of the road. Here they were under mortar and small arms fire, but the block had been cleared.

By 1030 hours traffic on the road began to move north, but about one hundred vehicles had been abandoned by their drivers who had made them unserviceable. Subsequently many of these vehicles were destroyed in a bombing attack by enemy aircraft.

After this action the greater number of the enemy dead were found to be clad in khaki uniforms and wearing felt hats of the type used by Gurkha and Burma Rifle units. They also had our equipment and rifles. The Japanese never scrupled to wear British uniforms when it suited them to do so, and in the absence of further evidence on this subject it would be therefore unprofitable to speculate on the exact identity of these corpses. It must, however, be remembered that the enemy force at the Pin Chaung had struck far to our rear, and the advantages of a complete disguise whilst carrying out this move are obvious.

The road block had been cleared, but this by no means put an end to Japanese activity. Attempts were made to turn the eastern flank of our position on the ridge in the road block area, whilst other parties of the enemy remained along the banks of the Pin Chaung where they busily consolidated their positions. They concentrated round the ford. In the evening a column of about one thousand men was observed moving south from the ford and was effectively shelled by 414 Battery, R.H.A.

Elements of 113 Regiment of the Chinese 38th Division were now arriving in the area. In view of the situation it had been decided to employ two regiments of 38th Division here, and these regiments were being hurried forward. As he had no artillery the services of 414 Battery, R.H.A., were placed at the disposal of Major-General Sun. It was arranged that the Chinese should attack the line of the Pin Chaung on the morning of April 18th.

Throughout the day the fatigued units of 1 Burma Division had been marching north towards Yenangyaung under most exhausting conditions. The heat was intense, there was no water, and the road was shade-less and very dusty. The men knew that ahead of them the enemy held the Pin Chaung crossing. Hostile aircraft kept our force under constant observation and carried out frequent bombing and machine-gun attacks. The sight of burnt-out vehicles and the complete lack of any support by our air forces was disheartening.

However, the Japanese air arm did not escape without loss during this period. For the four days ending with April 19th, 'B' Section of

3 Indian Light Anti-Aircraft Battery alone claimed to have hit seven aircraft. Several of these were seen falling.

1 Burma Brigade with a squadron of the 2nd Battalion Royal Tank Regiment and its attached company of the West Yorkshire Regiment formed the rearguard. The last elements of this did not arrive south of Yenangyaung until after midnight. Out troops had not been followed up by the Japanese.

Rations were scarce, and it was absolutely essential that men and transport animals should have water. Consequently, the force was concentrated south of Yenangyaung as near the river as possible. 13 Brigade was in the area around Milestone 360. South of it between Sadaing and Yonzeik was Magforce, whilst 1 Burma Brigade was south of the road junction at Milestone 358.

A signals detachment of 7 Armoured Brigade was with Headquarters 1 Burma Division and this furnished Major-General Bruce-Scott with his only wireless link with Burcorps. By this means he was able to speak with Lieut.-General Slim, and late on the night of April 17th plans were made to co-ordinate an attack with that to be carried out north of the Pin Chaung by the Chinese. These latter were to be halted on the Chaung to avoid the possibility of their being confused with Japanese troops. That this was a very real danger was demonstrated more than once during the next two days when the Japanese seized every opportunity of passing themselves off as Chinese. In spite of the fact that special recognition signals had been arranged with the Chinese and orders on this point issued to all troops, the Japanese on several occasions succeeded in this ruse.

Magforce was to attack Yenangyaung at dawn, the ridge north of Nyaunghla being its first objective. It was then to exploit forward with a view to covering the main advance of the Division along the by-pass road from Milestone 358. At the same time 13 Brigade would attack astride the by-pass road with its first objective as the ridge running east and west through Point 510. Then it was to move on Point 501 in Twingon, force the block there, and exploit towards the Pin Chaung. The rear of the Division would be covered by 1 Burma Brigade. 5 Mountain Battery was to support Magforce, and the remaining guns and the squadron of tanks were placed under command of 13 Brigade.

The country around Yenangyaung is barren and exceedingly broken. It is cut by many deep watercourses, always dry except in the monsoon season. In this shade-less, arid region the heat in April is very great and is exceedingly trying even when proper protection from the sun is to be had. Our troops were now to fight for two days under the blazing sun with a shade temperature of about 114°. Many of them were entirely without water or rations. The background to the battle was provided by the burning ruins of the town and the installations on the oilfields east of it.

At 0630 hours on April 18th the general attack of 1 Burma Division began. Advanced Divisional Headquarters moved to the Nyaunghla Stud Farm. On the left the 1st Battalion the Cameronians (Magforce) reached its objective astride the main road with little opposition, whilst the 5th Battalion 1st Punjab Regiment and the 1st Battalion 18th Royal Garhwal Rifles of 13 Brigade gained Point 510 and its ridge unopposed. From Point 510 the advance continued on Twingon, the 1st Battalion Royal Inniskilling Fusiliers being in reserve.

On Magforce front it was intended that the 7th Battalion Burma Rifles should continue the advance beyond the first objective, the attainment of which had secured the by-pass road leading north-east from Nyaunghla. No sooner had the Burma Rifles moved forward than the left-hand company sighted a pack column advancing south through Yenangyaung, some fifteen hundred yards distant. The company opened long range rifle fire, disclosed itself, and at once came under fire from a small bluff near the river. The Company Commander and several men were killed and the company fell back in confusion.

The right company of the Burma Rifles had moved into line on the east of the right company of the Cameronians. These two companies now advanced to the next ridge and, in doing so, came under considerable light machine-gun fire from another ridge to the north-east.

The third rifle company of the 7th Battalion Burma Rifles was ordered to out-flank this ridge and worked forward on to it. Throughout the engagement this company showed great enterprise and, although unable to clear snipers from the upper storeys of buildings, it effectively prevented the by-pass road from coming under small arms fire.

Lieut.-Colonel W.B. Thomas (The Cameronians), commanding Magforce, ordered a company of the 12th Battalion Burma Rifles to clear the bluff near the river, working up to it by a good covered approach. This company consisted of Gurkha reinforcements for 48 Brigade and had been temporarily attached to the 12th Battalion Burma Rifles. Coming under desultory mortar fire it broke and disappeared. The Officer Commanding the Battalion then established some of his troops on the rear edge of the bluff, but could not clear it.

During these operations the Forward Observation Officer of 5 Mountain Battery was with the forward troops, the guns being about three hundred yards further back. Targets were engaged at ranges between six hundred and fourteen hundred yards. Mortars were silenced, and houses containing snipers and observation posts shelled. Three enemy guns were successively engaged and put out of action after their smoke had been observed. Our gunners themselves sustained casualties including one officer killed and another badly wounded. The Battery only had forty rounds per gun, and the ammunition dump was now north of the Pin Chaung. Consequently, all targets were engaged with only one gun.

At 1000 hours a small column of our transport passed along the Nyaunghla by-pass road. It was followed later by another small column. This by-pass road was now safe except for possible long-range mortar fire.

At this stage the Japanese attempted to work south along the river bank and a platoon of the Cameronians was moved further west to deal with this threat. The platoon successfully held up the enemy until about 1515 hours when it was almost wiped out by mortar fire.

The bluff remained as the only threatening pocket of resistance and appeared to be held by a post of about ten men with two light machine-guns. The left company of the 7th Battalion Burma Rifles had reorganised and Captain O.W. Po, a Karen, made a gallant effort to clear the post. Leading a flank attack he had almost reached the top of the bluff when he was caught in the simultaneous burst of several grenades and was badly injured. His party withdrew after throwing its own grenades at the enemy. This appeared to silence the post, but later individual snipers worked forward into houses and were a considerable nuisance.

At 1315 hours 'A' Squadron of the 2nd Battalion Royal Tank Regiment, previously operating with 13 Brigade near Twingon, broke through to Nyaunghla from Obozu to assist the advance north. The Squadron Commander took his tank into the compound of a house where snipers were located and engaged them at short range, but the ground was unsuitable for tanks and the squadron shortly returned to 13 Brigade.

On the withdrawal of the tanks, men of a company of the 12th Battalion Burma Rifles on the left of the line began to discard their rifles and uniforms and to run south along the river. Lieut.-Colonel Thomas ordered the Cameronians to fire on deserters. In this way some of these troops were kept in position. The 12th Battalion Burma Rifles was of course a Territorial Unit. The left company of the 7th Battalion Burma Rifles now also became shaky, and this affected the general situation. Only the Cameronians could be counted on for offensive action. Parties of this Battalion attempted to clear snipers from the buildings along the

CHAPTER 18

front, but as these buildings were solid structures of brick no progress could be made. Two sections of the Cameronians entered the house compounds but there suffered very heavy casualties.

By this time 13 Brigade was fighting near Twingon. Consequently at 1530 hours Magforce was withdrawn by the Nyaunghla by-pass road. It re-joined the main body of the Division south of Twingon and then ceased to exist as a separate formation.

Around Twingon there had been heavy fighting. Having gained the ridge through Point 510, 13 Brigade went on across the oilfields and at 1000 hours the 5th Battalion 1st Punjab Regiment was approaching the Twingon ridge on which is Point 501. The Battalion was advancing on a wide front with all four companies forward, and when five hundred yards short of the ridge it came under heavy fire. Rifles, light machine-guns, mortars, and infantry guns opened on it. The Japanese were seen to be in prepared positions on the ridge. Several officers became casualties, and the Battalion suffered fairly heavily. The initial advance was held up, but a subsequent attack was more successful. By 1100 hours each company had gained a somewhat precarious footing on the ridge. Here the Battalion clung on until mid-afternoon and the Commanding Officer, Lieut.-Colonel K.D. Marsland, then asked Brigade Headquarters to send another Battalion through the position. Later, Battalion Headquarters received a direct hit from a mortar shell and Lieut.-Colonel Marsland was wounded.

A Japanese counter-attack now forced the Battalion to give ground with heavy casualties. The other two Battalions of the Brigade went forward to relieve the situation.

Round Twingon village the enemy was in considerable strength. The 1st Battalion Royal Inniskilling Fusiliers gained some ground but could not get into the built-up area of the village. Here the fighting was very close. Two companies of the Battalion under Major B.J. Boyle made their way round the village and pushed on to the Pin Chaung which they crossed with the object of establishing a bridgehead. They made contact with what they thought were the advanced elements of the Chinese. The recognition signal had been correctly replied to and the troops began to fraternise with the strangers who were in reality Japanese. They were surrounded and disarmed. Imprisoned in a neighbouring village they, with the exception of Major Boyle and another officer, escaped next day in the course of a counter-attack carried out by the Chinese and our tanks.

On the right of the Royal Inniskilling Fusiliers two companies of the 1st Battalion 18th Royal Garhwal Rifles continued the attack from the east of the by-pass road. After being held up by a high wire fence where severe casualties were suffered these companies entered the village. At 1700 hours the remaining two companies attacked from the west of the road. They advanced into the village and were there met by a large party of the enemy under an officer who stated that they were Chinese and asked for a senior officer to be called up. Our troops then manned the Japanese trenches. When it had been ascertained that there were no Chinese in the area the village was shelled for five minutes after which our troops advanced with tanks and burnt the village.

Throughout the day the infantry of 13 Brigade had been supported by the guns of 2 and 23 Mountain Batteries.

The road block south of the ford remained, and 'A' Squadron of the 2nd Battalion Royal Tank Regiment was unable to break through this. The Japanese still had a firm hold on both sides of the Pin Chuang ford.

During the afternoon all transport began to move up the by-pass road from Milestone 358, the head of the column being halted about a mile north of Point 510 where Divisional Headquarters was now established. At about 1630 hours the Divisional Commander proposed to Lieut.-General Slim that he should abandon his motor transport and fight his way out across country. The position was grave. Troops and animals were without water and suffering much exhaustion. However, Lieut.-General Slim ordered the Division to hold on. The Chinese 38th Division was to carry out a further attack on the following morning at first light and would cross the Pin Chuang west of the main road.

The attacks already carried out by the Chinese during that day had taken them to the north bank of the Pin Chaung except in the immediate vicinity of the main road and ford where they were unable to penetrate the Japanese defence. They had been assisted by the 2nd Battalion Royal Tank Regiment and 414 Battery, R.H.A. One tank was destroyed by an anti-tank gun in the area where the road block had existed on the night of April 16th/17th north of the ford.

Ordered to maintain his position Major-General Bruce-Scott formed a perimeter on the high ground astride the by-pass road just south of Twingon. Here his whole force was concentrated together with a mass of transport. There was no water in the area.

1 Burma Brigade was little more than a Brigade in name since the 1st Battalion Burma Rifles had lost heavily at Migyaungye, the 2nd Battalion King's Own Yorkshire Light Infantry at Myingun, and the remaining Battalions at the action on the Yin Chaung. This Brigade had not been engaged during the day and was employed in covering the

movement of the transport behind 13 Brigade. As the main transport column moved up the by-pass road from Milestone 358 Japanese were observed to be landing from the river about Nyaunghla.

Fortunately, hostile aircraft had not been very active. The broken nature of the country, the close fighting, and the smoke from demolitions no doubt hampered them. Our congested transport offered excellent targets and would have suffered heavily from aerial attack.

During the night the Japanese closed in on the north, west, and south of 1 Burma Division. On the east of the position the ground was precipitous and quite impassable for vehicles. The night passed quietly except that at intervals the enemy indulged in jackal cries at many points round our force. About half an hour before first light on April 19th enemy activity began.

The northern sector of the perimeter was held by 13 Brigade and this was attacked from the direction of Twingon village. The attack was accompanied by the usual screams, and machine-gun and mortar fire was directed on our position. 13 Brigade easily held the attack but it had a bad effect on some men of the Burma Rifles, the units of which were now in a nervous state. There was a certain amount of panic and considerable useless firing by our troops.

After daylight enemy machine-gun and mortar fire continued, the massed motor transport being a favourite target. Our own mortars and machine-guns retaliated. During the course of the morning there were, not unnaturally, a number of casualties within the perimeter.

Our attempt to force the road through Twingon was resumed early, the task again being undertaken by 13 Brigade supported by tanks. Soon after 0700 hours the 1st Battalion the Royal Inniskilling Fusiliers and a company of the 1st Battalion the Royal Garhwal Rifles went forward. Some progress was made, but neither infantry nor tanks could force the block. The Commander of 13 Brigade then ordered the 5th Battalion 1st Punjab Regiment to attack through the forward Battalions, but this order was subsequently cancelled. It was now about 1030 hours.

Meanwhile the 2nd Battalion King's Own Yorkshire Light Infantry and the 2nd Battalion 7th Rajput Regiment made a detour to the east of Twingon to assemble on the south of the Pin Chaung from which they were to attack Twingon from the north-east. They were to advance from the Chaung at 1145 hours, a fifteen-minute barrage being put down on the village at 1200 hours. The Rajputs had come under heavy mortar and machine-gun fire and only a few men made contact with the 2nd Battalion King's Own Yorkshire Light Infantry. The planned artillery preparation never materialised and eventually it was learnt that the attack had been cancelled by Burcorps. It was feared that the attack would clash with that of the Chinese who were to advance south along the west of the main road at 1230 hours. Crossing the Pin Chaung the Chinese would then attack Twingon from the north-west.

During the morning requests had been passed by Major-General Bruce-Scott through the Armoured Brigade wireless asking that the Chinese should also attack on the east side of the main road to help to clear the block. This attack had finally been promised for 1230 hours, then postponed to 1400 hours, then again to 1600 hours. In fact, the Chinese did attack at last from the north of the Pin Chaung at 1500 hours. In the morning, however, the 2nd Battalion Royal Tank Regiment had attempted to cross the Chaung and break through to the south. 'B' Squadron with 'D' Company of the West Yorkshire Regiment actually crossed at 1150 hours. It was then engaged by infantry with petrol bombs. Having disposed of this opposition it found itself confronted by a gun covering the road. Progress was halted, but contact was made with the 2nd Battalion King's Own Yorkshire Light Infantry on the east. At this point the West Yorkshire Company was recalled as all available infantry and tanks not already committed were required by Burcorps to proceed north to Gwegyo to hold the road junction there. The Japanese were reported to have occupied Kyaukpadaung, thirty-seven miles to the north-east. The occupying force later turned out to be Chinese and the erroneous report had a most unfortunate effect at a critical period of the Yenangyaung action. It prevented 'B' Squadron of the 2nd Battalion Royal Tank Regiment from continuing its forward move.

In the perimeter the position was precarious. The withdrawal of the 2nd Battalion King's Own Yorkshire Light Infantry and the 2nd Battalion 7th Rajput regiment involved the taking over of additional sectors by other units. The remaining companies of the 1st Battalion Royal Inniskilling Fusiliers were also employed on offensive tasks. A period of heavy accurate shell and mortar fire resulted in the disintegration for the time being of the 12th Battalion Burma Rifles and detachments of the Sappers and Miners. For a brief period, the 5th Battalion Burma Rifles was also out of control, but later the Battalion took over the sector vacated by the Sappers and Miners.

The heat of the blazing sun was again intense, and the lack of water and the scarcity of rations tried the exhausted troops highly. During the day some men died of exhaustion. It is no great wonder then that some of the weaker spirits attempted to leave the battlefield. These endeavours were only prevented by the efforts of British officers.

CHAPTER 18

At 1200 hours the Commander of 1 Burma Brigade reported to Major-General Bruce-Scott that his troops were unreliable. He was ordered to hold on until 1400 hours and then withdraw. At 1300 hours a somewhat similar report was received through the tanks from 13 Brigade. Men were moving down to the Pin Chaung. The tanks further reported that there was a by-pass track to the east along which vehicles might be got away if handled by really determined drivers.

It was evident that this was the last and only chance of saving the transport. Accordingly, the transport was formed up with guns in front and wounded in lorries next. The drivers of many vehicles could not be found and orders were given for the destruction or immobilisation of all non-essential vehicles. These orders were only carried put in part owing to the exhaustion of the whole force and lack of trained personnel to perform the work.

1400 hours arrived, and as there was still no sign of the Chinese Major-General Bruce-Scott confirmed the orders for withdrawal. 13 Brigade and 1 Burma Brigade were to cover the movement of the guns and transport. The motor transport started, then halted as the turn off to the by-pass track could not be found. Two tanks now acted as guides, and led by the Divisional Commander the transport moved out under mortar and gun fire. On the by-pass track one of the tanks was hit by a mortar shell, other vehicles were knocked out, and finally the loose sand of the track brought the whole column to a halt. It was abandoned. However, vehicles had travelled far enough to permit many of the wounded to be evacuated by tanks. Here the guns of 5 Mountain Battery carried on lorries were destroyed.

The two guns of 'B' Section 3 Indian Light Anti-Aircraft Battery were lost. Mortar fire knocked out one gun and the lorry towing the other. The section then endeavoured to extricate this gun, was surrounded and put up a fight against heavy odds until only two men remained unwounded. The five survivors including Captain Taylor then surrendered, but escaped when later in the day the Chinese with our tanks entered Twingon.

The Pin Chaung at a point some two miles north-east of Twingon was eventually reached by the main body. Near this point the village of Thitpyubin was held by the Japanese and some of our units came under light machine-gun fire. Here again the Japanese posed as Chinese troops. A platoon of the 1st Battalion Burma Rifles was deceived by the ruse and captured.

The Chaung was crossed at 1600 hours, some further machine-gun fire was encountered north of the Chaung, and the Division then reassembled that evening and night in the area about Milestone 372 on the Yenangyaung-Kyaukpadaung road.

For three days the Division had been subjected to great strain and had undergone excessive physical hardships. There had been many casualties. Yet wounded British, Indian, and Burman troops all bore their sufferings without complaint and with heroism. Their only shelter from the sun had been the shade afforded by lorries, and in their case the deprivation of water had been felt even more acutely. As an indication of how severe had been the lack of water it is stated that when transport animals smelt the water of the Pin Chaung during the withdrawal on April 19th they became quite uncontrollable.

As a fighting formation 1 Burma Division was now of no value until it had rested and reorganised. Much valuable motor transport and equipment had been lost, and the campaign had reached a stage when many of these losses were irreplaceable. Bofors guns, four 3·7 howitzers, four 25 pdrs., most of the 3" mortars were sacrificed, and four tanks had been destroyed. 1 Burma Division had suffered casualties to the extent of about twenty per cent of its personnel.

At 1500 hours on April 19th the Chinese supported by 'B' Squadron of the 2nd Battalion Royal Tank Regiment and a troop of 414 Battery, R.H.A., attacked south across the Chaung. The attack was well executed, but of course too late to assist 1 Burma Division. The Chinese progressed slowly, but late that evening had gained Twingon. Our tanks killed many of the enemy, and the capture of Twingon resulted in the release of about two hundred British prisoners.

Next morning the Chinese 38th Division, still assisted by the 2nd Battalion Royal Tank Regiment, continued its offensive operations and penetrated to Yenangyaung. An enemy counter-attack from the east was held. That evening the Chinese were in position south of the Chaung. However, during the night Major-General Sun formed the opinion that the Japanese would attack in strength at first light on April 21st and decided to withdraw his force across the Pin Chaung. This movement was carried out and the Chinese 38th Division then fell back towards Gwegyo. It here covered 1 Burma Division which was moving to the area of Mount Popa, north-east of Kyaukpadaung.

The Japanese thrust at the oilfields had been a bold move facilitated by our inability to watch closely the whole length of the Taungdwingyi-Minhla line. Chinese assistance would have been invaluable in stopping the gaps. Without this assistance it had not been difficult for enemy columns to pass between our widely spaced positions. Once through these, a forward move by unfrequented tracks and under cover of night was unlikely to be observed.

CHAPTER 18

It is interesting to note that the final stage of the enemy advance on the Pin Chaung was probably carried out along the dry bed of the Paunggwe Chaung. Stragglers from 1 Burma Division in withdrawing from Yenangyaung on April 19th crossed this Chaung and observed that the stream bed was scored with the tracks of motor transport.

If the intention of the enemy was to secure Yenangyaung and the oilfields before we could carry out demolitions he failed signally. At the same time, by his rapid move far behind our line he did succeed at substantial cost to himself in inflicting very heavy punishment on 1 Burma Division. This was when we could ill afford to lose either men or material.

Whilst the battle of Yenangyaung was being fought the remainder of Burcorps had not been inactive. Strong columns were sent out from Taungdwingyi and Natmauk. Each consisted of one Battalion and a Squadron of the 7th Queen's Own Hussars. Their tasks were to demonstrate against the flank or rear of enemy forces pressing 1 Burma Division and, if possible, to draw off part of these forces.

The Natmauk column comprising the 2nd Battalion the Duke of Wellington's Regiment with tanks moved out along the Magwe road on the morning of April 17th. During the next three days there was contact with the enemy on this road, particularly near its junction with the Yenangyaung road. Here the Japanese had established a block. Our tanks inflicted heavy casualties on the enemy, but did not escape without loss. Two tanks were badly damaged, one tank crew being disabled by gas bombs. In a sharp infantry engagement near Kanbya the Duke of Wellington's Regiment inflicted several casualties on the enemy without loss to itself.

The Taungdwingyi column also began its operations on April 17th when tanks and the 1st Battalion 10th Gurkha Rifles proceeded west along the Taungdwingyi-Magwe road. No substantial force of the enemy was encountered, but several vehicles and their occupants passing along the road were dealt with near Milestone 302. The column withdrew on Taungdwingyi on April 19th.

The operations carried out by these columns failed to relieve the pressure on 1 Burma Division at Yenangyaung.

Meanwhile, on April 17th, General Alexander had discussed with General Stilwell the possibilities of offensive action by the Chinese south of Pyinmana. General Alexander promised to make the 7th Queen's Own Hussars available for the operation and orders were issued for the Regiment to be prepared to move to Pyawbwe. However, on the following day it seemed clear that the projected attack by the

Chinese could not take place. The situation at Yenangyaung and in the Shan States where the Japanese advance against the Chinese VI Army was developing rapidly called for renewed consideration. Accordingly, on April 19th, General Alexander again met General Stilwell. Lieut.-General Slim was also present.

General Alexander stressed the importance of holding strongly the centres of communication on the line Chauk-Kyaukpadaung-Meiktila-Thazi. General Stilwell agreed, and it was arranged that the whole of the Chinese 38th Division should be placed under the command of Burcorps.

Plans for offensive action were again discussed. The deep penetration made by the Japanese 33rd Division at Yenangyaung appear to present a favourable opportunity for a counter-stroke. Owing to the nature and extent of the country this was beyond the capacity of Burcorps alone as considerable forces were required merely to locate the enemy should he elect to move into the jungle or off the main routes. General Stilwell consented to the employment of the Chinese 200th Division and one regiment of the 22nd Division for this counter offensive. Arrangements were made to set in motion the moves of these formations towards Kyaukpadaung and Ywamun as soon as possible. It was improbable that this force could be concentrated and ready for offensive action before the morning of April 22nd at the earliest. This was due to lack of transport and the difficulty of co-ordinating plans with the Chinese V Army.

The proposed operations were not carried out. Events in the Shan States were moving fast, and General Stilwell was compelled to divert the Chinese 200th Division and one regiment of the 22nd Division towards Taunggyi to prevent a Japanese break through to the west at that point. The remainder of the Chinese 22nd Division was ordered to concentrate in the Thazi area.

The general situation was critical and is discussed in detail in the next chapter.

Chapter 19

Effect of the Japanese advance through the Shan States on the situation south of Mandalay – General Alexander's plans in the event of the loss of Mandalay – Decision to fall back towards Kalewa with the object of protecting India – Problems of Supply – Withdrawal to the west bank of Irrawaddy begun – 2 Burma Brigade ordered to cover Myittha valley – Successful delaying actions at Meiktila and at Kyaukse – Decision to withdraw Chinese V Army to Katha – Destruction of the Ava bridge.

Events in the Shan States were now the dominating factor. The Chinese 55th Division covering the Mawchi-Loikaw-Taunggyi road had been destroyed south of Loikaw on the night of April 18th/19th. Since it had not been possible to effect any strong concentration of the widely dispersed Chinese VI Army behind the 55th Division there was only a small force available to oppose the hostile motorised column driving north. By the afternoon of April 20th, the Japanese had crossed the To Sai Kha and the Chinese were retiring on Hopong to take up a line east of that town. Taunggyi and the road through it to Thazi and Meiktila were open to the enemy. This constituted a grave and immediate threat to the Chinese and British forces in the area south of Mandalay.

Here the Chinese V Army had been forced out of Pyinmana on April 20th, and the 96th Division was very heavily engaged. The proposed counter-offensive by Burcorps and the Chinese 200th Division would have relieved this pressure, but it was essential to stop the gap at Taunggyi. Consequently 200th Division was on April 21st diverted east from Meiktila. It was accompanied by one Regiment of 22nd Division. On April 23rd it attacked the Japanese force holding Taunggyi.

To secure the centres of communication south of Mandalay, Burcorps made the following dispositions on April 21st:

38th Chinese Division to concentrate at Kyaukpadaung.
1 Burma Division (less 2 Burma Brigade on the west bank of the Irrawaddy) to be prepared to move to Taungtha.
17 Division to withdraw from Taungdwingyi, and later from Natmauk, to positions north-west and west of Meiktila at Mahlaing and Zayetkon.
7 Armoured Brigade to Meiktila, and there to come under command of the depleted Chinese V Army.

It now became necessary for General Alexander to give thought to the action to be taken should the Japanese effect a break-through in the Shan States, and on the possible loss of Mandalay. The problem facing him was far from easy.

Towards the end of March, the policy for the defence of Upper Burma in the event of the loss of Mandalay had been generally considered. At the direction of General Alexander an appreciation and outline plan had been drawn up. This appreciation and plan were approved by General Wavell on his visit to Burma at the end of March. The time had arrived for further consideration of the plan in the light of recent developments.

Briefly the plan contemplated that should Mandalay be lost the Allied forces would be disposed in the under-mentioned manner:

(a) Chinese VI Army.
   (i) Troops east of the river Salween to withdraw on Puerh in China.
   (ii) Troops west of the river Salween to withdraw towards Hsipaw and Lashio.
(b) Chinese V Army to withdraw astride the Mandalay-Lashio road.
(c) Imperial Forces.
   (i) To maintain touch with the Chinese, 7 Armoured Brigade and one composite British Infantry Brigade of 17 Division to accompany the Chinese V Army.
   (ii) 17 Division, less the above-mentioned Brigade, to withdraw on the axis Mandalay-Shwebo-Katha covering the newly projected road between India and China via the Hukawng valley.
   (iii) 1 Burma Division to cover the approaches to India through Kalewa.

CHAPTER 19

An Operation Instruction was issued to Burcorps early in April, and administrative arrangements were put in hand to implement this plan.

During the early part of April, however, with the fast-changing situation it became apparent that it would be impossible to accumulate in Lashio or beyond it, sufficient stocks of rice to feed the Chinese armies for more than a few weeks. The gradual loss of the main rice producing areas of Burma, the closing of rice mills and the difficulty of collecting the grain owing to the disintegration of the railways, and a famine in Yunnan, all contributed to this result. Consequently, on the plan as it stood, a withdrawal north of Mandalay would probably mean the starvation of the Chinese armies unless supplies could be sent in from China. This seemed highly improbable.

There was a better prospect of the Chinese obtaining food supplies in the Shwebo district. General Alexander decided, therefore, to invite the Chinese to withdraw some of their forces through Shwebo if it became necessary to abandon Mandalay.

Major-General T.J.W. Winterton, C.B.E., had succeeded Lieut.-General Hutton as Chief of Staff of the Burma Army at the beginning of April. Lieut.-General Hutton then went to India on a special mission to see the Commander-in-Chief. He discussed with General Wavell the question of a part of the Imperial Forces accompanying the Chinese in a withdrawal to China. General Wavell stated that he was prepared to accept a change in the plan if General Alexander thought it desirable. Lieut.-General Hutton returned to Burma on April 18th.

General Alexander was so impressed with the political considerations that he determined to give the Chinese the opportunity of accepting or refusing the assistance of British forces on the axis, Mandalay-Lashio. He met the Generalissimo's principal Liaison Officer, General Lin Wei, at Maymyo on April 21st, explained the situation in detail, and offered him 7 Armoured Brigade.

General Lin Wei agreed that the bulk of the Chinese V Army should move north via Shwebo, and that it would be better if no Imperial Forces withdrew towards Lashio. The tanks should be employed for the battle for Northern Burma on the most suitable ground which was on the west of the Irrawaddy towards Shwebo.

In view of this arrangement and of developments in the Shan States General Alexander now formulated a new plan and an Operation Instruction embodying it was issued to Burcorps on April 23rd. The contents of this Operation Instruction had been agreed by General Stilwell's staff at Maymyo.

This new plan envisaged certain dispositions on the west bank of the Irrawaddy, and also covering Mandalay.

These were:

(a) West of the River Mu.
Burcorps, less 7 Armoured Brigade. 1 Burma Division was to be astride the River Chindwin with a strong detachment covering the approach to Kalewa via the Myittha valley on the west bank of the Chindwin.

(b) Between the Mu and Irrawaddy rivers.
7 Armoured Brigade and the Chinese 38th Division.

(c) In and south of Mandalay and holding the crossings over the River Myitnge.

Chinese 22nd, 28th and 96th Divisions.

It will be realised that a withdrawal from the Meiktila area would uncover the communications with Mandalay of any Chinese force about Kalaw-Taunggyi and would prevent its withdrawal through Mandalay. The plan therefore contemplated that all Chinese forces east of the Mandalay-Pyawbwe railway would move towards Lashio.

It must here be emphasised that General Alexander had no intention of withdrawing the large forces mentioned above across the Irrawaddy unless compelled to give up Kyaukpadaung and Meiktila. Arrangements, already described, had been made to cover these places strongly. At the same time General Alexander had to consider the dangerous bottleneck of the Ava bridge, the only bridge over the Irrawaddy and the sole crossing place for tanks. The approaches to the bridge ran through Mandalay and were very vulnerable to air attack. Mandalay had already become a favourite target for hostile aircraft. The city was burnt out and lay in ruins. Its railway facilities had been seriously impaired.

To allow the Allied forces to be pushed into the loop of the Irrawaddy below Mandalay and to be compelled to fight with this obstacle behind them was a situation to be avoided. General Alexander decided, therefore, that the moment to put his plan into operation was when his advanced forces had to fall back from Meiktila. To delay longer would involve dangerous congestion at the Ava bridge.

To eliminate as far as possible the Ava bridge bottleneck steps had been taken earlier in April to construct ferries over the Irrawaddy. A ferry was also constructed across the Myitnge river. The Irrawaddy was in fact crossed by 1 Burma Division by ferry, and this formation did not use the Ava bridge.

CHAPTER 19

Owing to the uncertainty of the situation in the Shan States General Alexander's plan did not provide for the further withdrawal beyond Mandalay of the Chinese 22nd, 28th and 96th Divisions. No decision could then be made whether they would fall back northwards or towards Lashio, but it was still hoped to cover the Hukawng Valley.

The Japanese thrust through the Shan States progressed rapidly and the operations connected with this area are detailed in a later chapter. Loilem fell to the enemy on the evening of April 23rd, and although the Chinese 200th Division recaptured Taunggyi on April 24th this did not hold up the Japanese drive on Lashio. There was considerable panic in rear areas in the Shan States, but a certain amount of order and confidence was restored by Brigadier Martin who was sent to Lashio by General Alexander.

Under orders of General Stilwell, the Chinese 28th Division moved from Mandalay towards Lashio, but the disorganisation of the railways slowed up this movement. At the same time General Alexander took steps to protect his rear by sending a detachment from the Bush Warfare School and the British Infantry Depot at Maymyo, to hold the Gokteik Gorge on the Lashio road. He also moved his Rear Headquarters from Maymyo to Shwebo on April 23rd.

On April 25th General Alexander met General Stilwell at Kyaukse. Here he learnt that the Japanese were advancing from Pyinmana on Pyawbwe, and that the Chinese 96th Division holding the front was breaking up. As one regiment of 22nd Division was in the Shan States, Meiktila, which should have been strongly held, was devoid of infantry. General Stilwell was not sanguine about the operations in the Shan States, and General Alexander formed the impression that Chinese resistance on the Pyawbwe front was likely to collapse very soon. This belief was correct. The Japanese were north of Pyawbwe before the day was out.

General Alexander therefore issued orders for the plan of withdrawal north of Mandalay to be put into operation on the night of April 25th/26th. He also ordered Burcorps to provide a rearguard on the Axis Meiktila-Mandalay and to cover the withdrawal of the much-battered Chinese 22nd and 96th Divisions. The evacuation of units and installations remaining in Maymyo was begun. Advanced Army Headquarters moved from Maymyo to Shwebo on April 26th.

The situation had clarified sufficiently for a decision to be made on the future role of the Imperial Forces. The capture of Lashio by the enemy was only a matter of time. There would then be nothing to prevent the fall of Bhamo and the consequent turning of our communications with Myitkyina. It was quite impossible for General Alexander to disengage any troops for the defence of Bhamo. The condition and now depleted numbers of the Chinese troops south of Mandalay precluded the possibility of any lengthy stand on the Mandalay-Irrawaddy line, and with the Japanese in Bhamo the rear of such a line would be in grave danger.

In these circumstances General Alexander decided that his main object must be the defence of India. There were also the subsidiary objects of maintaining touch with the Chinese, retaining a position for re-entry into Burma, and the desirability of extricating as much as possible of the Imperial Forces. This decision was made on April 26th.

Upon the abandonment of the Mandalay-Irrawaddy line General Alexander now planned to fall back towards Kalewa, leaving two Brigades astride the Chindwin to delay the enemy as far as south as possible. A strong detachment would cover the Myittha valley. The remainder of the Imperial Forces would move on Kalewa via Ye-U leaving a detachment to cover this route. If possible, some portion of the Chinese Armies, and particularly the hard fighting 38th Division, was to be taken back to India with the British troops.

The question of maintenance was one of difficulty. Preparations were put in hand for making the rough jungle track from Ye-U to Shwegyin of the Chindwin river fit for motor transport. Although this track linked up with the projected road to India from Kalewa through Tamu little work had been done on it, and it still remained scarcely better than a bullock cart route. A stretch of thirty miles was waterless. The length of the track was approximately one hundred and twenty miles, or eight marches. Provision was now made for stocking this track with supplies and water, Major-General Wakely, Commander Lines of Communications Area, being placed in charge of the work.

The condition of the road between Kalewa and Tamu was also such that once the monsoon set in the movement of stores south of Tamu would have to be via the Chindwin river and its tributary, the Yu. The maintenance capacity of this route was not known in any detail at Burma Army Headquarters, and therefore it was not known what force could be maintained south of Tamu.

It was estimated that the stocking of the track from Ye-U to Shwegyin would take seven days. General Alexander was accordingly anxious to hold the Mandalay-Irrawaddy position for this period, although doubtful of the possibility of doing so. He urged his administrative staff to accelerate arrangements as much as possible. The now acute shortage of transport made it necessary to withdraw vehicles from all possible sources including 7 Armoured Brigade and other units of Burcorps. Drastic steps were taken to effect this, the dumping of kit and all stores not having an immediate fighting value being enforced. Fortunately supplies already accumulated in the Shwebo-Ye-U area by the foresight of the 'Q' staff were ample for requirements. The Administrative Services rose to the occasion nobly, and the problem of distributing supplies and water along the track was tackled with vigour. Dumps of rations, water, and petrol were established at likely staging camps. Further supplies were pushed forward to Shwegyin, the crossing place on the Chindwin, a few miles south of Kalewa.

Whilst these palms and arrangements were going forward Burcorps was in action south of Mandalay.

During this period of the operations Burcorps had to contend with considerable activity on the part of rebel Burmans and enemy agents. It was learnt that the Japanese were employing Indian troops captured in Malaya for espionage and Fifth Column purposes. An Indian National Army had been formed from these traitors. The enemy had also induced captured men of the Burma Rifles to act as spies and a party of these was taken by the Chinese 38th Division. All units were in consequence warned of the necessity of exercising extreme vigilance when stragglers or escaped prisoners entered out lines. In the Taungdwingyi-Natmauk area 17 Division had been much troubled by the activities of Burman malcontents, and there was frequent sabotage of telephone lines. A 'Peace' party of Burmans including a Buddhist monk and with a Japanese leader had been intercepted. At Mahlaing, north of Meiktila, no sooner had 17 Division Headquarters been established than fires were started in the town. Drastic action was taken against looters and fire-raisers, who were shot.

On April 25th Burcorps was on the general line Chauk-Kyaukpadaung-Thabyegon-Meiktila. This was held by the Chinese 38th Division on the east, the dividing line being east of Kyatkon. 1 Burma Division was in reserve in the area Taungtha-Myingyan with 2 Burma Brigade on the west bank of the Irrawaddy about Yenengyat. 7 Armoured Brigade had rejoined Burcorps. It was in the Meiktila area south of which at Pyawbwe the Chinese 22nd Division was being encircled by superior enemy forces.

That day the 7th Queen's Own Hussars operating on the road between Meiktila and Pyawbwe were in contact with the enemy. At 1200 hours a scout car met three Japanese tanks of the Cruiser class about one mile north of Pyawbwe out of which place Chinese troops were then streaming. On receipt of this information a patrol of a troop of tanks was sent forward, and in the evening an enemy motorised column with guns and mortars was encountered on the road thirteen miles south of Meiktila. The column was engaged at point blank range, the tanks running down its length. Many casualties were inflicted and several lorries were knocked out without any loss to the tanks. As it was growing dark the action could not be continued long enough to be decisive.

There being no Chinese troops in Meiktila to meet the Japanese advance from Pyawbwe, General Alexander that evening ordered Burcorps to move a Brigade of 17 Division to Meiktila forthwith. 63 Brigade at once marched for that place, and 7 Armoured Brigade from its harbour five miles north sent the 1st Battalion West Yorkshire Regiment into the town. Orders were also issued to 7 Armoured Brigade to continue to hold the area until the night of April 26th to enable the Chinese to withdraw to Wundwin where they would entrain.

The general withdrawal from the Kyaukpadaung-Meiktila line began that night. The Chinese 38th Division was ordered to withdraw by the road Popaywa-Taungtha to Tada-U south-west of the Ava bridge, this movement being covered by 1 Burma Division which in turn would fall back on the Sameikkon ferry. Behind its covering force at Meiktila 17 Division would retire to Ondaw across the Ava bridge. It was intended to take up strong lay-back positions at Myittha (south of Kyaukse) and at Kyaukse.

2 Burma Brigade was originally intended to fall back from Pakokku on Monywa, detaching a column to withdraw on Kalemyo by a route west of the Chindwin and thus denying the Myittha valley to an enemy force known to be advancing up the west bank of the Irrawaddy. On April 27th it was reported that this force was in Salin, sixteen miles north-west of Yenangyaung. An advance party of Thakins was then at Sinbyugyun. It should here be noted that in this area from Pakokku westwards gangs of Thakins and dacoits were active. Villages were looted and road bridges destroyed.

Reliable information being received that the enemy force west of the Irrawaddy intended to move through the Myittha valley to cut the Kalewa-Tamu road the role of 2 Burma Brigade was modified. The Brigade was ordered to fall back from Pakokku via Pauk to Tilin and to prevent any enemy movement up the Myittha valley. These instructions were subsequently embodied in a Burcorps Directive issued on April 28th.

CHAPTER 19

The same Directive also detailed the dispositions for the remainder of Burcorps formations after the crossing of the Irrawaddy. These were to the following effect:

(a) Having crossed the river by the Sameikkon ferry 1 Burma Division (less 2 Burma Brigade) was to march on Monywa where 13 Brigade would cross the Chindwin river to operate south and south-west from Salingyi. 1 Burma Brigade would move by steamers from Monywa to Kalewa to undertake the defence of that bridgehead. One Brigade (63 Brigade) of 17 Division was to come under command of 1 Burma Division to operate south from Chaung-U and also to protect the road Sagaing-Monywa.
(b) 17 Division (less one Brigade) having crossed the Irrawaddy by the Ava bridge would undertake the defence of the area Myinmu-Allagapa and prevent enemy infiltration between Allagapa and the Mu river.
(c) The Chinese 38th Division was to hold the area Sagaing-Ondaw preventing crossings of the Irrawaddy at Amarapura or Tada-U.
(d) 7 Armoured Brigade was to support the Chinese 38th Division, detaching one squadron for operations in the Chaung-U area.

2 Burma Brigade marched out of Pakokku at 1830 hours on April 28th. The following night it was at Pyinchaung.

Unopposed, the remainder of 1 Burma Division and the Chinese 38th Division carried out their crossings of the Irrawaddy. 1 Burma Division completed its crossing by the evening of April 28th, and then issued a warning order for the onward march to the Monywa area to begin on the evening of April 29th. Subsequently this move was postponed to the evening of April 30th on the representation of the Commander 13 Brigade that his troops should not march before 0700 hours on that day because of their tiredness and the loss of kit by the 1st Battalion 18th Royal Garhwal Rifles and Brigade Headquarters.

It will be noted that from the night of April 28th/29th the approach from Pakokku to Monywa along the west bank of the Chindwin had been left unprotected. The delay in the march of 1 Burma Division from the Irrawaddy opposite Sameikkon towards Monywa extended this danger period for Monywa with results that will subsequently become apparent.

Meanwhile 17 Division and 7 Armoured Brigade maintained contact with the enemy on the main Meiktila-Mandalay road. On the morning of April 26th, a patrol of the 7th Queen's Own Hussars again came upon a Japanese motorised column, this time at Kandaung about seven miles along the road south of Meiktila. Once more the Japanese were taken by surprise and considerable damage was inflicted on them before they went to ground in the village. A company of the 1st Battalion West Yorkshire Regiment was then sent forward from Meiktila to clear the village, but the attack was held up by enemy aircraft which pinned our infantry to the ground.

By this time the element of surprise had been completely lost. Eventually the attack went in at 1730 hours, the infantry being carried on tanks to within a hundred yards of the village. Our advancing troops came under mortar fire but entered the village and began to clear it. It was then decided to fire the village, and this was done by the guns of 'D' Troop 414 Battery, R.H.A.

The enemy now withdrew to a patch of jungle south of Kandaung and a further attack was made by the infantry company supported by tanks. Here was a much larger force of Japanese than was expected and the attack was held up by heavy light machine-gun and mortar fire. The company was ordered to withdraw, but the two forward platoons never received this order. Held to the ground by fire they were charged by an overwhelming force of Japanese. The platoons split into small groups and withdrew at dusk. The losses of the West Yorkshire Regiment had been one officer wounded, three other ranks killed, two wounded and two missing.

In these operations we lost two tanks, but it was estimated that the Japanese losses were one hundred and fifty killed, and that twelve enemy lorries and one gun had been destroyed.

During the day the remainder of 7 Armoured Brigade together with 63 Brigade had moved back to Wundwin. That night the 7th Queen's Own Hussars and the 1st Battalion West Yorkshire Regiment evacuated Meiktila, withdrawing to the Wundwin position.

Major-General Cowan had now assumed command of the rearguard. His orders were that 63 Brigade was to hold on at Wundwin until 1800 hours on April 27th when it would fall back in motor transport behind the lay-back at Kyaukse. Here 48 Brigade was in position.

After the rough handling the Japanese had received south of Meiktila it was not expected that they would press their advance. However, at about 0700 hours on April 27th a patrol of the 2nd Battalion Royal Tank Regiment came under anti-tank fire from the village of Ngathet near Milestone 350 on the main road. Two tanks were knocked out and the village was then shelled by the guns of 414 Battery, R.H.A.

Subsequently four enemy tanks were observed north-west of Ngathet and were promptly engaged by 'B' Squadron of the 2nd Battalion

Royal Tank Regiment. A short but fierce action followed in which exact observation was very difficult owing to the thin scrub covering the country. Hits were obtained on at least one enemy tank whilst our vehicles remained unscathed.

The day was an unsatisfactory one for our tanks which were employed in preventing the enemy from engaging 63 Brigade about Wundwin. The scrub enabled the Japanese infantry and guns to advance unseen although the movement of tanks could not be similarly concealed. The enemy thus was in a position to bring his guns up very close and our tanks were subjected to constant shelling and threats of out-flanking. This forced them repeatedly to withdraw for short distances throughout the day, but they succeeded in covering 63 Brigade which had come in for considerable attention from enemy bombing aircraft.

At 1630 hours 17 Division announced that no transport for 63 Brigade would be available before midnight and that the Wundwin position must be held until that hour, or the resources of 7 Armoured Brigade utilised for the withdrawal of the infantry. It was considered that once 63 Brigade became involved it would be very difficult for it to disengage. Consequently, by utilising tanks and other vehicles, 7 Armoured Brigade contrived to ferry all infantry to Kume where proper motor transport was found. The 2nd Battalion Royal Tank Regiment continued to act as rearguard whilst this movement was in progress.

7 Armoured Brigade then went on to cross the Ava bridge for the Ondaw area. The 7th Queen's Own Hussars joined 48 Brigade at Kyaukse. 63 Brigade took up a new position covering the road and railway bridges across the Myitnge river south of Mandalay. 16 Brigade had reached the Ondaw area on April 27th.

48 Brigade had begun to arrive in Kyaukse on the morning of April 26th. Immediate steps were taken to occupy and improve as strong a defensive position as possible. It was the intention to impose here sufficient delay upon the enemy to permit the safe passage of the Irrawaddy by all our forces, and also to give the depleted Chinese 22nd and 96th Divisions ample breathing time and an opportunity of concentrating in the Mandalay area.

Kyaukse had been burnt out and devastated by hostile aircraft. Dead Burmans and cattle lay about in the streets. The country round Kyaukse was mainly a mixture of open paddy fields and banana groves, whilst jungle was dense on the banks of the Zawgyi river. The ground near the main road was cut by numerous irrigation channels, the road itself being raised on an embankment. Adjoining the eastern outskirts of the town was a long ridge running due east. Its extent was too great to include it entirely within a Brigade defensive position. On this ridge our gunners found excellent observation posts. It was known that the main bulk of the Japanese 33rd Division was now on the front of 1 Burma Division to the west, and consequently the roads from that direction were potential approaches for mechanised forces.

The position covered the west, south, and east of the town in a wide arc. On the south-west the 1st Battalion 4th P.W.O. Gurkha Rifles held a line south of the irrigation channels that took off from the Zawgyi river. The right of the Battalion was swung back to deny encirclement, and its left stopped just short of the railway line. From this point the combined Battalion 7th Gurkha Rifles continued the defences to the river at a point some five hundred yards south of the town. The 2nd Battalion 5th Royal Gurkha Rifles, F.F., then held a line for about one thousand yards along the north bank of the river swinging back to cover the long ridge on the east of Kyaukse. It held Point 816, near the centre of the ridge, a strong patrol being thrown out to protect its eastern end. The 1st Battalion 3rd Q.A.O. Gurkha Rifles was in Brigade reserve on the north-eastern outskirts of the town, behind the 1st Battalion 4th P.W.O. Gurkha Rifles. The total Brigade strength was about seventeen hundred, all Battalions being much reduced in numbers. As in the earlier action at Kokkogwa the available signalling resources were practically nil. There was no wireless, and only one helio and two lamps were available. This absence of signalling equipment was not peculiar to 48 Brigade, all formations being similarly situated. It naturally much hampered the efficiency of the defence, and communication by runner inevitably delayed the carrying out of essentially urgent operations.

Supporting the infantry were the 7th Queen's Own Hussars with one company of the 1st Battalion West Yorkshire Regiment, one troop of 414 Battery, R.H.A., one troop of 'A' Battery 95 Anti-Tank Regiment, R.A., and 1 Field Battery of 1 Indian Field Regiment, I.A. 70 Field Company Bengal Sappers and Miners provided demolition parties.

The anti-tank guns were placed in pairs. One pair in depth covered the main road behind the bock mentioned later, the other covered the good tank country in front of the 1st Battalion 4th P.W.O. Gurkha Rifles.

Fields of fire for the infantry were improved, banana plantations and undergrowth being cut back and thinned out. Even after this work had been carried out many covered approaches for the enemy still existed. The area to the west of the main road in front of our positions was inundated by the opening of a water-cut. A road block was constructed at a bend in the road near a culvert just south of our forward defence lines. In addition to the pair of anti-tank guns, mortars also covered this block.

CHAPTER 19

During the night of April 27th/28th 63 Brigade passed through the position, and so, too, did the last elements of the Chinese V Army.

At dawn on April 28th infantry patrols were pushed well out to the flanks, and one of these patrols reported armed Burmans moving in the jungle west to east. Tanks and a patrol of the 7th Gurkha Rifles went south along the main road. Here, about ten miles south of Kyaukse, the tanks engaged a column of transport and later came under anti-tank gun fire which necessitated a slight withdrawal. A troop of our tanks was then heavily bombed from a low altitude by hostile aircraft. One tank was destroyed.

In the evening a tank trap a Milestone 399 was ordered to be manned. Two lorry-borne guns with a small escort of fourteen men of the 7th Gurkha Rifles proceeded to the position and were at once in action against five Japanese tanks. One of these was knocked out, but enemy infantry now marched up both sides of the road. After engaging the Japanese with light automatic fire and grenades our small force fell back on Kyaukse.

The enemy followed up and was soon in contact with our main position astride the road. Patrols approached the block soon after 2100 hours and were promptly wiped out by the 7th Gurkha Rifles with automatic fire and bombs.

At 2200 hours the enemy put in an attack on the east of the road. It was a bright moonlight night and our fire was held until the Japanese were within a hundred and fifty yards. They were then driven back in confusion, leaving some twenty-five dead and others screaming with pain.

Towards midnight the sound of bullock carts and motor transport approaching the river on the front of the 5th Royal Gurkha Rifles was heard. Vehicle headlights were seen. The turning off point from the main road was known and our 25 pounders opened up on this whilst 2" mortars fired on the transport near the river. Afterwards a Gurkha who had been captured by the enemy and later escaped reported that our fire did great execution in what he judged to be Regimental Headquarters.

At 0030 hours another attack was launched on the 7th Gurkha Rifles east of the road. This time the Japanese were allowed to advance even closer. Then every weapon was brought to bear, and the Japanese were routed with a loss of another forty killed. At the same time a subsidiary attack north of the Zawgyi river against the eastern face of our position was easily repelled by the 5th Royal Gurkha Rifles.

The enemy now waited for the moon to set and at 0515 hours, when it was very dark, attacked east of the road for a third time. Again, heavy fire broke up the advance, and the shouts and screams that came out of the darkness indicated that the Japanese had been greatly demoralised.

During the night enemy patrols endeavoured to advance west of the road and astride the railway. They were dealt with very easily.

At dawn patrols of tanks and infantry went forward to clear the front and flanks of our position and to ascertain if any encircling movements were in progress. To the west one patrol with a gunner Observation Post went as far as Panan. On the east another patrol went round the north side of the long ridge.

Meanwhile at 0900 hours a counter-attack was carried out by a company of the 7th Gurkha Rifles, the objective being the burnt-out village of Htanaungbinhla in front of our forward defence lines between the road and railway. It was hoped to trap a number of the enemy here. A gunner officer was in the forward defence lines and fired his guns by direct observation. The Battalion mortars also supported the counter-attack.

A party of the enemy was known to have taken refuge in the culvert just south of the road block. Accordingly, this was mortared whilst our guns fired on the centre and southern portions of the village. The infantry then advanced. From the culvert one or two Japanese attempted to flee but were intercepted. The remainder were trapped, and later thirty-eight corpses were pulled out. There were no survivors.

There was no holding the 7th Gurkha Rifles. They went through the village destroying the enemy. Those Japanese who ran away were caught by the fire of the remainder of the Battalion from the forward defence lines.

At the southern end of Htanaungbinhla the company gave the enemy a final burst of fire, then halted and reorganised. It had only lost one killed and three wounded. Over one hundred enemy dead were counted. In addition, three 2" mortars, five automatics, numerous rifles and revolvers, and a Japanese flag had been taken.

Brigade Headquarters had received orders for a withdrawal that night, but the exact time was dependent on the movement of certain Chinese troops. It was evident that the withdrawal might be difficult. The enemy, identified as the Japanese 18th Division, had at least one regiment deployed and had begun the usual encircling movement. A patrol of the 5th Royal Gurkha Rifles thrown out to the east reported contact with the enemy. This hostile force was dispersed by shell fire and suffered heavy casualties. During the afternoon another Japanese force, estimated at a strength of four hundred, was at Panan and west of that village. Here, too, the Japanese were engaged by our guns. Possibly, therefore, 48 Brigade would have to fight its way out of Kyaukse.

Throughout the day enemy artillery was active. Our guns were shelled, and the long ridge was continuously searched for gunner observation

CHAPTER 19

posts. These were gallantly maintained in spite of casualties and the work of our own guns was not interrupted. Soon after midday the Japanese guns shortened their range and began to fire on our infantry. At 1400 hours a most intensive and accurate barrage was put down on Brigade Headquarters. Although enemy aircraft were overhead this position had possibly been communicated to the enemy by Burmese spies. It had been well concealed. Battalion Headquarters of the 4th Gurkha Rifles, also concealed in dense jungle, was similarly shelled.

It was noted that the enemy was employing heavier guns than had hitherto been met in Burma and the fire, singularly ineffective, was the most concentrated experienced by our troops during the campaign. They endured it well.

Shortly after 1530 hours two companies of Japanese advanced on Htanaungbinhla. They were caught by machine-gun fire and made little headway. The attack petered out.

Orders had now been received from Divisional Headquarters that the Brigade was to be withdrawn at 1800 hours or as soon as possible. Although contact with the enemy was close, and a withdrawal at 1800 hours involved a movement in daylight, Brigadier Cameron decided to break off the action at that hour. The plan for this had been carefully worked out. It was executed speedily and with perfect timing.

At 1700 hours enemy activity increased and Japanese aircraft began to dive-bomb and machine-gun our troops. These attacks caused no damage. Two tanks of the 7th Queen's Own Hussars moved forward across the main road bridge at 1730 hours and at once had the effect of deadening hostile fire.

Before 1800 hours the troops in the forward defence lines began to thin out and first line motor transport moved off. The railway bridge across the Zawgyi river had been destroyed earlier in the day, and at 1800 hours precisely the main road bridge was blown. The deafening explosion had an electrical effect. All firing ceased as though both sides had received an order to do so. There was an eerie silence.

Then our guns opened on the enemy forward positions and the tanks followed suit. Our infantry remaining south of the river crossed it by wading. The two forward tanks covered this movement, and immediately afterwards swung west along a road skirting the river to cross it by a subsidiary bridge which was then blown. Other tanks covered the broken bridges. Our guns shortened their range to shell the recently evacuated forward defence lines.

The 1st Battalion 3rd Q.A.O. Gurkha Rifles had formed a lay-back at a hummock near the road just north of the town, and by 1815 hours the other Battalions were passing through this position. Five minutes later our tanks in Kyaukse were withdrawn but continued to act as rearguard to the Brigade which marched to an embussing point.

As the last of the tanks withdrew up the main road the bridge over the Zawgyi near Milestone 410 was blown. Not long afterwards 63 Brigade demolished the road and rail bridges across the Myitnge river. The demolition of the railway bridge was not very successful.

In the action at Kyaukse 48 Brigade, a weary skeleton of its proper self, had fought magnificently. It had been splendidly supported by our tanks and guns. A conservative estimate put the Japanese losses at five hundred killed. Our own casualties were ten killed and wounded.

If the enemy thought that the Imperial Forces in Burma were no longer in a fit condition to fight, he was disillusioned at Kyaukse. Notwithstanding his superior numbers and ample artillery support he had been halted in no uncertain manner when fighting us on ground of our own choice. His 18th Division now made no attempt to follow up or force the Myitnge position.

48 Brigade crossed the Ava bridge and concentrated at Myinmu near the confluence of the Mu river with the Irrawaddy.

During April 29th Mandalay had been cleared by Burcorps of as much of its accumulation of stores as possible. Shortage of transport made this difficult and much had to be destroyed, whilst other stores were made over to the Chinese.

On this day too, the situation regarding the future movement of the Chinese forces in the Mandalay area crystallised. At a meeting at Shwebo between Generals Alexander and Stilwell the latter stated that the remnants of the Chinese V Army would move north on Katha when Mandalay was given up. They would probably then fall back on Bhamo, but General Stilwell was uncertain on this point and he was awaiting the Generalissimo's instructions. The capture of Lashio, then imminent, might force the withdrawal of the Chinese V Army to India.

General Stilwell further stated that exhaustion made it impossible for the Chinese 96th Division to fight south of Mandalay. He proposed, therefore, to move this Division by train to Myitkyina as soon as possible. This left only the Chinese 22nd Division to cover Mandalay and hold the crossings over the Myitnge river. Consequently, only a delaying action could be fought on that line. The 22nd Division would then continue its withdrawal up the east bank of the Irrawaddy to Singu, crossing to the west bank by ferry at that point.

General Stilwell requested that the Chinese 38th Division should revert to his command to cover the withdrawal of the Chinese V Army.

CHAPTER 19

General Alexander felt obliged to agree to this request, although the withdrawal of the 38th Division must uncover the flank of Burcorps when it moved into position west of the Irrawaddy.

Whilst this meeting was taking place the Japanese were on the outskirts of Lashio, and before the day was closed had entered the town to get astride our main line of communication with China. Ahead of them, almost unguarded, lay the road to Bhamo and Myitkyina.

The Chinese 22nd Division was very weak. Apart from the heavy losses it had sustained one of its regiments was with the 200th Division in the Shan States. On April 30th only one Battalion was on the Myitnge position, the remainder of the Division being south of Mandalay in the Amarapura-Myohaung area where, as a senior officer reported, "it was looting to its hearts content".

In view of the danger to the Ava bridge and the unsatisfactory Chinese arrangements for the defence of the Myitnge position 63 Brigade fell back to cover the bridge. This it did after 49 Brigade had passed through it north of the Myitnge river. It then took up positions east of the bridge, a platoon being left on the Myitnge line.

During April 30th 63 Brigade remained on the east bank of the Irrawaddy, but it was evident that the destruction of the Ava bridge could not long be delayed. Japanese tanks were reported to be advancing on Mandalay from Lashio, other hostile forces were closing in from the south, and the Chinese 22nd Division was in no condition to fight.

After darkness that night the last elements of the Imperial Forces crossed the great bridge, and at 2359 hours it was blown. Two of its huge spans collapsed into the Irrawaddy.

We had entered upon the final phase of the campaign.

Chapter 20

Japanese appear unexpectedly at Monywa – Attack on Headquarters of 1 Burma Division – Attack on and capture of Monywa – Serious results thereof – Our attempts on May 1st and 2nd to recapture the town – Heavy fighting on its outskirts – Decision to break off the action – Withdrawal of 1 Burma Division on Ye-U – Minor operations north of Monywa – Japanese proceed up the Chindwin river – 16 Brigade hurried to the Kalewa area – March of 2 Burma Brigade by Pauk and Tilin to Kalemyo.

On the evening of April 30th Monywa was garrisoned by a detachment of the 1st Battalion the Gloucestershire Regiment about one hundred strong, and the river patrol of the Royal Marines. In the town were a number of refugees waiting for steamers to carry them up the Chindwin. At Alon, six miles out of Monywa, was a party of eighty surplus officers, and over two thousand four hundred clerks and servants with their women and children sent off from Army Headquarters at Shwebo the previous evening. This party also awaited transport up the river.

The civil authorities still functioned at Monywa. That day Burcorps Headquarters had opened at Songon, sixteen miles to the north, whilst Headquarters 1 Burma Division was at Ma-U four miles south-east of the town.

At 1910 hours machine-gun, mortar, and shell fire was directed on Monywa from the opposite bank of the river. No warning whatsoever had been received of the approach of the Japanese who had entered the village of Ywashe in motor vehicles accompanied by seven tanks. They were opposed by two men of the Royal Marines forming part of a guard of a launch moored on the west bank of the river. These two were last seen firing a Bren gun at the enemy transport.

CHAPTER 20

It is stated that fire was opened across the river by the enemy to prevent the escape of a steamer moored on the west bank. The serang in charge of this vessel cast off furtively in an attempt to cross to Monywa where his wife was. This move drew heavy fire from the Japanese and disclosed the threat to Monywa.

Spasmodic fire was maintained on the town throughout the night; and the enemy effected a crossing of the river to the south, setting up a road block between the town and Headquarters of 1 Burma Division.

At 2045 hours as soon as it was informed of the situation Burcorps issued orders to 1 Burma Division that Monywa was to be cleared of the enemy as soon as possible. It was then believed that Monywa had already been captured. 1 Burma Division was ordered to concentrate at Chaung-U, and 48 and 63 Brigades were placed under its command. 63 Brigade was expected to arrive at Chaung-U the following morning. 16 Brigade was to proceed to Ye-U immediately by the quickest route. The brigade was then in process of moving south from Ondaw to Muwa near Myinmu and, in fact, did not begin its movement towards Ye-U from Muwa until the following night. Meanwhile, on receiving information of the attack on Monywa, Army Headquarters ordered one squadron of 7 Armoured Brigade to move on the town via Ye-U, and a second squadron to support 1 Burma Division about Chaung-U. These orders were issued at 2359 hours of April 30th.

At about 0500 hours on May 1st a mixed party of Japanese and Burmans attacked 1 Burma Division Headquarters at Ma-U. The protective platoon, composed of raw Burmese troops, bolted; but a stout fight was put up by the officers, clerks, and batmen. These withdrew fighting and went north of the railway line. Taking secret documents and ciphers with them they then made their way across country to Chaung-U.

At Monywa in the early morning a dozen enemy aircraft made a thorough reconnaissance of the town from a height of one hundred feet. The shelling increased, most of it being concentrated on the area of the landing stage. Three large launches were then observed to be coming up the river. They pulled into the west bank and troops at once rapidly embarked in them, probably a couple of hundred men in each. The launches began to cross the river.

Monywa was now defended by the small detachment of the 1st Battalion the Gloucestershire Regiment, about twenty Royal Marines, and F.F.1, which had been sent by Burcorps to the town during the night. On the south-eastern outskirts were some Sappers and Miners of 1 Burma Division which had also detailed Lieut.-Colonel Thomas of the Cameronians to organise the defence of the town. This handful of troops opened small arms and light automatic fire on the approaching launches, and as soon as they did so they in turn came under heavy shell and mortar fire from the opposite bank of the river. Despite this, our Bren guns must have caused many casualties on board the launches although an enemy landing could not be prevented. Once the Japanese were ashore, they were soon in possession of the town.

In thus securing Monywa the Japanese made good use of the period when the direct line of approach from Pakokku lay unprotected. They had entered that town after the withdrawal of 2 Burma Brigade on the night of April 28th. Obviously well supplied with information they struck suddenly at Monywa when they knew that it lay open to them. The organised nature of the attack on the town and on Headquarters of 1 Burma Division indicated an arranged plan and not a haphazard dash. At the same time, by firing on Monywa for about twelve hours before carrying out their attack, the enemy largely discounted the element of surprise and gave us valuable time within which to group our forces against this unexpected threat. Even so, on May 1st, the road to Ye-U lay unguarded save by the small force that had fallen back from Monywa. During the day this force was joined by a squadron of the 2nd Battalion Royal Tank Regiment which had moved on receipt of orders from Army Headquarters.

The numerical weakness of all our formations and units during the latter phase of the campaign has been frequently mentioned. The operations about Monywa were conducted by 1 Burma Division, but it must be borne in mind that this was far short of its proper strength and that all its units were much depleted.

Neither of the two available Brigades of 1 Burma Division was within striking distance of Monywa towards which they were marching. They were south of the Monywa-Myinmu road, and the shortage of motor transport precluded the possibility of ferrying. The most conveniently situated formation was 63 Brigade since it could be taken forward by rail.

63 Brigade was being hurried towards Monywa from the area of the Ava bridge. It entrained in the very early hours of May 1st. Arriving at Kyehmon, eight miles south-east of Monywa, the leading Battalions at once took up a defensive opposition astride the main road with the 1st Battalion 10th Gurkha Rifles on the north and the 2nd Battalion 13th Frontier Force Rifles on the south. An advance then began towards Monywa.

East of Ma-U the Frontier Force Rifles encountered opposition. This was overcome after the Battalion had sustained a few casualties. The

CHAPTER 20

advance of the Battalion then continued, but beyond Ma-U the advance was again halted. Here opposition was heavy and the Battalion was held to the ground.

The 1st Battalion 11th Sikh Regiment went forward through the Frontier Force Rifles, and at 1500 hours took up an outpost line west of Ma-U. After dark positions were altered and a perimeter camp was formed round Ma-U.

During the day the infantry were supported by a squadron of the 7th Queen's Own Hussars, and one tank had been lost. There had been no artillery support.

Meanwhile 13 Brigade had arrived at Ma-U and received orders for a dawn attack next morning. 1 Burma Brigade was now at Chaung-U. It was to continue its march to Monywa at 0500 hours and was to join in the attack.

The Japanese were active that night round the perimeter at Ma-U. Flares and tracer ammunition were fired by patrols and the usual noises indulged in. Two attacks were made on the Frontier Force Rifles, but these were successfully repulsed.

Events at Monywa were discussed at a meeting on the evening of May 1st between Generals Alexander and Stilwell at Ye-U. At this town were now assembled Army Headquarters, and Headquarters of Burcorps and 17 Division.

General Stilwell agreed that a withdrawal from the Mandalay-Irrawaddy line could no longer be delayed. The situation created by the Japanese occupation of Monywa was serious since it cut off all the Imperial Forces west of the Mu river from the direct approach to Ye-U through Monywa. It also denied the use to us of the Chindwin, prevented the move of any of our forces across the river, and opened to the Japanese the means of cutting our line of withdrawal through Kalewa.

It was further agreed that the situation required the withdrawal of 7 Armoured Brigade from its position in support of the Chinese 38th Division east of the River Mu. Orders were therefore issued for 7 Armoured Brigade to move forthwith on the axis Ye-U–Monywa.

The withdrawal from the Mandalay-Irrawaddy line was ordered to begin at once.

General Stilwell informed General Alexander that he intended to withdraw the Chinese V Army to the Katha area, but he was uncertain of his further plans. Preparations were, however, in hand for a possible withdrawal to India.

This was the last occasion when General Alexander met General Stilwell before the close of the campaign. Owing to the failure of

General Stilwell's wireless it was not possible to communicate again with him. He made his way to India by a route further north than that taken by the Imperial Forces.

On May 2nd the operations about Monywa were resumed. It was now intended to attack the town on a two Brigade front, 63 Brigade advancing north-west astride the road and railway, and 13 Brigade moving on the town from Zalok down the road from Kyaukka. Its first objective was to be the railway line, and it was then to continue through the town to the river bank.

1 Burma Brigade would not be available until the early afternoon and was to support the attack of 63 Brigade.

To each Brigade front a Mountain Battery was allotted and also a Field Battery (less a troop) of 1 Indian Field Regiment, I.A. The squadron of tanks of the 7th Queen's Own Hussars was to co-operate with 63 Brigade.

The town of Monywa lent itself to defence. Surrounded by flat, open country, much of it paddy land, it gave its defenders excellent fields of fire and good command of all approaches. The sparse vegetation of the dry zone afforded scanty cover for our attacking force. The Japanese had not been slow to seize upon these advantages, and were in strong positions in buildings and other points of vantage on the outskirts of the town.

13 Brigade carried out a night march from Ma-U to Zalok. Starting at 0400 hours it reached the latter village at first light, changed direction, and at once began its advance on Monywa.

The 5th Battalion 1st Punjab Regiment on the north of the road was on a two-company front with its third company in reserve. The Battalion had no fourth company. South of the road the 1st Battalion 18th Royal Garhwal Rifles was also on a two-company front. The 1st Battalion Royal Inniskilling Fusiliers was in reserve, and the attack was supported by artillery. The village of Shaukka, one mile north-east of the railway station, was found to be clear of the enemy; and the advance continued across the flat, open country towards Monywa.

Approaching the railway line, the Royal Garhwal Rifles encountered the enemy in a village south of the road, cleared this, and went on. Fifty yards short of the railway the Battalion was brought to a halt by heavy automatic and mortar fire, the right leading company suffering many casualties.

The Japanese with mortars and automatic weapons were strongly entrenched along the railway line, and had a mortar and one infantry gun behind a stout wall covering the level crossing. A palm grove eight hundred yards south of the road was also well defended.

CHAPTER 20

The Royal Garhwal Rifles put in an attack astride the road to turn the position at the level crossing. The attack made no progress. Our guns, however, forced the mortar covering the level crossing to be withdrawn.

North of the road the 5th Battalion 1st Punjab Regiment met similar opposition and was unable to gain the railway line or the station which was just north of the level crossing. Here, too, there had been heavy casualties. The Battalion mortars shelled the station, and then at about 0830 hours one company worked its way forward and without loss to itself dislodged the enemy from the station. Two hours later this company was forced to withdraw.

Once again, the station changed hands. The Punjabis retook it at 1200 hours, holding on until 1400 hours when superior numbers compelled them to fall back for a second time. North of the station our troops had never been able to reach the railway.

The situation on 13 Brigade front in mid-afternoon was that our troops had been brought to a definite halt on a line just east of the railway. The Royal Garhwal Rifles had driven the enemy from the palm grove and now held it. But along the railway line itself the Japanese were in strong positions. They had excellent observation, and ranges appear to have been worked out on the whole of the Brigade front. Any movement by our men brought down heavy and accurate mortar and other fire.

The advance of 63 Brigade from Ma-U began at 0840 hours. Here, the 1st Battalion 11th Sikh Regiment moved astride the road to Monywa with the 1st Battalion 10th Gurkha Rifles on its right. The 2nd Battalion 13th Frontier Force Rifles was in reserve.

During the advance the left forward company of the Sikhs observed enemy movement on the west bank of the Chindwin and hostile craft on the river itself. These were engaged by the Battalion mortars and machine-guns and by our artillery. Some vessels were sunk.

The two forward companies of the Battalion then went through the village of Ywathit on the outskirts of Monywa and found it apparently clear of the enemy. As Battalion Headquarters and the two rear companies entered Ywathit they came under heavy fire from buildings in the village and trees surrounding it. At the same time, just ahead of our leading troops, a tree previously prepared for felling crashed across the main road making an effective block.

Ywathit was cleared of the enemy, although two or three snipers continued to harass the attack until the village was fired. The snipers died in the flames.

The road block was covered by numerous mortar and machine-guns and the leading companies of the Sikhs suffered severe casualties, mainly from mortar fire. They were brought to a halt about a hundred yards from the Japanese position.

The two rear companies now moved up on the right and left of the forward companies. On the left an advance was attempted up the river bank, but was soon held up by heavy fire. The company working forward on the right fared no better.

The Battalion clung on grimly to its positions, but in face of its great losses it could do no more. 'B' Company, the left forward company, had only sixteen unwounded men out of its original strength of ninety.

At 1400 hours two companies of the 2nd Battalion 13th Frontier Force Rifles were sent forward as a reserve to the Sikhs.

Tanks of the squadron of the 7th Queen's Own Hussars were employed against the block. They were unable to force it.

On the right, the 1st Battalion 10th Gurkha Rifles was held up outside the town. In the early afternoon two companies went forward to attack but were repulsed with loss.

1 Burma Brigade had been moving up from Chaung-U during the morning. This Brigade consisted of the 1st Battalion the Cameronians, the 2nd Battalion The King's Own Yorkshire Light Infantry, and the 2nd Battalion 7th Rajput Regiment. The 1st Battalion 4th P.W.O. Gurkha Rifles also joined it that morning from 48 Brigade. The 1st and 5th Battalions Burma Rifles had been withdrawn from the Brigade into Divisional Reserve after the Yenangyaung operations. These two Battalion were now each of a strength of less than two hundred.

The Brigade attacked at 1545 hours on a two Battalion front. It passed through 63 Brigade, but the left flank of its attack avoided the road block. The 1st Battalion 4th P.W.O. Gurkha Rifles advanced between the main road and the railway, whilst on the right of it the 2nd Battalion 7th Rajput Regiment advanced northwards along the east of the railway which formed the dividing line between the two Battalions. The two Battalions were in reserve.

Just prior to the advance of 1 Burma Brigade several small launches and native craft were seen crossing the river. Our artillery together with infantry machine-guns and mortars opened fire on these, and at least three vessels were sunk.

Both Gurkhas and Rajputs came under heavy fire. The Rajput attack went wide to the north-east away from the railway, but direction was restored and eventually contact was made with the 1st Battalion

CHAPTER 20

18th Royal Garhwal Rifles. The Rajputs were now astride the railway south of the station.

The 1st Battalion 4th P.W.O. Gurkha Rifles was held up by machine-gun fire from the area of the railway station and a hollow pagoda near it. These targets were shelled by the Battalion mortars and those of the 1st Battalion 11th Sikh Regiment.

Meanwhile, at about 1500 hours, 13 Brigade had received an order to withdraw to Alon. This order came through an officer of 7 Armoured Brigade who stated that he had received it from the Army Commander. The order was passed by 13 Brigade to Divisional Headquarters. About 1700 hours 13 Brigade began its withdrawal, the movement being effected without opposition.

The Commander of 1 Burma Brigade had also been ordered to stop his attack and to hold on to gains already made. On his representing that the attack should be allowed to continue an extension of time until 1900 hours was given by Divisional Headquarters. Both forward Battalions of 1 Burma Brigade were preparing to advance on the railway station and the area west of it. The enemy at this time employed captive Indians to shout to our troops that they were friendly Chinese and that firing should cease. This caused some delay.

However, owing to the earlier order to cease the advance the impetus of the attack could not be revived, and the prior withdrawal of 13 Brigade would have increased the difficulty of the task of 1 Burma Brigade in any further advance.

At 1900 hours 1 Burma Brigade and 63 Brigade withdrew down the road to Ma-U; the 2nd Battalion 7th Rajput Regiment falling back to Zalok and re-joining its Brigade later. The withdrawal was not followed up although enemy mortars and machine-guns were active.

The Divisional transport escorted by the Battalions of the Burma Rifles during the day had by-passed Monywa, moving round it by cross-country tracks. The column was frequently dive-bombed by hostile aircraft. Towards evening the 1st Battalion the Cameronians was also detailed to cover the movement of the column.

48 Brigade which had been held in readiness at Myinmu to take part in the operations if required, was ordered to proceed to Ye-U via Shwebo. This it did.

A certain mystery surrounds the order to break off the attack on Monywa passed to 13 Brigade. That this order came through an officer of 7 Armoured Brigade is certain, but both Army Headquarters and Burcorps disclaim knowledge of it. At the time when the attack was halted the Japanese were streaming out of Monywa and crossing to the west bank of the Chindwin. From evidence found by our troops on the outskirts of the town it was plain that the enemy had sustained severe casualties. However, as the transport of 1 Burma Division had been safely got away there was no particular advantage in continuing a costly operation.

The Brigades of 1 Burma Division carried out an arduous night march along rough bullock cart tracks through Zalok and Ettaw, and early on May 3rd concentrated in an area north of Alon on the Monywa-Ye-U road.

This area on the previous day had been held by 7 Armoured Brigade with the 1st Battalion West Yorkshire Regiment. There was also a small detachment of the Gloucestershire Regiment and F.F.1, from Monywa. In the evening there arrived a small force under Lieut.-Colonel Bagot of the 1st Battalion the Gloucestershire Regiment. In addition to his own Battalion Lieut.-Colonel Bagot had under him F.F.7, one troop of 15 Mountain Battery, and a Battery of 77mm guns. This force took up a lay-back position south of Budalin astride the road and railway.

Tank patrols were maintained about Alon on May 2nd round which village some snipers appeared. They were dealt with by the 1st Battalion West Yorkshire Regiment which also took punitive action against a neighbouring village where the crew of a tank of the 7th Queen's Own Hussars had been murdered by Burmese.

From about Alon, too, our troops fired on barges and other craft moving up the Chindwin. It was evident that the Japanese were losing no time in exploiting their success and that our line of communications which necessarily cut the river near Kalewa was seriously threatened.

1 Burma Division now began its withdrawal on Ye-U, the point from which the track to the Chindwin began. Through Ye-U must pass the whole of the Imperial Forces still remaining on the east bank of the Chindwin.

On May 3rd 7 Armoured Brigade covered the movement of 1 Burma Division and assisted in ferrying troops into Ye-U. The road was patrolled by the 7th Queen's Own Hussars who had a brush with some Burmese. The 2nd Battalion Royal Tank Regiment operating from the Alon area watched the northern and north-eastern exits from Monywa, whilst the 1st Battalion West Yorkshire Regiment observed the river and again employed its mortars on hostile craft moving upstream.

Towards evening when all marching infantry were clear of the Alon area our tanks began to fall back on Budalin. This encouraged the enemy to follow up the withdrawal, and at 1830 hours one squadron

CHAPTER 20

of the 2nd Battalion Royal Tank Regiment was in action east of the road against enemy tanks and anti-tank guns. The engagement was broken off, but two of our tanks were forced to make a wide detour to the east. One of these was subsequently lost by falling into a nullah in the dark.

At 0400 hours on May 4th tanks were heard approaching the layback south of Budalin, and were first assumed to be the two tanks mentioned in the preceding paragraph. When about one hundred yards distant these tanks opened fire. This was returned by our own tanks. The enemy fighting vehicles turned round and withdrew but had succeeded in setting alight to a tank of the 2nd Battalion Royal Tank Regiment. It was later established that the enemy had here been using tanks captured from us.

Following on this incident the Japanese shelled our positions with artillery and mortars. The mortars of the 1st Battalion the West Yorkshire Regiment replied with success, silencing those of the enemy. No attack developed, and after the last elements of 1 Burma Division were clear of Budalin Lieut.-Colonel Bagot withdrew his force.

After this engagement at Budalin the enemy did not again attempt to harass the withdrawal to Ye-U which was completed on the same day.

As an indication of hostile activity behind our lines the experience near Monywa of an officer of 1 Burma Division is worth recording. On May 3rd when at Milestone 8 north of Alon this officer leant against a haystack and was surprised to find that in it were concealed supplies of some kind. Pulling these out he discovered them to be belts of Japanese machine-gun ammunition.

The two Brigades of 17 Division not engaged at Monywa had already arrived at Ye-U, 16 Brigade arriving on May 2nd and 48 Brigade the following day.

In addition to any craft they themselves had the Japanese secured shallow draught vessels at Monywa. As it was evident that they were now moving up the Chindwin it was essential for us to secure Shwegyin, Kalewa, and Kalemyo at once. Consequently 16 Brigade was hurried forward in motor transport along the Ye-U-Shwegyin track to cover the Kalewa area. Brigade Headquarters and the 4th Battalion 12th Frontier Force Regiment (for Kalemyo) left on the night of May 2nd/3rd. The remaining Battalions left next day. The 1st Royal Battalion 9th Jat Regiment was to hold Shwegyin; the 2nd Battalion the Duke of Wellington's Regiment and the 7th Battalion 10th Baluch Regiment were to undertake the defence of Kalewa.

On the night of May 3rd/4th there was some sniping of the perimeter camp near Ye-U. At one time the firing was heavy. It came from a northeasterly direction. Whether Japanese or Burmese were responsible for this was not established.

Whilst the operations recounted in this chapter were proceeding, 2 Burma Brigade was marching towards the Myittha valley. It then consisted of the 2nd and 8th Battalions Burma Rifles and F.F.8. It moved with bullock cart and mule transport.

Arriving at Pauk on May 1st the Brigade was now in the centre of a disaffected area. Thakin elements were active. Pauk itself had been looted and burnt, bridges along the road for some distance west of Pauk had been systematically destroyed, dacoits were numerous in the district. A party of about one hundred and fifty armed Burmese in improvised uniforms was encountered by the Brigade Intelligence Officer when he was alone some miles east of Pauk. This party was assumed to be marching for Pakokku. F.F.8 on May 1st was engaged with a hostile force near Pauk. As a result of this engagement F.F.8 largely disintegrated, and it is uncertain whether the opposition it encountered was Japanese or Burmese. Possibly it was composed of the Thakin party just mentioned.

After a difficult march 2 Burma Brigade on May 12th made contact with the Chin Hills Battalion of the Burma Frontier Force near Natchaung, south of Kalemyo. It was then picked up by motor transport and ferried onwards along the road to Tamu. Bullock carts were destroyed and all transport animals were handed over to the Chin Hills Battalion.

2 Burma Brigade had marched from Pakokku to Natchaung, a distance of two hundred and sixteen miles, in fourteen days. It was the hottest period of the year, the Brigade had already in the earlier part of April carried out arduous marches, its movement was hampered by slow moving bullock cart transport, and the track was by no means good. All marches were made by night, defensive positions being manned by day. Having regard to these factors the performance was a good one.

If the Japanese had intended to carry out a dash for Kalemyo by this route they had been forestalled by 2 Burma Brigade. After leaving Pauk the Brigade made no contact with hostile elements, and there is no evidence that a Japanese advance along this route was initiated.

Chapter 21

General Alexander ordered to withdraw his force north of Tamu – The withdrawal to Shwegyin – Japanese advance up the Chindwin – Action at Shwegyin – Final stages of the withdrawal north of Tamu – 4 Corps assumes operational control of all Burma Army troops.

Following upon the despatch of 16 Brigade down the Ye-U-Shwegyin track our troops began their general withdrawal along this route. Around Ye-U, the single point of entry, there was necessarily considerable congestion. Once again enemy aircraft were presented with favourable targets, but they took singularly little advantage of this fact. They had been active over Shwebo and in a series of raids destroyed it when it was occupied by Army Headquarters. Throngs of refugees at Kyaukmyaung on the Irrawaddy had been heavily bombed. So, too, were most of the towns on the railway between Sagaing and Katha. At Ye-U aerial attacks were largely confined to the bridge that had been constructed across the Mu river just outside the town. After its first few miles the Ye-U-Shwegyin track entered dense jungle, and it was no doubt this that protected the heavy traffic that began to pass along it from the first days of May.

General Alexander's plan contemplated the holding of a line south of Kalewa and it was known that 1 Indian Infantry Brigade was marching into Burma from Manipur Road via Palel and Tamu. Its leading echelon was due in Kalewa on May 12th, but when it was learnt that our forces in Burma were falling back on Kalewa the march of 1 Brigade beyond Palel was countermanded by G.H.Q., India. It was not considered possible to maintain it in Kalewa in addition to the troops from Burma that would be in the area.

On May 3rd, however, India stated that a force could not be maintained in the Kalewa area, and General Alexander was ordered to take his troops back to motor transport road-head one march north of Tamu as rapidly as the tactical situation permitted. The message to the Burma Army added that maintenance further south than Tamu could not be carried put, and that echelons of about three thousand daily could be dealt with at road-head.

On the same day General Alexander received a visit at his Headquarters at Kaduma from Major-General Sun, commanding the Chinese 38th Division. This Division as rearguard to the Chinese V Army was carrying out a difficult task in its withdrawal north, and Major-General Sun was anxious that his movements should be co-ordinated with those of Burcorps. Orders to this effect had already been issued, but Lieut.-General Slim was now again told that he must not withdraw from the Ye-U area until the Chinese rearguard had passed north of Shwebo.

Evacuation of sick and wounded by rail and river to Myitkyina had been going forward. From Myitkyina casualties were being flown to India, but the rapid advance of the Japanese through the Shan States and the threat to Myitkyina closed this route. Casualties still with the main body of our troops and at the hospitals in Shwebo had to be taken out on the only route now available.

No less than two thousand three hundred sick and wounded were sent out by motor transport along the Ye-U-Shwegyin track. They endured great suffering, but the fact that they were safely evacuated is evidence of the efficiency and tireless devotion of the Medical Services.

1 Burma Division with 7 Armoured Brigade, less 7th Queen's Own Hussars, held the rearguard position on the line of the canal about Ye-U whilst lay-backs were to be provided by 17 Division at Yaduma, Pyingaing, Shwegyin, and Kalewa.

On May 5th at 1700 hours the rearguard withdrew to Kaduma, the tanks of the 2nd Battalion Royal Tank Regiment covering this movement and the blowing of demolitions along the track. Next day the tanks patrolled from Kaduma back to the canal near Ye-U but no contact with the enemy was made.

1 Burma Division then continued its withdrawal towards Shwegyin, but 1 Burma Brigade broke off from the Division and carried out a flank march up the east bank of the Chindwin through difficult and waterless country. Leaving Pyingaing on May 8th it moved by Indaw to Pantha and there crossed the Chindwin. It then continued its march by Yuwa and the Yu river to Tamu, arriving at the latter place on May 16th.

13 Brigade crossed the Chindwin on May 9th and that day began its march on Tamu.

From Kaduma 48 Brigade formed the rearguard and was supported by the 7th Queen's Own Hussars. Motor transport by this time was very short but enough was available to move 63 Brigade to Shwegyin.

CHAPTER 21

Simultaneously with this, 48 Brigade with Burma Military Police and F.F. units which were close-piquetting the route, marched forty miles from Kaduma to Pyingaing in thirty hours.

The dry sandy bed of the Maukkadaw Chaung which flows through Pyingaing gave an excellent approach from the Chindwin, and the country was ideal for the establishment of a road block. To prevent any attempt by the Japanese to set up such a block a strong force was posted at the confluence of the Chaung with the Chindwin. This force consisted of Commando personnel and one company from the 2nd Battalion 5th Royal Gurkha Rifles F.F., and another from the combined Battalion 7th Gurkha Rifles. It was commanded by Major Holdaway of the 7th Gurkha Rifles.

This force withdrew independently up the east bank of the river on the morning of May 9th after our rearguard was clear of Pyingaing. That village was abandoned by us on the afternoon of May 8th, the 7th Queen's Own Hussars leaving at 1500 hours.

The passage of the Imperial Forces through the vast and well-nigh uninhabited forests of the Chindwin was a remarkable achievement. General Alexander says in his Despatch, "Anyone seeing this track for the first time would find it difficult to imagine how a fully mechanised force could possible move over it". There is no doubt that only the urgent necessity of the occasion impelled the employment of this route. It crossed and re-crossed and sometimes followed for considerable distances the sandy beds of innumerable Chaungs. Often the deep sand brought vehicles to a standstill; some of them could not be extricated. Between Tawgyin and Pyingaing was a difficult hill section with many rickety bridges of brushwood or bamboo. Here, until the Engineers set to work to straighten out sharp hairpin bends, traffic became inextricably blocked. The Engineers also improved the going along the stream beds by laying corduroy tracks, and opened up a water point in the sand of the dry Maukkadaw Chaung near Pyingaing.

Traffic control posts were established and sections of the track were organised for two-way and one-way traffic. Only the most persistent vigilance and insistence upon road discipline kept the track open. Every mile of the dense forests it traversed was littered with the wrecks of vehicles that had broken under the strain.

Not only were we now racing the Japanese to Shwegyin. The breaking of the south-west monsoon was imminent. The first heavy stores would render the Chaungs impassable and turn the broken surface of the track into a quagmire. It was essential, therefore, to gain the Chindwin as quickly as possible.

There was no shortage of rations along the route, and there was also sufficient petrol to carry all vehicles to Shwegyin. There was food too, for refugees, some of them being families. General Alexander was not prepared to abandon these unfortunate people either to the enemy or to the tender mercies of the local population. They were carried to Shwegyin in military vehicles whilst many of the troops carried out forced marches.

From Shwegyin all troops, motor vehicles, and guns had to be transported to Kalewa by steamer. There were six of these steamers, each with a carrying capacity of some six or seven hundred men, but only on an average two lorries and two jeeps. This meant that few vehicles could be ferried across the Chindwin with the result that the transport problem from Kalewa onwards was acute. There was then barely sufficient transport to carry essential equipment and ammunition and to evacuate the wounded; but the establishment of staging camps stocked with supplies sent from India by motor transport eliminated the necessity for units to carry rations. The G.P. Transport Company from India proved invaluable.

The embarkation point at Shwegyin was a small sandy bay where the Shwegyin Chaung entered the river. It was overlooked by steep jungle-clad hills. In this bay the Engineers had built a jetty. A rise in the river submerged this, and there was much difficulty in loading on to the steamers the few vehicles and guns that could be taken. On May 9th the Engineers constructed a more serviceable jetty.

The track approached the bay through a cup-like depression in the hills to the north-east. This depression, known as the 'Basin', was about half a mile long and some four hundred yards broad at its widest point. Like the bay it was commanded by escarped forest covered hills. Its southern end opened on to the bay at the point where the Shwegyin Chaung joined the river. The flat land within the Basin afforded the only parking space for vehicles and as the withdrawal proceeded here was collected a vast agglomeration of transport and equipment.

Enemy aircraft had located the activity at Shwegyin. On May 7th they bombed and burst a protective boom that was placed across the Chindwin some two miles downstream, and on May 9th they bombed Shwegyin. At least two Japanese aircraft were hit by our anti-aircraft fire and crashed in the jungle.

These attacks much restricted the work of ferrying by day, and many of the native crews were now only prepared to operate at night.

On the night of May 9th 63 Brigade and 7 Armoured Brigade, less 7th Queen's Own Hussars, crossed the river to Kalewa. Before embarking,

CHAPTER 21

the 2nd Battalion Royal Tank Regiment destroyed its tanks which had rendered such splendid service during the campaign. One squadron of the Battalion which had been unable to cross that night remained in Shwegyin with its vehicles un-destroyed. To relieve the congestion in the Basin many units, guns, vehicles, and animals were retained in a harbour about two miles down the track near Mutaik, north-east of Shwegyin. Here were also Advanced Headquarters 17 Division, and the rearguard made up of the 7th Queen's Own Hussars, the 1st Battalion the West Yorkshire Regiment, and 48 Brigade.

Despite the endeavours of Royal Marines, officers of the Irrawaddy Flotilla Company, staff officers and others organising embarkation the lack of facilities made the work of loading vehicles onto the steamers painfully slow. On May 9th it was estimated that several days were still required for the clearance of all sick and wounded, troops, guns, animals, and vehicles and equipment not earmarked for destruction. The animal transport of both Divisions still awaited ferrying across the river.

The 1st Royal Battalion 9th Jat regiment carried out the duties of covering troops at Shwegyin. The Battalion now consisted of three weak companies, one of them on the west bank of the Chindwin. A large party from the Battalion was also continuously employed in cutting firewood for the steamers.

Defensive positions were manned at the north end of the Basin where the track entered it through a long defile. The heights overlooking the east and southern sides of the Basin were protected, and there were posts astride the defile of the Shwegyin Chaung and on the hills immediately to the south of the confluence of the Chaung with the Chindwin.

Downstream, covering the boom near Gaundi, were the 5th Battalion 17th Dogra Regiment and a handful of Royal Marines. Both banks of the river were held and patrols went forward for some miles along the west bank.

The defence of the Basin was numerically weak, and on May 9th Major-General Cowan decided to strengthen the garrison there. Accordingly, the Battalion of the 7th Gurkha Rifles were detailed to reinforce the Jats. It arrived in the Basin after dark on May 9th and was to take over the defensive positions the following morning.

Meanwhile, unknown to our force, the enemy had landed near Kywe, a village on the east bank of the river some eight miles below Shwegyin. This was on the afternoon of May 9th. Men, ponies, equipment, and one or more infantry guns had been put ashore from fast moving landing craft, one of which flew the Thakin flag. No sooner was the disembarkation completed than the landing craft turned downstream, presumably for the purpose of bringing up more troops already on the Chindwin on slower moving vessels. After dark another and larger enemy force landed at Ingongyi on the west bank of the river almost opposite Kywe.

The first hostile force that landed at Kywe was estimated to number about seven hundred. It probably marched due north to the village of Thanbaya thus avoiding our covering troops astride the river at Gaundi. North-west of Thanbaya a path along a dry tributary streambed would give easy access to the lower reaches of the Shwegyin Chaung. An advance from the direction of Thanbaya does not appear to have been expected by us.

The landing of this large hostile party was observed by Major Calvert and others of Major Holdaway's force. It was then growing dark and owing to the exhaustion of his men Major Holdaway decided not to attack, but to march due north to the track and re-join 48 Brigade at Shwegyin. Major Holdaway was out of touch with the platoons and porters carrying the wireless set. Consequently, no information about the proximity of the enemy was conveyed to our troops at Shwegyin.

The march through the jungle proved very exhausting, there was no water, and in the dark parties lost contact. Eventually Major Holdaway's force was split up. A small party got through to Shwegyin to take part in the fighting there. Others disappeared and were not heard of again. Major Holdaway himself was drowned when swimming the Chindwin under fire. The remainder joined our main body on the Tamu road.

Meanwhile, at 0545 hours on May 10th just as the 1st Royal Battalion 9th Jat Regiment had stood to in the half-light there were bursts of light machine-gun fire down the Shwegyin Chaung. The Japanese then attempted to advance towards the landing stage and into the Basin. Our own machine-guns and mortars checked this movement.

As the light grew enemy fire intensified. Crossing to the north of the Shwegyin Chaung the enemy made some progress down the defile of the Chaung towards the Chindwin, suffering heavy casualties in so doing. Mortar shells were now falling in the Basin. There was heavy sniping from the south.

Checked in their attempt to gain the jetty the Japanese began to work along the ridge dominating the eastern side of the Basin, whilst still maintaining pressure in the area of the Chaung. The Jats were hard pressed, and the 7th Gurkha Rifles went forward to reinforce all their positions.

Fighting was very confused on the hill tops to the south and east of the jetty and the Basin. Approaches were often precipitous, and in places the dense undergrowth reduced fields of fire to a few yards. Many small counter-attacks were put in by our troops as the enemy from time to time secured dominating positions on the hills. On one occasion men of the 7th Gurkha Rifles trapped about twenty Japanese in a nullah and destroyed them with bombs, and there is no doubt that the enemy casualties were heavy in their attempts to break through our lines.

The Bofors guns of 3 Indian Light Anti-Aircraft Battery I.A., were in position in the Basin. These guns for a considerable time were the only artillery support for our Infantry. When a Company of the 7th Gurkha Rifles went forward to the ridge east of the Basin their covering fire was of great assistance as our troops scaled the cliff-like hill. Here the Japanese had established themselves on a prominent knoll and could not be dislodged. However, Bofors and mortar fire kept them subdued, although one party of the enemy actually entered the Basin and for a time threatened Headquarters of the 1st Royal Battalion 9th Jat Regiment. They were driven out by the Jats and 7th Gurkha Rifles.

Meanwhile Major-General Cowan had gone forward from Mutaik to the Basin to ascertain the situation. He and his party came under automatic fire and his A.D.C. was wounded. Major-General Cowan then ordered 48 Brigade to move on the Basin from Mutaik. It was also to cover the track between these two places and the approach to the path up the east bank of the river by Kongyi to Kaing, the village opposite Kalewa.

The route between Mutaik and the Basin was close-piquetted by the 1st Battalion 3rd Q.A.O. Gurkha Rifles (now only a single company in strength) and the 1st Battalion 4th P.W.O. Gurkha Rifles. The latter Battalion was only just in time to prevent the enemy from cutting the track just north of the Basin. It then held off repeated attacks by the Japanese and was well supported by the Battalions 3" mortars and a section of 12 Mountain Battery. Picquet positions were held throughout the day and were supported by tanks of the 7th Queen's Own Hussars. Isolated parties of the enemy were engaged along the picquet line by infantry and tanks.

The 2nd Battalion 5th Royal Gurkha Rifles F.F., marched down the track to the Basin and was held in reserve at its northern entrance. A squadron of the 7th Queen's Own Hussars also entered the Basin.

Firing from near Mutaik 1 Battery of 1 Indian Field Regiment I.A., now supported our infantry. Despite the fact that only an inaccurate ¼" map was available some most effective shooting was carried out.

The general situation in the early afternoon was that north of the Basin we covered the track, and the path towards Kaing through Kongyi. Round the Basin and on the hills above the jetty the Jats and 7th Gurkha Rifles were holding on grimly. Only on the knoll on the eastern edge of the Basin towards its southern end did the Japanese command our positions.

On this knoll the enemy had brought up an infantry gun, and from here was directing the fire of his mortars. These latter were shelling the jetty and the Basin. However, before the infantry gun could open fire it was knocked out by a series of direct hits from a Bofors gun. After this incident hostile mortar fire was also much reduced, and at least one mortar was put out of action by Bofors guns of 3 Indian Light Anti-Aircraft Battery.

If further evacuation of troops and material was to be carried on it was essential that the enemy be cleared from the knoll, and at about 1400 hours a further attack was made on this position by the 7th Gurkha Rifles. Despite desperate attempts to dislodge the enemy the attack failed.

Meanwhile enemy pressure on the positions about the Chaung covering the jetty had increased, and the Jats were hard put to it to hold this ground. Accordingly, a two Company attack by the 2nd Battalion 5th Royal Gurkha Rifles F.F. was planned, both to sweep this area and to recover the knoll. The attack was to be made at 1650 hours.

During the day it had not been possible to use the jetty, and the crew of some of the steamers could not be induced to work. However, three steamers continued to operate the ferry by drawing in beneath an almost sheer cliff, some two hundred yards upstream. Here troops continued to embark. All sick and wounded were evacuated although it was with great difficulty that some of these men were sent down the cliff face. The three steamers were commanded by Messrs Murie and Hutcheon of the Irrawaddy Flotilla Company, and Lieutenant Penman of the B.R.N.V.R. The skill and determination of these three officers and the manner in which they kept their native crews in hand was most praiseworthy.

Enemy reconnaissance aircraft were active, but our anti-aircraft guns kept them at a distance. No bombing attacks were attempted. Once again, the difficulty of the country and the close nature of the fighting probably deterred Japanese aircraft from attempting to support their troops.

The attack planned for 1650 hours was cancelled. Satisfied that the ferry could not be operated from the jetty that night and that the numbers of the enemy had increased Major-General Cowan decided to fall back towards Kalewa along the Kongyi path.

The evacuation of Lines of Communication and other unwanted troops remaining in the area began at once. The path was over precipitous hills and known to be exceedingly difficult. Consequently, only the minimum of equipment could be carried. In the Basin and on

CHAPTER 21

the track towards Mutaik was the greater part of what remained of our motor transport, much of it still loaded with kit and equipment, rations, and ammunition. Apart from the artillery already mentioned there was also present 1 Heavy Anti-Aircraft Regiment R.A., B.A.F., 8 Indian Anti-Tank Battery, 8 Heavy Anti-Aircraft Battery R.A., one troop of 5 Indian Anti-Tank Battery and 15 Mountain Battery. Some of these units had not been actively engaged that day. Their guns could not be taken along the path and must be destroyed.

At 1700 hours guns and mortars began wasting down their ammunition. Heavy fire was directed on all the Japanese positions. This had a quietening effect on the enemy and the withdrawal of non-essential elements proceeded without interruption. At 1930 hours the path to Kongyi was reported clear, and zero for the withdrawal of covering troops was fixed at 1955 hours.

Two lay-backs were established by the 2nd Battalion 5th Royal Gurkha Rifles F.F., to protect the withdrawal of the forward troops through the northern exit of the Basin. The picquets along the track were to close in behind and follow the rear Battalion.

At 1955 hours every gun in the area increased its rate of fire. Ten minutes later they put down a devastating barrage on the positions evacuated by the Jats and the 7th Gurkha Rifles and on the hills surrounding the Basin.

Of this phase of operations and of the barrage a War Diary says: "The chief contribution came from the Bofors whose tracer shells lit up the descending darkness. It was a cheering sound the like of which we had not heard during our time in Burma. At 2015 hours the guns ceased fire, and five minutes later we received the order to go. As we left the Basin enormous fires were getting a good hold on the dumps of stores and ammunition, tanks and lorries. It was an eerie sight in the gathering gloom and distressing to think so much material had to be left behind. From the Japanese there wasn't a sound. They had apparently had enough! "

It was as well that the enemy had drawn off, for it soon became apparent that the path to Kongyi was hopelessly blocked. It was packed with troops and animals and the rear Battalions could make no movement up to it. They were halted along the track north of the Basin.

The same unit War Diary continues: "We were surrounded by cliffs three hundred feet high on two sides, difficult enough to climb by day, impossible to take against opposition at night. The 3rd Gurkha Rifles held the third side behind us, and on the fourth, to the east, ran the track back to Burma. On this track were several ammunition lorries burning furiously, lighting us up as we sat there.

Small arms and mortar ammunition were exploding continuously for some three hours afterwards. Our only exit was up the narrow path on which, at the moment movement was negligible .... So there we were a sitting target".

Mules found it almost impossible to follow the steep and narrow path in the darkness. Many fell over the edge of it, others were pushed off to clear the way for troops. Progress was at the rate of about one mile an hour and it was dawn before the rear of the column was at Kongyi. There was no sign of the enemy.

During the day the troops were ferried across from Paunggyaung to Kalewa, whilst mules were ferried over the river from Kaing.

A noteworthy feature of the arduous night march was the bringing out of a section of its guns by 12 Mountain Battery. Many mortars and much lighter equipment had been abandoned, and the carriage of these guns along the path to Paunggyaung was an outstanding performance.

On the other side of the river the 5th Battalion 17th Dogra Regiment with other covering troops there had carried out an equally difficult night march from Gaundi to Kalewa.

Our total casualties in the Shwegyin action were difficult to estimate. In the area of the Basin there were about one hundred and fifty, and were therefore probably less than two hundred in all. On the other hand, records of 17 Division state of the enemy: "In the jungle no one could tell his casualties from shell fire but, from the infantry assaults, one hundred and seventy bodies were counted". Having regard to these figures and to the nature and extent of the fighting the first Japanese force that landed at Kywe must have been considerably augmented.

There was no further contact with the Japanese. The last action of the campaign had been fought.

48 Brigade together with the 2nd Battalion the Duke of Wellington's Regiment left Kalewa on the night of May 11th, proceeding by steamer to Sittang and arriving there on May 14th. The Chindwin fleet was then sunk and the troops marched to Tamu.

The main body of the Imperial Forces withdrew on Tamu along the track from Kalewa, through the Kabaw valley. 63 Brigade as rearguard left Kalewa on May 12th and marched through Tamu on May 19th.

In the Chin Hills to the south-west and forward of the main Imperial Force the tracks into India were covered by the Chin Hills Battalion, Burma Frontier Force. This Battalion continued unsupported to protect the approaches to India along the western side of the Kale and Kabaw valleys. Our nearest troops to the Battalion were then over a hundred miles away.

CHAPTER 21

The first heavy rains of the monsoon fell on May 12th. By a narrow margin, therefore, had General Alexander extricated his troops. Had the campaign continued east of the Chindwin for any length of time after May 12th it is certain that only a very small proportion of the force could have survived a withdrawal to India.

As it was, dysentery and malaria were to take a heavy toll of exhausted men. The final stages of the withdrawal into Assam were carried out in heavy rain and in conditions that would have tried even the fittest. The troops of the Burma Army were now anything but fit. Passing through Lokchao and Palel formations went into rest camps in the Imphal area.

The Army had brought out of Burma very little in the way of equipment or transport. It reported to G.H.Q., India that it had ten twenty-five pounder guns, four anti-tank guns, fourteen 3·7" mountain guns, all with little or no ammunition; no tanks, about fifty lorries, and thirty jeeps. All vehicles were badly in need of maintenance.

On May 20th IV Corps assumed operational command of all troops of the Burma Army. General Alexander's command then ceased to exist.

At Imphal the Kachins, Chins, and Karens remaining with the Burma Rifles were given the option of returning to their own homes. The majority of men elected to do so. Each man received three months' pay, his rifle, and fifty rounds of ammunition.

In the rest areas about Imphal living conditions, at first, were very bad. Transport facilities onwards from railhead at Manipur Road were limited, and as India was still faced with a shortage of troops it was not possible to withdraw from forward areas the force coming out of Burma. Food and medical arrangements were defective.

Billets were provided for some troops; others camped in the open. There was an acute shortage of tents, ground sheets, blankets, mosquito nets and clothing. Inclement weather and the attacks of mosquitoes found easy victims. Almost universal illness resulted. An entry under June 1st in the War Diary of 17 Division said: "Majority of troops ill with malaria, very few fit men left". Hospital accommodation and facilities were inadequate to cope with the stream of sick men.

Yet it is on record that the spirt of the troops remained good, and many of them after a brief spell of rest continued to serve in forward areas. Having learned a hard lesson at the hands of a clever and seasoned enemy they were now in a better position to deal with him.

Chapter 22

Operations carried out by the Chinese Expeditionary Force in April and May 1942 – The Japanese thrust through Karenni and the Shan States – Collapse of the VI Army – Occupation of Bhamo and Myitkyina – Operations south of Mandalay – Withdrawal of V Army and 38th Division to China – Conduct of Chinese forces during their withdrawal – Failure of British and Chinese to co-operate fully.

The operations conducted by VI Army and other troops of the Chinese Expeditionary Force in the Shan States and Karenni were largely independent of those carried out by V Army on the front south of Mandalay. Here, in April 1942, V Army was employed in opposing the Japanese advance from Toungoo. Behind it in Mandalay was concentrating LXVI Army. The leading troops of this Army, 38th Division commanded by General Sun Li Jen, entered Burma in the first week of April. From Mandalay the Division was sent to the British sector about Yenangyaung in support of Burcorps. Its operations are recorded in the description of events on the British sector. Its place in Mandalay was taken by 28th Division. Headquarters LXVI Army and 29th Division of that Army did not enter Burma until the end of April.

Before describing the Chinese operations south of Mandalay in April it is desirable to detail the course of events in Karenni and the Shan States. These had a decisive bearing upon the whole of the Burma Campaign and were directly responsible for the withdrawal of the Allied forces from Burma.

There was little co-operation between V and VI Armies, and in spite of the fact that 55th Division was weak and the Japanese were known to be advancing on Mawchi 3 Regiment of 55th Division was retained by V Army at Thazi for some time. It did not rejoin its Division at Loikaw until April 14th.

CHAPTER 22

1 Regiment of the Division was in Karenni disposed in depth along the road Mawchi-Bawlake-Loikaw. A Battalion of 2 Regiment had also been moved up to Loikaw when 3 Regiment went to Thazi. There were accordingly four Battalions, possibly one thousand rifles in all, in Karenni to meet the Japanese thrust along the Mawchi road.

The Karen Levies west of Mawchi could not delay the Japanese advance for long and the town was occupied by the enemy on April 4th. The company of Chinese troops there fell back on Kemapyu without offering much resistance. Demolitions along the road were blown but not covered by the retiring force.

1 Regiment now concentrated in the Bawlake-Kemapyu area which was one of considerable natural strength, but the Chinese were not prepared to take offensive measures against what was at that time probably quite a small force of the enemy. This force formed part of the Japanese 56th Division.

General Liang had reported the situation to VI Army Headquarters on April 6th. He asked for immediate reinforcements. General Kan was at Lashio on a conference, and it was not until April 9th that the remaining two Battalions of 55th Division which were in Army Reserve about Loilem were ordered to move into Karenni.

Just previously to this it had been decided to concentrate 93rd Division (less one strong regiment to hold the Mongpayak area) and one regiment of 49th Division at Loikaw. Owing to the long distances involved and the lack of motor transport such a concentration would necessarily take a long time. The regiment of 49th Division was to march across country, whilst 93rd Division was intended to be moved by motor transport. It was suggested to General Kan by the Chief Liaison Officer of VI Army that these troops should march to Takaw where they could be picked up by motor transport. This would expedite the transfer of 93rd Division to the danger zone. The suggestion was rejected. The shortage of transport, the bottle-neck of the Takaw ferry, and the poor condition of the road and vehicles made the transfer a slow one. In addition, further delays were caused by the Chinese diverting to other purposes the transport vehicles allotted to them for the move.

From Kemapyu 1 Regiment was forced back to Pasawng, and shortly afterwards to positions covering the suspension bridge across the Htu Chaung just above its confluence with the Nam Pawn river. Here it was relieved by 2 Regiment and went back to Bawlake and Namphe, where Field Headquarters of 55th Division had been established.

Throughout these operations the Chinese appear to have done little to protect their right flank although there was always the possibility of a Japanese encircling movement from this direction. This actually occurred on April 16th after several direct attacks on the Htu Chaung positions had failed. In these engagements both sides incurred considerable casualties. The Japanese in their outflanking movement crossed the Htu Chaung north of the Chinese positions and thus compelled 2 Regiment to withdraw to a line just south of Bawlake. Next day, April 17th, the Japanese continued their cross-country advance on the west of the road and cut it between Namphe and Bawlake. In this latter place was now only 2 Regiment. The remainder of the Division, including 3 Regiment, was at Namphe. Casualties had been fairly heavy and at this stage the effective strength of the Division was probably not more than four thousand.

At 0300 hours on April 18th, 3 Regiment was ordered to counter-attack the enemy east of Namphe. Heavy fighting took place during the day. VI Army Headquarters had been established at Loikaw, and here, on the evening of April 18th, arrived one Battalion of 93rd Division. It was immediately sent forward to Namphe in motor lorries. Information was also received that 145 Regiment of 49th Division had arrived at the To Sai Kha bridge on the road north of Loikaw.

That night telephone and wireless communications between VI Army Headquarters and 55th Division suddenly ceased. The Chinese force in the Namphe-Bawlake area had been cut off. Early next morning Japanese armoured vehicles were encountered at Ngwedaung, nine miles south of Loikaw. It was evident that 55th Division had been overrun. In Loikaw were only a few guards and a company of Sappers. These were disposed to cover the two bridges over the Balu Chaung and to carry out demolitions. Army Headquarters then left for the To Sai Kha bridge across the Nam Tamhpak. The bridge was prepared for demolition.

Karen Levies were in contact with a Japanese force at Yado, and there was a possibility that the enemy would carry out an outflanking movement along the Mongpai-Pekon road and thus reach the Thazi-Loilem-Kengtung road behind the Chinese. A strong patrol was sent to Mongpai to prevent this. It was too late, and the Japanese were already in possession of the road.

The enemy approached To Sai Kha, and on the afternoon of April 20th crossed the bridge which had not been demolished. The Chinese retired on Hopong and took up a strong position some twelve miles to the east, astride the road at Htamsang. The available force was small, consisting of the remnants of 145 Regiment, some Army troops, and a Battalion of 93rd Division. There were few anti-tank guns.

CHAPTER 22

The enemy was in contact with the Chinese at Hopong on the evening of April 21st. Next morning the Japanese were attacking the Htamsang position. Hostile aircraft now began to take an active part in the operations on this front. The Chinese positions and approaches to them were almost continuously bombed during day-light hours. Loilem was also subjected to heavy dive-bombing attacks and a large part of the town was destroyed by fire.

That night the Chinese withdrew to a position at Kawng Nio, about eight miles west of Loilem. This was a position of great natural strength, but the Japanese outflanked it by moving along tracks to the south of the road. The Chinese were not in sufficient strength to stop this movement and, although their forward troops continued to hold out, the Japanese were in possession of Loilem on the evening of April 23rd. General Kan and the remaining elements of his force, amounting to about three hundred men, took up a defensive line on the Lashio road near Panglong.

At this time units of 93rd Division approaching from Kengtung were only some twenty miles distant from Loilem. Hearing of the fall of that town they withdrew to Takaw. Here they were met by General Kan who had marched across the hills with a bodyguard. From Takaw these remnants of VI Army moved to Kengtung where was concentrated what remained of 49th and 93rd Divisions. These were joined by General Chen and about a thousand men of 55th Division who had made their way across country from the Bawlake area. VI Army then retired into China, and Kengtung was occupied by the Thais.

Meanwhile, the fight in the Shan States had been maintained for a short period by other Chinese troops. Whilst advancing on Loilem the enemy had also occupied Taunggyi with a mixed force reported to consist of Japanese and Burmans. This force opposed an advance by 200th Division and one regiment of 22nd Division of the Chinese V Army moving east from Thazi. On the afternoon of April 23rd, the enemy positions west of Taunggyi were attacked under the personal direction of General Stilwell, and on April 24th the town was retaken. Next day 200th Division captured Hopong, and the enemy were estimated to have suffered five hundred casualties. Loilem was then occupied by the Chinese.

The situation now was very confused, but further north 28th Division had been ordered back from Mandalay to the Hsipaw-Lashio area. It was accompanied by some tanks and anti-tank guns of V Army. With the exception of one regiment these troops succeeded in reaching the area by April 26th. The remaining men of 28th Division, moving by road, was informed that the Japanese were in Hsipaw. Turning north just east of Maymyo it made for Mogok.

Headquarters LXVI Army and part of 29th Division had arrived in Lashio and the Army Commander, General Chang, assumed command of all Chinese troops in the area. On April 27th, 28th Division was moved south of Hsipaw to Namon fifteen miles distant on the Loilem road. At 2300 hours that night it was in contact with a small lorry-borne force of the enemy which was compelled to retire. However, fearing that his own small force would be outflanked, the Commander withdrew on Lashio.

During this period motor transport and armoured vehicles of V Army from the front south of Mandalay were pouring through Lashio on their way to China. Nothing of this force was diverted for use against the oncoming Japanese, although General Chang was desperately short of troops and elements of his Army had still to arrive from China.

The Chinese destroyed their very considerable remaining stores left in Lashio. On April 29th after heavy fighting they fell back on Hsenwi, and later took up positions astride the road covering Kutkai.

The Japanese occupied Lashio the same day. Their force was estimated at thirty light tanks, about a dozen 75 mm guns, and two Battalions of infantry.

The total force now available to General Chang could not now have exceeded three thousand men and little resistance was made to the continued advance of the enemy. The Chinese withdrew into China through Kutkai and Wanting, having fought at both these places, whilst the Japanese pressed on towards Bhamo. On the road to this town the Shweli river was a major obstacle.

The Shweli river was bridged at Manwing, the bridge being held by the Northern Shan States Battalion, Burma Frontier Force. This Battalion had been stationed in Lashio until the evacuation of that place. The necessary preparations for demolitions were made, but no officer trained in demolitions remained at the bridge. On May 3rd the enemy advanced in a column of lorries with machine-guns mounted on the vehicles. The covering troops were rushed, the fuses of the demolition charges were damp and would not ignite, and the bridge was lost. Further demolitions along the road had not been carried out and the Japanese went on to Bhamo. They occupied that town on May 4th. On May 8th they were in Myitkyina, no opposition being offered to them.

To complete the story of the Shan States operations it is necessary to refer briefly to the further movements of the Chinese 200th Division with its attached regiment of 22nd Division. From Loilem this force moved on to Hsipaw. Finding that the enemy held Lashio too strongly to be attacked it turned south-west and re-occupied Maymyo. From that place it went north to Mogok with the object of cutting its way out to China. At Mogok was the remaining regiment of 28th Division.

Myitkyina is roughly four hundred and twenty miles due north of Bawlake, and the Japanese advanced over this distance in three weeks. In the earlier stages of this operation the Japanese 56th Division was employed. Later the Japanese 18th Division also probably operated in the Shan States area. These Divisions had entered through Rangoon when considerable reinforcements were brought into the country early in April.

The failure of the Chinese VI Army to hold the advance of the Japanese has been attributed by a Liaison Officer attached to that Army to the following reasons:

(i) The fact that the poorly trained and comparatively weak 55th Division had to meet the thrust. In addition, the Division was widely dispersed.
(ii) Lack of transport and the failure of the Chinese to make the best use of what was available.
(iii) The reluctance of Senior Officers to assume responsibility. Even with rapidly changing situations officers would not countermand existing orders save upon the highest authority. Lack of adequate communications aggravated this state of affairs.
(iv) Consistent failure to initiate offensive action. The Chinese were content to be attacked in their defensive positions which invariably were on a narrow front in the immediate vicinity of the main roads. Fully allowing for a shortage of troops they made singularly little effort to protect their flanks, even when it was known that there were tracks along which the enemy could carry out turning movements.

It is now necessary to consider the operations undertaken in April by the Chinese V Army on the front south of Mandalay. Here, upon the withdrawal of 200th Division from Toungoo, the line was established by 22nd Division at Swa south of Yedashe.

The Japanese had been severely handled in the Toungoo fighting. Early in April their troops in this area were reported to have obtained reinforcements including artillery. Air action continued to be heavy, and on April 3rd both Pyinmana and Yamethin were severely bombed. After a brief interval the Japanese continued their forward movement and by

April 5th were attacking 22nd Division in Yedashe, where a Battalion of 66 Regiment was surrounded. There was hard fighting. In spite of enemy pressure, the Chinese only gave ground slowly. The Japanese were held on the Swa river at Thagaya, and again at Yeni. The Chinese then withdrew towards Pyinmana where General Tu was anxious to stage a 'Changsha' battle. The plan for this involved the employment of all three Divisions. One was to act as a forward screen, another was to hold Pyinmana as a strong point, whilst the third was to be held in reserve to deliver a counter-attack after the Japanese had carried out their inevitable pincer movement round the leading Division. The weakness of the plan was that the Japanese with their almost complete air superiority were aware of the Chinese dispositions and refused to fall into the trap.

Early in April an important meeting took place in Maymyo between the Generalissimo and General Alexander. The Generalissimo insisted that there must be no further retirements and undertook to stand at Pyinmana if the British would hold a line through Taungdwingyi and south of Magwe. General Alexander pointed out that Burcorps could not hold such a wide front, whereupon the Generalissimo promised to send one Division across the Yomas to Taungdwingyi.

This promise was never implemented and the fault was General Tu's. He was anxious to carry out his 'Changsha' plan and did not obey General Stilwell's order. Only a single Battalion went to Taungdwingyi. The result was that Burcorps was too thin on the ground, and the enemy passed through our line to cut off 1 Burma Division at Yenangyaung.

General Stilwell was determined to help the British and accordingly moved 38th Division from Mandalay to the support of Burcorps. Elements of this Division were able to render considerable assistance in the fighting round Yenangyaung.

Meanwhile the Japanese had refused to enter General Tu's trap. Finding that they were unlikely to launch a direct attack on Pyinmana, General Stilwell agreed to send 200th Division to help Burcorps in a counter-attack in the Kyaukpadaung area. He was afraid that enemy pressure up the Irrawaddy valley might result in the outflanking of V Army from the west.

Great difficulty was experienced in transferring 200th Division to its new area. Both British and Chinese insisted that they were helpless and unable to provide the necessary lorries. By the time that the Division had reached Meiktila the threat against VI Army had become so serious that General Stilwell was compelled to divert the Division

CHAPTER 22

to the Shan States. Leading it in person he launched the attack on Taunggyi on April 23rd.

It has already been stated that the Japanese in Burma had been heavily reinforced, and with the arrival of fresh troops they continued their pressure on V Army. The Japanese 18th Division was now identified on this front.

On April 20th the Chinese were forced out of Pyinmana, and on that day 96th Division was fighting twelve miles to the north of the town. The Division had sustained heavy casualties and the Japanese had worked round behind it. Next day the Division was fighting in Kyidaunggan. One regiment was surrounded. Behind it 22nd Division was holding Pyawbwe. One of its regiments had accompanied 200th Division to the Taunggyi area.

Moving by a road to the west of Pyawbwe an enemy force of tanks and armoured cars began to encircle that town on the afternoon of April 25th. The same evening British tanks surprised a column of Japanese lorry-borne troops several miles north of the town. 22nd Division withdrew.

The remnants of the two Chinese Divisions passed through 7 Armoured Brigade which covered their retirement. As a fighting force these Chinese Divisions had almost cessed to exist and were reduced to less than half their effective strength.

Opposed to a considerably superior force of the enemy they had been in constant action since early in April. They had fought well. The British (48 Brigade) were in position at Kyaukse, and 22nd Division was to occupy the line of the Myitnge river to defend Mandalay.

The campaign had now entered upon its final phase. In the Shan States VI Army had disintegrated and the British with the Chinese 38th Division were withdrawing across the Irrawaddy. It was arranged that 93rd Division with Army troops and some motorised units should also cross the Irrawaddy and move north through Shwebo. 22nd Division was to follow the east bank of the river through Mandalay to Singu, where it would cross the Irrawaddy to Kyaukmyaung, there re-joining 93rd Division. 38th Division was to act as rear guard to V Army.

The original intention was to withdraw the whole force on Katha and Myitkyina. When it became apparent that Bhamo and Myitkyina were imperilled by the Japanese advance through the Shan States this plan was modified to the extent that the V Army would make for India if it could not go north.

On April 29th and 30th the last elements of the Allied forces crossed to the west bank of the Irrawaddy with 22nd Division covering the east bank and Mandalay. At 2359 hours on April 30th the Ava Bridge was blown. The 22nd Division was then withdrawing through Mandalay. The road and rail bridges over the Myitnge river had previously been demolished.

The Chinese were in contact with the enemy in the foot-hills to the east of Mandalay, but the withdrawal to Singa was not followed up and the river was crossed without opposition. Kyaukmyaung and points along the railway on the west bank of the river were repeatedly attacked by enemy aircraft which now enjoyed unchallenged supremacy. These bombing attacks did much to complete the disorganisation of the railway and to interfere with the withdrawal northwards.

Realising that the Japanese had already reached Myitkyina, General Tu with his Headquarters and what remained of 22nd and 96th Divisions left the railway line about Naba and struck north-west through the Hukawng valley, eventually reaching India. 38th Division, in much better fighting condition than the two Divisions of V Army, turned south from Naba and regained contact with the Japanese at Wuntho where an engagement was fought. Then, with 113 Regiment as rearguard, the Division crossed the hills to the Chindwin river. Here at Paungbyin, on May 14th, it encountered a Japanese force moving up the Chindwin. Crossing the river, the Division, less 113 Regiment, arrived in the Imphal area on May 24th. 113 Regiment was cut off east of the Chindwin, and all efforts to cross the river were checked by the Japanese.

General Stilwell with members of his Headquarters and a bodyguard made his way independently across the Chindwin to India.

No account of the retirement of the Chinese forces from Burma would be complete without a reference to their general conduct during this final period of the campaign. They displayed a complete disregard for their Allies and the needs of the Civil population and refugees. Their stragglers were in an ugly mood and would brook no interference with their actions. Wholesale looting took place in all the towns and villages through which they passed. Disregard for the proper operation of the Railways increased. Refugees and British casualties and nurses were ejected from trains which were commandeered by force. Threats to shoot even the most senior railway officials were freely made. Armed guards were placed over others. In several cases Chinese interference with the running of the Railways was directly responsible for serious accidents resulting in numerous casualties. On the ill-stocked evacuation routes to India the Chinese appropriate to themselves supplies intended for the use of all persons passing over the routes. There was more than one instance in which a direct and serious clash with British elements was barely avoided.

Undoubtedly the assistance rendered by the Chinese Expeditionary Force led to a prolongation of the brief campaign in Burma. Without this aid the British alone must have been speedily enveloped after the fall of

CHAPTER 22

Rangoon. At the same time, it cannot be said that the British and Chinese worked in close accord. They did not, and some of the reasons for this failure have already been detailed. One of the main reasons would seem to have been the entire ignorance of each Army of the methods and organisation of the other. Not unnaturally the Chinese conducted themselves in Burma as they had been accustomed to do in China.

There had been no prior liaison and interchange of ideas or information, with the result that when the Chinese forces entered Burma the British were unprepared to assimilate them. Their lack of administrative services, their cumbersome system of command, the method (not always confined to junior officers) of emphasising a request with a significant pistol gesture, and other matters if studied and appreciated in advance could undoubtedly have been more satisfactorily met. Previous liaison, too, would have led to a further understanding of the difficulties existing on both sides. In addition, it would have warned our own liaison staff of the Chinese indifference to a close observance of administrative programmes and timetables.

The Chinese imagined that in Burma they had found a land well stocked with all the necessities and many of the luxuries of life. They could not understand that the British were desperately short of many of the supplies essential for the waging of a campaign. This is well illustrated by the S.S. *Tulsa* incident. This vessel arrived in Rangoon from America in January 1942 with a cargo of Lease/Lend munitions. It carried anti-aircraft guns and equipment, light automatic guns, and motor vehicles. Of all these the Army in Burma was in urgent need. The Generalissimo had already stated that all China's resources were at the disposal of China's allies, and accordingly the Governor of Burma, Sir Reginald Dorman-Smith, endeavoured to arrange with the American Lease/Lend officials that some of the most urgent requirements of the Burma Army should be met from the *Tulsa* cargo. Pending settlement of this question the cargo was, as a safety measure, removed as rapidly as possible from the dock area. General Yu Fe Pang, the Chinese representative in Rangoon, gave the Generalissimo the false impression that the goods had been seized and there were serious repercussions, although eventually a compromise was arranged and part of the *Tulsa* cargo became available to Burma.

This failure on the part of the Chinese to realise the shortage of supplies persisted throughout the campaign. Until it was too late, they did not appreciate the necessity of utilising everything they possessed in keeping open the port of Rangoon so vital to their needs. Later, when the shortage of motor transport was acute, they did not make available for general use the very large number of vehicles that had been concentrated in Lashio for employment on the Burma Road.

General Alexander had laid down a policy that all resources must be pooled, but it was not always easy to persuade the officers directly responsible to pass on to the Chinese a portion of their meagre supplies. The shortage of transport and the failing railway system also made it difficult always to carry out the transfer. In the case of petrol, we did definitely hoard our resources. The Chinese were naturally eager to transport to China as great a quantity of petrol as they could. Our policy was to hold as much as possible in the way of reserves. The result was that large quantities had finally to be destroyed or left for the Japanese.

Over this matter of supplies there were faults on both sides. The Chinese were consistently excessive and overbearing in their demands. The British, on the other and, were inclined to be niggardly and certainly put their own requirements first.

However, despite misunderstandings and differences of opinion, there is no doubt that the Chinese were sincere in their anxiety to take part in a joint defence of Burma. Only those who knew the Chinese, and Chinese history, can realise the significance of the step taken by the Generalissimo in offering the maximum possible number of troops and his readiness to place them under British command.

Not unnaturally the Generalissimo expected us to supply what the Chinese lacked in aircraft, munitions, administrative and medical services. Possibly, too, he expected a more comprehensive liaison service, and the delay in General Dennys' appointment was most unfortunate.

The disappointment of the Chinese at the British failure to produce sufficient troops or aircraft for the defence of Rangoon and the Burma Road requires to be appreciated, especially as their own ready and early offers of ample reinforcements were not promptly accepted. Our change in command, coming when it did, cannot have inspired confidence. It was probably responsible for the Generalissimo calling for the assistance of General Stilwell.

Had a firm front been established in Burma, and had the Chinese been able to meet the Japanese on equal terms, the campaign might well have represented the turning point of the war in the Far East. Consequently, if we had reason to be disappointed in the Chinese it must be remembered that they had also good reason to be disappointed in us.

Chapter 23

Events in Arakan and more particularly in Akyab – Civil unrest – Air attacks on Akyab – Japanese advance into Arakan – Encounters with the Japanese – Evacuation of Akyab – Organisation of Karen Levies – Resistance by Karen Levies and Karens of the Burma Rifles to Japanese advance on Mawchi from Toungoo – Commando units – Evacuation of Myitkyina – Indiscipline of members of armed forces on the northern evacuation routes to India.

An account of the First Burma Campaign would be incomplete without some reference to events in Arakan, and more particularly in the area of the port of Akyab. Some details of the work carried out by the Karen Levies and the Commandos, and of events in the Bhamo-Myitkyina area at the close of the campaign are also necessary.

Akyab as a point of entry into Burma was of negligible importance. It was of value, however, as an air base, whilst its proximity to India and position on the Bay of Bengal made it a prize of considerable importance to the enemy. It was necessary, therefore, to deny it to him as long as possible.

Akyab, for the defence of which G.H.Q. (India) had assumed direct responsibility, was also the centre of a rice producing area. It had several large mills, and its main export was the grain crop of Arakan.

Prior to the fall of Rangoon, the Japanese invasion of Burma had no vital effect on Akyab. At the end of January 1942 its defences had been augmented by the arrival of the 14th Battalion 7th Rajput Regiment which relieved 23 Garrison Company. The Battalion was commanded by Lieut.-Colonel O.C. Munckton. Indian refugees from Rangoon and Lower Burma, crossing to the Arakan coast through the Taungup Pass from Prome, were crowding into the port. In the latter part of February, the R.A.F. forced to evacuate the Rangoon airfields, strengthened its force in Akyab.

After the capture of Rangoon by the enemy our own activities in Akyab increased. It was organised as a naval base under Commodore Graham, R.N. commanding Burma Coast. Here were now stationed the R.I.N. sloops *Sutlej* and *Indus*, and four L.N.D. vessels. From the base there operated five, armed motor launches manned by personnel of the B.R.N.V.R. To prevent enemy infiltration these launches were on continuous patrol amongst the many islands and numerous creeks along the coast. Our force was wholly inadequate for this purpose, and it was not assisted by the absence of maps and charts accurate enough for the navigation of inland waters.

The task was not made any easier by the hordes of Indian refugees streaming out of Burma. The evacuation of these unhappy people was perforce undertaken by the naval authorities who, from the end of March to the beginning of May, sent by sea thirty-five thousand persons to India from Akyab and the small island port Kyaukpyu.

At the latter place this work was carried out in addition to his patrolling duties by Sub-Lieutenant H.C.G. Brown, B.R.N.V.R. With the crew of his launch and the aid of a few military stragglers from the front in Burma he restored order in Kyaukpyu and dealt with the thousands of refugees arriving at the port. As was not uncommon throughout Arakan many of these fugitives had been attacked, maltreated, and robbed by the local people.

In view of the importance of Akyab as an air base it was decided early in March to strengthen further our forces there. The occupation of the Andaman Islands by the Japanese was expected, and Akyab was the one base from which our air force could operate. Accordingly, Headquarters 109 Brigade with the 6th Battalion 9th Jat Regiment and the 9th Battalion 7th Rajput Regiment together with anti-aircraft guns were despatched to Akyab, arriving there on March 18th.

On March 23rd the enemy occupied the Andamans from which a small Garrison had already been evacuated on March 12th under orders by Abdacom. Although they were not occupied by the enemy until March 23rd the fact that they could not be defended constituted a serious threat to the security of shipping entering Rangoon river and was one of the factors bearing on the question of the evacuation of Rangoon. On March 23rd, too, Akyab was subjected to a heavy air raid, this being repeated the following day. Just previously the Magwe airfield had also been attacked. The result of the raids was the virtual extinction of our air force in Burma, and the decision was made to employ Akyab only as an advanced landing ground. Headquarters 109 Brigade and the two newly arrived Battalions were at once withdrawn. The remaining military garrison then consisted of the

14th Battalion 7th Rajut Regiment one section 67 Heavy Anti-Aircraft Regiment, and two troops of 1 Indian Light Anti-Aircraft Regiment.

From this period onwards Akyab, its airfields and harbour, and the naval craft based on it were subjected to frequent air attacks. The first raids immediately resulted in a drop both in military and civilian morale. There were numerous desertions amongst the troops and the civil police. Despite the protests of the naval and military authorities the Commissioner, Arakan Division, evacuated with nearly all his civilian officers on March 30th. The Deputy Commissioner of Akyab, Oo Kyaw Khine, and some telegraph officers elected to remain at their posts; but civil administration throughout Arakan was now wholly at an end.

Arson was not infrequent in the port. Rice mills were fired, and a large conflagration threatened the important oil installations of the Burmah Oil Company Limited. Civil unrest in Akyab and throughout Arakan increased. On April 13th Oo Kyaw Khine declared the town and island of Akyab to be under martial law. At the same time, he was active in visiting unsettled areas in an endeavour to restore order.

Deserters from the Burma Frontier Force and the Burma Military Police joined the forces of unrest and, together with a gang of Arakanese, took part in the massacre of Indians, mostly women and children, at Gopethaung on April 19th. The general state of disorder was particularly marked south of Kyauktaw, and east of the Kaladan river. Roused by these attacks Indians began to band themselves together and retaliated on their enemies.

In their frequent air raids on Akyab the Japanese did not escape loss. Several of their aircraft were destroyed. On the other hand, on April 6th, H.M.I.S. *Indus* was sunk by a direct hit from a bomb.

The morale of our troops continued to be poor. The crew of the *Indus* after she was sunk refused to man military evacuation launches which had been deserted by their Chittagonian crews. Special R.I.N. crews sent from Bombay took up the same attitude. Malaria was very prevalent, and on April 21st the War Diary of the 14th Battalion 7th Rajput Regiment recorded that no less than one hundred and forty-two men were sick in hospital or in quarters.

From about mid-April the prevailing unrest had become of a defiantly rebellious nature, and patrols of the Rajputs engaged in several skirmishes against parties of Thakins and others. On April 21st the Deputy Commissioner telegraphed a message to the following effect to the Burma Government: "This is report on situation in Akyab District. State of open rebellion exists which should be quelled and could be quelled only by military as owing to breakdown of civil (Administration) what is left of civil police is grossly unreliable. In Kyauktaw and Akyab sub-divisions gangs of rebels supported by deserters from Frontier Force with large quantities of arms and ammunition and the extreme section of Arakan National Congress have done incalculable damage to life and property. Arson and looting are rampant and the ground is being prepared for enemy infiltration".

The existing garrison of Akyab and the naval patrols were of course quite inadequate to deal effectively with the situation or to prevent the advance of the enemy.

On April 11th Sub-Lieutenant Brown, patrolling from Kyaukpyu, learnt that two hundred and fifty armed Burmans with Japanese officers, had arrived at Taungup on the previous day. They had launches and boats. This party proceeded to work its way up the coast via An to Minbya, a centre of rebel activity.

Towards the end of April enemy aerial activity increased, and there was now no doubt that a hostile force was concentrating in the Minbya area for an advance on Akyab. On May 1st two motor launches of the B.R.N.V.R. were separately engaged by this force near Minbya. Four field guns were reported to have been employed by the enemy and casualties were suffered on board the launches.

Next day the enemy was in Kyauktaw and Ponnagyun. A Rajput patrol was sent out that evening in launches to locate the forces. Meanwhile the launch of the Deputy Commissioner, Oo Kyaw Khine, had that day been fired on near Ponnagyun. Oo Kyaw Khine, whose devotion to duty had been of the highest order, was killed.

On the morning of May 3rd, the vessels of the Rajput patrol were fire on by machine-guns on a reach of the Kaladan river below Ponnagyun. Several men were hit. The fire was returned and one of the launches brought its two-pounder gun into action.

That day Akyab was subjected to a series of air raids, one of them by twenty-seven heavy bombing aircraft. This particular raid did appreciable damage to buildings, military stores, and equipment. Rations, mortars, and four armoured carriers were destroyed, and the reserve ammunition of the garrison was blown up. About twenty casualties were also sustained.

The role of the Akyab Garrison was to defend the airfields as long as possible. If a serious attack was made on the port, demolitions were to be carried out and the garrison to be withdrawn overland towards Chittagong.

Lieut.-Colonel Munckton, commanding the garrison, now considered that the retention of the port was no longer within the capacity of his

CHAPTER 23

force. The troops were in a low state of training; in addition, they were debilitated by malaria and shaken by the air raids. Recent encounters with the enemy indicated the presence of regular Japanese troops who would probably attack Akyab before the morning of May 4th. The coast road was flooded and the inland route was already threatened, if not cut, since the Japanese were at Ponnagyun.

Having regard to this state of affairs Lieut.-Colonel Munckton determined to carry out an evacuation by sea that night. Demolitions were ordered to be effected.

Guns and heavy equipment were loaded on to the ships *Heinrich Jessen* and *Hydari*, and after dark troops were embarked. Naval demolitions were carried out in the port and surplus vessels sunk. In the early hours of May 4th our forces abandoned Akyab.

The loyalty of the Karens towards the British has always been a marked national characteristic. They have no love for the Burman who, in pre-British times, regarded them as a subject race. Speaking generally, the Karens were strong supporters of the British during the campaign, although one section of the community was reported to have pro-Japanese leanings. The religion of the majority of these people is Christianity. Their politics are often coloured by their religion, and by no means all the missionaries working amongst them had British sympathies.

Karenni lies astride the Salween north of Papun, but the Karens are to be found in all the hill districts of the Salween south of the Shan States, in the Pegu Yomas, and in the Irrawaddy delta. Their knowledge of the thinly populated areas mainly inhabited by them and their jungle craft are great. The organisation of these hill people for intelligence work and as irregulars would have been invaluable, yet nothing substantial was done until it was much too late. This was an instance of the absence of pre-arranged planning against the possibility of a Japanese invasion.

It was not until the Japanese entered Burma that any effective steps were taken to enlist the general aid of the hill tribes. Even in the case of the Chins and Kachins the time proved too short to meet the existing emergency, although these hill men were to establish their value in a later stage of the war. With the Karens the results achieved within a brief period showed how dismally we had failed to employ the excellent material available to us. We were at least a year too late.

At the end of 1940 and in 1941 a small force of Karen Levies was raised by S.F. Hopwood for intelligence work on the frontier and in Thailand. This body of men obtained very useful information in the Karenni area and in the adjoining part of Thailand.

In February 1942 Forest Officers and others with an intimate knowledge of the Karens made contact with influential elders for the purpose of raising Levies. The general direction of the work was under the Oriental Mission, an organisation formed for the conduct of operations through irregulars and behind the enemy lines. By that time the Japanese were across the Salween. Many of the Karens were out of touch with us and in enemy occupied territory. In some cases, no more could be done than to distribute a scanty supply of rifles and guns with a little ammunition.

However, in spite of difficulties, a substantial number of Levies was raised. Five hundred of them were under Captain Boyt, a Forest Manager of Messrs Steel Brothers and Company Limited. These men patrolled the jungle tracks and paths in an area between the Thai Frontier and the Sittang valley. Captain Boyt's Diary says: "The Karen villagers under their leaders were keen and hardworking and some five thousand square miles of wild jungle country was completely covered by these Levies. Unfortunately, only about fifteen per cent of the men could be armed with rifles and shot guns, but the remainder armed themselves with their efficient cross bows which were, on occasions, more effective than firearms".

Of other similar forces Captain Boyt states: "in Bawgalaygyi McCrindle had recruited about the same number and was doing excellent work in an area of some fifteen hundred square miles ... Captain Seagrim (Burma Rifles) was down on the Papun-Shwegyin line and extended his activities to points well south of this line. I was in touch with Seagrim who had about two hundred and fifty well-armed Levies under him. To the north of the Mawchi road Cecil Smith had recruited seventeen hundred and fifty men, well organised into companies but only about eight per cent were issued with fire arms owing to lack of stocks ..... Summing up, in the short space of three weeks we had three thousand Levies on the ground, doing first class work, patrolling, doing intelligence, decimation of Burmese spies (some fourteen men were executed) hiding of supplies, successful attacks on villages held by the enemy, helping stragglers from the Sittang and Bilin battles, etc. Later, we were able to give valuable help to the Chinese VI Army when 13 Brigade left, and all Mawchi road demolitions were taken over by the Levies".

It was on the road between Toungoo and Mawchi that Karens of the 1st Battalion Burma Rifles and Karen Levies were seriously engaged with the Japanese. The Karens of the Burma Rifles had been detached from their Battalion at Toungoo where they took part in holding the

CHAPTER 23

Japanese surprise attack on the Kyungon landing ground. These men were under the command of Captain Thompson and were armed with rifles and fifty rounds of ammunition apiece. They also had four Thompson sub-machine carbines.

On April 2nd this force of Burma Rifles was covering the demolished road bridge at Paletwa on the road to Mawchi. Here it encountered a motorised Japanese force with armoured cars and estimated at some eight hundred men in strength. Captain Thompson had one hundred and thirty-five men in all.

Allowing Japanese scouts to pass through their position, fire was opened on the main body at twenty yards range. Many casualties were inflicted on the enemy. Then, when his left flank was overrun, Captain Thompson withdrew. The road was blown in places and numerous booby traps laid. Wooden bridges were destroyed.

Next day Captain Thompson's force with Levies under Captain Boyt was in position just west of Kyichaung astride the road. Levies were patrolling to the north and south. At 0230 hours on April 4th the Japanese attacked. They employed mortars to which there could be no reply. An advance against the left flank followed. This was stopped by rifle fire. The Burma Rifles then put in a counter-attack, but weight of numbers compelled a withdrawal after more than forty casualities had been sustained. Only fifty-eight men of the Burma Rifles remained, and the enemy strength was now about twelve hundred.

The Chinese VI Army then took over the defence of the area round Mawchi, but the Karens continued to carry out patrols. On April 5th they gave warning of an attempt by the enemy to by-pass Mawchi to the north. Later, when the Japanese had gained Mawchi and were moving north along the road from Kemapyu, Levies and the remaining Karens of the Burma Rifles were patrolling and covering the tracks west of the main road. They were in contact with the Japanese at Yado and warned the Chinese of this threat to their right flank.

This brief account indicates that the Karens played a by no means negligible part in the campaign. That they did not render greater services was due entirely to our own lack of provision. Properly organised and better armed they would have been able to offer serious resistance to the Japanese thrust that shattered the Chinese VI Army.

Three Special Service Detachments (Commando) were formed from the personnel of the Bush Warfare School. These units comprised specially trained and selected British officers and men, expert in Guerilla warfare and demolition work. Towards the end of March these units were placed under the command of Col. Wingate who, in view of his experience in Abyssinia, had been asked for by General Hutton to organise what were afterwards called Long Range Penetration Groups. Unfortunately, conditions were such that it was not possible in the available time to organise anything very effective. However, Col. Wingate put his Burma experience to good use at a later date.

Two of these Commandos were employed in the Southern Shan States where they carried out one or two minor operations. Later, on the arrival of the Chinese VI Army, they remained to co-operate with these forces. In the final phase of the campaign they did much useful demolition work. The operations of the Commando on the Irrawaddy valley front have been described.

The success of deep penetration units depends to a large extent on their operating in a friendly country, and this condition did not exist in Burma at that time. Furthermore, as the Army was cut off from India, the only source of supply for suitable personnel was the depleted British Battalions. In consequence, it was not possible to utilise these valuable Commando units to the full.

When the Japanese break-through occurred in the Shan States small parties of men from the Bush Warfare School, the only troops available, were sent to the Gokteik gorge to prevent a hostile advance on Maymyo. Later these small parties were reinforced by convalescents and other men from the British Infantry Depot. In early May some of these men were again employed to cover the mouth of the Maukkadaw Chaung on the south flank of the Ye-U-Shwegyin track.

When Japanese air attacks towards the end of April rendered impossible the further regular employment of the Shwebo airfield, sick and wounded were sent by rail and river to Myitkyina for evacuation to India by air. Early in May there were also in Myitkyina numerous civilian refugees awaiting air transport to India.

On May 6th enemy aircraft twice bombed Myitkyina aerodrome. Two R.A.F. aircraft taking in wounded and evacuees were caught on the ground and destroyed. Most of the passengers and crew were killed or wounded. These raids put an end to evacuation by air and about two thousand refugees, including many Anglo Indians, were stranded.

The only organised unit in this area was the Bhamo Battalion if the Burma Frontier Force. This was really a depot battalion consisting of recruits and details and could not be regarded as fit for serious operations. Wholesale desertions from this battalion meant that no formed body of troops was available for the defence of the Bhamo-Myitkyina road. No attempt was made to hold it, nor were demolitions carried out.

CHAPTER 23

At many points this road lent itself to defence, and demolitions would have imposed substantial delay on the enemy motorised force.

Along the railway between Shwebo and Myitkyina were at that time thousands of refugees, military personnel, and causalities.

On May 7th Myitkyina was evacuated. Next day a force of about three hundred Japanese entered the town.

North of Myitkyina demolitions had been prepared along the road to Sumprabum. These were blown by a small band of officers, mainly of the Oriental Mission. No other opposition could be made to a further enemy advance.

With a high sense of duty Brigadier N. Upton, C.B.E., Commander Northern Sub Area, remained at his post. A sick man, he died at Fort Hertz at the end of June. His gallant services were acknowledged by the award of the Companionship of the Distinguished Service Order.

It now remained for the refugees and military personnel along the railway north of Shwebo and from Myitkyina itself to make their way overland to India. The great majority of them followed the route through the Hukawng valley to Assam, others employed tracks further to the south, a handful crossed by the difficult Chaukan pass. The full sad story of this evacuation is set out in several official reports and it is not proposed to repeat it here. Only one aspect of it calls for mention.

The conduct of military officers and men on these routes was the subject of much adverse criticism. It appears to have been wholly justified.

There were parties of troops that marched out in formed bodies under officers. Chins of the Frontier Force were particularly good in this respect. They retained their discipline to the last. On the other hand, many, and particularly Indians, largely Burma Frontier Force personnel, were only too ready to shoulder aside civilians in their anxiety to reach safety. Stores and villages were looted and refugees robbed, and the threat of arms was freely employed.

Of many officers it is said that they, too, were only concerned for their own safety. They made no efforts to organise stragglers or to assist in the evacuation of civilians, of whom large numbers were women and children. There were others who nobly discharged their responsibilities. Taken as a whole, however, the tale is a sorry one and does no credit to the armed forces.

Chapter 24

The Air Garrison of Burma – Its inadequacy – Strength of the Japanese air force opposed to it – Air attacks on Rangoon – Our successes – Air support for early operations of 17 Division – Withdrawal from Rangoon – Formation of Burwing and Akwing – Heavy reverses at Akyab and Magwe – Termination of R.A.F. activities based on Burma – Operations from Loiwing and India – Our air losses and those of the Japanese compared.

It has already been indicated that the employment of aircraft was always visualised as playing a large part in the defence of Burma. Here, again, the requirements of Burma were subordinated to other demands considered to be of a more pressing nature. The result was that in December 1941 the air garrison of the country was entirely negligible and wholly incapable of withstanding any heavy or long sustained attacks upon it.

The R.A.F. in Burma consisted of No. 67 Squadron with a strength of about sixteen Buffalo aircraft, and No. 4 Indian Flight equipped with a few obsolete machines. The only other flying unit in the country was the Communications Flight. This had two Moth type aircraft belonging to the Burma Volunteer Air Unit. No. 4 Indian Flight was stationed at Moulmein, the others at Mingaladon near Rangoon.

There was also present in Burma the personnel of No. 60 Squadron without its aircraft which were in Malaya when war broke out. Although pressed to return these the C.-in-C. Far East refused to do so stating that they could not be spared.

In addition to the above, there was in Burma the Third Squadron of the American Volunteer Group which with twenty-one Tomahawk aircraft was based on Mingaladon for the defence of Rangoon. The primary role of the A.V.G. under Colonel (later Brigadier General) C.L. Chennault was the defence of the Burma Road, its operational base being Kunming. Impressed with the importance of defending Rangoon

CHAPTER 24

adequately the Generalissimo specially detached the Third Squadron for the protection of that city.

When hostilities began the R.A.F. was commanded by Group Captain E.R. Manning, D.S.O. Subsequently the command of the enlarged Allied air forces (Norgroup) in Burma was assumed by Air Vice-Marshal D.F. Stevenson, C.B.E., D.S.O., M.C.

The main line of airfields with attendant satellites was Victoria Point, Mergui, Moulmein, Rangoon (Mingaladon and Zayatkwin), Toungoo, Heho, Namsang, Lashio, and Loiwing. This last was an American built airfield on the Chinese side of the frontier, north of Lashio.

This line faced the enemy in Thailand across the intervening jungle-clad and mountainous belt along the frontier. Hence, except in the case of Rangoon, adequate warning of the approach of hostile aircraft was impossible. Had this main line of airfields been sited in the Irrawaddy valley warning would have been satisfactory and possible as long as communications in the Sittang valley and along the Rangoon-Mandalay railway remained in our hands.

There were other airfields at Akyab, Magwe, Meiktila, Shwebo and Myitkyina. Some of these were still under construction but all with the possible exception of Meiktila were brought into service. In general, the airfield development and construction undertaken by the Government of Burma showed an extremely good state of affairs. All airfields had one or two all-weather runways fit for modern aircraft of the heaviest type, and all-weather satellites were provided for most airfields. During the period of the campaign, too, the flat paddy lands of Burma were dry. Provided labour was available a runway suitable for fighter and bomber aircraft could be quickly prepared on these. The weakness of the lay-out, however, was in the lack of adequate warning for the main line of airfields. The construction of these airfields had been carried out by the Burma Public Works Department. During the campaign this Department was also responsible for the maintenance of airfields.

The Burma Observer Corps provided an efficient warning system within limits, but it was necessarily tied to existing telegraph and telephone lines. Consequently, it could not fill the wide gaps where no means of communications existed.

At the outset of the campaign anti-aircraft defence was very weak. It consisted of one Battery of the Burma Auxiliary Force. The arrival of the British and Indian light and heavy Batteries later made it possible to organise a weak scale of defence at vital points, but the defence was never in sufficient strength to provide adequate protection for all these points such as airfields. Light automatic defence against low flying aircraft was provided at some aerodromes by hurriedly trained detachments of the Burma Auxiliary Force armed with ·5 Browning machine-guns. Elements of the R.A.F. Regiment arrived too late to be of service except in Akyab.

The Air Ministry programme for the defence of Burma visualised six Fighter Squadrons, seven Bomber Squadrons, two Army Co-operation Squadrons, and one General Reconnaissance Squadron. Air Vice-Marshal Stevenson who took over the Air Command on January 1st, 1942, in an early appreciation estimated fourteen Squadrons as the fighter force requisite to meet the probable Japanese air strength. But only the mixed equivalents of two Fighter Squadrons, one Bomber Squadron, two Army Co-operation Squadrons, and one-third of a General Reconnaissance Squadron joined action with the enemy in the course of the campaign. Of seven Radio Direction Finder Stations proposed only one existed.

In addition to No. 67 Squadron the R.A.F. fighter force later consisted of Nos. 17, 135 and 137 Squadrons, these last three being equipped with Hurricanes. There were never enough Hurricanes available in Burma to equip No. 67 Squadron with them, and many of those machines received were obsolescent, worn-out Hurricane I aircraft. Consequently, the maximum number of these aircraft ever in action against the enemy was about thirty, i.e., the equivalent of two Squadrons. The strength fell away rapidly due to lack of reinforcing aircraft, proper operational facilities, and absence of spares. On February 15th 1942 there were only fifteen serviceable Hurricanes, and on March 5th only six. For similar reasons the available effort of the A.V.G. fell away until in March 1942 it was between seven and ten.

For the Bomber offensive No. 113 Squadron personnel with Blenheim aircraft, arrived in Rangoon in January and early in February 1942. There were never enough Blenheim's for the equipping of No. 60 Squadron. Consequently, the average daily bomber effort was about six.

General Reconnaissance was carried out by Nos. 3 and 4 Flights of the Indian Air Force. No. 3 Flight was equipped with Wapiti and Audax aircraft, and No. 4 with Blenheim I aircraft. Subsequently No. 139 Squadron R.A.F. en route for Java was held up in Burma. It was equipped with Hudsons, but there was no personnel or equipment, and the Hudsons were maintained by Nos. 3 and 4 Indian Flight.

Army Co-operation was carried out by No. 1 Indian Co-operation Squadron and No. 28 Army Co-operation Squadron, both being equipped with out of date Lysander aircraft.

The units of the Indian Air Force mentioned above were on active service for the first time in their history. They proved their efficiency and gallantry on several occasions. No. 1 Indian Squadron carried out forty-one bomber sorties against enemy aerodromes and direct support targets, and two Lysander were shot down by enemy fighters. Accurate bombing was achieved. The General Reconnaissance aircraft did much useful work.

In the opening stages of the campaign, and whilst the offensive in Malaya was in full progress, the enemy strength within close range was estimated at a minimum effort of one hundred. Our available effort on January 31st 1942, was thirty-five. Japanese bombers and fighters were disposed at the following airfields in Thailand:

Prachuab Girikhan	10
Mesoht / Tak	40
Bangkok	70
Lampang / Chiangmai	30

Singapore fell on February 15th, but even before that date the enemy air strength had risen. After that he continued to bring up reinforcements and by March 21st was estimated to have a minimum strength of four hundred based largely on the Burma airfields, south of the line Tharrawaddy-Toungoo and also in Thailand. Intelligence reports from China and other sources indicated the presence of some fourteen Regiments of the Japanese Army Air Force. This gave him an effort of at least two hundred and sixty. On March 21st our total effort was forty-two of which fourteen were at Akyab.

The Japanese employed three types of fighter aircraft; the Army 97 with a fixed under-carriage; the Army O.I. (an Army 97 with slightly improved performance and a retractable under-carriage) and the Naval 'O' Fighter. The former two were manoeuvrable with a top speed of two hundred and seventy miles an hour at fifteen thousand feet and had a climb of two thousand five hundred feet per minute. Armament consisted of two machine-guns.

The Navy 'O' had two 20 mm guns in addition to two machine-guns, and was much superior in performance to the Army 97. It had a top speed of three hundred and fifteen miles an hour at ten thousand feet, a good climb, and good manoeuvrability. It was slightly inferior to the P. 40 and Hurricane II at medium heights, and above twenty thousand feet the Hurricane II was definitely superior. None of the three types had self-sealing tanks or armour all had a radius of action of over two hundred and fifty miles instead of the one hundred and thirty-five miles of the Hurricane II, and were also fitted with jettisonable petrol tanks which increased their radius to over five hundred miles.

The Japanese Army 97 heavy bomber was mostly employed. It had a radius of seven hundred and fifty miles and with a full load of petrol its lift was one and a half tons of bombs. It had no self-sealing tanks or armour.

Japanese fighter aircraft were able to reach out over great distances and to destroy first line aircraft on the ground. Consequently, unless airfields had a good warning system, enemy fighters achieving surprise, would come in and cause great damage to first line aircraft by low-flying attacks. This form of attack could be met by a good ground defence, but in Burma we were extremely weak in this respect.

Enemy bombers with their range and bomb lift had a wide choice in their selection of objectives. Operating in formations of not less than twenty-seven, with a pattern of some twenty-seven tons of small light Anti-Personnel and High Explosives bombs, they caused great damage to first line aircraft and P.O.L. even though dispersal and anti-blast protection had been provided.

We were much inferior to the enemy in numbers, in the vital factor of the restricted range of our fighters, and in the range, bomb lift, and speed of our bombers. On the other hand, the enemy suffered the grave disadvantage of not having armour and self-sealing tanks. In addition, the Hurricane II and P. 40 in the air battle were decisive against the ill-defended Army 97 Bomber, were much superior to the Army 97 fighter, and slightly superior to the Naval 'O'. Our Blenheim bomber with its power-operated turret gave a good account of itself against enemy fighters.

To sum up, fighter for fighter, we were much superior. It was only when we were heavily outnumbered, had received no warning, and were without proper airfield protection that the enemy was able to get a decision.

Enemy aircraft raided Tavoy on December 11th but their bombs did little damage. On December 13th three air attacks were made on Mergui. On the same day a heavy raid was carried out against Victoria Point. Thereafter there was little or no enemy air activity until December 23rd when between seventy and eighty bombers with an escort of some thirty fighters attacked the Mingaladon airfield and Rangoon. Another attack in about the same strength was made forty-eight hours later on December 25th.

A severe set-back was inflicted on the enemy in these two operations against Rangoon by the P. 40s of the A.V.G. and the Buffaloes of

CHAPTER 24

67 Squadron R.A.F. Not less than thirty-six enemy first line bombers and fighters were claimed as destroyed on these two days. On each occasion bombs were dropped by the enemy at Rangoon and Mingaladon, but no substantial damage was done although on December 23rd the Rangoon Wharves and shipping area were attacked. There were, however, very heavy civilian causalities in Rangoon on December 23rd, some two thousand four hundred persons being killed. This resulted in the general exodus of labour and the almost complete stoppage of work in the port. In the first raid there were a few R.A.F. casualties on the ground, and three P. 40s were shot down. On the second occasion four R.A.F. fighters were lost.

On January 3rd and 4th 1942 two further significant air actions were fought. On January 3rd nine enemy aircraft attacked Moulmein, and as the raiders returned to their aerodromes, they were overtaken by three A.V.G. fighters. Three of the raiders were destroyed in the air and so, too, were four that had landed.

The next day over thirty Japanese fighters attempted to break through to Rangoon. They were intercepted by the A.V.G. and driven off with loss.

The enemy now abandoned his daylight attempts on Rangoon and for the next three weeks or so resorted to night bombing, his effort varying from one or two bombers up to sixteen.

It had become apparent that the main duty of the small Allied fighter force in Burma at that time was to defend Rangoon with its important airfields and base facilities, and the arriving and departing sea convoys. There were no important military operations then in progress.

To carry out this task against a numerically superior and constantly growing air force it was necessary to reduce the scale of air attacks on Rangoon, and to meet attacks in sufficient force to inflict a high casualty rate on the enemy.

To reduce the scale of enemy air attack a portion of our fighter aircraft from the advanced bases of Moulmein, Tavoy, and Mergui attacked the enemy wherever found. Further, to weaken him by a dispersal of his fighters for protection of widely separated points, daylight bombing of and attacks on objectives were made as far apart as Chiangmai, Mehongsohn, Chiang Rai in the north, and Singora and the Thai railway system running down to Malaya in the south. Enemy airfields were searched and attacked if aircraft were present. Attacks were also made on motor transport, launches, trains and formations of troops.

This policy of attack was maintained throughout the earlier period of the Burma Campaign. It reduced the scale of attack against Rangoon and, later, against our troops. At least fifty-eight enemy bombers and fighters were destroyed on the ground by our own fighters, and further considerable losses must have been inflicted by our bombers in their attacks on grounded enemy first line aircraft. This form of action was ultimately reduced in effort when the strength of the Buffalo Squadron fell to only two or three serviceable aircraft and the P. 40s were suffering from a shortage of equipment. The effective range of the Hurricanes only allowed them to engage the closest enemy objectives.

The air battle over Rangoon lasted from December 23rd 1941 until February 25th 1942. During this period thirty-one day and night attacks were made. Between January 23rd and 29th a second attempt was made to overwhelm our small fighter force, the enemy using at least two hundred and eighteen aircraft, mostly fighters. During those six days some fifty of his bombers and fighters were destroyed. He at once went back to night operations, but made a last attempt to attain air superiority over Rangoon on February 24th and 25th. His scale of attack then was one hundred and sixty-six bombers and fighters, and the Allied Forces claimed to have destroyed thirty-seven of his aircraft with another seven probably destroyed. On the second day, February 25th, the A.V.G. claimed to have shot down no less than twenty-four aircraft. Such wastage had been inflicted on the enemy that thereafter he did not attempt to enter the warning zone round Rangoon until the city had been evacuated and the Mingaladon airfield was in his hands. Thus, the safety of our convoys bringing in final reinforcements was assured, and the demolitions in Rangoon and Syriam and the final evacuation were carried out without any interference from enemy aircraft.

In the defence of Rangoon one Squadron of P. 40s of the A.V.G., a half Squadron of Buffaloes, and the equivalent of two Squadrons of Hurricanes, which did not all arrive until midway through February, inflicted a claimed loss of one hundred and thirty bombers and fighters on the enemy with another sixty-one claimed as probably destroyed. The greater portion fell to the guns of the A.V.G. which fought with ready devotion and resolute gallantry.

Much of the fighting by 17 Division in Tenasserim took place in close jungle country and it was often impossible for supporting aircraft to see the enemy or its own troops. Navigators could not pin-point their targets with accuracy since there were no suitable land-marks. In addition, recognition of Japanese troops was difficult owing to the use of captured uniforms and native dress, and their employment of bullock carts, launches, and private motor cars. However, promiscuous bombing of the jungle was known to have a good effect and this was carried out.

CHAPTER 24

On January 20th, the attack on the Kawkareik position began. Air action in support of the troops holding the position was difficult owing to the density of the jungle. Neither our own troops not the enemy could be seen. Accordingly, the enemy landing ground and base depot at Mesoht were attacked by bombers and fighters. Reconnaissance was also made towards Tavoy with the object of locating our own troops and the enemy in that area.

The withdrawal from Kawkareik took place on January 22nd, and on January 21st and 22nd Blenheims attacked Raheng aerodrome and village and Mesarieng. Fighter escort was provided with the object of clearing the air for short periods over the Army front and providing support for the bomber operations. A strong escorted formation of enemy bombers attacked Moulmein and was intercepted by the escort of our bomber raid on its outward journey. As a result, seven enemy bombers and nine fighters were destroyed.

From January 23rd to 30th frequent low visual reconnaissance flights were made by our fighter aircraft over the battle area, the Japanese lines of communication, and the Tenasserim coast. But information was difficult to obtain over the jungle-clad areas, and in more open country the enemy only moved by night. Our bomber force, a daily average of about six, acted in support of the Army.

On the nights of January 24th, 27th, and 28th our bombers attacked the main base at Bangkok dropping a total of 42,000 lbs of bombs. They had previously bombed Bangkok in the early morning of January 8th within a few hours of their arrival in Burma.

During January the main objective of the Japanese air force, outside Rangoon, had been Moulmein. The main target was the aerodrome, and seven attacks were delivered between January 3rd and 22nd.

After the withdrawal of our land forces from Moulmein all available bombers and such fighters as could be spared were used for direct Army support. Attacks were made on river craft on the Salween; and batteries, enemy concentrations, troops, landing stages, railway stations, barracks and stores were all attacked. Fighters, operating at a great distance from their base, attempted to intercept enemy raids on our forward troops. Raids were carried out on Kado, Martaban, Paan, Moulmein, Minzi, Heinze, and the roads from Thaton to Martaban and Duyingeik.

The Japanese air force supported its land forces and from February 8th to 12th bombers attacked our troops between Paan and Thaton, but generally with little effect. Four raids by bombers were also made on the Toungoo aerodrome on February 3rd and 4th.

Air operations in support of the Army continued at the maximum intensity possible during the withdrawal to the Bilin and Sittang positions, and 17 Division was much heartened by the excellent air support it received during the operations on the Bilin river. With the loss of Moulmein our forward air base in this area had been lost, and all operations had been carried out from Rangoon. But our warning system in Tenasserim was being rapidly rolled up, and the interception of aircraft supporting enemy troops was impossible unless the attacks took place when our fighters happened to be over the line at the time.

On February 21st an enemy transport column of more than three hundred vehicles was reported on the road between Bilin and Kyaikto. The whole fighter effort of the Rangoon defence and what bombers were at readiness were ordered to attack at 1625 hours. A total of thirty-eight fighter sorties and eight Blenheim sorties were engaged in the attack. Direct hits were reported on vehicles, accompanied by many fires. The village of Kyaikto through which the column was passing was set on fire.

As already related in an earlier chapter, some of these heavy attacks fell on our own troops. The reason for this mistake is not known, but the dense jungle in which the opposing forces were operating and the paucity of our communications may have accounted for it.

On this day enemy aircraft were active over the Sittang area, the effort being estimated at ninety fighters and twelve bombers. The area of the Sittang bridge was the scene of the heaviest attacks.

On February 19th Mandalay was attacked for the first time. The attack was carried out by ten enemy bombers.

The urgent need for air reinforcement was stressed by the A.O.C. to General Wavell when the latter visited Burma at the end of January and again early in February. The main requirements were two reinforcing Hurricane Squadrons, two reinforcing Blenheim Squadrons, sixteen Blenheims for the equipping of No. 60 Squadron, and allocations of twenty-four Hurricanes and twelve Blenheims a month from the command flow of maintenance aircraft. But at that time the needs of Malaya and the Dutch East Indies were also of vital importance. Again, Burma suffered.

On February 15th Singapore fell, and the implications for Burma were very serious. But already the threat to Rangoon had developed, and when our forces fell back to the Sittang line the continued maintenance of Rangoon as an air base became dangerous. Save for limited R.D.F. and Observer Corps posts, warning facilities had all gone.

On February 20th instructions were given for the withdrawal of 17 Division across the Sittang river, and the evacuation of non-essential civil personnel from Rangoon was ordered. General Hutton indicated to the Air Officer Commanding that it might become necessary to

CHAPTER 24

withdraw the Army northwards into Central Burma. Arrangements were accordingly made to base a mixed wing on Magwe and another mixed wing on Akyab. These were to be supplied from a base organisation in India.

The size of the Magwe Wing was fixed on the maintenance already available in Burma. On the fall of Rangoon there would be no sea or overland communication between Magwe and India. Akyab could be maintained by sea.

The decision to base the air force in Northern Burma on Magwe was taken because Magwe was covered by two lines of Observer Corps telephone lines down the valleys of the Irrawaddy and the Sittang respectively. Magwe was also the only aerodrome from which the withdrawal of the Army from Rangoon up the Irrawaddy valley could be suitably protected. South of Magwe on this line were no bases of any kind for the operation of modern fighters and bombers with high wing loading. Magwe itself had no accommodation, no pens, and no dispersal. Work on its improvement was at once put in hand.

The possibility of having to cover the withdrawal of the Army had been foreseen, and a number of 'kutcha' strips were cut into the hard paddy lands along the Rangoon-Prome line. The location of these strips was kept as secret as possible. They fulfilled a double purpose. At night all first line aircraft were flown from the parent airfields at Mingaladon and Zayat Kwin to these strips. They were flown off the strips before dawn. Thus, the location of the fighting force was not readily obvious to the enemy and the possibly damaging results of accurate enemy night bombing of Mingaladon were avoided.

It was very essential to maintain air superiority over Rangoon until the final phase of the important demolitions of oil and other plant in the area had been completed and the troops withdrawn. Thereafter it was equally necessary to cover the movement of the Army away from Rangoon up the Prome road. To control the requisite fighter and bombing offensive action during these operations a special 'X' Wing Headquarters was formed under Group Captain N. Singer, D.S.O., D.F.C.

On February 21st at 1800 hours the telephone system in Rangoon ceased to function, but the observer centre in the Central Telegraph Office was at once manned with R.A.F. personnel. Thus, a limited warning system was continued. There also still remained the single R.D.F. set, of the wrong kind and now worn out.

On February 23rd the Sittang bridge was blown, and on the following two days the enemy made his last attempt to secure air superiority over Rangoon. As has already been recorded the attempt failed. Thereafter the enemy fighter force was occupied purely defensively over the areas in which his advance was taking place. To keep the enemy on the defensive our bombers operated in the same areas, and our fighters attempted to make interceptions.

During this period our effort both in fighters and bombers dwindled rapidly. This was due to lack of maintenance and spares, and the numbers that were shot up in the air battle. On February 17th our fighter effort, Hurricanes and P. 40s, was forty-four, and that of our bombers, sixteen. On February 28th our fighter effort was under ten, that of our bombers twelve. The figures rose again for the early part of March.

In the first days of March the enemy had followed our troops across the Sittang. Fighting took place around Pegu, whilst other enemy forces were infiltrating through the lower Pegu Yomas towards the Prome road. Hurricanes on reconnaissance observed this movement. The enemy did not attempt any further air attacks on Rangoon, although they took place against Maymyo, Toungoo, and Bassein, and considerable activity was maintained over the battle area.

On March 2nd the R.D.F. set was moved to Magwe, and the only warning then available in the Rangoon area was by observation from Military posts and airfields. A 'Jim Crow' Hurricane was kept over Rangoon by day. The fighter force, as a protection against being surprised on the ground, was moved to the newly prepared strip known as 'Highland Queen' near Hmawbi. The bombers operated from Magwe, using 'Highland Queen' and 'John Haig' strips as advanced bases. To give the impression that the force was still at Mingaladon dummies and wrecked fuselages were parked there on the runways.

On March 6th an enemy formation of at least twenty aircraft, protecting Japanese troops moving through the Yomas towards the Prome road, overshot its mark and by accident discovered the 'Highland Queen' strip. Our fighters, some bombers, and general reconnaissance aircraft were on the ground. Luckily the enemy shooting was bad. Some Hurricanes were able to take off and to beat off the attack. Two of our aircraft were destroyed on the ground, but the raid might well have made a decisive end to our small air force.

In the last days of the defence of Rangoon the bomber effort was directed against the enemy wherever he could be found. Fighters accompanied bombers to shoot up enemy objectives. 96,800 lbs of bombs were released, and troop concentrations, trains, transport columns, and boats on the Sittang were attacked with satisfactory results.

On March 6th Headquarters of 'X' Wing was moved from Rangoon to Zigon, the first strip from which operations could be carried

CHAPTER 24

out in support of the withdrawal of the Army along the Prome road. A demolition party then destroyed all facilities at Norgroup Headquarters in Rangoon and at the Mingaladon aerodrome.

The column of our Army withdrawing up the Prome road on March 8th was reported by air crews to be some forty miles long, mostly motor transport vehicles and tanks, and offered an admirable target for enemy bomb action in country where there was little or no cover. There was also no possibility of getting off the long straight tarmac road. From Zigon the R.A.F. maintained fighter patrols over the line to Rangoon, whilst escort was provided for the sea convoy that left the port with the final demolition parties.

The rough surface of Zigon was unsatisfactory for Hurricanes, and on the night of March 8th 'X' Wing moved to Park Lane, a strip north of Prome. Neither Zigon nor Park Lane was located by the enemy who carried out reconnaissance over our eastern airfields, obviously searching for our air force.

Meanwhile attacks on enemy objectives in support of the Army were being carried out, Rangoon and the Sittang valley were kept under observation, and our old air bases were watched for signs of the arrival of the enemy air force.

On March 9th Air Vice Marshal Stevenson received orders from the Air Officer Commanding-in-Chief, Air Forces in India, to maintain the two mixed wings at Magwe and Akyab, and also to organise the air defences in India of Calcutta, Asansol, and Tatanagar, and the Digboi oil installations in Assam, and to continue from India offensive bombing operations in support of the Army in Burma. Reconnaissance over and the attack of enemy surface vessels in the Bay of Bengal was also to be carried out.

The mixed wing (Burwing) at Magwe comprising No. 17 Hurricane and No. 45 Bomber Squadrons, the elements of an Army Co-operation Flight, the numerically weak Second Pursuit Squadron of the A.V.G. which had relieved the Third Squadron, and the R.D.F. station under the command of Group Captain Seton-Broughall was placed under the operational control of General Alexander on March 18th.

The mixed wing (Akwing) at Akyab then consisted of No. 135 Squadron armed with obsolete Hurricane Is and one Hurricane II, a general Reconnaissance Flight, and a small Air Communications detachment.

On 17th March Air Vice Marshal Stevenson flew to Calcutta where his Headquarters reopened.

On March 20th, when a reconnaissance disclosed more than fifty enemy aircraft on the Mingaladon airfield, the Japanese scale of air attack in Burma was estimated at a minimum of four hundred. In an effort to reduce this, an attack on Mingaladon was planned for the following morning. Ten Hurricanes and nine Blenheims of Akwing took off. The Blenheims were intercepted by Naval 'O' fighters forty miles north of Rangoon but fought their way into Mingaladon. They dropped their bomb lift of 9,000 lbs on the runways among enemy aircraft and then fought their way back to Tharrawaddy. Eighteen enemy fighters were encountered, two of them were shot down, two more were claimed as probably destroyed, and two damaged. Most of our aircraft were hit but none shot down, and the only casualty was one pilot wounded.

Meanwhile the Hurricanes carried out a low flying attack. Nine enemy fighters were destroyed in air combat, whilst sixteen bombers and fighters were destroyed on the ground. Some of our Hurricanes were badly shot up and one of them crashed on our side of the line through lack of petrol.

This was a magnificent air action and O.C. Burwing prepared to repeat the attack that afternoon. While final preparations were in progress enemy aircraft themselves launched a heavy attack on Magwe.

Over a period of some twenty-five hours Magwe was attacked in force six times. In all, the scale of attack reached about two hundred and thirty fighters and bombers which included one hundred and sixty-six Army 96 and 97 medium and heavy bombers. Some two hundred tons of bombs were accurately released in patterns during these attacks.

We had twenty-one fighters present at Magwe on March 21st when it was first attacked, but as a result of the action fought at Mingaladon that morning the number of serviceable aircraft ready to take the air was only twelve.

At 1330 hours twenty-one enemy bombers escorted by ten fighters bombed and machine-gunned the airfield. Our fighters intercepted and destroyed four aircraft with one probable and one damaged, but the weight of the attack got home. This was followed by further raids at 1410 hours and 1430 hours. The scale of attack for the day was fifty-nine bombers and twenty-four fighters.

Next morning another attack developed at 0845 hours. Twenty-seven bombers with an escort of ten fighters attacked the airfield, and a quarter of an hour later similar formations repeated the raid. No warning of these raids had been received, but the Japanese formations were engaged by two Hurricanes that had been sent off to intercept a high-flying reconnaissance aircraft heard earlier over Magwe.

Again, considerable damage was done. The runways were rendered unserviceable, communications were broken down, and a number of

CHAPTER 24

bombers and fighters were destroyed on the ground. At this stage of the action only three P. 40s and three Hurricanes remained flyable, the Hurricanes alone being operationally serviceable. The Commander of the A.V.G. Second Pursuit Squadron then reported to Group Captain Seton-Broughall that, in view of the absence of warning and the scale of attack, he was compelled by the terms of his instructions from General Chennault to withdraw his remaining flyable aircraft to refit. That afternoon the A.V.G. flew the P. 40s to Loiwing, the airfield on the Chinese frontier north of Lashio.

At 1330 hours two of the three remaining Hurricanes were sent up but failed to intercept enemy reconnaissance aircraft. Whilst they were returning to land at 1430 the enemy again attacked with two waves of twenty-seven and twenty-six bombers respectively, each accompanied by fighter escort.

In all these attacks nine Blenheims and at least three P. 40s were destroyed on the ground, five Blenheims were rendered unserviceable, and three Hurricanes had been destroyed in air combat. The remaining aircraft were flyable but unserviceable owing to normal unserviceability or damage from enemy action. These, except the P. 40s, were flown out to Akyab.

This grave reverse was due to our weakness in fighters, the serious defects in the warning system, and the complete absence of aircraft pens and bad dispersal arrangements at the Magwe airfield. There were no Observer Corps posts to the west and north-east of Magwe, an outflanking avenue used by the enemy in his attacks. It is understood, however, that for some of these attacks some warning was actually received but owing to the failure of land lines did not get through to the aerodrome in time.

Early on March 23rd Burwing left Magwe for Lashio and Loiwing for refitting. Loiwing was the only remaining aerodrome where a reasonable warning system still existed, but it was at a great distance from the area where the Army was operating.

The hurried abandonment of the Magwe airfield and the resulting cessation of all air support for Burcorps and the Chinese Armies led to a definite drop in morale in the Allied forces. This was probably accentuated by the knowledge that earlier in the campaign signal successes had been scored over the Japanese in the Rangoon area. Troops now found it hard to understand why air protection was no longer afforded them, and the unopposed attacks by enemy aircraft were a source of depression.

It was proposed to remedy the faults of the Magwe warning system and to put the airfield in a proper state of defence to enable Burwing to return to it for operations. But the enemy advance prevented this scheme from being carried out.

Owing to the difficult nature of the country only the outlines of communication existed at Akyab where Observer Corps warning was poor. On March 23rd, 24th, and 27th the enemy repeated the tactics employed at Magwe and overwhelmed the small R.A.F. force at Akyab. Our fighters intercepted on two occasions, inflicting a loss of four enemy aircraft destroyed and three probably destroyed for a cost of six Hurricanes. On March 27th, although warning had been received, low flying fighters caught our force on the ground. Two Hurricanes got into the air and engaged; one being shot down. Seven Hurricanes and a Valencia were destroyed on the ground. After this Akyab was only employed as an advanced landing ground for refuelling, and to enable our Hudson reconnaissance aircraft to reach the Andaman Islands.

The actions at Magwe and Akyab in effect terminated the R.A.F. activities based on Burma. The supply of aircraft now became the critical factor, and it was essential to build up the air defence of North Eastern India and Ceylon. The lack of warning and increasing weight of the enemy attack would only have resulted in the piecemeal destruction of any small force that could be maintained in Burma.

However, Burwing continued as an organisation and bombers were flown in to Loiwing and Lashio to operate for a few days. They then returned to Calcutta. Eight Hurricanes flown in on April 6th to Loiwing only lasted for a few days.

On the rapid advance of the Japanese on Lashio towards the end of April, Burwing was withdrawn to China to provide refuelling parties at main Chinese air bases. The personnel of No. 17 Squadron withdrew to India via Myitkyina.

The Japanese in Burma had been reinforced on April 6th when a convoy of ships reached Rangoon. It was this reinforcement that enabled the enemy to throw fresh troops into the attack and to speed up his advance. The passage of this convoy had been covered by vigorous air attacks on Ceylon and our shipping in the Bay of Bengal. Our air force was unable to prevent its passage. Fortress aircraft of the U.S.A.A.C., however, attacked with five and a half tons of bombs an enemy force in the Andamans and straddled a cruiser and a destroyer. Night flying attacks were also made on the convoy in Rangoon, and fires and explosions were caused in the dock areas.

After the Magwe air action the enemy air force widely extended its patrols and attacked targets not only near the battle zone but also far behind it. Taunggyi, Prome, Mandalay, Lashio, Loiwing, Meiktila,

CHAPTER 24

Maymyo and several other places were accorded the main weight of the enemy bomber attack. Great damage mainly to civilian property resulted, with considerable moral effect on local populations. But the enemy did not follow up his air actions at Magwe and Akyab by heavy and long-sustained attacks on our ground forces, although considerable support was given by Japanese aircraft to their troops operating both against us and the Chinese. The extent of the Magwe and Akyab successes does not appear to have been fully appreciated. The bases at Toungoo, Heho, Namsang, Lashio and Loiwing were constantly searched and attacked, but except for the last-named they were unoccupied. Between March 28th and April 5th enemy flying boats based on the Andamans began attacks on our shipping in the Bay of Bengal.

Our bombers and fighters continued in action over Burma, but fighter section was limited to sorties that could be made within the range of the Mohawk Squadron based at Dingan. Bomber action was exerted from the same aerodrome and from Texpur and the Calcutta air bases. Chittagong was used as a forward landing ground. Long range bombers of the U.S.A.A.C. also took part, and fifty-eight raids were made in support of our withdrawing army. Most of the bombing took place on the right flank of General Alexander's forces; but three protective raids were made on the Chinese front, and places such as Mongpawn, Laikha, and Kongchaiping were attacked. The Chinese front was of course covered by the A.V.G. operating from bases in China. They had bombed airfields in Thailand, notable Chiangmai on March 24th, and their constant attacks on advancing Japanese mechanised columns enabled the Chinese forces to consolidate their positions on the Salween front in May.

The airfields at Mingaladon, and later Akyab and Myitkyina when occupied by the enemy, were subjected by us to a harassing scale of attack. Operations against Akyab and Myitkyina were particularly successful, the airfields being made untenable by destruction of enemy first line aircraft on the ground. These latter operations, however, had no material effect on the campaign. We had already withdrawn from Burma.

In the final stages of the withdrawal of our army the enemy attempted an outflanking movement along the Chindwin river. Steamers, launches, and barges were concentrated at Monywa for this purpose. These craft and the Monywa landing stages were bombed on May 4th and 5th. This supporting action by our aircraft must have imposed delay and difficulty on the abortive Japanese encircling movement.

The work of No. 31 Air Transport Squadron must be mentioned. This was equipped with D.C.2 and later some D.C.3 aircraft. The daily effort was about three, and heavy transport requirements had to be met. Wounded were evacuated from Magwe, Shwebo and Myitkyina in turn as the battle moved north. A very large number of civilians was evacuated when there were no wounded to move. In all, two thousand six hundred wounded and an additional six thousand other persons were flown to India. Many thousands of refugees were streaming out of Burma along the difficult routes across the mountains into Assam. Food and medical stores were urgently required on all these routes both for refugees and troops. With the help of the American Air Force nearly one hundred and ten thousand pounds of supplies were dropped.

According to the available records of Norgroup in this campaign two hundred and thirty-three enemy fighters and bombers were claimed destroyed in the air. Of these the A.V.G. claimed one hundred and seventy-nine and the R.A.F. fifty-four. Fifty-eight were claimed destroyed on the ground, thirty-eight by the A.V.G. and twenty by the R.A.F. Seventy-six were claimed probably destroyed, forty-three by the A.V.G. and thirty-three by the R.A.F. The main brunt of the fighting was borne by the P.40 Squadrons of the A.V.G. they were first in the field with pilots well trained and with good fighting equipment. Their gallantry in action was the admiration of all the Allied services in Burma.

Our fighter losses in air combat were sixteen P.40s and twenty-two Buffaloes and Hurricanes, but fortunately the majority of pilots were saved. There were two substantiated incidents of Japanese fighter pilots attacking and killing our fighter pilots who were making parachute descents.

Eight of our bombers failed to return from operations, and our losses on the ground were seventeen fighters, twenty-three Blenheims, four Hudsons, and seven transport and communication aircraft.

Comparable with the total of two hundred and thirty-three enemy fighters and bombers claimed by us to have been shot down in air combat the Allied losses were forty-six. Thus, an average of slightly more than five enemy aircraft were claimed shot down for each of our aircraft lost. We also destroyed more of the enemy's aircraft on the ground than those destroyed of ours. We made no claim in respect of aircraft destroyed on the ground by bombing attacks but the numbers must have been high.

Chapter 25

Matters of Civil Administration affecting the military situation – General failure to place Civil and Military Administration on a war time basis before opening of hostilities – Evacuation – Work on the Burma-Assam road – Martial Law – Military Administration and other matters – The Base – Transport and Supply – Ordnance – Transportation and Movement Control – Denial of Railways and River Services – Lack of general Denial Scheme – Signals – Medical Services – Matters affecting discipline and morale – Morale of Burma Units – Casualties.

In considering matters of Civil and Military administration it is necessary to refer once again, very briefly, to the general situation in Burma immediately prior to the outbreak of hostilities with Japan. Incidentally, it is not proposed to discuss the Civil Administration save in so far as its actions affected the campaign.

Before December 1941 the possibility of war with Japan was realised, but it was by no means regarded as a probability. In Chapter 4 the military appreciation of the situation has been discussed. In short, this was that in the event of war with Japan the invasion of Burma was a somewhat remote further possibility and that the main danger was from aerial attack.

How far these views were justified is another question, but they certainly were the views of His Majesty's Government in the United Kingdom and of the responsible Command. It was upon this reading of the situation that the Government of Burma made its preparations for a possible emergency.

As with the Army in Burma there can be little doubt that the recent Separation from India with the introduction of a large measure of Self-Government adversely affected the administration. The Defence Department was newly created, and the general policy of Burmanisation of Government Services did not make for efficiency. Burma had been fortunate in that it had escaped all knowledge of a large-scale war in modern times, but this ignorance on the part of officials and people alike now proved a handicap.

In spite of the complete absence of assistance from His Majesty's Government much work was done both by the Army authorities and Civil Administration to prepare for war. The resources of both were, however, so thin that many of these preparations were incomplete, or the resultant organisation was so weak that it just melted away under the stress of war. There were, too, many notable omissions. Some of these might have been remedied if the work had been taken in hand earlier.

For all who cared to read, the writing on the wall was clear as soon as Japan entered Indo-China in September 1940. We had just received a bitter lesson in unpreparedness in the European Theatre of War. Thereafter readiness for war against Japan was a plain duty, and the question may well be asked if the Supreme Commander in Singapore ever warned the Burma Government or the G.O.C. Army in Burma, to prepare for a full-scale invasion.

As far as is known no Directive was issued either by the Commander-in-Chief, Singapore or by His Majesty's Government setting out what preparations were to be made in Burma to meet invasion. His Majesty's Government did increase its financial aid to Burma for defence purposes, but form a military point of view no material help was given to the Burma Government.

Having regard to these facts, and to the limited resources of the Burma Government and the inadequate staff of the G.O.C., it would be unfair to criticise the authorities for what was not done. Admittedly more could have been done had the necessary knowledge and staff been available.

It may be mentioned that the defenceless state of Burma and the need for the provision of adequate staff and services to organise its defence had been the subject of repeated representation by G.H.Q., India, to the War office. It is clear now that the demand made by C.G.S. India (General Hutton) when he visited the War Office in 1940, and again by General Wavell in the summer of 1941, that Burma should be placed under India, was the only correct solution. In the event this was only done after the outbreak of war with Japan when it was too late to undertake many of the necessary measures.

By our unpreparedness we lost to a large extent all the advantages of fighting in our own country, a country we should have known intimately

CHAPTER 25

and whose resources were at our disposal. Prior to the outbreak of war with Japan there was not the close co-ordination that should have been established between civil and military departments. No arrangements existed for the militarisation of transport and other essential services, or for the organisation of the country as a whole against attack. The provision of an overland link with India was not regarded as an urgent matter calling for prompt and affective action. The great local knowledge of innumerable government servants and other reliable persons was invaluable; no plan existed for bringing it into immediate use. Little was done to raise irregular fighting forces amongst hill-men such as the Karens. The immediate provision of an adequate number of guides and interpreters for troops operating in a strange country and ignorant of its language had not been arranged. Even the supply of maps was grossly inadequate. Many were out of date, and units sometimes found themselves without any maps at all. When a few were available they were frequently on the scale of ¼" to a mile.

There had been a complete failure to comprehend the full implications of an invasion. Burma was never visualised as one vast battle-ground, rather were any possible hostilities with Japan seen merely as an affair of frontier operations.

This lack of pre-war constructive forethought and preparation was to hamper us through the whole course of operations. In place of communications and local resources, Intelligence Services and all the specialised knowledge of the country ready organised against the invader, we were thrown back upon series of hasty improvisations. Some of these withstood the strain tolerably well, others failed. But improvisation should not have been required at all.

A major lesson of the campaign, therefore, was the necessity for the placing of both Civil and Military Administration on a war footing before the opening of hostilities. Peace time systems cannot adapt themselves at once to war conditions, and the speed of modern warfare does not permit of a leisurely change.

Speaking generally, civil officers European, Burman and Indian stood by their posts when the emergency arose. They were, however, handicapped by the defection of many subordinates whom fled at the first bombing of back areas by hostile aircraft. The result was a breakdown of Police and essential services. It was not to be expected that many of the lowest paid rank of servants would remain steadfast. They were bound by no particular ties of loyalty and to them the coming of the Japanese meant nothing more than a change of masters. Possibly it is matter for surprise that so many did carry on with their duties.

Man were often concerned not only for their own safety but for that of their wives and families. Here the Civil Government was faced with a difficult problem which it had considered but found to be insoluble.

Pre-arranged plans for the removal to safety areas of the women and children of essential public servants might well have created alarm and despondency, that bugbear of all Governments in time of emergency. On the other hand, it has to be remembered that Burma was unprepared for war. When it broke upon its people the repercussions were even more alarming than the frankest of forebodings could have been.

The mass evacuations that took place were beyond the most strenuous efforts of the Civil Authorities to keep under complete control. At times they seriously impeded troop movements, brought about a breakdown in some essential services when they were most required, led to outbreaks of cholera which infected the troops (although energetic military measures checked the spread of the disease), and facilitated the infiltration off enemy agents through our lines.

It was not the Civil Administration alone that was confronted with this problem. In as much as it affected the military situation it was the duty of the staff of the Army in Burma to have considered the matter of the evacuation of families before the outbreak of war. To prepare for the worst always lays one open to the charge of defeatism, but there was a full knowledge of the lack of preparedness of the country. Consequently, the probable course of events was clear. As will be seen this question of evacuation and the anxiety of men folk for their families was to touch the Army very closely.

The work on the road intended to link Burma with the Assam road and rail system was begun in a small way in December 1941 with the improvement of existing tracks between Kalewa and Tamu. This work was undertaken in the first instance by the Deputy Commissioner and such P.W.D. help as could be provided locally and with local resources. The original proposal put to the Government of Burma was for a road from Tamu to Sittang and thence to the railway near Wuntho. It was not until January 1942 that this project was abandoned as impracticable, and the easier though longer alignment to Kalewa and thence to Ye-U was adopted.

The work had not originally been given a high military priority and the P.W.D. was fully occupied with military works elsewhere, particularly communications in the Tenasserim area and numerous landing grounds throughout the country. With the growing threat of invasion, the urgency of the work was recognised, it was given first priority, and endeavours were made to organise an adequate P.W.D. staff.

CHAPTER 25

The dislocation caused by the enemy advance, and the collection of tools, plant, and labour delayed the start of serious work.

Tools, plant, material, labour, and rations were always a difficulty. Even when they could be collected down-country limited transport delayed arrival on the site. In accordance with orders from India the exit of refugees by this route was sought to be limited to five hundred persons a day. But those who passed through had a disturbing effect on labour which tended to join in the exodus. Cholera broke out. In addition, work on the Indian side of the frontier did not progress as fast as was expected, and consequently the help promised from India was not forthcoming in time.

The P.W.D. staff lived and worked under extremely hard conditions. It was faced with innumerable difficulties yet carried out great improvements on the very rough existing tracks. Without the work that was done it is certain that the Imperial Forces could not have withdrawn to India by the route they followed. That more was not achieved was certainly not the fault of the officers in charge of the project.

The original failure to appreciate the urgent necessity of a link with India was a grave mistake, especially as the question had been raised by G.H.Q. (India) several months before. So, too, was the delay in advancing the work with all the resources at our disposal as soon as its vital nature became apparent. Every effort should at once have been bent to the task and the strongest measures taken to enforce its completion. If Burma was to be held the road was an essential life line. After the fall of Rangoon, the lack of it was strangling in its effect. The Allied armies were virtually cut off from reinforcements and supplies. Had the road been completed in time to become an effective line of communication events in Burma may well have taken a very different course.

Under certain circumstances even a limited use of the road would have been of great assistance. It is never very profitable to speculate in matters of this kind, but had we retained our hold on the oilfields and on some of the grain producing areas the maintenance problem of the Allied forces would have been much reduced. In such cases the supply of ammunition, essential stores, and equipment might well have been brought in by air and the Assam-Burma road. If circumstances had not forced a withdrawal before the monsoon broke, it is obvious that this would have been carried out under circumstances of very great difficulty in the absence of an all-weather road. The existence of such a road would also have greatly facilitated the movement of refugees which it was not very successfully sought to curtail in the interests of road construction.

Throughout the earlier part of the campaign the Government of Burma was opposed to the institution of Marital Law which in the minds of the people was associated with the existence of a state of rebellion. Its effects, therefore, might have been unfortunate. It had also recently been decided by His Majesty's Government and the Government of India to adopt a new attitude towards Martial Law, and in desiring to delay its application the Burma Government was following the policy laid down. Later, however, certain Special Security Regulations were introduced with the effect but not the name of Martial Law. Much of the area to which they were applied was already in the hands of the enemy. Nevertheless, this attitude on the part of the Government made little difference. Order was enforced by the Military from the early days of the campaign. Before the evacuation of Rangoon, a Military Commandant was appointed, and looters were shot or otherwise punished. Similar action was taken in Mandalay; whilst in forward areas occupied by the Imperial Forces and the Chinese Armies, spies, Fifth Columnists, fire raisers, and similar criminals were summarily executed. As the line receded and civil authority progressively ceased to function, military authority necessarily took its place.

In a previous chapter reference has been made to the change of Command just after the opening of active operations. The new Commander never had an opportunity to organise the defence and secure the administration on a sound footing. Even without considerable reinforcements or administrative units he could probably have done much if placed in command earlier and provided with an adequate staff. As matters stood neither Commander nor Staff could fully appreciate the defence problem or take stock of available resources before becoming engaged in active operations.

That there was not a breakdown in Military Administration was due to the efforts of the Administrative Staff which kept its overworked machine functioning throughout the campaign in face of almost insuperable difficulties. Matters were in fact so serious that Lieut.-General Hutton, both as G.O.C.-in-C. and afterwards, had to devote much of his time to a solution of these problems. Major-General E.N. Goddard, M.V.O., O.B.E., M.C., was in charge of administration, and his successful effort to keep the machine at work were the admiration of all concerned.

At no time were there sufficient administrative units. Transport, Supply, Medical, Movements and Transportation, Provost Rest Camps, Mess, Ordnance and Labour units were all less than the number requisite for the force. Improvisation with all its attendant troubles was

CHAPTER 25

the only remedy. The problem would have been less complicated if the administrative plan had been drawn up before active operations began.

Some administrative and other matters together with the problems to which they gave rise are discussed hereunder.

One of the main difficulties confronting the Ordnance and all Supply Services was the absence of a secure Base. Before the outbreak of hostilities Rangoon was the sole Base and no similar installations had been sited in Upper Burma. The course of operations at once proved Rangoon to be far too far forward, whilst the advance of the Japanese entailed early organisation of another Base. The dislocation of labour and railways following on the bombing of Rangoon in December 1941 together with a shortage of other transport made the establishment of a new Base far from easy. Such a Base should have been created in Upper Burma before active operations began.

The Army was too highly equipped with motor transport at the expense of animal transport. In the main the terrain demanded a very comprehensive employment of pack animals. The absence of these in adequate numbers tied our force to the main supply routes and had a marked influence on the course of the campaign. We were unable to disregard roads and could not move across country with the same freedom that the Japanese did. This fact gave the enemy an advantage in his offensive movement and largely dictated the nature of our defence.

Although our force was over-equipped with motor transport this does not imply that there was a sufficiency of such transport. There was not.

Units often landed without their transport which sometimes did not even sail in the same convoy. In some cases, troops had to be sent into battle as soon as they landed. Consequently, transport was necessarily improvised. This lowered fighting efficiency and therefore morale, and not infrequently resulted in the loss of much equipment and kit.

It is of interest to note that the 1st Battalion the Gloucestershire Regiment, stationed in Rangoon at the outbreak of the war, completely equipped itself with Chinese Lease/Lend and other motor vehicles abandoned prior to the evacuation of the city. Permission had been sought from the Chinese to move vehicles from the parks about to be destroyed by the U.S.A. authorities. This permission was refused. Nevertheless, with commendable resource, the Battalion acquired transport from the burning parks, and eventually had one hundred and fifty new vehicles including several 5-ton lorries, eight American Armoured Scout cars, and 'Jeeps'.

Vehicles for Supply Services were lamentably short. Prior to the outbreak of hostilities transport arrangements had been carried out with hired and requisitioned vehicles. When operations began hired transport became unreliable. Vehicles were then bought, requisitioned, or acquired from Lease/Lend material. Only a proportion of M.T. units could be equipped as the heavy losses in Tenasserim and at the Sittang had to be made good. The loss of transport continued to be great at road blocks and through bombing. After the evacuation of Rangoon such losses were irreplaceable. As the Chinese Armies were virtually without transport and since it was our duty to supply these Armies with rations the added strain on our limited number of motor vehicles was severe. It must be remembered, too, that the distances to be travelled, particularly in the Shan States, were very long.

Much transport might have been saved from loss by the creation of a service of 'Road Officers' who would have functioned on all roads. Their duties would have covered the enforcing of road discipline, the direction of drivers who had lost their units, the carrying out of minor repairs, and the salvage of abandoned vehicles. Such a service could not be introduced owing both to lack of personnel and vehicles.

Due to the general shortage of transport and to our almost continual withdrawals, stocks of supplies were generally far forward, the main problem being to back-load surpluses and to get supplies into safe Bases. The rule rather than the exception was lay-backs based on an administrative time-scale fixing the number of days supplies to be held in forward localities. Only during the first short periods of stabilisation could maintenance forward be carried out.

North of Rangoon the absence of lateral communications and the difficulty of persuading the crews of river craft to proceed downstream added to the supply problem. Road convoys were sent out from Mandalay.

The enormous task of supplying rice and other commodities for the Chinese has already been frequently referred to. After the evacuation of Rangoon and the loss of its important mills this task increased. Up-country resources were limited and unorganised.

Very large quantities of supplies had been collected at Prome together with thousands of tons of rice both here and on the main railway line to Mandalay. Local resources were exploited to the full and an Army Purchasing Agency, based on the peace-time organisation of Messrs Steel Brothers & Company Limited, was functioning. The administrative plan required the holding of a considerable amount of supplies in Prome. Much of these were lost when we evacuated that town.

Prior to this, at the end of March, a review of the stock situation had been prepared. It was then estimated that, by revising the scale of rations, stocks of imported and locally acquired supplies, plus possible future purchases of indigenous supplies, would be sufficient to feed the Army for six months from April 1st. This estimate was subject to the proviso that sources of supply could be held and that no loss of stocks took place. In fact, the loss of the areas south of Mandalay, the destruction of stocks by air bombing in that city, and the earlier losses in Prome much reduced our supplies.

For the last phase of the campaign with commendable foresight supplies had been dispersed in depth on the Lashio-Mandalay Railway, on the railway from Shwebo northwards, and at Monywa and Kalewa on the Chindwin. The decision to fall back on India resulting in the withdrawal of Hospital and Administrative units from the Maymyo area, together with the movement of large numbers of evacuees, Chinese troops, and supplies, threw additional heavy burdens on the railway services which were already fully stretched. As late as April 22nd supplies and bombs were being despatched by rail in the opposite direction to stations on the Lashio branch. Much of the supplies east of the Irrawaddy, therefore, could not be transferred across the river and were handed over to the Chinese or destroyed. The sudden attack on Monywa cut off the stocks held at that town, but sufficient remained in the Shwebo area for the maintenance of the Imperial Forces on the Ye-U-Shwegyin track. After our forces crossed the Chindwin supplies were received from India.

The supply of petrol, oil, and lubricants was a source of unending anxiety. Not only the requirements of the Imperial Forces, but also those of the Chinese Armies and the Civil Administration had to be met. On the fall of Rangoon, the only source of supply was the oilfields which were not on the railway. Very few tank lorries were available and there was a shortage of containers. The prompt return of the latter became a vital necessity. Apart from direct distribution by road, oil barges and steamers went from the oilfields to Mandalay where all filling possible was done ex bulk.

Rangoon Arsenal was itself unsuitable as a Base. It was intended for the maintenance in Burma of a small force of two Brigades, and until the outbreak of hostilities the Ordnance staff was not warned to provide for more than an additional Division. Consequently, stores and equipment were entirely inadequate for the forces that later arrived. Units arriving incompletely equipped could not have deficiencies made up. Had the Chinese Government not released to us a supply of automatic weapons and three-ton lorries the situation would have been even far worse than it was.

The Ordnance staff at Army Headquarters on the opening of the campaign consisted of an Administrative Officer (D.O.S.) and two officers on the engineering side. The Arsenal itself was working with an entirely civilian staff of clerks and labourers. As a result, after the bombing of Rangoon on December 23rd, 1941, the majority of the civilians disappeared never to return. There was always a shortage of military personnel.

The Arsenal itself had no facilities for handling large quantities of stores, and being very near to the Mingaladon airfield was subject to constant air attack. For these reasons various subsidiary depots were opened in Rangoon and its environs. With the small staff available this was difficult.

Ammunition was dumped in a rubber estate near Milestone 18 on the Prome road. On the evacuation of Rangoon lack of transport made it necessary to destroy much of this ammunition. Similarly, a large portion of other stores, mainly tentage and hospital reserves, had to be destroyed. Stores held in sheds near to Pazundaung creek were lost through arson before we abandoned Rangoon.

The only Base workshop facilities available consisted of the repair plant of a civilian motor agency in Rangoon. In the course of the campaign the Lashio workshops of Messrs Watson and Son Limited were taken over. There was a shortage of trained personnel but many suitable men were obtained from the Burma Auxiliary Force and British Battalions, of course to the detriment of the fighting efficiency of these units.

A fully rail served Base Ordnance Depot under construction at Meiktila was completed and opened up before the evacuation of Rangoon; at the same time work was pressed forward on an ammunition dump under construction by the Engineering Department of the Railways five miles north of Pyinmana. Later, a Central Ammunition Dump was established at Tonbo in the Shan foothills near Mandalay. Our continued withdrawals necessitated a further removal to Katha where the Ordnance Depot was eventually made over to the Chinese. Its ultimate fate is not known.

Prior to the outbreak of hostilities, no plan existed for the militarisation of the transportation services. The Burma Railways Battalion, B.A.F., was only intended to meet security requirements during periods of internal disturbances.

Soon after his arrival in Burma early in 1941 His Excellency Sir Reginald Dorman-Smith asked His Majesty's Government for the services of a transport expert. Such an expert could not be made available as Burma was not considered to be on a very high level of priority. Work on the co-ordination of transport was then done by the Burma Government.

After the outbreak of war, it was proposed that Sir John Rowland, lately Chief Railway Commissioner and at that time Director of Construction of the Burma-China Railway, should be placed in charge of transportation. For various reasons nothing came of this proposal, partly because it was thought preferable to appoint an officer with military transportation experience.

In December 1941, in response to an appeal from Army Headquarters, a decision was made in India to form a Transportation Directorate for Burma and to send such personnel as could be made available. Eventually Colonel F.J. Biddulph, Deputy Director of Transportation, Iraq, was appointed Director and arrived in Burma on January 27th 1942. Colonel J.N. Soden, also from Iraq, had been appointed Director of Movements and landed in Rangoon on January 3rd. The absence of previous planning rendered it inevitable that these officers should have no knowledge of Burma, a fact that did not render their unenviable task easier.

For the proper functioning of the Transportation and Movements Directorate personnel trained in military duties were essential. To a very large extent they were not available, and it was necessary to utilise the services of such officers as were in Burma. Many of these, taken direct from their ordinary civil occupations, carried out their duties most creditably.

The Burma Railways and the Irrawaddy Flotilla Company were highly organised and well equipped for peace-time requirements. They had large staffs of experienced and qualified officers. The same remarks apply to the Commissioners for the Port of Rangoon, the public body responsible for the maintenance and operation of the Port. In each case the subordinate staff consisted almost entirely of Indians.

Very early in the campaign the unreliability of civilian labour had been clearly demonstrated. Air raids and a reluctance to work in forward areas soon led to desertions. Reference to this state of affairs has been made frequently in this narrative.

In January 1942 Army Headquarters asked India to supply Railway, Docks, and I.W.T. units to remedy this situation. At that time the development of transportation in Iraq was considered vital, and India was also faced with her own defence problems. As with fighting troops, only a very limited number of units were available; and of these, three arrived in Burma, Headquarters No. 2 Docks Operating Group, No. 213 Docks Operating Company, and Headquarters No. 3 Railway Construction and Maintenance Group. In addition, a number of I.W.T. crews and locomotives drivers and firemen were flown in towards the end of the campaign.

As no other units were to be found in India it was suggested that staffs should be obtained from officers in Burma and that units be raised locally. It was far too late to do very much, but Headquarters No. 3 Docks Operating Group was available for recruiting and a Company was formed from casual labour in Rangoon. It was an example of what could have been done had militarisation been part of a comprehensive plan. Employed at once on dock work it received military training in spare time. The issue of three hundred Italian rifles greatly increased the morale of the unit. In his report the Director of Transportation says, "Even this modicum of military training, the possession of uniform and arms, and the cohesion afforded by working as a unit with their own officers amply demonstrated the value of a military organisation in war. The Company worked through air raid alerts whilst their civilian comrades were under cover. Later on, during the last two weeks in Rangoon, only a proportion of the Company absented themselves at a time when there was a wholesale desertion of civilian labour".

An attempt at militarisation at so late a date did not commend itself to those in control of the transport organisations concerned. Difficulties were many and the effectiveness of the step at this stage was questioned. Consequently, there was no general militarisation of the Transportation Services.

That a change in the control of the Railway was necessary was indicated on February 24th when the Chief Railway Commissioner is reported to have declared in Rangoon that "the Railways are finished and not another train can be run". He feared that increased desertions would occur in the grades of menial and lower subordinate staff.

The situation could not be accepted. The Governor sanctioned immediate militarisation of the Railway south of Toungoo, and afterwards extended this to the whole railway system. Officials of the Burma Railways were commissioned, the Deputy Traffic Manager (Transportation) being appointed Director of Railways. These officers together with the remaining loyal staff maintained the essential Railway Services till the end of the campaign. In justice, however, it must be said that militarisation under the circumstances was in name rather than fact for the Army authorities found it impossible to feed, pay, clothe, or arm the staff. There can be no doubt, however, of the advantage of militarisation even in such circumstances. The morale of the personnel undoubtedly improves, they feel that they and their dependents will be looked after by the army and that if they become casualties, they will become entitled to war pensions, etc.

In the evacuation of Rangoon and throughout the remainder of the campaign there was always sufficient transportation for all personnel and goods brought to loading points. This was despite the defection of railway and river steamer subordinate staff. The limiting factors were lack of motor transport and the absence of labour for handling goods. In consequence quantities of stores had to be abandoned in Rangoon and elsewhere, yet a sufficiency of what was available was got away to enable the Army to live and fight. Had the campaign been further prolonged the loss of these stores would doubtless have been felt.

During the latter stages of the campaign Transportation Services were maintained under increasingly difficult circumstances. The disregard of the Chinese Armies for normal methods, their and our own lack of interpreters, and their continued interference with the conduct of the Railways not infrequently resulting in serious accidents, all made for disorganisation. The Chinese suspicion of civilians working trains, and their habit of requiring compliance with their wishes by a threat of force led to further desertions amongst subordinates. So, too, did the increasing air attacks on centres of communication.

Important Railway Stations on the main line Toungoo to Mandalay were frequently bombed, sustaining considerable damage. An engineering train in charge of an officer and with supervisory staff and labour, rations, equipment, and stores undertook essential repairs, moving up and down the line as required.

An air attack on April 3rd resulted in the wrecking of the Mandalay railway yard, though the station buildings received only minor damage. Telephonic and Telegraphic communication was destroyed and was at the time irreparable. Working at night the railway staff repaired and brought into use six tracks, thus allowing the removal of a number of locomotives and loaded wagons, which were despatched up-country. Thereafter, limited facilities at the small junction of Myohaung, three miles to the south, had to be used for the reception, marshalling, and despatch of trains.

This was partly responsible for the halting of all through movements for twenty-four hours on two separate occasions during the most critical period of the withdrawal at the end of April.

As each town was bombed, the main lines of communication would fill with a fresh spate of refugees. Mandalay was a great clearing centre for these unfortunates. Forty thousand of them were sent north by river to Kyaukmyaung and Myitkina; others travelled to the north by railway; yet another great stream went west towards India by way of the Chindwin river route. These mass movements further impeded the normal work of the military transportation.

That the Railway Services continued to function under chaotic conditions is a tribute to those officers and subordinates who stood by their posts. In the last days of April, when the desertions of operating personnel became very serious, administrative control was assumed by Sir John Rowland; and the activities of the Railways were maintained as long as was humanly possible.

On the Irrawaddy and Chindwin rivers it became increasingly difficult to obtain crews to go downstream, or even up the river to Bhamo. More and more were the minds of would-be deserters turning to the Chindwin river as a route of escape to India.

From Prome northwards the staging system of clearance was adopted on the river. No loaded craft were left for the enemy. The Irrawaddy Flotilla Company had been requisitioned by the Government on March 1st 1942, the General Manager of the Company acting as the Director of I.W.T. By his personality he retained the services of sufficient crews who with the assistance of military personnel complied with all civil and military demands. There were, however, periods of considerable anxiety, as when the enemy unexpectedly seized Monywa and cut off part of the Chindwin Fleet. However, the majority of the steamers escaped and there were enough craft to operate the Shwegyin-Kalewa ferry.

Until January 1942 the Movements Staff in Burma was very small. On the erroneous assumption that the initial Japanese advance would be through Kengtung and the Shan States the greater part of such staff as existed was in that area where most of its few officers had been detailed for other duties.

One of the great difficulties that the Movement Control Directorate had to overcome was the complete ignorance of Commanders and staffs of its duties and functions. Movements were carried out with a total disregard for the Directorate. The usual overseas expedition is accompanied by some Movement Control staff, but in Burma the staff assumed its duties after the campaign had begun. Peace-time methods were still in force, and it was some time before a proper control of movements could be introduced.

The disembarkation of troops in Rangoon, the transfer to Upper Burma of the Base organisation and of the great accumulation of stores in Rangoon, and the movements of the Chinese Armies were heavy tasks for an attenuated Movements staff. In addition, arrangements had to be made for the move to Upper Burma of essential stocks of supplies for civil needs.

CHAPTER 25

One of the best administrative achievements of the campaign was the disembarkation of troops in Rangoon, particularly after February 21st. Lack of civil dock labour, frequent changes of orders, and transportation difficulties tested the staff to the full. Yet disembarkation was quickly and successfully carried out.

After the loss of Rangoon, Movement Control problems increased. Railway Stations being the main targets for hostile aircraft, Transportation and Movement Control officers existed dangerously. As the railway line was usually destroyed and officers had no independent transport, upon a withdrawal they often only got away by good fortune or resource. The destruction of telephone and telegraph lines made communication difficult and, as in other branches of the Army, contact had to be maintained by personal visits or a courier service. This did not make for efficiency.

Examples emphasising the importance of strict compliance with Movement Control orders were furnished during the campaign. In spite of continuous orders to the loading services that railway wagons must be labelled, barely a single wagon despatched from Rangoon bore a label. There were no staff officers available at depots in Rangoon to check this. The resulting congestion on the railway at Mandalay and south of it was overwhelming. The Mandalay yards were full to capacity, and there were seventeen freight trains stabled at adjoining stations. Sorting teams had to open and label every wagon before unloading or resorting could be carried out.

The heavy damage sustained in the Mandalay railway yard on April 3rd was very largely attributable to the non-labelling of wagons containing R.A.F. bombs. Shortly after the air raid wagons which had caught fire touched off a wagon-load of these bombs, the subsequent explosion causing more damage than did the raid itself.

The experience of both the Transportation and Movements Directorates pointed clearly to the necessity for the early planned militarisation of transportation services and to the provision of an adequate and efficient Movements staff from the outset of the campaign. The necessary organisation for the movement of fighting troops with equipment and stores is as essential as the presence of the troops themselves. The campaign proved the danger of relying on civil transportation services staffed by men without military training and not bound by ties of military discipline, yet exposed to dangers comparable to those encountered by troops fighting in forward areas. Japanese dominance of the air established not only this fact, but also the further fact that under the circumstances prevailing in Burma a high standard of 'toughness' is most desirable amongst those whose duties require them to remain constantly in the neighbourhood of the main targets for hostile aircraft.

As the Imperial Forces withdrew towards Upper Burma demolitions of river craft and on the railways were carried out.

The main portion of the Irrawaddy Flotilla Company's fleet was scuttled at Mandalay, and between that place and Katha. Over one hundred power-craft were sunk at or near Mandalay. Further sinking's were made at Kyaukayaung, and on May 3rd forty-four power-craft were scuttled at Katha. The fate of a few vessels left at Bhamo and Myitkyina is unknown. The greater part of the Chindwin fleet was sunk at Sittang on May 14th.

On the railways, demolition was more thorough in the earlier stages of the campaign. Comparatively little damage was done to main line bridges in relation to their importance. The speed of the Japanese advance combined with lack of engineer units and labour difficulties accounted for this, and many bridges scheduled for destruction were not, in fact, destroyed. It should be noted, however, that the main line to Mandalay ran through the area taken over by the Chinese. Rolling stock in general was abandoned undamaged. Some wagons were burnt by Commando units.

Locomotives were usually immobilised by the removal of connecting rods and the destruction of injectors and other boiler fittings. Fire boxes were sometimes damaged by lighting up under empty boilers. Systematic destruction of the boilers and cylinders does not appear to have been carried out except by Commando units. It was estimated that well over a third of the locomotives owned by the Burma Railways were immediately or soon available to the enemy, whilst others of those immobilised were probably repaired and put into use at an early date. Many of the undamaged locomotives were either handed over to the Chinese when they took over sectors of the railways, or were abandoned in the final stages of the campaign. At that time neither the Chinese nor the Imperial Forces carried out all the demolitions that could or should have been done.

The Japanese were in a position to operate important sectors of the railway very soon after occupying the areas they served. This was entirely due to our failure and that of the Chinese to put into effect a comprehensive policy of demolitions.

It was not only upon the railways and water-ways that general denial was not carried out. Enormous quantities of rice, both milled and un-milled, were left in godowns, mills, and villages. Valuable timber was

CHAPTER 25

abandoned in stacks or rafts, rubber plantations with their factories and smoke houses were often left untouched; the destruction of rice and timber mills was only spasmodic; livestock including elephants, a favourite means of transport with the enemy, was left behind.

The systematic and controlled burning of towns and villages would have saved us many casualties from snipers, hampered the work of spies and Fifth Columnists, and prevented heavy losses of stores in fires caused by air bombing.

Since a wholesale denial scheme was not enforced the supply problem of the enemy not only in Burma but elsewhere was eased. There is no doubt that more demolition work could have been done if a detailed plan had been prepared in advance and the task had been entrusted to a special organisation. Denial was carried out as far as possible, but Divisional Engineers were too much occupied on other requirements to give this matter detailed attention.

We had neither the time, material, nor personnel to carry out a comprehensive 'scorched earth' policy. The task would have been enormous and it is improbable that it would have been made much difference to the length of the campaign.

There was also the effect on the civil population to be considered. The policy of the Burma Government, with which the G.O.C. concurred, was not to interfere with the food supplies of the people. A general scorched earth policy would have spread panic and disaffection, and resulted in a large-scale evacuation of the bulk of the population. Added to the existing stupendous refugee problem this would have had most serious effects on the conduct of operations. Nor would it have rendered any easier the eventual re-occupation of Burma. The turn of popular opinion against the Japanese invader, which by all accounts has already taken place, might have been transferred by such action into permanent active hostility to the British.

Signal communication in the field was never easy to maintain although the Signals Services acquitted themselves well. Again, the limited shortage of equipment was to blame. Early losses led to the rapid worsening of the situation and in the final stages of the campaign the shortage had become acute.

Save for the slow system of runners, widely dispersed detachments and companies were frequently out of touch with their Headquarters. Patrols were unable to send back information at once, and were sometimes lost owing to sudden withdrawals orders which could not be passed to them in time. Higher formations were regularly compelled to maintain contact by couriers or liaison officers. It is obvious that where, as in Burma, operations essentially involve continuous movement the rapid communication of information or orders is vital. It must be remembered, too, that our forces were operating over very great distances and in a country of few roads and with large areas of jungle. Our inability to ensure rapid signal communications was therefore a very heavy handicap.

The Burma Government Posts and Telegraph Department rendered great assistance to the Army. The normal peace-time signal system in Burma fell very short of military requirements, and on the outbreak of hostilities the Department was hard put to it to expand existing telephone connections. In the course of the campaign the staff of the Department was militarised. The conferring of military status, with the knowledge that dependants had acquired the right to military pensions on the death of an official on active service, did much to maintain morale. Members of the Posts and Telegraph Department were conspicuous in carrying on at their tasks when other essential services were failing.

The conditions of the campaign and the pre-war Burma policy regarding the Medical Services placed these services under a considerable strain, and the shortage of medical officers resulted in much hardships to the sick and wounded. Medical units of the Army in Burma had been raised but were quite inadequate for their work.

The Indian Hospital Corps was satisfactory. Its Burma counterpart failed badly owing to mass desertions. Inferior personnel such as sweepers, cooks, and other menials was always lacking in numbers as soon as hostile air raids began.

Medical officers were deficient. Medical conscription had been accepted but while it produced a number of doctors the country had been caught up in the confusion of bombing and evacuation before it could become fully effective. Many potential medical officers were thus lost.

This general lack of personnel resulted in the understaffing of units and the overworking of those of all classes who remained at their posts. Many displayed much resource and initiative in surmounting obstacles and keeping the service functioning, but inevitably the men in hospital suffered.

Again, shortage of transport was a serious handicap. Two Motor Ambulance Sections arrived without vehicles. One improvised section never had more than fifteen cars. All were Fords and all broke their half-shafts. Field Ambulances arrived without transport. In withdrawals valuable equipment was lost when transport from pooled sources was not available.

CHAPTER 25

Three improvised Ambulance Trains were made up. Being non-corridor they were not good, but proved of great value and saved the situation many times. Without these trains medical evacuation must have collapsed. Several river steamers and launches of the Irrawaddy Flotilla Company were also converted into Hospital Ships towards the end of March. These, too, did excellent work. Incidentally, it is only fair to record that hostile aircraft appear to have respected the Red Cross markings on these vessels.

Mention has already been made of the fact that our own limited medical facilities had to be employed for the Chinese Armies. These had practically no medical organisation of their own, and it was necessary to provide them not only with stores and equipment, but with medical units, staffs, and even accommodation in our own hospitals, trains, and ships.

The problem of evacuating sick and wounded to India was a constant source of anxiety. After the loss of Rangoon casualties were evacuated by air first from Shwebo, and later from Myitkyina. In the early part of April when such evacuation was easy sufficient aircraft were not available, and the numbers of sick and wounded accumulated in the hospitals. Towards the end of the month evacuation from Shwebo became impossible, and many casualties were on the Irrawaddy en route for Myitkyina when the Japanese captured Lashio. It was impossible then to make any change in the plan. When Myitkyina fell many of those not yet evacuated made their way across country to India. The evacuation of the large number of casualties from Shwebo by the Ye-U-Shwegyin track has been related in a previous chapter.

After the evacuation from Rangoon the medical services were constantly fighting the threat of a serious outbreak of cholera amongst the troops. About Prome and Mandalay and on the evacuee routes to India the primitive and insanitary conditions under which hordes of refugees existed led to the appearance of this dread complaint. In the Mandalay area particularly, deaths amongst Indians were heavy. The troops were affected, but vigorous preventive measures kept the disease under control and there was no general epidemic. Having regard to the very difficult circumstances under which the medical services functioned this was a noteworthy achievement.

The lack of Provost, Rest Camp, and Mess Units tended to break down administration and, therefore, to impair discipline. No canteen organisation existed before the war, and the absence of amenities was a potent contributory factor in lowering the morale of both officers and men. During the campaign a Chief Amenities Officer was appointed, and in the face of many difficulties was able to provide something in the way of comforts for the troops.

Constant withdrawals necessarily caused much straggling, and the need for a fully organised Provost service was acute, and was strongly represented to India on several occasions. The complete absence of any Provost personnel rendered it very difficult to maintain road discipline or to cope with stragglers. Eventually Provost Units were improvised locally.

Non-provision of Mess Units contributed towards some extraordinary results. At Army Headquarters officer's civilian servants retained with them their wives and families. These moved with Headquarters from Rangoon to Maymyo, and later to Shwebo. There were also at Headquarters many families of clerks and other employees. When the withdrawal to India was decided upon the problem of moving these women and children arose. That they had not been sent away earlier was due to lack of transport.

In the result, these women and children suffered many casualties in the bombing of Shwebo. They were then sent to Monywa for evacuation up the Chindwin, but on arrival by train at Alon near Monywa on the morning of April 30th they found that movement up the Chindwin had already ceased. At Alon they then formed the target for another bombing attack and suffered further casualties. Eventually with their menfolk they made their way across country to India by the Ye-U-Shwegyin track and other routes.

This campaign must have been the only one in modern times in which a British Army has had attached to it a large following of women and children. It was an unhappy state of affairs and, apart from other drawbacks, certainly affected efficiency.

The general unpreparedness of the Army in Burma and the lack of much essential equipment of all kinds meant decreased efficiency from the outset of the campaign. Several other factors, too, affected morale and discipline. Many of the troops, both local and Indian, were young recruits only partially trained; officers were often inexperienced and with insufficient knowledge of the languages spoken by the men. Frequent changes in the composition of Brigades, brought about by an acute shortage of troops, did not encourage that important element, esprit de corps. It is significant that this always remained high in 7 Armoured Brigade and 48 Brigade, formations which were well-trained, though not for jungle warfare, and were maintained virtually intact. The utterly strange conditions of jungle warfare brought about by short-sighted methods of training, and the straggling resulting from contact with an enemy superior in jungle fighting methods and often in greater force were causes of depression. So, too, were the continued withdrawals, the knowledge that with the fall of Rangoon the Army was in effect cut off, and the air dominance enjoyed by the enemy in the latter phase of the operations. Most troops were employed without periods of rest as there was no reserves with which to carry out reliefs. A long and arduous retreat in the face of a superior enemy is the severest of trials for even the most seasoned troops. It is not surprising, therefore, that there were many desertions, and there can have been few units that were not thus affected to some extent. Yet this by no means applies to our forces as a whole. The last actions proved the ability of exhausted men to fight with courage and determination. This was demonstrated at Monywa and Shwegyin, whilst the holding of Kyaukse by 48 Brigade and its supporting troops must rank high as a model of a delaying action.

The conduct of certain Battalions of the Burma Rifles and of other Burma units has given rise to much criticism. The majority of units included a very large number of well-nigh raw recruits, whilst the Burma Frontier Force and Military Police were required to carry out tasks for which they had never been intended or trained. Undoubtedly desertions were heavy. They began in the opening phases of the campaign, and it is possible that the bad example then set reacted adversely on other troops.

The drastic measures taken to comb out unreliable elements from the Burma Rifles undoubtedly had a good effect, the losses in personnel being compensated by an increased reliability of units. When the Army in Burma comes to be reconstructed this important lesson is one to be remembered. The composition of the post-war Army will call for much careful consideration if past weaknesses are to be avoided.

Desertion is inexcusable under any circumstances, but the causes of its prevalence in the locally raised troops in Burma are of interest. Burmese and Karens were affected largely by the fact that the country was being overrun by the invaders and that their families and homes were passing into enemy hands. They knew, too, that there was some animosity towards the British cause amongst the civilian population, and this increased their apprehension for the safety of relatives. In addition, Burmese soldiers were subjected to a certain amount of political pressure. These were factors causing desertions. Chins and Kachins were not strongly affected by similar considerations. After the campaign when their units were disbanded many Chins and Kachins of the Burma Rifles joined bodies of Levies.

Indian, Anglo-Indian, and Anglo-Burman personnel with families in the country also suffered considerable anxiety. In their case they feared not only the advent of the Japanese but definite acts of hostility on the part of the Burmese people. Owing to lack of transport there was no general evacuation of their families out of Burma, and some of these men deserted the forces to accompany their relatives either to places of safety or to India. These considerations no doubt affected Indian personnel of the Burma Frontier Force and Military Police most of whom had families in Burma.

It is unnecessary to labour the point. It must be evident that a soldier fights better when he is assured of the personal safety of his wife and children. If he is fighting in an area which makes it possible for him to rejoin his family and to escort it to safety the temptation to do so is very great. In Burma many fell to the temptation, and it is probable that the same thing will happen elsewhere.

The families of the two British Battalions stationed in Burma at the outbreak of hostilities were concentrated in Maymyo. Some if these were flown to India. Others left Burma at the time of the final withdrawal.

If it had been possible to evacuate British, Anglo-Indian, Indian and Anglo-Burman military families out of the country before the fall of Rangoon much of the uneasiness felt by the troops concerned would not have arisen. This remark does not apply to Burmans and Karens who would probably not have accepted such a measure.

No definite figures are available, but many military families or members of them, particularly those of men in the Burma Frontier Force and Burma Military Police, were lost on the overland routes to India. Leaving Burma late, these families were exposed in full to the terrible conditions encountered on these routes. This fact gave rise to an understandable feeling of bitterness at the absence of effective arrangements for the safe evacuation of the dependents of the fighting troops.

The casualties sustained by our forces in the campaign have not yet been fully ascertained. Information about Prisoners of War in Japanese hands is very meagre, and for this and other reasons nothing is known of the large number of men posted as 'Missing'. The loss of many records in Burma has complicated the situation. Returns continue to come in from units. As a consequence, the Casualty Lists are subject to constant revision. The figures given hereunder must therefore be regarded as merely provisional and subject to amendment.

Officer casualties amounted to about four hundred. Sixty-three are reported to have been killed in action, seventy died of wounds or disease, one hundred and twenty-six were wounded, one hundred and fifteen were originally stated to be 'Missing'.

CHAPTER 25

Other casualties, as at present known, were as follows:

	Killed	Wounded	Missing	Died of Wounds	Wounded & Missing	Prisoner of War	Presumed Dead etc	Total
British Units.	273	556	647	75	49			1600
Indian Army Units. V.C.Os.	60	60	80			3	3	206
Other Ranks.	649	1678	5291			181	57	7856
Army in Burma Units.	239	114	3052	10	12			3427
							Grand Total	13089

The large proportion of missing is no doubt partly accounted for by the fact that in jungle warfare, where withdrawals are frequent, the majority of the killed and many of the wounded are necessarily shown under this head. No figures of the losses of the Chinese Expeditionary Force are to be had and no assistance is to be extracted from the brief Chinese official account of the campaign. At Toungoo and elsewhere on the Sittang valley front south of Mandalay, V Army suffered severely; in Karenni and the Shan States VI Army and the other formations engaged, admittedly had heavy losses. The number of missing men must have been very high in Karenni and during the closing phases of the operations. Having regard to these factors the casualties of the Chinese may well have been not much less than our own, although such an estimate must be little better then guess work.

The Japanese, obviously for propaganda purposes, have published details of their own and the Allied losses. These details are demonstrably false. For instance, the Japanese claim that the Allied dead left on the battlefields numbered close on twenty-five thousand. At the same time, they modestly place their own loss in killed at under thirteen hundred, and at just over three thousand in wounded.

Chapter 26

Careful Japanese preparations for invasion – Unscrupulous methods of passing themselves off as friendly troops – Wearing of native dress – Burmese assistance to the enemy – General attitude of the Burmans – Japanese treatment of prisoners – Japanese tactical methods and our replies to them – Limitations of Japanese tactical methods – Their general failure to exploit successes – Causes of our failure to hold Burma – Conclusion.

The Japanese invasion of Burma was carefully planned. It was part of the larger Japanese offensive against Allied possessions in the Far East, and as such received considerable prior thought and organisation on the part of the enemy High Command. After the outbreak of hostilities Japanese commentators made no secret of the fact that for a year before the war their country was fully informed of the strength, dispositions, and likely defence plans of its potential enemies. Consequently, it was possible to estimate accurately the attacking forces required for each theatre of operations and to draw up full plans for invasion.

China was long utilised as a proving ground for arms and equipment and a training ground for personnel. The constant rotation of officers and men through the ranks of the Divisions in China built up a great reserve of experienced troops. Many of these were then employed in the formation of new Divisions. Units and Commanders were selected for their special tasks months in advance and were concentrated in training areas where terrain and climate approximated to those of the regions where they were to fight. Thus, the force designated for the Philippines carried out frequent landing operations along the South China coast in 1941, whilst the Divisions chosen to attack Hongkong were trained in night fighting and the storming of pill boxes in the hills near Canton.

Throughout 1941 preparations went forward. Commentators have been frank in describing the negotiations with Thailand for the landing

CHAPTER 26

of troops on the Kra Isthmus, the use of railways, and the storing of supplies. These admissions reveal both the double-dealing of Thailand and the completeness of Japanese arrangements.

Steps were taken to combat the feeling prevalent amongst the Japanese that they were inferior to the Western Powers in technical skill. The alleged superhuman courage and devotion to duty of the Japanese soldier were emphasised and constantly repeated, and the offensive spirit of the armed forces encouraged. The degeneracy and soft living of the West were asserted. The result of all this was the development of a great confidence in the fighting services, not only amongst the personnel themselves, but also in the people at large. This alone was excellent preparation for war.

In Burma, as elsewhere, steps were taken to prepare the country for the coming of the invader. The Japanese took advantage of and exploited in a masterly manner the political situation in Burma.

Broadcasts from Tokyo in Burmese, other propaganda measures, contacts with disaffected persons all helped to foster an anti-British spirit. To be accepted as a liberator and the champion of freedom was sufficient for the purpose of Japan. Naturally enough, the fact that Burma was to become a dependency of Nippon was not proclaimed. During the invasion period the Japanese people were regaled over and over again with alleged descriptions of the throngs of happy natives who turned out to welcome their invading troops. This was obvious propaganda. Doubtless the tales were much embellished, but they did have some substratum of truth. There were elements in the population ready to receive the Japanese, and the arrival of enemy troops naturally put these elements in the ascendant.

Preparations for the intended campaign appear to have been most detailed. That the Japanese force invading Burma was well supplied with information and maps and was accompanied by men acquainted with the terrain is certain. In crossing the frontier, it employed little known tracks. Thereafter such tracks across difficult country were regularly utilised. Outstanding examples of this were the outflanking march of the 33rd Division on the Sittang Bridge, the advance on Rangoon through the Pegu Yomas, and the long march through our lines to the Pin Chaung north of Yenangyaung.

Rubber boats, outboard motors, and special landing craft were in readiness for use on waterways. Railways were speedily repaired and in operation. Even peace propaganda parties were at once at work amongst the people. Excellent knowledge of the resources of the country facilitated use of local transport available. Special currency notes had been printed in advance and were promptly put into circulation. All this was indicative of the thoroughness of the Japanese plan of invasion.

The Japanese concept of war is simple. It is limited by no rules. Tricks and stratagems which until recent times were regarded by civilised nations as improper have always commended themselves to the Japanese. If an action will secure an advantage then it is fully justified.

In Burma the enemy looked upon the wearing of uniform as no more than a convenience. Whenever it was expedient to do so his troops passed themselves off as Chinese, Burmese or our own men. There were several instances of this. There were also the unexplained incidents at Moulmein, when some of our gunners at the northern end of the town were attacked by men believed by them to be personnel of the Burma Rifles; and at the road block north of the Pin Chaung where many enemy dead were found to be clad in khaki uniforms with the Burma Rifles and Gurkha type of hat and armed with our rifles.

The wearing of Burmese dress by Japanese soldiers was not infrequent. This disguise facilitated infiltration and free movement behind our lines. When employed in conjunction with the ordinary bullock cart, it would enable quite considerable numbers of men with machine-guns and mortars to pass through our positions. It is not improbable that certain incidents in which Burmans were stated to be involved were in fact attributable to the Japanese.

At the same time there can be no doubt that there were Burmans actively engaged on the side of the enemy. Apart from the Japanese-sponsored and organised Burma Independence Army there were many sympathisers who took active steps to assist the invaders. In addition, there were many who took advantage of the unsettled condition of the country to indulge their proclivities for robbery and murder and the flaunting of such established authority as still existed.

It is quite impossible to estimate the strength of the Burma Independence Army, but it must have numbered several thousands. It was first identified in the fighting around Pegu. A boatload of its members was captured off the mouth of the Rangoon river. It certainly took part in the fighting at Shwedaung, and it was estimated at the end of March 1942 that four thousand organised Burmans were with the Japanese in the Prome area.

Since Burmans also took a prominent part in the actions at Shwegyin on the Sittang river, at Menzada, and at Letpadan it is not improbable that their Independence Army was engaged at these places. The Burmese themselves claim to have participated in the engagement near Pauk when F.F.8 was attacked. The Chinese reported the presence of Burmans in the enemy force at Taunggyi. They took part in the surprise attack on Headquarters of 1 Burma Division near Monywa. One of the craft used by the Japanese in their landing near Kywe for the attack on Shwegyin

CHAPTER 26

on the Chindwin river flew the Thakin flag. Burmans were therefore probably employed in that operation. It is known that the organisation of the Burma Independence Army was prepared before the invasion, and men were recruited as soon as the enemy entered Burma. In the ordinary course of events the Army must have grown with enemy successes.

This narrative has already set out many examples of treachery or hostility by Burmans and it would be possible to lengthen the list considerably. However, it is unnecessary to do more than to add one or two instances.

On March 14th an attempt was made to loot a train by a body of about five hundred Burmese armed with rifles, pistols and dahs. This was between Thazi and Mandalay. The timely arrival of a Chinese troop train prevented the looting of the train. The Burmans were dispersed with casualties.

The harbouring of Japanese by the local population of Padaung has been mentioned. Another case of this kind occurred at Pegu where the enemy appear to have sheltered in occupied houses near the Railway Station for many hours before attacking the rearguard of 48 Brigade.

When the 1st Battalion the Gloucestershire Regiment was acting as reconnaissance unit for 17 Division in the area south of Prome it found it exceedingly difficult to make contact with the enemy whose presence was known. The Battalion narrative of the campaign states: "The elusiveness of the enemy amongst the numerous villages in the neighbourhood was greatly facilitated by the disinclination of the local inhabitants to give us any reliable information". In this area, too, the enemy was welcomed by the people of Letpadan and other towns.

At Taungdwingyi, deserted on the arrival of the 17 Division, evidence was found in monasteries of Japanese propaganda and instructions. Japanese emblems and flags were discovered.

Near Mandalay, anti-aircraft gun positions were repeatedly disclosed to approaching enemy aircraft by the burning of the jungle around them. By the time our security police had arrived on the scene the Fifth Columnists responsible had generally vanished. On one occasion, however, Chinese troops were in the area. They promptly surrounded it and shot every Burman caught. The deterrent effect was good.

It is not suggested that all Burmans were traitors. They were not. The large mass of the people was probably indifferent to the course of the war. The one desire of these folk, was to be left in peace, a condition they were not to enjoy. Many fled from the towns and main lines of communication to escape the horrors of war. In the belief that the Japanese were destined to occupy the country they were terrified of doing anything that might anger their new masters. This coupled with the threats of the traitor element would suffice to prevent them from giving any assistance to the Allied forces. Similar reasoning and threats cowed those who were loyal, thus leaving the field free for the supporters of Japan.

A Senior Intelligence Officer who had long resided in Burma as a civilian and who served throughout the campaign with 17 Division has summed up the situation in the following words:

"There was absolutely no sign on the part of the population that I saw of determination or even wish to make things difficult for the invader, much less actively resist him .... On the other hand there can be no doubt that the Japanese did receive active help from a considerable number of the inhabitants, quite apart from those who actually joined them in arms, such as the Burma Independence Army. The main difficulty is to determine how much of this help was voluntary and how much was given under some form of compulsion.

I think a fairly clear distinction might be drawn between the townspeople and the population of villages some distance removed from the railway and the main roads. The latter were bewildered and frightened by the turn of events and did not look beyond their own safety. They were consequently fair game for forcible impressment by the Japanese as guides and porters. On the other hand they were quite ready to assist stragglers of our side provided they were not in danger of reprisals.

The townspeople being better informed and having already been affected by or implicated to some extent in both national and local politics must have quickly realised that they had two choices open to them, namely, to adopt a neutral attitude, entailing at least passive co-operation with the Japanese, or to co-operate actively in driving out the British."

After speaking of the furnishing of information to the enemy by Burmans he adds: "The opposite side of the picture is practically a complete blank. Except for a few loyal Karen villagers in the Pegu Yomas no single case was known to me of any Burman volunteering information about the Japanese. The general fear of reprisals prevented any attempt on our part of setting up post-occupational sources of information.

The fact that no voluntary help was obtainable from the population although the enemy had plenty of voluntary as well as forced assistance, and the fact that there were Burmans actually in arms against us makes it difficult to find any other term than 'hostile' for the population as a whole."

CHAPTER 26

Except for the conclusion which would classify the population as a whole as 'hostile'; this appears to be a very fair summing up of the Burmese attitude. The view expressed is that the greater part of the population was not actively hostile, it followed a generally passive 'do nothing' policy induced by terror of the invaders. This policy might almost be described as traditional with the Burmese who, with their country's earlier record of internecine warfare, have long realised the comparative safety afforded by concealment in the jungle.

It is inly proper, however, to put on record the fact that on occasions stragglers from our forces were assisted by Burmese people at considerable risk to themselves. In addition, officers of the Civil Administration do not agree that Burmans (other than Government Servants) never voluntarily brought in information concerning the enemy. The considered statement of the Intelligence Officer with 17 Division has been quoted, and there appear to be no military records of the furnishing of such information.

The brutal treatment of prisoners by the Japanese would seem to be part of a policy intended to break the morale of hostile forces. Not infrequently prisoners were murdered cold-bloodedly and not in the heat of battle. A captured Japanese diary established such murders at Moulmein. There were other authenticated cases at Padaung and elsewhere. Maltreatment of prisoners was often resorted to, particularly in the case of officers. On the other hand, if prisoners proved pliant, they were readily employed as spies.

The general tactics used by the Japanese against the Allies in the years 1940/1942 have been detailed in the textbook 'Japanese Tactical Methods'. It is therefore unnecessary to discuss them in detail here. Reference will only be made to special characteristics of the methods used by the enemy in Burma.

In the early stages of the campaign the greater part of the fighting took place in dense jungle; then followed the phase in the Irrawaddy valley and the dry zone. Here, except for the jungle strip about Shwedaung leading into Prome, the more open terrain allowed much greater scope to our own mobile units and suited us better. In the final phase on the Chindwin we were again fighting in thick jungle.

The Japanese troops employed in Burma were expert jungle fighters. As such they possessed a great advantage over our own men whose training in this respect was woefully deficient. The enemy regarded the jungle as of considerable assistance to himself; we looked upon it as a blinding, hampering obstacle. Untrained troops were confused by the Japanese methods of infiltration, their habit of simulating the presence of additional weapons and forces by the use of crackers and other means, and the rapid movement of small bodies of men along little-known tracks. The ability of Japanese troops to exist on a minimum of rations, to live on the country, to husband the ammunition they carried with them, and to improvise means of transport either by impressing bullock carts or utilising our own abandoned vehicles, all contributed to their mobility.

Japanese shock action troops were noticeably superior to other less trained men. They were individual fighters of initiative, exceptionally good at infiltrating into our rear areas where they caused confusion by frequently changing their positions and firing light automatics. They were generally well educated and were equipped with maps and pocket compasses.

Snipers also showed considerable enterprise. They concealed themselves in trees, in the roofs of houses, and in other vantage places where they waited patiently for favourable targets. Concealment, in fact, was a subject in which Japanese troops were highly trained. This was particularly the case in village fighting when, on several occasions, our troops found the enemy still in occupation after it was believed that a village had been cleared. Heaps of grain, drains, wicker-baskets, and other hiding places were skilfully employed. Much of the fighting during the campaign took place in villages and small towns. When they were to be attacked by us, bold and resolute leadership was called for. Roads were to be avoided and, wherever possible, covered approaches employed. Contact had to be well maintained, and a perfunctory search of houses and other places of concealment only meant that the Japanese faded out until the attacking troops had passed. The search therefore required to be very thorough. Often the only effective means of clearing a village was to burn it. 'Blitz' fire tactics were found to be most successful both in villages and jungle fighting. The Japanese were unwilling to face a heavy concentration of fire and often withdrew when subjected to it.

When moving by night the enemy made little or no use of scouts and often had no forward screen at all. When motor transport was employed headlights were normally used. As a result, his columns were caught by us and suffered heavy punishment.

Lying up by day the Japanese took few precautions for local protection. Here again we were able to surprise the enemy with excellent results. The attacks carried out by the 1st Battalion of the Gloucestershire Regiment at Letpadan and Paungde are examples of this.

There were several instances of close hand to hand fighting during the campaign, but as a general rule the enemy avoided this unless in superior numbers. At Martaban, Letpadan, Kokkogwa, Kyaukse, and elsewhere he fled when charged by our infantry.

CHAPTER 26

The Japanese had an intense dislike of shelling. The mere threat of our mortar fire was enough to silence their mortar and light automatic posts. It was found that even inaccurate shelling by us in the general direction of enemy mortars was sufficient to put them out of action for a time.

Our tanks also had a great moral effect on the enemy. In open country Japanese infantry went to ground and remained hidden until the tanks had passed well out of view. Their own tanks avoided trying conclusions with ours. It was only when they were in a position prepared to deal with tanks, as at a road block, that the Japanese stood against them. Hence, although the nature of the country rendered it impossible to employ the full mobility of the tank, we found even its limited use to be invaluable. In dense jungle it could not operate, and the bunds of paddy fields seriously hindered its progress; but whenever it could be used its functioning was most effective. Against road blocks, in stalking enemy support weapons, and in mopping up Japanese infantry fleeing from villages or other defended positions the tank was outstanding. It always established supremacy in 'no man's land'.

Enemy artillery displayed great lack of initiative. Obvious positions were shelled, and the shelling continued when positions were empty. Usually no attempt was made to search for alternative positions. Enemy infantry guns and mortars were well forward and came into action quickly and effectively. Shells, mortar bombs, and grenades excelled in noise but were of inferior lethal quality. It is possible that they were all designed for use against second class inexperienced Oriental troops, amongst whom infectious panic could be easily started.

Japanese aircraft operated largely according to a fixed routine. Except for their night raids on Rangoon they were never in the air in the early morning or after 1700 hours, and reconnaissance aircraft often carried out flights at fixed times. They were frequently able to operate at low altitudes and their ground to air communication appeared to be good. Japanese troops disclosed their positions to their own aircraft by displaying strips of material on the ground or hanging flags in trees.

Attacks on our troops were made by high level and shallow dive-bombing and by machine-gunning. The latter often appeared to be designed to draw fire or otherwise obtain disclosure of our positions. Attacks were generally made out of the sun even when there were disadvantages of approaching from this direction. The consensus of opinion was that Japanese aircraft did not press home their attacks on ground troops with the dash and determination displayed by the German Luftwaffe.

The enemy air force began the campaign by an attempt to destroy our own air force. This corresponded to the tactics employed by it in other theatres of war. However, this object was not achieved until the successful attacks on Magwe and Akyab had been carried out. Thereafter, the Japanese considerably extended the range of their aerial activities.

The most characteristic feature of Japanese tactics in Burma was the frequent employment of road blocks. The enemy was able to establish blocks generally as a result of our own weakness in strength. We had not the forces to protect vulnerable stretches of road behind our forward troops. Located at points where main roads passed through dense jungle or very enclosed country these bocks were concealed from long frontal observation. A road bend was a favourite location. When possible, defiles such as cuttings or ridges were chosen.

The object of the block was either to cut off our forward troops and transport or to protect the Japanese flank when an advance was in progress. The blocks themselves were never very substantial and consisted of damaged vehicles, a felled tree, or other readily available obstacle. Of themselves they were generally incapable of stopping our tanks although sufficient to halt a wheeled vehicle. They were, however, defended in strength. Covered by well sited mortars, guns employed in an anti-tank role, and light machine-guns they constituted a formidable obstacle. This became more difficult to clear as the road in front of it grew congested with damaged and burning vehicles, often double banked. This in turn hindered the deployment of our troops.

The frontage held astride the block was comparatively short, the enclosed country or thick jungle facilitating this. Hence small numbers of the enemy were able to defend these obstacles.

As the presence of a block was usually unsuspected until the enemy was ready to operate behind it our attacks in the first instance were invariably carried out piecemeal. Sometimes forward troops would by-pass the obstacle leaving the rest of the force on the wrong side. On occasion tanks smashed their way through, but lack of co-ordination and failure to keep the passage open would enable the enemy to close in again before infantry and transport had passed. This happened south of Pegu where some of our attacking infantry went wide round the block, and tanks went through it but failed to hold the passage for the remainder of the force.

Experience in Burma taught the necessity of attacking road blocks frontally. Such an attack had to be in strength and supported by all available fire power. Turning movements through the enclosed or jungle country were apt to lose direction, were difficult to co-ordinate, and called for a high standard of training not then possessed by our troops. A broad front was not necessary for a frontal attack. It was sufficient to secure a strip of ground astride the road wide enough to blind the fire of the enemy whilst our transport passed through. It was of course essential to hold both sides of the road by close picquetting or otherwise to prevent a return of the enemy to his dominating positions.

'Japanese Tactical Methods' deals with the defence of Lines of Communication in depth. Operations in Burma endorsed the principles there laid down.

On one occasion in Burma our line of communication ran laterally. This was from Magwe to Taungdwingyi. Here as elsewhere during the campaign the Brigade harbour was found to be the best method of protection. Battalion or smaller groups lent themselves to envelopment and annihilation by greatly superior numbers.

Our protracted withdrawal and lack of Intelligence Services threw a great mental and physical strain on troops and it was found that the Brigade harbour made less calls on its defenders than would the manning of a smaller post. The protection of animal and motor transport, dispersal against fire and aerial attack, and the tactical deployment of artillery all tended to increase the perimeter of a harbour. In a small defended position, the forward defence lines required so many men that reserves were quite inadequate to counter a heavy attack. Even in the Brigade harbour tenacious holding on by tired man was often the only remedy.

The defence of Kokkogwa by 48 Brigade was an excellent example of the strength of a Brigade harbour. On the other hand, it also instanced the Japanese method of by-passing a position that cannot be quickly overrun. In the case of Kokkogwa there was further illustrated the inherent weakness of a lateral line of communication across which the enemy quickly passed to divide our force.

Throughout the campaign the Japanese employed their customary methods of by-passing strong forces and carrying our wide encircling movements. At the same time their tactics were by no means as successful as they might have been. They appear to have been limited by:

(a) An advance to a fixed objective without any provision for the exploiting of a success.
(b) Lack of initiative in pursuit.
(c) Inability to deviate from a fixed plan.

The only real instance of the major exploitation of a success and of a fast-moving pursuit was the drive of the Japanese 56th Division through Karenni and the Shan States after the destruction of the Chinese 55th Division. With the Allied forces south of Mandalay heavily engaged, and securing itself against immediate attack by the occupation of Taunggyi, this Japanese force carried out a bold enterprise deserving of the success it gained.

On the other hand, not once but several times did the Japanese fail to take advantage of a most favourable situation. From our point of view the most crucial period of the campaign began with the withdrawal from the Bilin river. That withdrawal was begun not a moment too soon, yet was in time to permit the safe transfer of 17 Division to the west bank of the Sittang if it had been carried out with vigour. There were delays, and the ensuing battle for the Sittang Bridge was a disaster for us. Fortunately, it was a disaster not exploited by the enemy, possibly owing to his own heavy losses. By the failure of 17 Division to cross the river intact we were not able to prevent an early Japanese advance across the Sittang. Yet the Japanese could have crossed at once to secure an overwhelming victory. On February 23rd there were two Japanese Divisions on the east bank of the Sittang. Their immediate employment against the shattered and almost unarmed remnants of 17 Division then only supported by 7 Armoured Brigade must almost certainly have ensured the mastery of Burma by mid-March.

The blow did not fall and we gained sufficient time to reorganise. Less than a fortnight later, at Taukkyan, the enemy again neglected to seize an opportunity. Favourably situated to cut off the greater portion of the Imperial Forces in Burma he preferred to march on Rangoon. That port was his in any event.

After Taukkyan the most critical period of the campaign had passed. We were now compelled to retire northwards, but the enemy only advanced at the expense of a series of costly actions against ourselves and the Chinese. Never again, save in the Shan States, was he presented with a situation the exploitation of which would have helped him to an appreciably speedier conquest of Burma. The operations at Shwedaung, Yenangyaung, Monywa, and Shwegyin on the Chindwin resulted in the temporary cutting off of substantial portions of our force. Each time there was a failure to take full advantage of the initial success. This, coupled with the stubborn opposition of our troops, deprived the Japanese of anything more than a partial gain. But even complete success on any one of these occasions would have done little to shorten the campaign. The prospect of accomplishing this had vanished at Taukkyan.

The primary causes of our failure to hold Burma have become apparent in the course of this narrative. Briefly, these causes were our unpreparedness for invasion in practically every respect, but mainly in lack of troops and proper material of war; the necessary employment of wrongly trained, and in many cases only partially trained troops; the inadequacy of our air support; and the preparations, superior numbers, and specialised training of the enemy.

CHAPTER 26

In considering the question of numbers regard must be had to the low standard of armament and fire power of the Chinese. Unarmed men swelled their numerical strength. It has to be remembered too, that the Chinese VI Army was enormously dispersed. This was unavoidable if a protective screen was to be provided for the southern frontier of China east of the Salween. It meant, however, that the VI Army was never concentrated for battle, and the greater portion of it took no very active part in the campaign.

The campaign was distressingly short. Yet the Allied forces had achieved one result of the utmost importance. This has never received the appreciation it warrants. By delaying the advance of the Japanese until the onset of the monsoon in May our Armies effectively prevented an invasion of India early in 1942. India was then ill-prepared to withstand an attack, and a large-scale invasion at that time may well have been fraught with the gravest and most far-reaching consequences. That such a danger was averted was in itself no small success.

Neither the troops nor the Commanders of the Imperial Forces concerned were responsible for the loss of Burma. Our small forces were called upon to carry out a task far beyond their physical powers. In endeavouring to perform their duty they endured much and suffered heavily. Most units and formations were continuously in forward areas. There were no periods of recuperation. Through February, March, April and May they fought and marched, in intense and exhausting heat, without even the minor comforts of life. Continuous withdrawals and the unchallenged air supremacy of the enemy were causes of depression. So, too, was the feeing that with the fall of Rangoon had gone all possibility of aid. Despite all this, weary men continued gallantly to the end, and even on the Chindwin took a heavy toll of the invader.

From Moulmein to Tamu on the Assam border the shortest route followed by our troops was about eight hundred and fifty miles. The story of this long and arduous retreat has been told. It contains much of which Commanders and men of all ranks must be proud. It would be astonishing if the story did not also contain some account of matters where forethought was lacking, of errors of judgement, and failures in duty. Such things are inevitable, and from them important lessons may be learnt. They do not, however, detract from the record of the Imperial Force as a whole. In point of time we are still too near to the campaign to assess with accuracy its real importance. That can only be done with a full knowledge of all the surrounding circumstances. Yet one thing is certain. The stern and protracted fighting withdrawal of our Army, its courage and endurance, and its final extrication from Burma must go down to history as no mean achievement.

Appendix A

Army in Burma Location Statement for December 1st, 1941

1.
Headquarters Army in Burma	Rangoon.
2nd Echelon (Burma)	Rangoon.
Commando	Loilem.

2.
Headquarters 1 Burma Division	Toungoo.
1 Burma General Hospital (Headquarters and one Section)	Toungoo.
Divisional Signals	Toungoo.

1(A) Upper Burma Area.

Maymyo.
Headquarters Upper Burma Area.
Depot 2 Mountain Battery I.A.
Depot 2nd Battalion King's Own Yorkshire Light Infantry.
Upper Burma Battalion, B.A.F.
Headquarters and Two Sections, Burma Sappers and Miners.
Headquarters and Depot, Burma Signals.
10th Battalion Burma Rifles.
Militia Company.
Burma Regimental Records and Recruiting Centre.
Supply Depot.
7 Supply Depot Section, B.A.S.C.

ARMY IN BURMA LOCATION STATEMENT FOR DECEMBER 1ST, 1941

5 Independent Sub-Section Field Bakery, B.A.S.C.
5 Independent Sub-Section Field Butchery, B.A.S.C.
2 Remount Detachment.
British Military Hospital.
Burma Military Hospital.
Burma Army School of Education.
Schools of Instruction.
British Warfare School.

Mandalay.
Station Staff Officer.
One Company 1st Battalion the Gloucestershire Regiment.
7th Battalion Burma Rifles.
11th Battalion Burma Rifles.
3 Garrison Company (less one Platoon).
7, 11 Mechanical Transport Sections, B.A.S.C.
Supply Depot, B.A.S.C.
6 Supply Depot Section, B.A.S.C.
Burma Military Hospital with British Wing.
1 Ordnance Field Depot.
4 Supply Issue Section, B.A.S.C.
4 Independent Sub-Section Field Bakery, B.A.S.C.
4 Independent Sub-Section Field Butchery, B.A.S.C.

Meiktila.
12 Reinforcement Camp.
9th Battalion Burma Rifles.
14 Mess Unit.
Burma Military Hospital.

1(B) Central Area.

Akyab.
Detachment Rangoon Battalion, B.A.F.
Burma Frontier Force Aerodrome Guard.

Bridge 393 Mandalay – Rangoon Railway.
Two Sections, 11th Battalion Burma Rifles.

Chauk.
2 Garrison Company (less two Platoons)
Detachment 'D' Company, Upper Burma Battalion, B.A.F.

Kabyaung River Bridge.
Two Sections, 12th Battalion Burma Rifles.

Kanhla.
One Section, 1 Garrison Company.

Kutkai.
F.F.1.

Lanywa.
Detachment 'D' Company, Upper Burma Battalion, B.A.F.

Lashio.
Demolition Squad Upper Burma Battalion, B.A.F.
Burma Frontier Force, Aerodrome Guard.

Myitnge River Bridge.
One Platoon 11th Battalion Burma Rifles.

Namsam Falls.
Detachment 'C' Company Upper Burma Battalion, B.A.F.

Namtu.
'C' Company Upper Burma Battalion, B.A.F. (less detachments).

Pegu River Bridge.
Two Sections, 12th Battalion Burma Rifles.

Pyu River Bridge.
Two sections, 12th Battalion Burma Rifles.

Samon River Bridge.
Two Sections, 11th Battalion Burma Rifles.

Sinthechaung Bridge.
Two Sections, 11th Battalion Burma Rifles.

ARMY IN BURMA LOCATION STATEMENT FOR DECEMBER 1ST, 1941

Sittang River Bridge.
Two Sections, 12th Battalion Burma Rifles.

Swachaung Bridge.
Two Sections, 11th Battalion Burma Rifles.
Thayetmyo.
6, 7 Garrison Companies.

Tharrawaddy.
One Section, 1 Garrison Company.

Thegon.
One Section, 1 Garrison Company.

Toungoo.
Burma Frontier Force Aerodrome Guard.

Yenangyaung.
Headquarters 1 Garrison Battalion.
1 Garrison Company (less one Platoon).
Two Platoons 2 Garrison Company.
One Platoon 3 Garrison Company.
'D' Company Upper Burma Battalion, B.A.F. (less detachments).

Yonbinchaung Bridge.
Two Sections 11th Battalion Burma Rifles.

1(C) Rangoon Area.

Mingaladon.
Headquarters Rangoon Area.
1st Battalion the Gloucestershire Regiment (less two companies).
3rd Battalion Burma Rifles.
12th Battalion Burma Rifles.
Mechanical Transport Training Company and Depot, B.A.S.C.
3 Mechanical Transport Section, B.A.S.C.
Rangoon Arsenal.
'Z' Ordnance Detachment.
British Military Hospital (with Burma Wing).
Branch Veterinary Hospital.

Rangoon.
Station Staff Officer.

One Company 1st Battalion the Gloucestershire Regiment.
Rangoon Field Brigade, R.A., B.A.F.
Headquarters and Detachments 1 Heavy Anti-Aircraft Regiment, R.A., B.A.F.
Rangoon Battalion, B.A.F.
Burma Railways Battalion, B.A.F.
Detachment Burma Army Signals.
Headquarters 2 Garrison Battalion.
5 Garrison Company.
Rangoon University Training Corps, Burma Territorial Force.
Supply Depot, B.A.S.C.
4 Supply Depot Section, B.A.S.C.
Supply Personnel Depot, B.A.S.C.
1, 2 P.O.L. Sections, B.A.S.C.
Detention Hospital.
Burma Hospital Company Headquarters and Depot.
13 Field Accounts Office.
Medical Stores Depot.
Reserve Base Engineering Park.
2nd Echelon (India).
Embarkation Staff Officer.

Syriam.
One Battery 1 Heavy Anti-Aircraft Regiment, R.A., B.A.F.
4 Garrison Company.

1(D) 16 Indian Infantry Brigade Group.

Mandalay.
Headquarters 16 Indian Infantry Brigade.
16 Indian Infantry Brigade Employment Platoon.
16 India Infantry Brigade Signal Section.
1st Royal Battalion 9th Jat Regiment.
4th Battalion 12th Frontier Force Regiment.
1st Battalion 7th Gurkha Rifles.
43 Mule Company.
34 Supply Issue Section.
160 Supply Personnel Section.
2 Rail Head Supply Depot.
112 Field Bakery Sub Section.

ARMY IN BURMA LOCATION STATEMENT FOR DECEMBER 1ST, 1941

112 Field Butchery Sub Section.
3 Field Ambulance Troop.
37 Field Ambulance.
G. and Q. Sections Indian General Hospital.
'C' Field Hygiene Sub Section.
4 Mobile Veterinary Sub Section.
16 Indian Infantry Brigade Mobile Workshop Section.
139, 140 Mess Units.
40 Field Post Office.

Meiktila.
Malerkotla Field Company.

Rangoon.
135 Supply Personnel Section.
141 Mess Unit.

Taunggyi.
27 Mountain Regiment.
50 Field Park Company.

Maymyo.
5 Mountain Battery.

2(A) 13 Indian Infantry Brigade.

East Taunggyi.
Headquarters 13 Indian Infantry Brigade.
23 Mountain Battery, I.A.
13 Indian Infantry Brigade Employment Platoon.
13 Indian Infantry Brigade Signals Section.
1st Battalion 18th Royal Garhwal Rifles.
28 Animal Transport Company (Mule).
35 Supply Issue Section.
205 Indian Supply Section Field Bakery.
202 Indian Supply Section Field Butchery.
210 Supply Personnel Section.
Detachment 8 Motor Ambulance Section.
57 Field Ambulance.
1 Field Ambulance Mule troop.

2 Mobile Veterinary Section.
15 Mess Unit.
38 Field Post Office.

Loilem.
5th Battalion 1st Punjab Regiment.
2nd Battalion 7th Rajput Regiment.
17 Rail Head Supply Detachment.
Detachment, Burma Field Hygiene Section.
Detachment, 28 Animal Transport Company (Mule).
4 Casualty Clearing Station.

Mandalay.
Indian General Hospital.

2(B) Southern Shan Area.

Taunggyi.
Headquarters Southern Shan Area and Headquarters 1 Burma Brigade.
Headquarters Lines of Communication Area.
2 Mountain Battery, I.A. ⎫
5 Field Battery, R.A., B.A.F. ⎬ Leaving for Laikha
2nd Battalion The King's Own Yorkshire Light Infantry ⎭
56 Field Company (less three sections).
Brigade Signal Section (less two detachments).
Southern Shan States Battalion, Burma Frontier Force.
13th Battalion Burma Rifles (less two companies, less two platoons).
14th Battalion Burma Rifles.
Detachment 1 Animal Transport Company.
Detachment 2 Animal Transport Company.
1 Mobile Veterinary Detachment.
4, 5, 12 Mechanical Transport Sections.
1 Light Aid Detachment.
1 Company Field Ambulance (leaving for Laikha).
Burma Military Hospital (with British Wing).
2 Field Hygiene Section.
Field Supply Depot.
2 Supply Issue Section.
2, 3, 6 Independent Sub Sections Field Bakery and Butchery.

ARMY IN BURMA LOCATION STATEMENT FOR DECEMBER 1ST, 1941

4 P.O.L. Section.
2 Ordnance Field Depot.
Base Engineer Park.
Garrison Engineer.
Artizan Company, R.E.
2 Field Post Office (leaving for Laikha).
Three Civilian Labour Gangs.

Aungban.
Burma Frontier Force Satellite Aerodrome Guard.

Heho.
Burma Frontier Force Aerodrome Guard.

Kunhing.
One Company 13th Battalion Burma Rifles (less three platoons).

Kengtung.
One Company less two platoons 13th Battalion Burma Rifles.
5 Ordnance Field Depot.
R.E. Dump.
5 Mechanical Transport Section.
Field Supply Depot.
2 Light Aid Detachment.

Loilem.
F.F.4 (less one column).
Commando.
Outposts Southern Shan States Battalion, Burma Frontier Force.

Loimwe.
1st Battalion Burma Rifles.
Detachment Brigade Signals.
Outposts Southern Shan States Battalion, Burma Frontier Force.
F.F.3.
One Section 56 Field Company.
One Company 2 Field Ambulance.

Laikha Area.
209 Supply Personnel Section.

Mong Pan Area.
One Column F.F.4.

Mawchi.
F.F.5.

Monghpayak.
One Column F.F.3.
Mongping.
Detachment 13th Battalion Burma Rifles.
Namsang.
Burma Frontier Force Aerodrome and Satellite Aerodrome Guards and Columns.
Burma Frontier Force Mounted Infantry two troops.

Nammawngun.
One Section 56 Field Company.
Two Platoons 13th Battalion Burma Rifles.
One Company 5th Battalion Burma Rifles.
Field Supply Depot.
3 P.O.L. Section.
2 Supply Issue Section.
3 Light Aid Detachment.
4 Ordnance Field Depot.
R.E. Dump.
2 Casualty Clearing Station (less one section).
One Civilian Labour Gang.

Pangkhem.
5th Battalion Burma Rifles (less one company).
Detachment Brigade Signals.
2 Field Ambulance (less two companies).

Thamakan.
Burma Frontier Force Column and Mounted Infantry Troop.

Takaw.
One Section 56 Field Company.
One Platoon 13th Battalion Burma Rifles.
Detachment enrolled ferrymen.

ARMY IN BURMA LOCATION STATEMENT FOR DECEMBER 1ST, 1941

Tongta.
Detachment 13th Battalion Burma Rifles.

2(C) Tenasserim Area.

Moulmein.
Headquarters Tenasserim Area and 2 Burma Brigade.
Brigade Signal Section.
Tenasserim Battalion, B.A.F. (less one company).
12 Mountain Battery, I.A.
One Section 1 Field Company Burma Sappers and Miners.
One Section Artizan Works Company.
8th Battalion Burma Rifles.
Detachment Kokine Battalion Burma Frontier Force.
1 Animal Transport Company (less detachment).
1, 2, 4, 6, 8 Mechanical Transport Sections.
4 Light Aid Detachment.
1 Field Supply Depot.
1 Rail Head Supply Depot.
1 Supply Issue Section.
1 Independent Sub Section Field Bakery.
1 Independent Sub Section Field Butchery.
1 Field Ambulance.
1 Casualty Clearing Station.
1 Field Hygiene Section.
3 Ordnance Field Depot.
1 Field Post Office.
Station Staff Officer.

Mergui.
2nd Battalion Burma Rifles.
F.F.2.
Detachment Kokine Battalion Burma Frontier Force.
Detachment Supply Depot.
Burma Military Hospital.

Station Staff Officer.
Tavoy.
One Company Tenasserim Battalion, B.A.F.
6th Battalion Burma Rifles.

Detachment Kokine Battalion Burma Frontier Force.
Detachment 1 Animal Transport Company.
Detachment Supply Depot.
Burma Military Hospital.

Victoria Point.
Detachment Kokine Battalion Burma Frontier Force.

Thabawleik.
F.F.2.

Kawkareik.
4th Battalion Burma Rifles.

Appendix B

Army in Burma outline Order of Battle for December 8th, 1941

Headquarters Army in Burma.

I.
Army Formations.

Rangoon Area (Rangoon Fortress).
Area Headquarters.
Rangoon Field Brigade, R.A., B.A.F.
1 Heavy Anti-Aircraft Regiment, R.A., B.A.F.
1st Battalion the Gloucestershire Regiment (less one coy).
Rangoon Battalion, B.A.F. (less Akyab detachment).
Burma Railways Battalion, B.A.F.
3rd Battalion Burma Rifles.
12th Battalion Burma Rifles (less detachments).
4 Garrison Company.
5 Garrison Company.

Upper Burma Area.
Area Headquarters.
One Company 1st Battalion the Gloucestershire Regiment.
Upper Burma Battalion, B.A.F. (less two companies).
7th Battalion Burma Rifles.
9th Battalion Burma Rifles.
10th Battalion Burma Rifles.
11th Battalion Burma Rifles (less detachments).
3 Garrison Company (less one platoon).

Southern Shan Area.
Area Headquarters.
13th Battalion Burma Rifles.
14th Battalion Burma Rifles.
F.F.3.
F.F.4.
F.F.5.
Commando.

Central Area.
Area Headquarters.
Akyab Detachment Rangoon Battalion, B.A.F.
Two Companies Upper Burma Battalion, B.A.F.
Detachments 11th Battalion Burma Rifles.
Detachments 12th Battalion Burma Rifles.
1 Garrison Company.
2 Garrison Company.
One Platoon 3 Garrison Company.
6 Garrison Company.
7 Garrison Company.
F.F.1.

Tenasserim Area.
Area Headquarters.
Tenasserim Battalion, B.A.F.

16 Indian Infantry Brigade Group.
Brigade Headquarters.
27 Mountain Regiment, I.A.
5 Mountain Battery, I.A.
50 Field Park Company.
Malerkotla Field Company.
1st Royal Battalion 9th Jat Regiment.
4th Battalion 12th Frontier Force Regiment.
1st Battalion 7th Gurkha Rifles (to arrive).

II.
1 Burma Division.
Divisional Headquarters.

1 Burma Brigade Group.
Brigade Headquarters.
5 Field Brigade, R.A., B.A.F.
2 Mountain Battery, I.A.
2nd Battalion The King's Own Yorkshire Light Infantry.
1st Battalion Burma Rifles.
5th Battalion Burma Rifles.
F.F.3.

2 Burma Brigade Group.
Brigade Headquarters.
12 Mountain Battery, I.A.
2nd Battalion Burma Rifles.
4th Battalion Burma Rifles.
6th Battalion Burma Rifles.
8th Battalion Burma Rifles.
F.F.2.

13 Indian Infantry Brigade Group.
Brigade Headquarters.
23 Mountain Battery, I.A.
5th Battalion 1st Punjab Regiment.
2nd Battalion 7th Rajput Regiment.
1st Battalion 18th Royal Garhwal Rifles.

Appendix C

State of Infantry of 17 Division on Evening of February 24th 1942

Brigade	Battalion	British Officers	Viceroy's or Governor's Commissioned Officers	Other Ranks	Rifles	Bren Guns	Thompson Sub-machine Carbines
16.	2nd Battalion The King's Own Yorkshire Light Infantry	6	-	200	50	2	2
	1st Royal Battalion 9th Jat Regiment	8	10	550	50	-	2
	1st Battalion 7th Gurkha Rifles	6	4	290	50	2	-
	8th Battalion Burma Rifles	3	3	90	60	2	-
Total 16 Brigade		23	17	1130	210	6	4

STATE OF INFANTRY OF 17 DIVISION

46.	7th Battalion 10th Baluch Regiment	5	3	200	90	-	2
	5th Battalion 17th Dogra Regiment	1	3	100	70	-	-
	3rd Battalion 7th Gurkha Rifles	5	6	160	30	-	-
	2nd Battalion The Duke of Wellington's Regiment	16	-	300	150	4	6
Total 46 Brigade		27	11	760	340	4	8
48.	1st Battalion 3rd Q.A.O's Gurkha Rifles	3	4	100	40	5	8
	1st Battalion 4th P.W.O. Gurkha Rifles	12	18	650	600	30	30
	2nd Battalion 5th Royal Gurkha Rifles F.F.	6	6	215	30	2	2
	4th Battalion 12th Frontier Force Regiment	9	13	480	200	9	16
Total 48 Brigade		30	41	1445	870	46	56
Total for the Division	80	69	3335	1420*	56	68	
Approximate Deficiency	100	65	4600	6800	300	300	
Immediate Deficiency of Weapons	-	-	-	1700	120	100	

*Note the small number of rifles available.

Appendix D

Chinese Expeditionary Force, Burma 1942 Order of Battle – March 31st 1942

Commander-in-Chief – General Lo Cho-Ying

Expeditionary Army Troops.
36 Division   Commander Major General Li Chi P'eng
One Battalion 20th Gendarme Regiment.
Infantry 24th Engineers Battalion.

    Locations.
V Army.   Commander General Tu Yu Ming   V
Army Headquarters – Pyawbwe.
  22nd Division. Commander Major General Liao Yao Hsiang
   64 Regiment   }
   65 Regiment   }
Yedashe/Kyungon
   66 Regiment   }
   Divisional Troops   }

  96th Division.   Commander Major General Yu Shao
   286 Regiment   }
   287 Regiment   }
Pyinmana
   288 Regiment   }
   Divisional Troops   }

  200th Division. Commander Major General Tai An Lang
   598 Regiment   }
   599 Regiment   }

CHINESE EXPEDITIONARY FORCE, BURMA 1942

Yezin
  600 Regiment
  Divisional Troops

  Training Depot.
  1 Reserve Regiment
  2 Reserve Regiment

  Army Troops.
  Cavalry Regiment
  Artillery Regiment
  Engineer Regiment
  Armoured Regiment
  Motor Regiment
  T.R. (1 Battalion)
  Signal Battalion
  A.A. Battalion
  Anti-Tank Gun Battalion
  Infantry-Gun Battalion
  Special Service Battalion
  1 Coy of Fire Brigade
  1 Coy of Drivers
  Field Hospital
  1st Battalion of 10th Artillery Regiment (attached)
  1st Battalion of 18th Artillery Regiment (attached)

  VI Army   Commander Lieut.-General Kan Li Chu   VI
Army Headquarters – Loilem
  49th Division.   Commander Major General Peng Pi Sheng
  145 Regiment
  146 Regiment
  147 Regiment
  T.M. Battalion
Mongpan Area
  Engineer Battalion
  Transport Battalion

  55th Division. Commander Lieut.-General Chen Mien Wu
  1 Regiment
Karenni
  2 Regiment
  3 Regiment

Loilem
  T.M. Battalion
  Engineer Battalion
Thazi
  Transport Battalion

  23rd Division.   Commander Lieut.-General Lu Kuo Ch'uan
  278 Regiment
  279 Regiment
  T.M. Battalion
Kengtung Area
  Engineer Battalion
  Transport Battalion

  Army Troops.
  Liu Kuan-lung Detachment (277 Regiment from 93rd Division but strengthened)
  Special Services Battalion
  Engineer Battalion
  Transport Battalion
  Signal Battalion
  1st Battalion 13th Artillery Regiment (attached)
  5th & 6th Coys of 52nd Artillery Regiment (attached)

The following Chinese Army entered Burma during April 1942.

  LXVI Army   Commander General Chang Chen
  28th Division   Commander Major General Liu Po Lung
  82 Regiment
  83 Regiment
  84 Regiment

  29th Division   Commander Major General Ma Wei Chi
  85 Regiment
  86 Regiment
  87 Regiment

  38th Division   Commander Lieut.-General Sun Li Jen
  112 Regiment
  113 Regiment
  114 Regiment

  Army Troops
  1st Battalion 18th Artillery Regiment
2 Coys 1st Battalion Firing Corps

Appendix E

Order of Battle Army in Burma 1st April 1942

1. Burma Corp (Burcorps).

Corps Troops

7 Armoured Brigade Group.

7 Hussars
2 R. Tanks
414 Battery R.H.A.
'A' Battery 95 Anti-Tank Regiment R.A.
1 West Yorks.
13 Light Field Ambulance
65 Company R.A.S.C.
114 Butchery Independent Sub-Section R.I.A.S.C.
7 Armoured Brigade Light Repair Section
7 Armoured Brigade Recovery Section
2 R.T.R. Light Aid Detachment
7 Hussars Light Aid Detachment
8 Field Post Office.

Artillery.
8 Anti-Aircraft Battery R.A.
3 Indian Light Anti-Aircraft Battery (less one troop)

Engineers.
1 Field Company Burma Sappers and Miners
17 Artizan Works Company I.E.

18 Artizan Works Company I.E. (less one section)
6 Pioneer Battalion I.E.

Signals.
1 Burma Corps Signals
212 Line Construction Section 'M' L of C Signals

Infantry.
Special Service Detachment No. 1 (Commando)

Supply and Transport.
59 G.P. Transport Company R.I.A.S.C.
17 Divisional Troops Transport Company (less detachment)
47 Mule Company R.I.A.S.C.
4 Field Ambulance Troop R.I.A.S.C.
1 Local Transport Company (formed from 20 M.A.S. and impressed vehicles)
22 Motor Ambulance Section R.I.A.S.C.
115 Supply Personnel Section R.I.A.S.C.
1 and 18 Supply Personnel Sections B.A.S.C.
Lower Burma Supply Section B.A.S.C.
112, 114 and 115 Bakery Independent Sub-Section R.I.A.S.C.
1 Bakery Independent Sub-Section B.A.S.C.
Lower Burma Bakery Section B.A.S.C.
Lower Burma Butchery Section B.A.S.C.
1 Butchery Independent Sub-Section B.A.S.C.
1 Rail Head Supply Detachment B.A.S.C.
2 P.O.L. Section B.A.S.C.

Medical
1 Burma Field Ambulance
1 Burma Field Hygiene Section
7 Anti-Malarial Unit (Indian)
2 Burma Depot Medical Stores

Labour Misc.
Two Coys, 18 Aux. Pnr. Bn. 2 and 7 Burma Labour Coys
85 Field Post Office
Mess Units
Advanced Base Stationery Depot (Burma)

1 Burma Division.

ORDER OF BATTLE ARMY IN BURMA 1ST APRIL 1942

1 Burma Brigade.
2/7 Rajput
1 Burma Rifles
2 Burma Rifles
5 Burma Rifles

2 Burma Brigade.
5/1 Punjab
7 Burma Rifles

13 Indian Infantry Brigade.
1/18 R. Garhwal Rifles

Divisional Troops.

Artillery.
H.Q. 27 Mountain Regiment
2 Mountain Battery
23 Mountain Battery
8 Anti-Tank Battery

Engineers.
50 Field Park Company
56 Field Company Sappers and Miners (less two sections)
Malerkotla Field Company

Signals.
1 Burma Divisional Signals

Infantry.
Special Service Detachment No. 2 (Commando)

Supply & Tpt.
1 Burma Division Headquarters Transport Section B.A.S.C.
3, 5, 9, 11 and 12 Mechanical Transport Sections B.A.S.C.
8 Motor Ambulance Sections R.I.A.S.C.
2 Animal Transport Company B.A.S.C.
28 Mule Company R.I.A.S.C.
1 Field Ambulance Troop R.I.A.S.C.
35 Supply Issue Section R.I.A.S.C.
1, 2 and 3 Supply Issue Sections B.A.S.C.

202 Butchery Independent Sub-Section R.I.A.S.C.
2 Cattle Supply Section B.A.S.C.

Ordnance.
7 Mobile Workshop Company I.A.O.C.
48 Infantry Brigade Workshop Section I.A.O.C.

Medical.
2 Burma Field Ambulance
57 Field Ambulance (Indian)
2 Burma Field Hygiene Section

Vet.
1 (Burma) Mobile Veterinary Detachment
2 (Indian) Mobile Veterinary Section

Postal.
1, 2 and 7 Field Post Offices (Burma)
38 Field Post Office (Indian)

Provost.
1 Burma Division Provost Unit

17 Indian Division.

16 Indian Infantry Brigade.
1 D.W.R.
1/9 R. Jats
7/10 Baluch Regt.
4/12 F.F.R.

48 Indian Infantry Brigade.
1 Cameronians
1/3 G.R.
2/5 R.G.R.
1/4 G.R.
1/7 G.R.
3/7 G.R.

63 Indian Infantry Brigade.
1 Inisks.

ORDER OF BATTLE ARMY IN BURMA 1ST APRIL 1942

1/11 Sikhs
2/13 F.F.R.
1/10 G.R.

Divisional Troops.

Artillery.
1 Indian Field regiment
H.Q. 28 Mountain Regiment
5, 12, 15, 28 Mountain Batteries
5 Anti-Tank Battery

Engineers.
24, 60, 70 Field Companies Sappers and Miners

Signals.
17 Indian Divisional Signals

Infantry.
1 Glosters
5/17 Dogra
8 Burma Rifles
1, 2, 3 Frontier Force Detachments B.F.F.
Royal Marine River Patrol
Rangoon Battalion Burma Military Police
Special Service Detachment No. 3 (Commando)

Supply and Transport.
46 Indian Infantry Brigade Transport Coy R.I.A.S.C.
17 Divisional Headquarters Transport Section R.I.A.S.C.
Detachment 17 Divisional Troops Transport Coy R.I.A.S.C.
24 Mechanical Transport Section B.A.S.C.
45 Mule Company R.I.A.S.C.
5 Field Ambulance Troop R.I.A.S.C.
34, 36, 46 and 66 Supply Issue Sections R.I.A.S.C.
3 Butchery Independent Sub-Section B.A.S.C.
1 Cattle Supply Section B.A.S.C.

Medical.
23, 37, 50 Field Ambulance (Indian)
22 Field Hygiene Section (Indian)

Ordnance.
59 Mobile Workshop Company I.A.O.C.
46 and 63 Indian Infantry Brigade Workshop Sections I.A.O.C.

Veterinary.
4 (Indian) Mobile Veterinary Section

Provost.
17 Indian Division Provost Unit

Labour.
17 Auxiliary Pioneer Battalion (less two coys)

Postal.
40, 82, 97 and 100 Field Post Offices (Indian)

Army Troops.

Artillery.
1 Heavy Anti-Aircraft Regiment R.A., B.A.F.
Detachment Rangoon Field Brigade R.A., B.A.F.

Engineers.
1 Burma Artizan Works Company
Depot and Training Company Burma Sappers and Miners

Signals.
Depot and Training Centre, Burma Army Signals

Infantry.
Depot, British Infantry
9 and 10 Bns. The Burma Rifles
Bhamo Bn. The Burma Frontier Force
Chin Hills Bn. The Burma Frontier Force (less detachment)
Myitkyina Bn. The Burma Frontier Force
Northern Shan States Bn. The Burma Frontier Force
Southern Shan States Bn. The Burma Frontier Force
Reserve Bn. The Burma Frontier Force
Kokine Bn. The Burma Frontier Force (less detachments)
Karen Levies

ORDER OF BATTLE ARMY IN BURMA 1ST APRIL 1942

Supply and Transport.
56 Mechanical Transport Section R.I.A.S.C.
A.H.Q. Mechanical Transport Section B.A.S.C.
Mechanical Transport Training Centre B.A.S.C.
Animal Transport Depot B.A.S.C.
Base Supply Depot
H.Q. 15 Supply Personnel Company R.I.A.S.C.
135, 138, 153, 164 and 169 Supply Personnel Sections R.I.A.S.C.
4, 9, 12, 14, 15 and 16 Supply Personnel Sections B.A.S.C.
2 Rail Head Supply Detachment R.I.A.S.C.
3, 7 and 8 P.O.L. Sections B.A.S.C.
78 P.O.L. Section R.I.A.S.C.
Supply Personnel Depot
5 Supply Issue Section B.A.S.C.
22 and 23 Supply Personnel Sections B.A.S.C.
5 and 6 P.O.L. Sections B.A.S.C.
3 and 4 Cattle Supply Sections B.A.S.C.

Medical.
1 Burma Casualty Clearing Station   ⎫
4 Burma General Hospital   ⎪ on loan
3 Field Laboratory   ⎬ to Chinese
2 Burma Staging Section   ⎪ Expeditionary
One section 41 Indian General Hospital ⎭ Force
Depot Indian Hospital Corps
Depot Burma Hospital Corps
H.Q. Detachment R.A.M.C.

Ordnance.
Vehicle Distribution Group (Burma)

Survey.
6 Indian Field Survey Company

Misc.
Officer Cadet Training Unit
Burma Army Schools of Instruction
Burma Army School of Education
Bush Warfare School
Burma General Service Corps Depot
1, 2 and 3 (Railway) Field Service Security Secs.

Line of Communication Defence Troops and Units.

Artillery.
2 Indian Anti-Tank Regiment (less two batteries) (no guns)
8 (Indian) Heavy Anti-Aircraft Battery
One Troop 3 (Indian) Light Anti-Aircraft Bty.
Rangoon Field Brigade R.A., B.A.F. (no guns)

Engineers.
1 Field Company Burma Sappers and Miners
56 Field Company Sappers and Miners
6 Pioneer Battalion I.E.
18 Artizan Works Company
107 and 108 C.R.E. Works (Indian)
310 Workshop and Park Company
1 and 3 Engineer Stores Base Depots
Engineer Stores Depot

Signals.
213 Section 'M' L of C Signals
Detachment Burma Frontier Force Signals
Burma Posts and Telegraphs L of C Signals

Infantry.
2 K.O.Y.L.I.
3, 4 and 6 Bns. The Burma Rifles
11, 12, 13 and 14 Bns. The Burma Rifles B.T.F.
Tenasserim Bn., Burma Aux Force
Rangoon Bn., Burma Aux Force
Burma Railways Bn., Burma Aux Force
Upper Burma Bn., Burma Aux Force
Mandalay Bn., The Burma Frontier Force
Detachments Kokine Bn., The Burma Frontier Force
Detachment Chin Hills Bn., The Burma Frontier Force
1, 3, 4 and 5 F.F. Detachments, The Burma Frontier Force
M.I. Detachment, The Burma Frontier Force
Headquarters 1 and 2 Garrison Battalions
1, 2, 3, 4, 5, 6, 7, 8 and 9 Garrison Companies

Supply and Transport.
1, 2 and 3 Aux Mechanical Transport Coys B.A.S.C.

ORDER OF BATTLE ARMY IN BURMA 1ST APRIL 1942

7, 13, 14, 15, 25 and 26 Mechanical Transport Secs. B.A.S.C.
H.Q. 'A' and 'B' Sections, 3 Mechanical Transport Company B.A.S.C.
'C' and 'D' Sections, 3 Mechanical Transport Company B.A.S.C. (personnel only)
16, 17, 18, 19 and 20 Mechanical Transport Sections B.A.S.C. (personnel only)
21 Motor Ambulance Section R.I.A.S.C.
3 Field Ambulance Troop R.I.A.S.C. (personnel only)
43 Mule Company R.I.A.S.C. (personnel only)
1 Animal Transport Company B.A.S.C. (personnel only)
H.Q. 1, 3, 4 and 5 Supply Personnel Companies B.A.S.C.
2, 3, 5, 6, 7, 8, 10, 11, 13, 17, 19, 20, 21, 24, 25 and 26 Supply Personnel Sections B.A.S.C.
114, 115, 116, 167, 209 and 210 Supply Personnel Sections R.I.A.S.C.
4 Supply Issue Section B.A.S.C.
3, 4 and 5 Rail Head Supply Detachments B.A.S.C.
17 Rail Head Supply Detachment R.I.A.S.C.
1, 4, 9, 10, 11, 12, 13 and 14 P.O.L. Sections B.A.S.C.
68 P.O.L. Section R.I.A.S.C.
2, 3, 4, 5, 6, 7, 8, and 9 Bakery Independent Sub-Sections B.A.S.C.
112 and 205 Bakery Independent Sub-Sections R.I.A.S.C.
2, 4, 5, 6, 7, 8 and 9 Butchery Independent Sub-Sections B.A.S.C.
5, 6 and 7 Cattle Supply Sections B.A.S.C.

Medical.
1, 2, 3, 5, 6, 7 and 8 Burma General Hospitals
41, 59 and 60 Indian General Hospitals (less one section 41 I.G.H.)
1, 2 and 3 Field Laboratories (Burma)
2 Burma Casualty Clearing Station
4 Indian Casualty Clearing station
1 and 2 Ambulance Trains
Hospital Ships:
Mysore (staffed by 8 C.C.S.)
Kalaw (staffed by 8 C.C.S.)
Fano (staffed by 31 Indian Staging Section)
Ebro (staff of 3 Amb. Train)
Lady Innes
39 Field Ambulance (Indian)
3 Field Hygiene Section (Indian)
1 Burma Staging Section
2 British Staging Section
16 Indian Staging Section

British Convalescent Depot
10 Mobile X-ray Unit (Indian)
2 Ear, Nose and Throat Surgical Unit (Indian)
2 Ophthalmological Unit (Indian)
Base Depot Medical Stores (Burma)
13 Depot Medical Stores (Indian)
District Laboratory (Burma)
Dental Centre (Burma)

Ordnance.
Base Ordnance Depot (Burma)
Base M.T. Repair Depot (Burma)
1, 2, 3, 4, 5 and 7 Ordnance Field Depots (Burma)
16 Indian Infantry Brigade Workshop Section I.A.O.C.
1, 2, 3, 4, 5 and 6 Station Workshops (Burma)
1, 3 and 5 Light Aid Detachments (Burma)

Movement Control.
2 Movement Control Area

Veterinary.
Burma Military Veterinary Hospital

Remounts.
2 Remount Detachment (Indian)

Provost.
Provost Company (Burma)

Labour.
18 Aux. Pnr. Bn. (less two companies)
1 Burmese Labour Company
Lahu, Wa, Shan and Gurkha Labour Companies

Postal.
Base Post Office (Burma)
3, 5, 6 and 9 Field Post Offices (Burma)

Misc.
Stationery Depot (Burma)
Independent Rest Camp Sections
9, 10, 12 and 18 Reinforcement Camps
Mess Units